T0203129

Lecture Notes in Computer Science   13487

More information about this series at https://link.springer.com/bookseries/558

Jan Friso Groote · Marieke Huisman (Eds.)

Formal Methods for Industrial Critical Systems

27th International Conference, FMICS 2022
Warsaw, Poland, September 14–15, 2022
Proceedings

Editors
Jan Friso Groote 🆔
Eindhoven University of Technology
Eindhoven, The Netherlands

Marieke Huisman 🆔
University of Twente
Enschede, The Netherlands

ISSN 0302-9743   ISSN 1611-3349 (electronic)
Lecture Notes in Computer Science
ISBN 978-3-031-15007-4   ISBN 978-3-031-15008-1 (eBook)
https://doi.org/10.1007/978-3-031-15008-1

This Springer imprint is published by the registered company Springer Nature Switzerland AG
The registered company address is: Gewerbestrasse 11, 6330 Cham, Switzerland

Preface

The International Conference on Formal Methods in Industrial Critical Systems (FMICS), organized by ERCIM, is the key conference at the intersection of industrial applications and formal methods. The aim of the FMICS series is to provide a forum for researchers who are interested in the development and application of formal methods in industry. FMICS brings together scientists and engineers who are active in the area of formal methods and interested in exchanging their experiences in the industrial usage of these methods. FMICS also strives to promote research and development for the improvement of formal methods and tools for industrial applications.

This volume contains the papers presented at the 27th International Conference on Formal Methods in Industrial Critical Systems (FMICS 2022), which was held during September 14–15, 2022. The symposium took place in the beautiful capital of Poland, Warsaw, but could also be attended online. The conference was organized under the umbrella of CONFEST, alongside with the 33rd International Conference on Concurrency Theory (CONCUR 2022), the 19th International Conference on Quantitative Evaluation of Systems (QEST 2022), and the 20th International Conference on Formal Modeling and Analysis of Timed Systems (FORMATS 2022).

FMICS 2022 received 22 paper submissions. We selected a total of 13 papers for presentation during the conference and inclusion in these proceedings, resulting in an overall acceptance rate of 59%.

The submissions were reviewed by an international Program Committee (PC) of 28 members from a mix of universities, industry, and research institutes. All submissions went through a rigorous single-blind review process overseen by the Program Committee Chairs. Each submission received three review reports and was actively and thoroughly discussed by the PC.

The program of CONFEST 2022 included two FMICS invited keynotes. One by Sven Schewe from Liverpool University about reinforcement learning with guarantees, and one by Bas Luttik from Eindhoven University of Technology about railway innovations via formal modeling and verification.

We are grateful to all involved in FMICS 2022. We thank the authors for submitting and presenting their work at FMICS 2022 and the PC members and sub-reviewers for their accurate and timely reviewing. We also thank the invited speakers, session chairs, and attendees, all of whom contributed to making the conference a success. We are also grateful to the providers of the EasyChair system, which was used to manage the submissions, to Springer for sponsoring the Best Paper Award and for publishing the proceedings, and to the Steering Committee of FMICS for their trust and support. We thank the General Chair of CONFEST, Sławek Lasota, for providing the logistics that enabled and facilitated the organization of FMICS 2022.

July 2022

Jan Friso Groote
Marieke Huisman

Organization

Program Committee

Erika Ábrahám	RWTH Aachen University, Germany
Maurice ter Beek	ISTI-CNR, Italy
Simon Bliudze	Inria, France
Rafael C. Cardoso	University of Aberdeen, UK
Milan Češka	Brno University of Technology, Czech Republic
Hubert Garavel	Inria, France
Jan Friso Groote (Chair)	Eindhoven University of Technology, The Netherlands
Ernst Moritz Hahn	University of Twente, The Netherlands
Paula Herber	University of Münster, Germany
Marieke Huisman (Chair)	University of Twente, The Netherlands
Peter Höfner	Australian National University, Australia
Nikolai Kosmatov	CEA List, Université Paris-Saclay and Thales, France
Alfons Laarman	Leiden University, The Netherlands
Peter Gorm Larsen	Aarhus University, Denmark
István Majzik	Budapest University of Technology and Economics, Hungary
Rosemary Monahan	Maynooth University, Ireland
Thomas Neele	Eindhoven University of Technology, The Netherlands
Wytse Oortwijn	TNO-ESI, The Netherlands
Paweł Parys	University of Warsaw, Poland
Wojciech Penczek	Institute of Computer Science, Polish Academy of Sciences, Poland
Jaco van de Pol	Aarhus University, Denmark
Marco Roveri	University of Trento, Italy
Kristin Yvonne Rozier	Iowa State University, USA
Cristina Seceleanu	Mälardalen University, Sweden
Martina Seidl	Johannes Kepler University Linz, Austria
Jiri Srba	Aalborg University, Denmark
Alexander J. Summers	University of British Columbia, Canada
Ashutosh Trivedi	University of Colorado Boulder, USA
Elena Troubitsyna	KTH, Sweden
Naijun Zhan	Institute of Software, Chinese Academy of Sciences, China

Additional Reviewers

Backeman, Peter
Franken, Tom
Gora, Paweł
Grosen, Thomas Møller
Iwanicki, Konrad
Jin, Xiangyu
Kurkowski, Mirosław

Longuet, Delphine
Oda, Tomohiro
Schubert, Aleksy
Sidoruk, Teofil
Szekeres, Dániel
Wang, Qiang
Xu, Runqing

Contents

Invited Keynote Talks

Reinforcement Learning with Guarantees that Hold for Ever

Ernst Moritz Hahn[1] [iD], Mateo Perez[2] [iD], Sven Schewe[3] [✉] [iD], Fabio Somenzi[2] [iD], Ashutosh Trivedi[2] [iD], and Dominik Wojtczak[3] [iD]

[1] University of Twente, Enschede, The Netherlands
[2] University of Colorado Boulder, Boulder, USA
[3] University of Liverpool, Liverpool, UK
sven.schewe@liverpool.ac.uk

Abstract. Reinforcement learning is a successful explore-and-exploit approach, where a controller tries to learn how to navigate an unknown environment. The principle approach is for an intelligent agent to learn how to maximise expected rewards. But what happens if the objective refers to non-terminating systems? We can obviously not wait until an infinite amount of time has passed, assess the success, and update. But what can we do? This talk will tell.

1 Learning from Rewards

Model free reinforcement learning (RL) [16,19] refers to a class of algorithms, where an intelligent agent (sometimes many, but we stick with basic case) receives rewards. Such rewards serve as feedback; they can be received after termination, after a fixed period of time, or after every action. Reaping high rewards reinforces a given behaviour of the agent (hence the name), while behaviour that leads to low rewards is avoided.

What makes RL algorithms popular is their flexibility and generality. They can work without being provided with a model of the environment dynamics and can handle probabilistic environment behaviour – that is, Markov decision processes (MDP) are their natural domain.

The goal of an agent in its interaction with its environment is to learn an optimal *strategy*, which describes how she chooses actions in a way that maximises the expected value of the overall reward, usually the total or discounted sum of individual rewards or a single reward at the end of a finite run. Discounted and average rewards are typical of infinite horizon problems.

This work is supported in part by the National Science Foundation (NSF) grant CCF-2009022 and by NSF CAREER award CCF-2146563, and by the Engineering and Physical Science Research Council through grant EP/V026887/1. ■ This project has received funding from the European Union's Horizon 2020 research and innovation programme under grant agreements No 864075 (CAESAR) and 956123 (FOCETA).

J. F. Groote and M. Huisman (Eds.): FMICS 2022, LNCS 13487, pp. 3–7, 2022.
https://doi.org/10.1007/978-3-031-15008-1_1

The strategy of an agent describes what she does in each situation. Average, total, and discounted rewards usually lead to memoryless strategies, but strategies can take the history (i.e., the previous interaction with the environment) into account.

2 Learning with ω-Regular Objectives

Standard approaches to RL face natural difficulties when considering ω-regular properties [13,17] that, for example, occur when specifications in linear time temporal logic (LTL) [12] are used.

This is because the reward for an overall run of a system is binary (does/does not satisfy the specification), and its binary value cannot be determined after a finite prefix.

So, how can we learn in this case?

We suggest a layered approach, which consists of the following:

1. Translate the property into a formal acceptor, like a Büchi [2] or parity automaton, such that maximising the likelihood of winning on the *syntactic* product with the MDP is good enough for maximising the chance of satisfying the property [3,7,18].
2. Translate the formal acceptor into a reachability objective, such that maximising the chance of reaching a goal state leads to maximising the chance of acceptance [4].
3. Wrap this reward structure into a standard RL approach [16].

2.1 Good-for-MDP Automata

Finding the right type of automata has two major ingredients:

1. a limited level of nondeterminism, such that the resulting automaton is *good for MDPs* (see below) and
2. a simple acceptance mechanism.

The first ingredient is a technical requirement. Formally(-sh), an automaton is **good-for-MDPs** if, for *all* finite MDPs, its syntactic product MDP (which is the syntactic product of the finite MDP with the automaton) has the same likelihood to satisfy the acceptance condition as an optimal control of the MDP has to satisfy the objective [4].

In this syntactic product, the agent has more to do: she has to resolve the nondeterminism of the automaton as well as the choices of the original MDP.

Broadly speaking, this limits the type of nondeterminism the automaton can use: normally, an automaton can use unlimited look-ahead to resolve its nondeterministic choices, but this automaton has to take into account where the randomness of the MDP can take it. Moreover, it needs to react to almost all cases perfectly.

This is reminiscent of good-for-games automata [10], but they need to be able to deal with all (not merely almost all) interactions with their environment.

The relaxation to *almost all* allows for more automata. Indeed, one of the main differences between good-for-games and good-for-MDPs automata is that non-deterministic Büchi automata can always be used for the latter, while the former requires more complex acceptance mechanisms.

This brings us back to the second ingredient: a simple acceptance mechanism. This is a practical requirement rather than a technical necessity. It is due to the much higher cost of the further translation of complex acceptance mechanisms [8].

Standard translations to limit deterministic automata [7,18] produce nondeterministic Büchi automata that are good-for-MDPs [6], but it is equally simple to produce other good-for-MDP automata with attractive alternative properties, like never offering more than two choices [6].

After learning, the automaton states (and structure) turn into a finite state memory.

2.2 From GFM Büchi Automata to Reachability and RL

A parameterised translation from good-for-MDPs automata to rewards proves to be quite simple: for a given parameter $\lambda \in]0,1[$, whenever one passes an accepting state (or transition), go to an accepting sink with probability λ, and continue with a probability of $1 - \lambda$.

It is easy to see that the chance of reaching the accepting sink is at least the chance of satisfying the Büchi objective. But it also holds that, when λ goes to 0, the chance of reaching the accepting sink converges to the chance of satisfying the Büchi objective, and that optimal strategies for the reachability goal are stable, and optimal for the Büchi objective, for all sufficiently small values of λ.

This reachability objective can then be handled with standard RL techniques. We have used Q-learning, which would normally wrap the reachability objective into a discounted payoff objective to guarantee contraction.

3 Related Work

Reinforcement learning for ω-regular objectives has first been applied using deterministic Rabin automata [11,14]. While there are small examples where this method does not produce optimal results [4], they have paved the way for further exploration.

The translation through reachability [4] has been complemented by an integrated approach to discounted payoff that uses different discount factors for accepting and non-accepting transitions [1]. This can be mimicked by replacing the reduction to reachability by replacing the transition to an accepting sink by obtaining a reward while discounting the rest of the game with a factor of $1 - \lambda$, while not discounting otherwise. Wrapping this approach into another discount scheme for RL (in order to guarantee contraction) leads to the same set of different discount factors [5].

Suitable limit deterministic automata have been replaced by good-for-MDP automata [6]. While current approaches to obtain them from general nondeterministic Büchi automata hinge on breakpoint constructions, it is also possible (but expensive: PSPACE hard and in EXPTIME) to check whether or not an nondeterministic Büchi automaton is already good-for-MDPs [15].

The learning approach extends to Markov games [8], which need good-for-games automata [10], and thus parity objectives. While using games as such does not seem to be problematic, handling more powerful acceptance conditions comes at a cost, broadly speaking by using the small parameter λ in different powers.

Being able to handle games also paves the way for using alternating automata (so long as they are good-for-MDPs) for ordinary MDPs, which has proven to allow for efficient translations from deterministic Streett to alternating Büchi automata that are good-for-MDPs, while their translation to nondeterministic Büchi automata (GFM or not) is expensive [9].

References

1. Bozkurt, A.K., Wang, Y., Zavlanos, M.M., Pajic, M.: Control synthesis from linear temporal logic specifications using model-free reinforcement learning. In: 2020 IEEE International Conference on Robotics and Automation, ICRA 2020, Paris, France, May 31–August 31, 2020, pp. 10349–10355. IEEE (2020). https://doi.org/10.1109/ICRA40945.2020.9196796
2. Büchi, J.R.: On a decision method in restricted second order arithmetic. In: Proceedings of the International Congress on Logic, Methodology, and Philosophy of Science, 1960, Berkeley, California, USA, pp. 1–11. Stanford University Press (1962)
3. Courcoubetis, C., Yannakakis, M.: The complexity of probabilistic verification. J. ACM **42**(4), 857–907 (1995)
4. Hahn, E.M., Perez, M., Schewe, S., Somenzi, F., Trivedi, A., Wojtczak, D.: Omega-regular objectives in model-free reinforcement learning. In: Vojnar, T., Zhang, L. (eds.) TACAS 2019. LNCS, vol. 11427, pp. 395–412. Springer, Cham (2019). https://doi.org/10.1007/978-3-030-17462-0_27
5. Hahn, E.M., Perez, M., Schewe, S., Somenzi, F., Trivedi, A., Wojtczak, D.: Faithful and Effective Reward Schemes for Model-Free Reinforcement Learning of Omega-Regular Objectives. In: Hung, D.V., Sokolsky, O. (eds.) ATVA 2020. LNCS, vol. 12302, pp. 108–124. Springer, Cham (2020). https://doi.org/10.1007/978-3-030-59152-6_6
6. Hahn, E.M., Perez, M., Schewe, S., Somenzi, F., Trivedi, A., Wojtczak, D.: Good-for-MDPS automata for probabilistic analysis and reinforcement learning. In: Tools and Algorithms for the Construction and Analysis of Systems, pp. 306–323 (2020)
7. Hahn, E.M., Li, G., Schewe, S., Turrini, A., Zhang, L.: Lazy probabilistic model checking without determinisation. In: Proceedings of the 26th Conference on Concurrency Theory (CONCUR 2015), September 1–4, Madrid. LIPIcs, vol. 42, pp. 354–367. Schloss Dagstuhl - Leibniz-Zentrum für Informatik, Germany (2015)
8. Trivedi, A., Wojtczak, D.: Model-free reinforcement learning for stochastic parity games. In: Konnov, I., Kovács, L. (eds.) 31st International Conference on Concurrency Theory, CONCUR 2020, 1–4 September 2020, Vienna, Austria (Virtual Conference). LIPIcs, vol. 171, pp. 21:1–21:16. Schloss Dagstuhl - Leibniz-Zentrum für Informatik (2020)

9. Hahn, E.M., Perez, M., Schewe, S., Somenzi, F., Trivedi, A., Wojtczak, D.: Model-free reinforcement learning for branching Markov decision processes. In: Silva, A., Leino, K.R.M. (eds.) CAV 2021. LNCS, vol. 12760, pp. 651–673. Springer, Cham (2021). https://doi.org/10.1007/978-3-030-81688-9_30
10. Henzinger, T.A., Piterman, N.: Solving games without determinization. In: Ésik, Z. (ed.) CSL 2006. LNCS, vol. 4207, pp. 395–410. Springer, Heidelberg (2006). https://doi.org/10.1007/11874683_26
11. Hiromoto, M., Ushio, T.: Learning an optimal control policy for a Markov decision process under linear temporal logic specifications. In: Symposium Series on Computational Intelligence, pp. 548–555, December 2015
12. Manna, Z., Pnueli, A.: The Temporal Logic of Reactive and Concurrent Systems *Specification*. Springer, New York (1991). https://doi.org/10.1007/978-1-4612-0931-7
13. Perrin, D., Pin, J.É.: Infinite Words: Automata, Semigroups. Logic and Games. Elsevier, Amsterdam (2004)
14. Sadigh, D., Kim, E., Coogan, S., Sastry, S.S., Seshia, S.A.: A learning based approach to control synthesis of Markov decision processes for linear temporal logic specifications. In: IEEE Conference on Decision and Control (CDC), pp. 1091–1096, December 2014
15. Schewe, S., Tang, Q., Zhanabekova, T.: Deciding what is good-for-MDPS. CoRR abs/2202.07629 (2022), https://arxiv.org/abs/2202.07629
16. Sutton, R.S., Barto, A.G.: Reinforcement Learning: An Introduction, 2nd edn. MIT Press, London (2018)
17. Thomas, W.: Handbook of Theoretical Computer Science, Chap. Automata on Infinite Objects, pp. 133–191. The MIT Press/Elsevier, London (1990)
18. Vardi, M.Y.: Automatic verification of probabilistic concurrent finite-state programs. In: 26th Annual Symposium on Foundations of Computer Science, Portland, Oregon, USA, 21–23 October 1985. pp. 327–338. IEEE Computer Society (1985)
19. Wiering, M., van Otterlo, M. (eds.): Reinforcement Learning: State of the Art. Springer, Heidelberg (2012). https://doi.org/10.1007/978-3-642-27645-3

Supporting Railway Innovations with Formal Modelling and Verification

Bas Luttik[✉][iD]

Eindhoven University of Technology, Eindhoven, The Netherlands
s.p.luttik@tue.nl

It is a continuing challenge for European railway infrastructure managers to increase the capacity of the dense European railway network and to achieve cost reductions at the same time. Innovations developed to that effect rely heavily on digital technology. To cope with the ensued complexity, railway infrastructure managers are starting to appreciate more and more the use of formal modelling and verification techniques to support the development of these digital innovations. In my presentation I will discuss our contributions to two ongoing innovations in the railway domain: EULYNX and ERTMS/ETCS Hybrid Level 3.

EULYNX

The goal of the EULYNX[1] undertaking is to develop digital standardised interfaces between interlockings and trackside equipment (signals, points, level crossings, etc.). It is crucial that the standard is unambiguous, that it ensures all relevant safety requirements, and that compliance to the standard can be tested thoroughly. To this end, the FormaSig project[2]—a collaboration between railway infrastructure managers DB Netz and ProRail, Eindhoven University of Technology and the University of Twente—supports EULYNX with formal verification and model-based test technology.

The EULYNX standardised interfaces are defined using SysML internal block diagrams and state machine diagrams. The approach of the FormaSig project is to derive from these SysML models a formal model in the process specification language mCRL2 [10]. The mCRL2 toolset[3] then offers model-checking facilities to formally analyse the correctness of the interface model with respect to high-level requirements [6]. Moreover, since the semantics of an mCRL2 model is a labelled transition system, it also facilitates automated model-based testing of compliance of implementations to the standard in accordance with formal testing theory [13].

In a first case study, we have manually derived an mCRL2 model from the SysML models specifying the EULYNX Point interface [4]. A formal analysis of

---

[1] https://www.eulynx.eu.
[2] https://fsa.win.tue.nl/formasig/.
[3] https://www.mcrl2.org.

J. F. Groote and M. Huisman (Eds.): FMICS 2022, LNCS 13487, pp. 8–11, 2022.
https://doi.org/10.1007/978-3-031-15008-1_2

the model using the mCRL2 toolset revealed a deadlock caused by event buffers overflowing and a discrepancy in the interaction of the EULYNX standard with the underlying communication protocol. We also performed some preliminary model-based testing experiments using JTorX [2] to automatically generate tests from the mCRL2 model, running those tests on a simulator of the EULYNX interface. The case study showed the feasibility of our approach.

Our next step was to automate the translation of EULYNX SysML models to mCRL2. The precise semantic interpretation of the SysML models developed in EULYNX, however, is not fixed. To achieve maximal flexibility in our analysis, we have therefore set up the translation from SysML to mCRL2 such that it can be easily modified. At its core is a generic formalisation of the semantics of SysML state machines in the expressive mCRL2 language [3]. The automated translation interprets the SysML internal block diagrams, and renders the SysML model as a data object within the mCRL2 specification of SysML state-machine semantics. The translation framework, with an application to the EULYNX Point interface, is described in [5].

We are currently using the framework to analyse other EULYNX interfaces (level crossing, light signal, train detection). We observe that these other interfaces yield mCRL2 models with significantly larger state spaces. So we are investigating how we can use compositional state-space generation techniques [12] and symbolic model checking [11] recently developed for mCRL2. Also, we are experimenting with alternative semantic interpretations of the SysML models; the flexible set-up of the translation framework now pays off, because it allows us to experiment with variations of the state-machine semantics without changing the translation tool itself.

ERTMS/ETCS HL3

Level 3 of ERTMS/ETCS[4], the European standardised command and signalling system, introduces the concept of *virtual block*. Trains communicate their exact positions on the track to the trackside system through a radio connection, and the system computes movement authorities for trains ensuring that two trains never simultaneously occupy the same virtual block. This approach obviates the need for expensive train detection hardware. Moreover, since virtual blocks can be arbitrarily small, or even move along with the train, a capacity increase of the network is realised.

Transitioning to such a radically new train separation concept on the dense European railway network is an enormous challenge, because it requires the entire railway network and trains (passenger and freight) to be equipped with the enabling technology. To smoothen the transition, railway infrastructure managers are developing a hybrid version of ERTMS/ETCS Level 3 (HL3). It describes a train separation mechanism based on virtual blocks that is integrated with a traditional train detection system with train detection hardware.

---

[4] https://ertms.be/workgroups/level3.

The HL3 principles facilitate a partitioning of hardware protected track sections into so-called virtual subsections. Multiple suitably equipped trains can then be admitted on the same track section simultaneously, ensuring that they are never simultaneously occupying the same virtual subsection. For trains without the required equipment, the system still provides the traditional train separation mechanism. An added benefit of HL3 is that, by making use of the installed train detection hardware, it can recover from a failing radio communication between train and trackside.

There has been ample attention for the HL3 principles from the formal methods research community since version 1A of the principles [8] served as the ABZ 2018 case study (see [7] and references therein). At FMICS 2018 we reported on a formal analysis of the principles using mCRL2 [1]. That first version of our mCRL2 model formalised the core the principles; it ignored the influence of various timers that should prevent the system from qualifying a situation as hazardous too quickly. Since our presentation at FMICS 2018, we have updated the mCRL2 model to reflect version 1D of the principles [9], and also incorporated the behaviour of the timers. Our various analyses exposed potentially dangerous scenarios, especially also related to the behaviour of timers, and resulted in recommendations for improvement of the HL3 principles that were taken into account in subsequent versions. ProRail is using our mCRL2 model to simulate HL3 scenarios.

Acknowledgements. The contributions to EULYNX have been made in collaboration with Mark Bouwman from Eindhoven University of Technology and Arend Rensink, Mariëlle Stoelinga and Djurre van der Wal from the University of Twente; the research was funded by ProRail and DB Netz. The contributions to ERTMS/ETCS Hybrid Level 3 have been made in collaboration with Maarten Bartholomeus from ProRail and Rick Erkens and Tim Willemse from Eindhoven University of Technology; the research was partially funded by ProRail. The vision presented here does not necessarily reflect the strategy of DB Netz or ProRail.

References

1. Bartholomeus, M., Luttik, B., Willemse, T.: Modelling and analysing ERTMS hybrid level 3 with the mCRL2 toolset. In: Howar, F., Barnat, J. (eds.) FMICS 2018. LNCS, vol. 11119, pp. 98–114. Springer, Cham (2018). https://doi.org/10.1007/978-3-030-00244-2_7
2. Belinfante, A.: JTorX: a tool for on-line model-driven test derivation and execution. In: Esparza, J., Majumdar, R. (eds.) TACAS 2010. LNCS, vol. 6015, pp. 266–270. Springer, Heidelberg (2010). https://doi.org/10.1007/978-3-642-12002-2_21
3. Bouwman, M., Luttik, B., van der Wal, D.: A formalisation of SysML state machines in mCRL2. In: Peters, K., Willemse, T.A.C. (eds.) FORTE 2021. LNCS, vol. 12719, pp. 42–59. Springer, Cham (2021). https://doi.org/10.1007/978-3-030-78089-0_3

4. Bouwman, M., van der Wal, D., Luttik, B., Stoelinga, M., Rensink, A.: What is the point: formal analysis and test generation for a railway standard. In: Baraldi, P., di Maio, F., Zio, E. (eds.) Proceedings of ESREL 2020 and PSAM 15. Research Publishing, Singapore (2020). http://www.rpsonline.com.sg/proceedings/esrel2020/html/4410.xml
5. Bouwman, M., van der Wal, D., Luttik, B., Stoelinga, M., Rensink, A.: A case in point: verification and testing of a EULYNX interface. Formal Aspects Comput. (2022). https://doi.org/10.1145/3528207
6. Bunte, O., et al.: The mCRL2 toolset for analysing concurrent systems. In: Vojnar, T., Zhang, L. (eds.) TACAS 2019, Part II. LNCS, vol. 11428, pp. 21–39. Springer, Cham (2019). https://doi.org/10.1007/978-3-030-17465-1_2
7. Butler, M.J., Hoang, T.S., Raschke, A., Reichl, K.: Introduction to special section on the ABZ 2018 case study: Hybrid ERTMS/ETCS level 3. Int. J. Softw. Tools Technol. Transf. 22(3), 249–255 (2020)
8. EEIG ERTMS Users Group: Hybrid ERTMS/ETCS Level 3, ref: 16E045, Version: 1A, Date: 14/07/2017
9. EEIG ERTMS Users Group: Hybrid ERTMS/ETCS Level 3, ref: 16E042, Version: 1D, Date: 15/10/2020
10. Groote, J.F., Mousavi, M.R.: Modeling and Analysis of Communicating Systems. MIT Press, Cambridge (2014). http://mitpress.mit.edu/books/modeling-and-analysis-communicating-systems
11. Laveaux, M., Wesselink, W., Willemse, T.A.C.: On-the-fly solving for symbolic parity games. In: Fisman, D., Rosu, G. (eds.) TACAS 2022. LNCS, vol. 13244, pp. 137–155. Springer, Cham (2022). https://doi.org/10.1007/978-3-030-99527-0_8
12. Laveaux, M., Willemse, T.A.C.: Decomposing monolithic processes in a process algebra with multi-actions. In: Lange, J., Mavridou, A., Safina, L., Scalas, A. (eds.) Proceedings 14th Interaction and Concurrency Experience, ICE 2021, 18 June 2021. EPTCS, vol. 347, pp. 57–76 (2021). https://doi.org/10.4204/EPTCS.347.4
13. Tretmans, J.: Model based testing with labelled transition systems. In: Hierons, R.M., Bowen, J.P., Harman, M. (eds.) Formal Methods and Testing. LNCS, vol. 4949, pp. 1–38. Springer, Heidelberg (2008). https://doi.org/10.1007/978-3-540-78917-8_1

Certification

Formal Monotony Analysis of Neural Networks with Mixed Inputs: An Asset for Certification

Guillaume Vidot[1,2]([✉])[ID], Mélanie Ducoffe[1][ID], Christophe Gabreau[1],
Ileana Ober[2], and Iulian Ober[3][ID]

[1] Airbus Opération S.A.S, Toulouse, France
{eric-guillaume.vidot,melanie.ducoffe,christophe.gabreau}@airbus.com
[2] University of Toulouse, Institut de Recherche en Informatique de Toulouse,
Toulouse, France
{eric.vidot,ileana.ober}@irit.fr
[3] ISAE-SUPAERO, University of Toulouse, Toulouse, France
iulian.ober@isae-supaero.fr

Abstract. The use of ML technology to design safety-critical systems requires a complete understanding of the neural network's properties. Among the relevant properties in an industrial context, the verification of partial monotony may become mandatory. This paper proposes a method to evaluate the monotony property using a Mixed Integer Linear Programming (MILP) solver. Contrary to the existing literature, this monotony analysis provides a lower and upper bound of the space volume where the property does not hold, that we denote "Non-Monotonic Space Coverage". This work has several advantages: (i) our formulation of the monotony property works on discrete inputs, (ii) the iterative nature of our algorithm allows for refining the analysis as needed, and (iii) from an industrial point of view, the results of this evaluation are valuable to the aeronautical domain where it can support the certification demonstration. We applied this method to an avionic case study (braking distance estimation using a neural network) where the verification of the monotony property is of paramount interest from a safety perspective.

Keywords: Neural network verification · Monotony · Certification · Formal Methods

1 Introduction

Over the last years, neural networks have become increasingly popular and a reference method for solving a broad set of problems, such as computer vision, pattern recognition, obstacle detection, time series analysis, or natural language processing. Their usage in safety-critical embedded systems (e.g., automotive, aviation) is also becoming increasingly appealing. The aeronautical domain is known to be one of the more stringent. Indeed, products are ruled by binding regulation requirements to guarantee that the aircraft will safely operate in foreseeable operating

J. F. Groote and M. Huisman (Eds.): FMICS 2022, LNCS 13487, pp. 15–31, 2022.
https://doi.org/10.1007/978-3-031-15008-1_3

and environmental conditions. At the end of 2021, the European Union Aviation Safety Agency (EASA) released the first issue of a concept paper [5] to anticipate any application for AI-based products: it contains *a first set of technical objectives and organization provisions that EASA anticipates as necessary for the approval of Level 1 AI applications ('assistance to human') and guidance material which could be used to comply with those objectives.*

Among all the properties required to certify AI-based systems, robustness is of paramount importance and is a widely studied property in the machine learning and verification communities [2,14,16,18,21,23,24,27–29,31,32]. Although robustness is a critical property for classification tasks, we see the emergence of safety-related properties for regression tasks in many industries. For example, numerical models have been developed to approximate physical phenomena inherent to their systems [1]. As these models are based on physical equations, whose relevancy is asserted by scientific experts, their qualification is carried out without any issue. However, since their computational costs and running time prevent us from embedding them on board, the use of these numerical models in the aeronautical field remains mainly limited to the development and design phase of the aircraft. Thanks to the current success of deep neural networks, previous works have already investigated neural network-based surrogates for approximating numerical models [12,22]. Those surrogates come with additional safety properties linked to induced physics. One of them is the monotony which is motivated by the fact that monotonic functions are ubiquitous in most physics phenomena. For instance, one should expect that the estimate of a braking distance should be a monotonic function with respect to specific parameters such as the state of the brakes (nominal or degraded) or the state of the runway (dry or wet). Another case where monotony is relevant is in DNNs used for control. Today, state-of-the-art methods for enforcing partial monotony assume that if the property is not respected on the whole operational domain of the ML-based function, this puts at risk its certification (i.e., its compliance determination to certification requirements) and, therefore, its industrialization. We believe that this risk can be covered, especially for models that, in the future, would also be penalized for being too loose given the reference function. We propose an iterative method that measures and identifies the part of the domain for which the monotony property is violated, which can be used to demonstrate conformity to certification requirements.

2   Certification Preamble

As stated before, to certify a product, the following principle shall apply to the systems composing that product: each system performs its intended function and safely operates in foreseeable operating and environmental conditions. It means that even if the system performs a function with poor performance (this is obviously not desirable from an industrial viewpoint), it can be certifiable if the product's safety is guaranteed in the usage domain. Once that is said, a primordial principle emerges: the safety is to be considered at the system level,

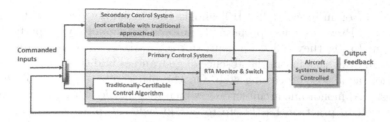

Fig. 1. Typical runtime assurance architecture proposed by NASA [20]

meaning that even if a specific algorithm is not robust in some areas of its input space, then the system can remain certifiable if one can demonstrate that any unsafe behavior is prevented or mitigated. One possible mitigation of this risk is the use of runtime assurance illustrated in Fig. 1 extracted from the NASA paper [20], which ensures the system's safety by the design of redundant control system architecture, where a certifiable function takes over the function not certifiable with traditional approaches when unsafe context is detected. This mitigation is relevant regardless of the technology used during the system development. Coming back to the specific context of ML-based development, the ability to formally define the areas of the input space where the safety properties of the model are not preserved can be a powerful asset in the compliance determination to certification requirements. The use of formal methods can save significant testing efforts while preserving the safe behavior of the function.

3   Related Work

In recent years, assessing the robustness of neural networks has been tackled with formal verification (i.e., sound algorithms demonstrating whether a property holds or not). Verifying properties on a neural network is challenging because neural networks are non-convex functions with many non-linearities, with hundreds to millions of parameters. Even if the type of architecture studied is restricted to piecewise-linear networks, it is known that this problem is already NP-hard [29]. There has been tremendous progress in the field of verification, from robustness proof of networks trained on MNIST to scaling up to CIFAR 10 and even TinyImagenet. These successes are particularly due to the collaboration of different communities that made it possible to formulate and tackle the robustness problem from different perspectives. Without being exhaustive, we can cite the methods that rely on Lipschitz-based optimization [32,33], input refinement [27] and semi-definite relaxations [21].

So far, the verification community has mainly tackled robustness verification from adversarial robustness [26] to computing the reachable set of a network [30] despite a few other properties that are highly relevant for the industry. Among those properties, partial monotony under specific inputs appears to be a key property, especially for regression tasks. Indeed, the need for monotony appeared in various contexts such as surrogate modeling [11], economics [6], fairness [13], or interpretability [19] and is thus a highly desirable feature in the industry. Previous works proposed to enforce the monotony property during the design; In [9], they relied on heuristics regularizers to promote monotony, whose main drawback lies in the absence of guarantees and therefore will require verification as a post-processing step. On the other side, [7] and [15] adopted hand-designed monotonic architectures, which may harden the training and not perform well in practice. Lastly, up to our knowledge, previous works mainly considered monotony under continuous inputs, while many industrial use-cases have monotony constraints on discrete inputs. One notable exception is the fairness verification in [25] that can be applied on both a discrete or a continuous input and holds similarity with monotony verification.

When it comes to continuous inputs, monotony is equivalent to verifying a property on the gradients on the whole domain. Indeed the sign of the gradient component corresponding to monotonous inputs should always be positive or negative. However, for a neural network with discrete inputs, the gradient sign condition is not necessary for the monotony to hold, even when the gradient can be computed by extending the input domain to reals. For piece-wise linear neural networks such as ReLU networks, we can base verification on the very definition of monotony (Definition 1), which can be cast as solving a mixed-integer linear programming problem. This method is complementary to the literature using the gradient condition and can verify monotony over discrete inputs.

Verifying the monotony is recognized to be more challenging than robustness since it is a global property on the whole domain rather than a local neighborhood [15]. However, we argue that applying partial monotony over the whole domain, which may affect the performance and put at risk the product's release, is a very drastic approach. Indeed, in an industrial context, it is necessary to balance quality and safety, especially as the systems will be constrained by other specifications than just monotony, such as accuracy. The solution we propose is a partitioning scheme that splits the operational domain into areas where the monotony property is respected and areas where it is (partially) violated; in the latter, the neural network's behavior could be mitigated. This possibility has been considered on a collision detection use case in [4] and studied at a higher level for the certification of a system before an ML component [17].

4   Monotony Analysis

In this section, we define the concept of *partial* monotony with respect to a set of inputs. Let $\mathcal{V}$ be a (finite) set of input features. For each feature $v \in \mathcal{V}$ we denote $\mathcal{D}(v)$ the domain in which v ranges. Hence, let $X = \times_{v \in \mathcal{V}} \mathcal{D}(v)$ be the input space, Y be the output space and $f{:}X{\to}Y$ be the neural network. Note that the features are generally of two types ($\mathcal{V} = \mathcal{V}_d \sqcup \mathcal{V}_c$):

- $v \in \mathcal{V}_d$ are features whose domain $\mathcal{D}(v)$ is discrete (*e.g.*, a finite set of labels or categorical values)
- $v \in \mathcal{V}_c$ are features whose domain $\mathcal{D}(v)$ is a real interval

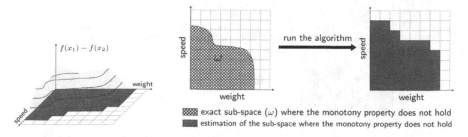

Fig. 2. Purpose of the algorithm through Example 1. In x_1 the runway is dry and in x_2 the runway is wet. The left plot represents $f(x_1) - f(x_2)$ where only the positive values are displayed (monotony property violated). The two plots on the right are the projection of these points on the plane composed of feature 1 and 2.

In this work, we are interested in monotony properties, which supposes that the set Y has an order relation denoted $\preceq$; usually, $Y \subseteq \mathbb{R}$ and $\preceq$ is one of the usual orders ($\leq$, $\geq$). The monotony property will be relative to a subset of discrete features, $\alpha \subseteq \mathcal{V}_d$ for which a partial order is defined on $\times_{v \in \alpha} \mathcal{D}(v)$, also denoted $\preceq$ without risk of confusion. For $x \in X$, let us denote $x{\downarrow}_\alpha$ the projection of x onto the dimensions in α, and $\bar\alpha = \mathcal{V} \backslash \alpha$.

Definition 1. *Monotony Property*
A function f is monotone with respect to an order $\preceq$ on the output domain Y and to a subset of discrete features $\alpha \subseteq \mathcal{V}_d$ endowed with a partial order defined on $\times_{v \in \alpha} \mathcal{D}(v)$ also denoted $\preceq$ (without risk of confusion) if and only if

$$\forall (x_1, x_2) \in X^2 : x_1 {\downarrow}_{\bar\alpha} = x_2 {\downarrow}_{\bar\alpha} \wedge x_1 {\downarrow}_\alpha \preceq x_2 {\downarrow}_\alpha \implies f(x_1) \preceq f(x_2)$$

4.1 Goal of the Analysis

Our analysis aims to identify the sub-spaces where the monotony does not hold using a MILP solver. Example 1 describes a toy example (a simplified version of the case study in Sect. 5) that we will use to explain the main concepts.

Example 1. <u>Setup:</u> Let f be a neural network estimating the braking distance of an aircraft based on its speed, its weight and the runway's state (dry or wet).
<u>Property:</u> *for the same speed and weight ($x_1{\downarrow}_{\bar\alpha} = x_2{\downarrow}_{\bar\alpha}$), the braking distance on a wet runway must be higher than on a dry one ($x_1{\downarrow}_\alpha \preceq x_2{\downarrow}_\alpha \implies f(x_1) \preceq f(x_2)$).*
<u>Goal:</u> Identify and quantify the input areas where the property does not hold.

If we plot $f(x_1) - f(x_2)$ versus the speed and the weight, the Definition 1 holds if and only if all the values are negative. The 3D plot in Fig. 2 shows a sketch of this example when the monotony property partially holds, *i.e.* $f(x_1) - f(x_2)$ is partially positive. To ease the visualization we only draw the positive values. The crosshatched area in the 2D plots are projections of the positive values of the curve on the plane representing the speed and the weight features and

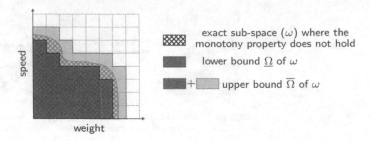

Fig. 3. Based on Fig. 2: representation of $\underline{\Omega}$ and $\overline{\Omega}$ considering Example 1 (Color figure online)

models the area where the monotony property is not respected, namely the Non-Monotonic Space Coverage denoted as ω. The rightmost 2D plot shows what we expect from our analysis on Example 1: identifying and estimating ω. To estimate ω, we partition the space (grid in Fig. 2) and then the monotony property is checked on each sub-spaces. The dark red area represents the identified sub-space where monotony issues occur, i.e., an over-approximation of ω. In addition, our approach provides a lower and upper bound of the size of ω relative to the whole input domain, respectively denoted as $\underline{\Omega}$ and $\overline{\Omega}$ (See Fig. 3).

Our approach can distinguish the sub-spaces where the monotony property does not hold (dark red area in Fig. 3) from the ones where it partially holds (orange area in Fig. 3). Hence, the lower bound is the dark red area, while the upper bound is the dark red and orange areas. The benefit of having a lower and upper bound, instead of just an overestimation, is to be able to assess whether our estimation is precise: large gaps between the upper and lower bound may reveal that our bounds are not representative of ω. The iterative nature of our approach overcomes this problem: we refine our space, which leads to a finer grid for the Fig. 3 and run again the MILP solver where the property partially holds to have a most accurate estimation of ω.

4.2 MILP Formulation

Neural Network Encoding. Let $f : X \rightarrow Y$ be a neural network composed of n layers with ReLU activations. The layer 0 corresponds to the input layer while the layer n to the output one. We use the MILP formulation proposed by [3], which uses the big-M method [8] to encode the ReLU activation. By convention, the notations in bold denote the MILP variables, and those not in bold denote constants. For $1 \leq i \leq (n-1)$, let C^i be the conjunction of constraints for the layer i:

$$C^i \triangleq \quad \hat{\mathbf{x}}^{\mathbf{i}} = W^i \mathbf{x}^{\mathbf{i-1}} + b^i \tag{1}$$

$$\wedge \, \mathbf{x}^{\mathbf{i}} \leq \hat{\mathbf{x}}^{\mathbf{i}} + M^i(1 - \mathbf{a}^{\mathbf{i}}) \qquad \wedge \qquad \mathbf{x}^{\mathbf{i}} \geq \hat{\mathbf{x}}^{\mathbf{i}} \tag{2}$$

$$\wedge \, \mathbf{x}^{\mathbf{i}} \leq M^i \cdot \mathbf{a}^{\mathbf{i}} \qquad \wedge \qquad \mathbf{x}^{\mathbf{i}} \geq 0 \tag{3}$$

$$\wedge \, \mathbf{a}^{\mathbf{i}} \in \{0, 1\}^{|\mathbf{x}^{\mathbf{i}}|} \tag{4}$$

where $\hat{\mathbf{x}}^{\mathbf{i}}$ and $\mathbf{x}^{\mathbf{i}}$ are the vector of neuron values at the layer i before and after the ReLU activation respectively. M^i is a large valid upper bound s.t. $-M^i \leq \hat{\mathbf{x}}^{\mathbf{i}}$ and $\mathbf{x}^{\mathbf{i}} \leq M^i$ [3]. W_i and b_i are, respectively, the weights and bias at the layer i, and $\mathbf{a}^{\mathbf{i}}$ is a binary vector that represents whether the neurons are activated or not. The Eq. (1) is the constraint for the affine transformation and the Eqs. (2)–(4) are the constraints encoding the ReLU activation. For the output layer n, there is no ReLU activation, then we have:

$$C^n \triangleq \quad \hat{\mathbf{x}}^{\mathbf{n}} = W^n \mathbf{x}^{\mathbf{n-1}} + b^n \tag{5}$$

It remains to encode the constraints of the input layer, which enforce the lower and upper bounds of the domain of the input features. Our analysis relies on a partition of the input space X, thus the encoding of the input layer will depend on it: let $\mathcal{P}$ be a partition of X, $p \in \mathcal{P}$ be a subset of X represented by a set of linear constraints (also denoted p). Hence, the neural network f is encoded as the conjunction of the constraints defined for each layer and p which is constraining the input layer:

$$C^f(p) \triangleq p \wedge \left(\bigwedge_{i=1}^{n} C^i \right) \wedge C^n \tag{6}$$

Monotony Property Encoding. Following Definition 1, we must encode f twice in MILP: C_1^f and C_2^f. Similarly to the encoding of the input space's constraints, we encode the monotony property regarding the partition $\mathcal{P}$. So, let $p_i, p_j \in \mathcal{P}^2$ be two sub-spaces of X such that $\exists x_1, x_2 \in p_i \times p_j$, $x_1 \downarrow_{\bar{\alpha}} = x_2 \downarrow_{\bar{\alpha}} \wedge x_1 \prec x_2$. Then, we have:

$$C^{mon}(p_i, p_j) \triangleq \left(\mathbf{x_1^0} \downarrow_{\bar{\alpha}} = \mathbf{x_2^0} \downarrow_{\bar{\alpha}} \wedge \ \mathbf{x_1^0} \downarrow_{\alpha} \preceq \mathbf{x_2^0} \downarrow_{\alpha} \right) \wedge \left(C_1^f(p_i) \wedge C_2^f(p_j) \right) \wedge \left(\hat{\mathbf{x}}_1^{\mathbf{n}} \leq \hat{\mathbf{x}}_2^{\mathbf{n}} \right) \tag{7}$$

$$C^{\neg mon}(p_i, p_j) \triangleq \left(\mathbf{x_1^0} \downarrow_{\bar{\alpha}} = \mathbf{x_2^0} \downarrow_{\bar{\alpha}} \wedge \ \mathbf{x_1^0} \downarrow_{\alpha} \preceq \mathbf{x_2^0} \downarrow_{\alpha} \right) \wedge \left(C_1^f(p_i) \wedge C_2^f(p_j) \right) \wedge \left(\hat{\mathbf{x}}_1^{\mathbf{n}} \geq \hat{\mathbf{x}}_2^{\mathbf{n}} + \epsilon \right) \tag{8}$$

The MILP solver may output either SAT, UNSAT or TIMEOUT. For (7) and (8), TIMEOUT means that the time limit is reached. C^{mon} checks whether the neural network f is monotonic:

- SAT: there is an assignment for $\mathbf{x_1^0}, \mathbf{x_2^0} \in p_i \times p_j$ which respects the monotony.
- UNSAT: the monotony is violated on the entire sub-space $p_i \times p_j$.

$C^{\neg mon}$ checks whether the neural network is not monotonic:

- SAT: there is an assignment for $\mathbf{x_1^0}, \mathbf{x_2^0} \in p_i \times p_j$ which violates the monotony.
- UNSAT: the monotony is respected on the complete sub-space $p_i \times p_j$.

To avoid having SAT for $C^{\neg mon}$ when $\hat{\mathbf{x}}_1^{\mathbf{n}} = \hat{\mathbf{x}}_2^{\mathbf{n}}$, we introduce the ϵ term (Eq. 8).

To determine for each sub-space $p_i \times p_j$ whether the monotony property holds, partially holds, or does not hold (see Fig. 3), we must solve successively $C^{\neg mon}$ and C^{mon} (see Sect. 4.3 for more detail).

Algorithm 1. Monotony analysis refinement

Require: T: the number of iteration of the procedure

1: $P_1 \leftarrow \{(p_i, p_j) \in \mathcal{P}^2 \mid \exists(x_1, x_2) \in p_i \times p_j,\ x_1 \prec x_2 \text{ and } x_1 \downarrow_{\bar{\alpha}} = x_2 \downarrow_{\bar{\alpha}}\}$

2: $\Omega_0 \leftarrow 0$ and $\widehat{P}_0 \leftarrow P_1$

3: $\Omega \leftarrow [\,]$, $\mathbb{P}^{\neg\text{mon}} \leftarrow \emptyset$, and $\mathbb{P}^{\text{partially mon}} \leftarrow \emptyset$

4: **for** t from 1 to T **do**

5: $\quad \widehat{P}_t \leftarrow \widehat{P}_{t-1} \wedge P_t$

6: $\quad (P_t^{\neg\text{mon}}, P_t^{\text{partially mon}}) \leftarrow \mathbf{F}(\widehat{P}_t)$

7: $\quad \underline{\Omega_t} \leftarrow \underline{\Omega_{t-1}} + \frac{|P_t^{\neg\text{mon}}|}{|P_t|}$ and $\quad \overline{\Omega_t} \leftarrow \underline{\Omega_t} + \frac{|P_t^{\text{partially mon}}|}{|P_t|}$ {See Fig. 4}

8: $\quad \Omega \leftarrow \Omega + (\underline{\Omega_t}, \overline{\Omega_t})$

9: $\quad \mathbb{P}^{\neg\text{mon}} \leftarrow \mathbb{P}^{\neg\text{mon}} \cup P_t^{\neg\text{mon}}$ and $\quad \mathbb{P}^{\text{partially mon}} \leftarrow P_t^{\text{partially mon}}$

10: $\quad \widehat{P}_t \leftarrow P_t^{\text{partially mon}}$

11: $\quad P_{t+1} \leftarrow \mathbf{partition}(P_t)$

12: **end for**

13: **return** Ω, $\mathbb{P}_{\neg\text{mon}}$ and $\mathbb{P}_{\text{partially mon}}$

4.3 Verification Procedure

As explained in Sect. 4.1, our verification procedure implies the partition of the space and the verification of each sub-space. In Algorithm 1 the monotony property is iteratively analyzed regarding a partition while refining this partition in the zone of interest to sharpen the analysis. Algorithm 2 details the verification run at each iteration.

Algorithm 1. The monotony is defined on the space X^2; however, we define earlier the partition $\mathcal{P}$ of X. Hence to verify the monotony on the complete space, i.e. X^2, we need to go through all the sub-spaces i.e. $p_i \times p_j, \forall(p_i, p_j) \in \mathcal{P}^2$. However, it may happen that the monotony does not apply to the sub-space (p_i, p_j) because there are no comparable elements within the sub-space: P_1, in Line 1, contains all and only the (p_i, p_j) including comparable elements. We denote the elements of P_1 and more generally, P_t, "monotony scenario".

We propose an iterative procedure where at each iteration we use, in Line 6, $\mathbf{F}(\cdot)$ (see Algorithm 2) to retrieve $P_t^{\neg\text{mon}}$ and $P_t^{\text{partially mon}}$. Then, we compute in Line 7 the metrics $\underline{\Omega_t}$ and $\overline{\Omega_t}$ for the iteration t, which respectively lower-bounds and upper-bounds ω; ω is the exact ratio of the space where f is not monotonic, which corresponds to the ratio of monotony scenarios where f is not monotonic. In Line 11, we refine the partition of the space for the next iteration: $\mathbf{partition}$ is the function that takes the current partition of the space and returns a finer partition; we suppose that all elements in the partition have the same size. Note that P_t gets finer and finer through the iterations: the more we refine, the more elements P_t will have. We highlight that in Line 5, the operator $\wedge$ applies the intersection between each subset of $\widehat{P}_{t-1}$ and P_t where P_t is a finer partition of the space than $\widehat{P}_{t-1}$. It allows to get the elements of interest ($\widehat{P}_{t-1}$) in the right level of details (P_t). For the first iteration, we run $\mathbf{F}(\cdot)$ on all the elements (initialization of $\widehat{P}_0$ to P). However, we only need to refine the sub-spaces where the monotony property is partially respected for the other iterations. Finally,

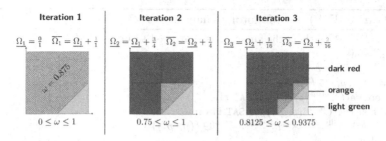

Fig. 4. Run of Algorithm 1 on Example 1 with the detailed computation of $\underline{\Omega}_t$ and $\overline{\Omega}_t$. The crosshatched area represents the sub-space the algorithm strives to estimate. (Color figure online)

the algorithm returns the lower and upper bounds of each iteration and all the sub-spaces where the monotony property does not hold or partially holds.

In Fig. 4 we run Algorithm 1 on Example 1[1]: α contains the runway's state, we partition X on α and we have a unique (p_i, p_j) in P_1; in p_i the runway is dry and in p_j wet. Then, the two axes represent features of $\bar{\alpha}$ (speed and weight) and the squares, the partition of the space. The crosshatched surface is the exact sub-space where the monotony property does not hold. The orange squares means that the monotony property partially holds, the dark red squares means it does not hold, and the light green squares means it holds. Through the iteration, we refine the partition (smaller squares) while running the verification only for the smaller squares (in solid lines) coming from a bigger orange square (in Line 5; $\widehat{P}_{t-1}$ is the orange square of iteration 2 and P_t is the small squares of iteration 3).

Algorithm 2. The verification function $\mathbf{F}(P)$ aims to analyze the monotony of f regarding P a subset of $\mathcal{P}^2$ which gathers the sub-spaces where the monotony property must be checked. Intuitively, the partition $\mathcal{P}$ and thus P can be seen as the level of details of the monotony analysis. Indeed, a finer partition $\mathcal{P}$ results in smaller sub-spaces in P; hence a more detailed analysis.

Then, from Lines 4 to 12, we identify in which sub-spaces $p_i \times p_j$ the neural network f partially respects or does not respect the monotony property and sort them in $P^{\text{partially mon}}$ and $P^{\neg\text{mon}}$. In Lines 4 and 5, solve($\cdot$) refers to any off-the-shelf MILP solver taking as input a MILP problem. Table 1 shows the interpretation of the monotony of f within the sub-space regarding every truth values of the conditions of Lines 4 and 5. Note that we arrive in Line 11 when the condition of Line 4 is False, and we jump to the next sub-space (or monotony scenario) because the monotony property holds for the current sub-space $p_i \times p_j$. Finally, we return the two sets gathering the sub-spaces where the monotony property does not hold and where it partially holds.

---

[1] Note that we simplify the crosshatched area's shape in order to know the omega value for the explanation.

Algorithm 2. $\mathbf{F}(P) \longrightarrow$ Monotony analysis of $P \subseteq \mathcal{P}^2$

Require: $P \subseteq \mathcal{P}^2$ gathers the sub-spaces that need to be verified.
1: $P^{\neg mon} \leftarrow \emptyset$
2: $P^{partially\ mon} \leftarrow \emptyset$
3: **for all** $(p_i, p_j) \in P$ **do**
4:    **if** solve($C^{\neg mon}(p_i, p_j)$) is SAT **then**
5:       **if** solve($C^{mon}(p_i, p_j)$) is SAT **then**
6:          $P^{partially\ mon} \leftarrow P^{partially\ mon} \cup \{(p_i, p_j)\}$
7:       **else**
8:          $P^{\neg mon} \leftarrow P^{\neg mon} \cup \{(p_i, p_j)\}$
9:       **end if**
10:   **else**
11:      Continue to the next (p_i, p_j) {Monotonic on the whole domain $p_i \times p_j$}
12:   **end if**
13: **end for**
14: **return** $P^{\neg mon}$ and $P^{partially\ mon}$ $\{\{P^{\neg mon} \cup P^{partially\ mon}\} \subseteq P\}$

Table 1. State of the monotony property regarding the condition of Lines 4 and 5

Case	Line 4	$C^{\neg mon}$	Line 5	C^{mon}	Monotony property on $p_i \times p_j$
1	True	SAT	True	SAT	partially holds
2	True	SAT	False	UNSAT	does not hold
3	False	UNSAT	-	-	holds

Non-monotonic Space Coverage. $\underline{\Omega_t}$ and $\overline{\Omega_t}$ are defined as the ratio of subspaces (monotony scenarios) where f has monotony issue over the total number sub-spaces in P_t (contains all the monotony scenarios):

Definition 2. *Lower bound and upper bound of ω*

$$\underline{\Omega_t} = \underline{\Omega_{t-1}} + \frac{|P_t^{\neg mon}|}{|P_t|} \quad (9) \qquad \overline{\Omega_t} = \underline{\Omega_t} + \frac{|P_t^{partially\ mon}|}{|P_t|} \quad (10)$$

On the one hand, $\underline{\Omega_t}$ takes into account only the sub-spaces where the monotony property holds not; hence, it lower-bounds ω. On the other hand, $\overline{\Omega_t}$ considers the sub-spaces where the monotony property holds not and partially holds; hence, it upper-bounds ω. Figure 4 details the computation of these metrics along with the iteration: at each iteration, the lower bound $\underline{\Omega_t}$ is represented by all the dark red squares and the upper bound $\overline{\Omega_t}$ by all the dark red and orange squares.

Example 2. Computation of $\underline{\Omega_t}$ and $\overline{\Omega_t}$ considering Example 1.

Iteration 1. We consider the entire space. Hence, we only have one sub-space where we assess the monotony property ($|P_t| = 1$). There is no dark red square, *i.e.* sub-space where the monotony property does not hold, which means that $|P_1^{\neg mon}| = 0$, then $\underline{\Omega_1} = 0$. We have one orange square: in this sub-space, the monotony property partially holds, then $|P_1^{partially\ mon}| = 1$ and $\overline{\Omega_1} = 1$.

Iteration 2. We partition the space in 4 smaller sub-spaces ($|P_t| = 4$) and run again the verification on each sub-space. We proceed similarly as previously for the computation of $\underline{\Omega_2}$ and $\overline{\Omega_2}$. We have 3 dark red squares ($|P_2^{\neg\text{mon}}| = 3$) and 1 orange square ($|P_2^{\text{partially mon}}| = 1$): $\underline{\Omega_2} = \underline{\Omega_1} + \frac{3}{4} = 0.75$ and $\overline{\Omega_2} = \underline{\Omega_2} + \frac{1}{4} = 1$.

Iteration 3. We refine the partition of the previous step, and we end up with 16 sub-spaces. However, we only run the verification on the sub-spaces coming from an orange square (Lines 5 of Algorithm 1), *i.e.*, a sub-spaces where f is partially monotonic. We have $\underline{\Omega_3} = \frac{3}{4} + \frac{1}{16} = 0.8125$ and $\overline{\Omega_3} = \frac{3}{4} + \frac{1}{16} + \frac{2}{16} = 0.9375$.

The Proposition 1 shows that the lower and upper bounds are tighter over the iterations: the more iterations we run, the closer to ω we are.

Proposition 1. *For any $t \geq 1$, we have*

$$\underline{\Omega_{t-1}} \leq \underline{\Omega_t} \quad (11) \quad and \quad \overline{\Omega_t} \leq \overline{\Omega_{t-1}} \quad (12)$$

Proof. For Eq. 11, from the facts that

$$\underline{\Omega_0} = 0 \quad and \quad \frac{|P_t^{\neg\text{mon}}|}{|P_t|} \geq 0 \quad and \quad \underline{\Omega_t} = \underline{\Omega_{t-1}} + \frac{|P_t^{\neg\text{mon}}|}{|P_t|},$$

we can deduce $\underline{\Omega_{t-1}} \leq \underline{\Omega_t}$.

Then, to prove Eq. 12, we need first to state some invariant: for the computation of $\overline{\Omega_t}$ (Algorithm 1, Line 7) we have,

$$\left(P_t^{\text{partially mon}} \cup P_t^{\neg\text{mon}}\right) \subseteq \hat{P}_t \quad (13)$$

Based on Eq. (13), we have:

$$\left|P_t^{\text{partially mon}} \cup P_t^{\neg\text{mon}}\right| \leq \left|\hat{P}_t\right|$$

$$\leq \left|P_{t-1}^{\text{partially mon}}\right| * \frac{|P_t|}{|P_{t-1}|} \qquad \text{By construction of } \hat{P}_t \text{ which is a finer partition of } P_{t-1}^{\text{partially mon}}$$

$$\underline{\Omega_{t-1}} + \frac{\left|P_t^{\text{partially mon}} \cup P_t^{\neg\text{mon}}\right|}{|P_t|} \leq \underline{\Omega_{t-1}} + \frac{\left|P_{t-1}^{\text{partially mon}}\right|}{|P_{t-1}|} \qquad \text{We divide both side of the inequality by } \left|\hat{P}_t\right| \text{ and add } \underline{\Omega_{t-1}}$$

$$\underline{\Omega_{t-1}} + \frac{|P_t^{\neg\text{mon}}|}{|P_t|} + \frac{\left|P_t^{\text{partially mon}}\right|}{|P_t|} \leq \overline{\Omega_{t-1}} \qquad P_t^{\text{partially mon}} \cap P_t^{\neg\text{mon}} = \emptyset$$

$$\underline{\Omega_t} + \frac{\left|P_t^{\text{partially mon}}\right|}{|P_t|} \leq \overline{\Omega_{t-1}}$$

$$\overline{\Omega_t} \leq \overline{\Omega_{t-1}}$$

5 Case Study: Braking Distance Estimation

5.1 Description of the Case Study

Our case study comes from the aeronautical industry. It is an R&D project consisting in training a neural network to estimate the braking distance of an

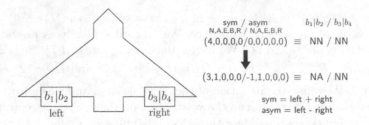

Fig. 5. Representation of the position of the four brakes on an aircraft denoted by $b_i \in \{N, A, E, B, R\}$. For example, we have NN-NN when all the brakes are in the normal state. Then if the state of one of the left brakes becomes *Altered*, we have NA-NN. Note that NA-NN≡AN-NN due to the choice of the representation of the brakes.

aircraft based on physical information. The R&D team provides us with a trained feedforward neural network composed of 2 layers (30 and 29 neurons on the first and second layers, respectively) and ReLU activation functions. There are 15 input features, including 13 discrete and 2 continuous. Among the discrete features, ten describe the state of the brakes. The aircraft has 4 brakes, and each brake has 5 possible modes: Normal (N), Altered (A), Emergency (E), Burst (B), and Released (R). Then, the network has 2 features for each mode: *(i)* the total number of brakes in a given mode (referred to as "symmetric") and *(ii)* the difference between the number of brakes on the left and right side of a given mode (referred to as "asymmetric"). From this information, we can find back the states of the pairs of brakes on the left and right sides of the aircraft (see Fig. 5), although the state of each individual brake cannot be retrieved. For clarity and since we have the equivalence between both notations, we will describe the state of the brakes using the form "b_1b_2-b_3b_4".

To show how to handle simultaneously several input features within the monotony property, we focus on the one involving the state of the brakes. We can textually express the monotony property as follows:

When the brakes' state deteriorates, the braking distance should increase.

To perform the monotony analysis, we need to define what *deteriorates* means formally. Relying on the system expert's knowledge, the following partial order applies to the different modes of the brake:

$$N \prec_b A \prec_b E \prec_b B \prec_b R \tag{14}$$

where $b_i \prec_b b_j$ means that the state b_j is more deteriorated than the state b_i. We can easily extend the partial order $\preceq_b$ on one brake to the state of an aircraft's brakes composed of 4 brakes. Let $S_1 = (b_1, b_2, b_3, b_4)$ and $S_2 = (b'_1, b'_2, b'_3, b'_4)$ be two states of an aircraft's brakes, we have

$$S_1 \prec S_2 \iff \forall b_i, b'_i \in S_1 \times S_2, \ b_i \preceq_b b'_i \text{ and } \exists b_i, b'_i \in S_1 \times S_2 \ b_i \prec_b b'_i \tag{15}$$

It means that S_2 is deteriorated compared to S_1 if and only if for all brakes in S_2, the brake's mode in S_2 is at most as good as its counterpart in S_1 and there exists a brake in S_2 whose mode is strictly worse than its counterpart in S_1.

5.2   Experimentation

Setup. Let $\mathcal{V}$ be the set of 15 input features described above, $X = \times_{v \in \mathcal{V}} \mathcal{D}(v)$ be the input space, $Y = \mathbb{R}^+$ be the output space, and $f : X \mapsto Y$ be the neural network estimating the braking distance of an aircraft. We consider the monotony property as formulated in Definition 1. As stated earlier, we are dealing with the monotony with respect to the brakes' space. Hence, $\alpha \subseteq \mathcal{V}$ is made up of the ten features describing the state of the brakes and the partial order $\preceq$ on $\times_{v \in \alpha} \mathcal{D}(v)$ is as defined in Eq. (15). We take advantage of the discrete nature of the brakes' features: a natural partition $\mathcal{P}$ is to enumerate all the possible values for the ten brakes features. We have $|\mathcal{P}| = 225$.

Monotony Analysis. We run Algorithm 1 for 5 iterations with the setup described above. The algorithm is explained in Sect. 4.3. Here we only focus on the partitions used for the analysis and the refinement strategy which are specific to the case study. Additionally, we will see how to capitalize on the data available at each iteration to perform some space exploration. P_1 is setup using $\mathcal{P}$, and $\preceq$; it represents the brakes' sub-space. Then our partition's refining strategy is to start with the remaining discrete features (second iteration) and then consider the continuous features (the last three iterations). For the discrete features, the partitioning consists in enumerating the possible values, while for the continuous features, it consists of a uniform partition (finer through the iterations). To illustrate the impact of the refinement on the level of details of the analysis, we detail the total number of sub-spaces in each partition P_t: $|P_1| = 10800$, $|P_2| = 259200$, $|P_3| = 6480000$, $|P_4| = 25920000$ and $|P_5| = 103680000$.

Based on the partition and the outcomes of $\mathbf{F}(\cdot)$, the algorithm yields at each iteration the metrics $\underline{\Omega_t}$ and $\overline{\Omega_t}$. Nonetheless, for our case study, we put in place visualization means (see Fig. 6). However, the relevant visualizations helping space exploration are case-dependent, so we do not propose any generic way to do it. Firstly, it might be relevant to visualize the sub-space composed of the features on which the partial order $\preceq$ is defined, i.e. α corresponding to the brakes' space. It is modeled as a graph where the nodes are the brakes' states (the elements of $\mathcal{P}$), and the edges are the transitions between the states modeled by the partial order $\prec$ (the elements of P_1) and with the outcomes of the first iteration, we can highlight (dashed line in Fig. 6) the transitions which violate the monotony property (in Fig. 6, we plot only a sub-graph as an example). Then, to include the information of the formal verification of the following iteration in the space visualization, we plot some features versus the difference of distances $f(x_1) - f(x_2)$ and visualize in which sub-spaces monotony issue occurs. These visualizations are helpful for exploration purposes after the analysis for the expert of the system (e.g., if the expert can identify some place of interest within the space and wants to know what happens there).

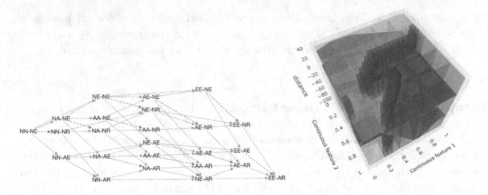

Fig. 6. Example of visualization of features in α (left) and $\bar{\alpha}$ (right).

Table 2. Values of $\underline{\Omega}$ and $\overline{\Omega}$ bounding the percentage of the space where the monotony property is violated.

Metrics	It.1	It.2	It.3	It.4	It.5
$\overline{\Omega_t}$	11.57%	4.11%	1.95%	1.72%	1.61%
$\underline{\Omega_t}$	0.03%	0.45%	1.12%	1.29%	1.39%

Metrics: Non-monotonic Space Coverage.

At each iteration, we compute $\underline{\Omega_t}$ and $\overline{\Omega_t}$, which bound the ratio of the space where f violates the monotony property (*i.e.* ω). The results are summarised in Table 2. In Fig. 7, we can clearly see the convergence of $\underline{\Omega_t}$ and $\overline{\Omega_t}$. At the first iteration, we can explain the notable gap between $\underline{\Omega_1}$ and $\overline{\Omega_1}$ by the coarse partitioning of the space. That is why, $\overline{\Omega_1}$ is large (numerous sub-spaces where the monotony property is partially respected) and $\underline{\Omega_1}$ small (only few sub-spaces where the monotony property does not hold). We can notice a significant drop of $\overline{\Omega_t}$ compared to the rise of $\underline{\Omega_t}$: there are more sub-spaces where the monotony property holds than not. Eventually the algorithm yields a narrow gap between the bounds; we obtain at the fifth iteration: $1.39\% \leq \omega \leq 1.61\%$. The stopping criterion of the algorithm may depends on various things such that the system's requirements (e.g. bounds precision, max value to not cross for $\underline{\Omega}$ or min value to reach for $\overline{\Omega}$).

Through these five steps, we analyze the monotony of f considering finer and finer partition of the space; we obtain: *(i)* metrics bounding the percentage of the space where the neural network is non-monotonic and *(ii)* the identification of the sub-spaces where the monotony issue occurs thanks to the formal verification on each elements of the partitions.

We run our experiments on MacBook Pro 8 core 2,3 GHz Intel Core i9 with 32 Gb of RAM. The MILP solver used is Gurobi 9 [10] and our monotony analysis took less than 10 h.

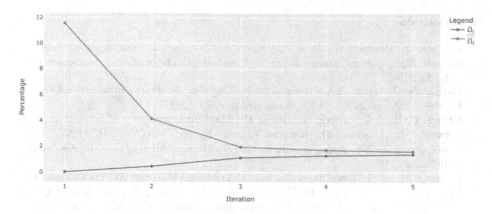

Fig. 7. Evolution of $\underline{\Omega_t}$ and $\overline{\Omega_t}$

6 Conclusion

This work develops an iterative method to assess the monotony of a neural network using a MILP solver. The monotony property defined is suited for discrete features. This iterative method allows for lower and upper bounding the space where the neural network does not hold the property and formally identifies these areas. This is a step further in the demonstration that neural networks can preserve important function properties and therefore in the capability to embed the ML technology in an aeronautical safety-critical system.

We applied this method on an aeronautical case study that consists in estimating the braking distance of an aircraft using a neural network mixing discrete and continuous inputs. We managed to quantify the percentage of the space where the neural network does not preserve the monotony property and to identify formally each sub-space where it occurs. In addition, we showed that we can capitalize on the available data to visualize the sub-spaces for helping the braking function's experts in processing the results of the algorithm.

Note that this work leaves room for some optimizations, such as using tighter big-M values in Eq. 2–3, or using asymmetric bounds, computed by incomplete methods such as [23, 31]. To the best of our knowledge, the scalability of complete method remains a challenge in the verification community and is mainly used with "shallow" neural networks. Thus, this method is mainly useful for small to medium networks used as surrogates or for control.

As an extension of this work, we plan to estimate the integral under the curve of $f(x_1) - f(x_2)$ in the sub-spaces where the monotony is violated by leveraging our definition of the monotony property. This would give a key indicator on the level of violation of the monotony property that could support the performance of the training phase. Another perspective would be to extend this work to continuous features by using the formulation of the monotony based on the gradient.

References

1. Biannic, J., Hardier, G., Roos, C., Seren, C., Verdier, L.: Surrogate models for aircraft flight control: some off-line and embedded applications. Aerospace Lab (12), 1 (2016)
2. Carlini, N., Wagner, D.A.: Towards evaluating the robustness of neural networks. In: IEEE SP, pp. 39–57. IEEE Computer Society (2017)
3. Cheng, C.-H., Nührenberg, G., Ruess, H.: Maximum resilience of artificial neural networks. In: D'Souza, D., Narayan Kumar, K. (eds.) ATVA 2017. LNCS, vol. 10482, pp. 251–268. Springer, Cham (2017). https://doi.org/10.1007/978-3-319-68167-2_18
4. Damour, M., et al.: Towards certification of a reduced footprint ACAS-Xu system: a hybrid ML-based solution. In: Habli, I., Sujan, M., Bitsch, F. (eds.) SAFECOMP 2021. LNCS, vol. 12852, pp. 34–48. Springer, Cham (2021). https://doi.org/10.1007/978-3-030-83903-1_3
5. EASA: Concept paper first usable guidance for level 1 machine learning applications (2021). https://www.easa.europa.eu/downloads/134357/en
6. Feelders, A.J.: Prior knowledge in economic applications of data mining. In: Zighed, D.A., Komorowski, J., Żytkow, J. (eds.) PKDD 2000. LNCS (LNAI), vol. 1910, pp. 395–400. Springer, Heidelberg (2000). https://doi.org/10.1007/3-540-45372-5_42
7. Gauffriau, A., Malgouyres, F., Ducoffe, M.: Overestimation learning with guarantees. arXiv preprint arXiv:2101.11717 (2021)
8. Grossmann, I.E.: Review of nonlinear mixed-integer and disjunctive programming techniques. Optim. Eng. **3**(3), 227–252 (2002)
9. Gupta, A., Shukla, N., Marla, L., Kolbeinsson, A., Yellepeddi, K.: How to incorporate monotonicity in deep networks while preserving flexibility? arXiv preprint arXiv:1909.10662 (2019)
10. Gurobi Optimization, LLC: Gurobi Optimizer Reference Manual (2022). https://www.gurobi.com
11. Hao, J., Ye, W., Jia, L., Wang, G., Allen, J.: Building surrogate models for engineering problems by integrating limited simulation data and monotonic engineering knowledge. Adv. Eng. Inform. **49**, 101342 (2021)
12. Jian, Z.D., Chang, H.J., Hsu, T.S., Wang, D.W.: Learning from simulated world - surrogates construction with deep neural network. In: SIMULTECH 2017: Proceedings of the 7th International Conference on Simulation and Modeling Methodologies, Technologies and Applications. SCITEPRESS (2017)
13. Karpf, J.: Inductive modelling in law: example based expert systems in administrative law. In: Proceedings of the 3rd International Conference on Artificial Intelligence and Law, pp. 297–306 (1991)
14. Katz, G., et al.: The marabou framework for verification and analysis of deep neural networks. In: Dillig, I., Tasiran, S. (eds.) CAV 2019. LNCS, vol. 11561, pp. 443–452. Springer, Cham (2019). https://doi.org/10.1007/978-3-030-25540-4_26
15. Liu, X., Han, X., Zhang, N., Liu, Q.: Certified monotonic neural networks. Adv. Neural. Inf. Process. Syst. **33**, 15427–15438 (2020)
16. Madry, A., Makelov, A., Schmidt, L., Tsipras, D., Vladu, A.: Towards deep learning models resistant to adversarial attacks. In: ICLR. OpenReview.net (2018)
17. Mamalet, F., et al.: White paper machine learning in certified systems. IRT Saint Exupéry - ANITI (2021)
18. Müller, M.N., Makarchuk, G., Singh, G., Püschel, M., Vechev, M.: PRIMA: general and precise neural network certification via scalable convex hull approximations. Proc. ACM Program. Lang. **6**(POPL), 1–33 (2022)

19. Nguyen, A.P., Martínez, M.R.: Mononet: towards interpretable models by learning monotonic features. arXiv preprint arXiv:1909.13611 (2019)
20. Peterson, E., DeVore, M., Cooper, J., Carr, G.: Run time assurance as an alternate concept to contemporary development assurance processes. NASA/CR-2020-220586 (2020)
21. Raghunathan, A., Steinhardt, J., Liang, P.S.: Semidefinite relaxations for certifying robustness to adversarial examples. In: Advances in Neural Information Processing Systems, pp. 10877–10887 (2018)
22. Sudakov, O., Koroteev, D., Belozerov, B., Burnaev, E.: Artificial neural network surrogate modeling of oil reservoir: a case study. In: Lu, H., Tang, H., Wang, Z. (eds.) ISNN 2019. LNCS, vol. 11555, pp. 232–241. Springer, Cham (2019). https://doi.org/10.1007/978-3-030-22808-8_24
23. Tjeng, V., Xiao, K.Y., Tedrake, R.: Evaluating robustness of neural networks with mixed integer programming. In: ICLR (2019)
24. Tsuzuku, Y., Sato, I., Sugiyama, M.: Lipschitz-margin training: scalable certification of perturbation invariance for deep neural networks. In: NeurIPS, pp. 6542–6551 (2018)
25. Urban, C., Christakis, M., Wüstholz, V., Zhang, F.: Perfectly parallel fairness certification of neural networks. Proc. ACM Program. Lang. 4(OOPSLA), 1–30 (2020)
26. Urban, C., Miné, A.: A review of formal methods applied to machine learning. arXiv preprint arXiv:2104.02466 (2021)
27. Wang, S., Pei, K., Whitehouse, J., Yang, J., Jana, S.: Formal security analysis of neural networks using symbolic intervals. In: 27th USENIX Security Symposium (USENIX Security 2018), Baltimore, MD, pp. 1599–1614. USENIX Association, August 2018
28. Wang, S., et al.: Beta-CROWN: efficient bound propagation with per-neuron split constraints for neural network robustness verification. In: Advances in Neural Information Processing Systems (2021)
29. Weng, T.W., et al.: Towards fast computation of certified robustness for ReLU networks. arXiv preprint arXiv:1804.09699 (2018)
30. Xiang, W., Tran, H.D., Johnson, T.T.: Output reachable set estimation and verification for multilayer neural networks. IEEE Trans. Neural Netw. Learn. Syst. 29(11), 5777–5783 (2018)
31. Xu, K., et al.: Automatic perturbation analysis for scalable certified robustness and beyond. In: NeurIPS (2020)
32. Zhang, H., Weng, T.W., Chen, P.Y., Hsieh, C.J., Daniel, L.: Efficient neural network robustness certification with general activation functions. In: Advances in Neural Information Processing Systems, pp. 4939–4948 (2018)
33. Zhang, H., Zhang, P., Hsieh, C.J.: Recurjac: an efficient recursive algorithm for bounding jacobian matrix of neural networks and its applications. In: Proceedings of the AAAI Conference on Artificial Intelligence, vol. 33, pp. 5757–5764 (2019)

Generating Domain-Specific Interactive Validation Documents

Fabian Vu$^{(\boxtimes)}$, Christopher Happe, and Michael Leuschel

Institut für Informatik, Universität Düsseldorf, Universitätsstr. 1,
40225 Düsseldorf, Germany
{fabian.vu,leuschel}@uni-duesseldorf.de

Abstract. In state-of-the-art approaches, requirements are gradually
encoded into the model, with each modeling step being *verified*. Once
the modeling and verification process has finished, code generation is
usually applied to generate the final product. Finally, the generated
code is *validated*, e.g., by executing tests, or running simulations. At
this point, stakeholders and domain experts are actively incorporated
into the development process. Especially in industrial applications, *validation* is as important as *verification*. Thus, it is important to integrate
the stakeholders' and the domain experts' feedback as early as possible. In this work, we propose two approaches to tackle this: (1) a static
export of an animation trace into a single HTML file, and (2) a dynamic
export of a classical B model to an interactive HTML document, both
with a domain-specific visualization. For the second approach, we extend
the high-level code generator B2PROGRAM by JavaScript, and integrate
VISB visualizations. An important aspect here is to ease communication
between modelers and domain experts, which is achieved by implementing features to share animated traces, and giving feedback to each other.

1 Introduction and Motivation

Verification checks the software for bugs, tackling the question "Are we building the software correctly?" [17]. Just as important is validation, which checks
whether the stakeholders' requirements are fulfilled and thus tackling the question "Are we building the right software?" [17].

An important aspect of validation is the dialogue between modelers and
stakeholders or domain experts. The latter are usually not familiar with the formal method and notation, while the modeler only has limited knowledge about
the domain. Animation and visualization of scenarios is an important enabling
technology: a domain expert can grasp the behavior of a model by looking at
visualizations, without having to understand the underlying mathematical notation. Even for modelers, visualization is important; some errors are immediately

This research is part of the IVOIRE project funded by the "Deutsche Forschungsgemeinschaft" (DFG) and the Austrian Science Fund (FWF); grant # I 4744-N. Sect. 3
is part of the KI-LOK project funded by the "Bundesministerium für Wirtschaft und
Energie"; grant # 19/21007E.

J. F. Groote and M. Huisman (Eds.): FMICS 2022, LNCS 13487, pp. 32–49, 2022.
https://doi.org/10.1007/978-3-031-15008-1_4

obvious in a visual rendering, while they can remain hidden within the mathematical, textual counterpart.

In this paper, we tackle one further hurdle that domain experts or stakeholders face: in addition to lacking knowledge and experience with formal notations, they typically also lack the knowledge to drive the particular tool, or possibly even install it. In this article we propose two solutions to this:

- a static export of an animation trace into a single HTML file, that can be sent by email and rendered in any current browser. This export is available for all models supported by PROB [23], and enables the user to navigate within the trace.
- a dynamic export of a classical B model (and optionally pre-configured traces), to an HTML document which can also be rendered in a current browser. This export uses the high-level B code generator B2PROGRAM [35] which is extended by JavaScript. While not applicable to all models, the export is completely dynamic: a user can freely navigate the model's state space, not just one pre-configured trace.

First, we present validation workflow in Sect. 2. Section 3 describes the static export of an animation trace into a single HTML file. In Sect. 4, we describe a dynamic export of a classical B model (including a VISB visualization) to an interactive HTML document. Section 5 demonstrates how this work improves validation of requirements by domain experts, and communication between modelers and domain experts. Finally, we compare our work with related work in Sect. 6, and conclude in Sect. 7.

Background. PROB [23] is an animator, constraint solver, and model checker for formal methods, such as B, Event-B, Z, TLA+, CSP, and Alloy. PROB2-UI [3] is a JavaFX-based graphical user interface which has been developed on top of PROB. Two features of PROB2-UI are especially relevant for this work: the persistent storage and replay of traces, and VISB.

VISB [38] is a tool to create interactive visualizations of formal models using SVG images and a glue file. The VISB glue file defines the main SVG image, as well as observers and click listeners which link the graphical elements with the model's state. Using VISB, a user can view the model's current state graphically, and execute operations by clicking on visual elements. Many features have been added in response to feedback from academic and industrial uses since VISB's original publication [38]. New features include iterators for groups of related SVG objects, multiple click events for SVG objects, dynamic SVG object creation, and SVG class manipulation for hovers. Furthermore, VISB's core has been reimplemented in Prolog and integrated into PROB's core. Thus, VISB can now be used from PROB's command-line interface directly (without PROB2-UI [3]).

B2PROGRAM [35] is a code generator for high-level B models, which targets Java, C++, Python, Rust, and also TypeScript/JavaScript now. Unlike other B code generators, the model does not have to be refined to an implementable subset of B, called B0. This enables code generation from a formal B model at various abstraction levels for validation and demonstration purposes. B2PROGRAM is implemented using the STRINGTEMPLATE [29] engine which allows targeting multiple languages with a single code generator. This is achieved by mapping each construct to a template which is rendered to the target code.

2   Validation Workflow

Figure 1 shows a typical formal methods workflow: A system or software is modeled step-by-step until all requirements are encoded. Furthermore, the model is refined until reaching an implementable subset of the modeling language (e.g. B0 in the B method). Each development step of the model is verified by provers such as ATELIERB [7], or by model checkers such as PROB. After finishing the modeling process, a low-level code generator (e.g. an ATELIERB B0 code generator) is applied to generate the final program from a verified model.

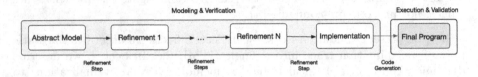

Fig. 1. Typical Formal Methods Workflow

In our opinion, software is often validated too late during the development process, possibly after generating the final code. Figure 2 describes the approach followed by this work: We extend the high-level B code generator B2PROGRAM [35] by JavaScript generation and supporting VISB [38] visualizations. In particular, an HTML document is generated, supporting early-stage validation (e.g. running scenarios) by a domain expert. As result, domain experts are integrated into the development process at an early stage.

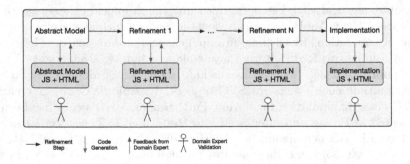

Fig. 2. Workflow: Code Generation for Validation

While Fig. 2 is also feasible with existing animators like PROB, our approach enables communication via "interactive validation documents", where the model's formal aspects are hidden and no formal methods tool has to be installed by the domain expert.

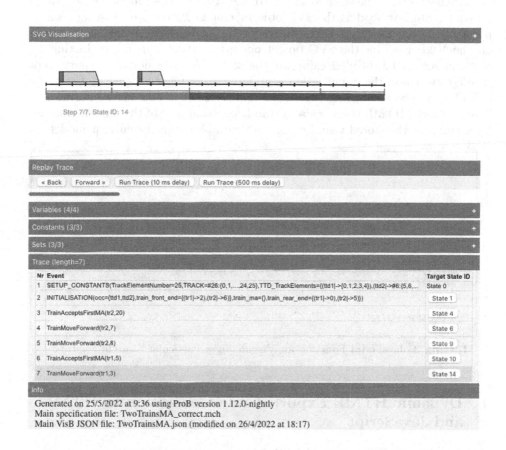

Fig. 3. Static VISB Export of Trace from Railway Domain

3   Static VisB HTML Export

In this section, we present another new feature of VISB to export a trace as a standalone HTML file containing the visualization of the entire trace. This approach is supported by all formalisms in PROB. The trace can either be constructed interactively in the animator or automatically by model checking or simulation. The HTML file enables the user to navigate the trace, and inspect the visualization of each state in the trace, without installing PROB. The model's variables and constant values are also accessible. Furthermore, the trace can be replayed automatically at different speeds. An example export can be seen in Fig. 3.[1]

This feature has been used for the communication of modelers with domain experts, e.g., in follow-on projects of the ETCS Hybrid Level 3 [15].

When exporting the trace to an HTML file, a JavaScript function is generated for each state, hard-coding the SVG objects' changed attributes. Listing 2 shows parts of the function that is generated for the state shown in Fig. 3. Focusing on the VISB item for the SVG object `occupied_ttd_polygon` (see Listing 1), one can see its hard-coded value for the state. When a domain expert steps through the trace, the visualization is updated according to the current state by executing the corresponding function. Figure 3 also contains meta-information. Thus, a stored HTML trace is also a standalone snapshot of the model. One can later compare the stored visualization and variables with the current model.

```
1  {
2    "id":"occupied_ttd_polygon",
3    "attr":"points",
4    "value":"svg_set_polygon(OCC_TE,100.0/real(TrackElementNumber+1),100.0,2.0)"
5  }
```

Listing 1. VISB Item for Occupied Section on Track

```
1  function visualise14(stepNr) {
2    setAttr("visb_debug_messages","text","Step "+stepNr+"/7, State ID: 14");
3    setAttr("occupied_ttd_polygon","points","0.0,0 0.0,2.0
4              42.30769230769231,2.0 42.30769230769231,0 100.0,0");
5    ...
6    highlightRow(stepNr);
7  }
```

Listing 2. JavaScript Function for Visualizing a Particular State in Figure 3

4   Dynamic HTML Export: Code Generation to HTML and JavaScript

Instead of generating a static HTML file consisting of a single trace, we now present a second approach which allows a domain expert to interact with the model. This approach is only supported for (a subset of) classical B. In this section, we describe how interactive HTML documents are generated technically. As state values are **computed** in JavaScript dynamically, a domain expert can explore alternate paths, and not just the exported one.

Figure 4 shows the infrastructure for code generation to HTML and JavaScript. In addition to the B model, B2PROGRAM also expects the VisB glue file and the associated SVG visualization as input. To support JavaScript, we extend B2PROGRAM by TypeScript as described in our previous work [35]. Here, we decided not to generate JavaScript directly, but to generate TypeScript

---

[1] A more complex one is available at https://www3.hhu.de/stups/models/visb/ train_4_POR_mch.html.

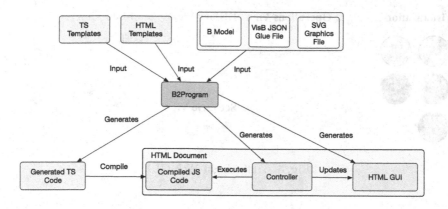

Fig. 4. Code Generation from B Model and VisB to HTML and JavaScript

code as an intermediate step, which is then transpiled to JavaScript. As Type-Script supports stricter typing, it is easier to debug during development, and to detect errors at compile time. Following the steps described in [35], we first implement TypeScript templates, and the B data types in TypeScript.

Listing 3 shows a TypeScript template which is used for code generation from INITIALISATION. For code generation, B2PROGRAM's current implementation could be used directly without extending the code in B2PROGRAM. Using the STRINGTEMPLATE engine in B2PROGRAM, this applies to almost all constructs. The main effort was to implement the B data types including the B operators in TypeScript. Listing 4 shows an example of code generation of INITIALISATION tl_cars := red; tl_peds := red to TypeScript.

In addition to TypeScript templates, we also implemented HTML templates from which the graphical user interface (GUI) is generated. B2PROGRAM also generates a controller for the GUI and the translated B model. The controller's task is to execute operations in the translated model, and to update the GUI based on the model's current state.

```
1  initialization(properties, values, body) ::= <<
2  constructor() {
3      <properties; separator="\n">
4      <values>
5      <body>
6  }
7  >>
```

Listing 3. TypeScript Template for INITIALISATION

```
1  constructor() {
2      this.tl_cars = new colors(enum_colors.red);
3      this.tl_peds = new colors(enum_colors.red);
4  }
```

Listing 4. Generated TypeScript Code from INITIALISATION in Traffic Light

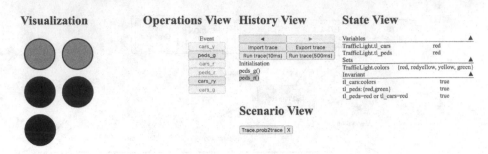

Fig. 5. Traffic Light Web GUI

4.1   Graphical User Interface

Figure 5 shows the GUI that is generated from a formal model which is now explained in detail.[2] The GUI is inspired by PROB2-UI [3] and consists of its main views.

VisB View. On the left-hand side, one can see the domain-specific VISB visualization. Its features include (1) graphical representation based on the model's current state, and (2) interaction with the model, i.e., executing an operation by clicking on a graphical object.

Listing 5 shows a VISB item defining an observer on the model's state. Here, the SVG object **peds_red** should be filled **red** when the variable **tl_peds** is equal to **red**, otherwise **black**. As described in Sect. 3, values for the graphical objects' appearances are hard-coded in the static HTML export. To allow interactive animation, the visualization has to be updated based on the current state dynamically. For this purpose, the B expression is translated to JavaScript, and is thus evaluated at runtime (and not statically hard-coded as described in Sect. 3). The generated for Listing 5 is shown in Listing 6.

```
1  {
2     "id":"peds_red",
3     "attr":"fill",
4     "value":"IF tl_peds = red THEN \"red\" ELSE \"black\" END"
5  }
```

Listing 5. Example of VisB Item

```
1  _svg_vars["peds_red"] = document.getElementById("traffic_light")
2                          .contentDocument.getElementById("peds_red")
3  _svg_vars["peds_red"].setAttribute("fill",
4     (_machine._get_tl_peds().equal(new colors(enum_colors.red)).booleanValue() ?
5     new BString("red") :
6     new BString("black")).getValue());
```

Listing 6. Code Generation from Listing 5 to JavaScript

---

[2] The example is also available at https://www3.hhu.de/stups/models/visb/ TrafficLight/TrafficLight.html.

```
1   _svg_events["peds_red"] = document.getElementById("traffic_light")
2                          .contentDocument.getElementById("peds_red");
3   _svg_events["peds_red"].onclick = function() {
4      transition = _machine["_tr_peds_r"]();
5      ... // Check whether transition is feasible
6      var parameters = [];
7      var returnValue = _machine.peds_r(...parameters);
8   }
```

Listing 7. Code Generation from {"id":"peds_red", "event":"peds_r"} to JavaScript

For VISB events, B2PROGRAM generates a click listener on the SVG object which checks whether the corresponding B event is enabled, and executes it afterward. This makes it possible to interact with the model by clicking on the graphical element. {"id":"peds_red", "event":"peds_r"} defines a click event on peds_red, triggering the peds_r event. The generated code is shown in Listing 7.

Other Views. The HTML document also contains views to execute operations (*operations view*), to show the currently animated trace (*history view*), to store animated traces (*scenario view*), and to view the model's state in mathematical notations (*state view*). Although mathematical notations are difficult for a domain expert to understand, it is still important to debug the model. Code generation for executing an operation via the *operations view*, and displaying the state textually is analogous to the VISB observers is done similar to the VISB events and VISB observers respectively. There are also buttons to import, and export an animated trace represented in PROB2-UI's format. In Sect. 5, we demonstrate how this improves communication between modelers and domain experts.

4.2 Applicability of JavaScript Code Generation

Another important aspect is the applicability of JavaScript code generation. Here, we focus on the limitations and the performance.

Limitations. As the JavaScript code generator is based on B2PROGRAM, it shares the same restrictions that are discussed in [34,35].

For quantified constructs, B2PROGRAM only accepts models where the bounded variables are constrained by the first predicates: For bounded variables $a_1 \ldots a_n$ constrained by a predicate P, the first n conjuncts of P must constrain the bounded variables in the exact order they are defined. This allows assigning a value to a bounded variable directly, and iterating over a set to constrain this variable. B2PROGRAM also forbids set operations on infinite sets, or storing them in variables.

Using B2PROGRAM for simulation, non-deterministic constructs such as ANY, CHOICE, and non-deterministic assignments are translated by B2PROGRAM, only choosing one execution path [35]. Regarding this work, traces executing operations with those constructs can not be animated precisely. B2PROGRAM only allows top-level PRE and SELECT as non-determinism [34] for model checking. Inner guards, e.g., inner SELECTs cause problems when calculating enabled transitions (discussed in [34]). Regarding this work, a superset of actually possible transitions is shown to the user; those inner guards are checked when the user tries to execute the operation.

In conclusion, some models must be rewritten according to these rules; still, there are also models where it is not possible. So, B2PROGRAM can be used at an early development stage; but especially at a very early stage, some models are too high-level for B2PROGRAM. One must then refine the model further to enable B2PROGRAM for validation, or use the static export from Sect. 3. Note that B2PROGRAM supports a significantly larger subset than B0 code generators.

Performance. In the previous work [35], we already compared Java and C++ code generation with PROB. To achieve a good performance, we implement the B data types BSet and BRelation using persistent data structures (similar to Java and C++, see [35]). For JavaScript we use the Immutable[3] library, which also makes use of structural sharing [2].

We have benchmarked the models from [35] for PROB[4] and Java[5] again and compared with JavaScript[6]. As explained in [35], those selected models range from small to very large ones, covering various performance aspects. Each benchmark is run five times on an ASUS Vivobook 14 (R465JA-EK278T, 8 GB RAM, 1.2 GHz Intel i3 processor with two cores), and afterward, the median runtime is taken. The results are shown in Table 1.

Table 1 shows that the JavaScript benchmarks also outperform PROB. Train and Sieve are models with many set operations where JavaScript is less than one magnitude faster than PROB. For other benchmarks, JavaScript is also two or three magnitudes faster than PROB. JavaScript and Java benchmarks are usually in the same order of magnitude. Although JavaScript is an interpreted language, our new backend for B2PROGRAM performs very well; it seems that the JIT compiler in NodeJS can optimize efficiently.

Note, however, that Table 1 are benchmarks for simulation or trace-replay, *not* for animation, i.e., we measure the performance of executing the model on long-running paths where operations parameters are provided explicitly. In animation, the tools need to compute *all* enabled transitions and present them to the user. In this use case, PROB with its constraint-solving capability can be much faster than B2PROGRAM (discussed in [34]). For example, for the automotive case study in Sect. 5, PROB can be up to three orders of magnitude faster at computing all enabled transitions presented to the user. Still, for all the case studies, the performance of B2PROGRAM was sufficient for interactive exploration.

---

[3] https://immutable-js.com/.
[4] PROB CLI Release Version 1.1.1.
[5] OpenJDK 64-Bit Server VM (build 25.332-b03, mixed mode).
[6] NodeJS 17.6.0.

Table 1. Simulation Runtimes (PROB and Generated Java and JavaScript Code) in Seconds with Number of Operation Calls (op calls), Speed-Up Relative to PROB

Lift		PROB	Java	JavaScript
$(2 \times 10^9$ op calls)	Runtime	> 1200	9.25	21.38
	Speed-up	1	> 129.73	> 56.13
Traffic		PROB	Java	JavaScript
Light	Runtime	> 1200	3.6	63.82
$(1.8 \times 10^9$ op calls)	Speed-up	1	> 333.33	> 18.8
Sieve		PROB	Java	JavaScript
(1 op call,	Runtime	69.62	6.37	28.31
primes until 2 Million)	Speed-up	1	10.93	2.46
Scheduler		PROB	Java	JavaScript
$(9.6 \times 10^9$ op calls)	Runtime	> 1200	6.01	5.42
	Speed-up	1	> 199.67	> 221.4
sort_m2_		PROB	Java	JavaScript
data1000 [30]	Runtime	11.79	0.96	0.28
$(500 \times 10^3$ op calls)	Speed-up	1	12.28	42.11
CAN Bus		PROB	Java	JavaScript
(J. Colley,	Runtime	242.12	3.69	3.49
15×10^6 op calls)	Speed-up	1	65.62	69.38
Train [1]		PROB	Java	JavaScript
$(940 \times 10^3$ op calls)	Runtime	67.94	6.14	9.49
	Speed-up	1	11.07	7.16
Cruise		PROB	Java	JavaScript
Controller	Runtime	> 1200	8.99	19.50
$(136.1 \times 10^6$ op calls)	Speed-up	1	> 133.48	> 61.54

5 Case Studies

This section demonstrates how this work (1) makes it possible for a domain expert to validate requirements, and (2) improves communication between the modelers and the domain experts. We will study two case studies: a pitman controller from the automotive domain [24], and a landing gear from the aerospace domain [20].

Pitman Controller. Based on the specification by Houdek and Raschke [16], we use the pitman controller model by Leuschel et al. [24]. This model encodes a subset of requirements from the specification which contains the key ignition, the pitman controller, the blinking lights, and the hazard warning lights.

In the following, we focus on *sequence 7* which is given in the specification [16]. *Sequence 7* validates the turn indicator's and the hazard light's behaviors. In particular, events for tip blinking, direction blinking, and the hazard warning lights are executed, and the desired behavior is checked afterward.

Figure 6a shows parts of *sequence 7* from [16] after animation by a modeler in PROB2-UI. The sequence's feasibility in the model has already been shown by Leuschel et al. in [24]. Based on this sequence, we outline how our approach helps to improve communication between modelers and domain experts.

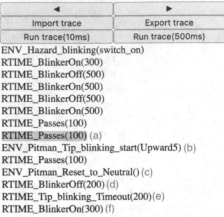

Position ▲	Transition
103	RTIME_BlinkerOff(delta=500)
104	RTIME_BlinkerOn(delta=500)
105	RTIME_BlinkerOff(delta=500)
106	RTIME_BlinkerOn(delta=500)
107	RTIME_Passes(delta=100)
108	RTIME_Passes(delta=100)
109	ENV_Pitman_Tip_blinking_start(newPos=Upward5)
110	RTIME_Passes(delta=100)
111	ENV_Pitman_Reset_to_Neutral
112	RTIME_BlinkerOff(delta=200)
113	RTIME_Tip_blinking_Timeout(delta=200)
114	RTIME_BlinkerOn(delta=300)
115	RTIME_Passes(delta=100)
116	RTIME_Passes(delta=100)
117	ENV_Hazard_blinking(newSwitchPos=switch_off)
118	RTIME_Nothing(delta=300, newOnCycle=FALSE)
119	RTIME_Nothing(delta=100, newOnCycle=FALSE)
120	RTIME_Nothing(delta=100, newOnCycle=FALSE)
121	RTIME_Nothing(delta=100, newOnCycle=FALSE)
122	RTIME_Nothing(delta=100, newOnCycle=FALSE)

History View

◀   ▶
Import trace   Export trace
Run trace(10ms)   Run trace(500ms)

ENV_Hazard_blinking(switch_on)
RTIME_BlinkerOn(300)
RTIME_BlinkerOff(500)
RTIME_BlinkerOn(500)
RTIME_BlinkerOff(500)
RTIME_BlinkerOn(500)
RTIME_Passes(100)
RTIME_Passes(100) (a)
ENV_Pitman_Tip_blinking_start(Upward5) (b)
RTIME_Passes(100)
ENV_Pitman_Reset_to_Neutral() (c)
RTIME_BlinkerOff(200) (d)
RTIME_Tip_blinking_Timeout(200)(e)
RTIME_BlinkerOn(300) (f)

(a) PROB2-UI

(b) Interactive Validation Document; (a) – (f) added manually; links to Figure 7

Fig. 6. Parts of Sequence 7 in History Views

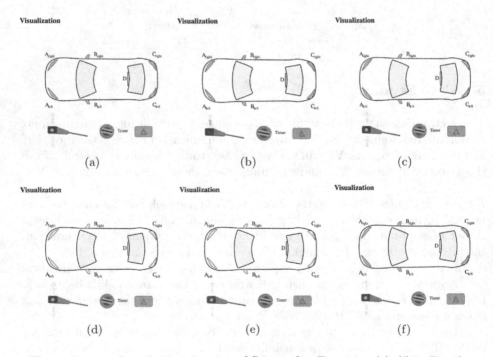

Fig. 7. Domain-Specific Visualization of States after Executing (a)–(f) in Fig. 6b

To ensure that the modeler has not misunderstood the requirements, he or she can then export the trace to a domain expert, who could load this trace into the generated HTML document (see Fig. 6b). The domain expert can then inspect whether the correct behavior was indeed implemented by the modeler.

A critical point in the sequence is to validate that "if the warning light is activated, any tip-blinking will be ignored or stopped if it was started before." (requirement **ELS-13** in [16]) This part of the animation is shown in Fig. 6b. With help of the domain-specific visualization (see Fig. 7), the domain expert can easily approve that the desired behavior has indeed been implemented. Furthermore, the dynamic export allows a domain expert to inspect alternate paths with the same behavior, to establish a stronger guarantee.

Landing Gear. The landing gear model [20] by Ladenberger et al. is modeled based on the specification by Boniol [5]. For the demonstration, we use the refinement level which includes gears, doors, handle, switch, and electro-valves. To be able to use B2PROGRAM, we have manually translated the Event-B model to classical B. Figure 8 shows parts of the generated GUI from the landing gear model which contains the VISB view and the history view. The domain-specific VISB view shows a hydraulic circuit consisting of the handle, the switch, and the electro-valves.

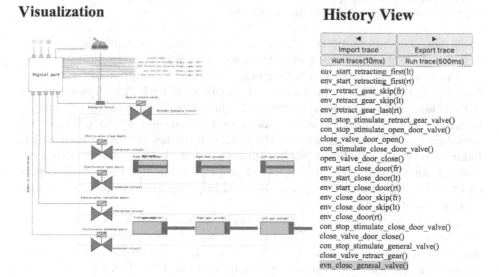

Fig. 8. Retraction Sequence with Hydraulic Circuit as Domain-Specific Visualization

Using the operations view (which we omitted here due to space reasons), a domain expert, e.g., an engineer can animate traces representing desired requirements. In this example, the domain expert has animated the *retraction sequence* from the specification. This trace can then be exported for ProB2-UI, to be used by a modeler. It can also be converted for use by another domain expert more focused on other aspects of the model. For instance, Fig. 9 shows an alternate domain-specific visualization with gears and doors. The second domain expert can

Visualization

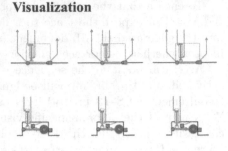

Fig. 9. Retraction Sequence with Gears and Doors as Domain-Specific Visualization

import the trace created from Fig. 8. Thus, our approach does not only improve communication between modelers and domain experts, but also between domain experts from different perspectives.

6   Related Work

In the following, we compare this work with existing tools that integrate domain experts in the software development process.

Requirements. Automatic translation of natural language requirements makes it possible to involve domain experts more directly in the validation process. An example is the requirements language FRETish [14] supported by the tool FRET [13]. Using FRET, the domain expert can write FRETish requirements in natural language which are translated to linear temporal logic (LTL). To further improve communication between modeler and domain expert, FRET supports visualizing and simulating the underlying LTL formulas. A similar approach is followed by the tool SPEAR [8]. In contrast, our work does not yet enable the domain expert to directly validate formal properties. Instead, the domain expert can run scenarios for certain properties, and inspect the behavior in a domain-specific visualization.

Other works support writing high-level domain-specific scenarios for execution on a formal model, e.g., Gherkin and Cucumber for Event-B to run scenarios using the ProB animator [9,32]. This allows a domain expert to write scenarios in natural language, execute them, and check the behavior afterward. As the base of communication, modelers and domain experts must agree on the events' meaning in natural language. Furthermore, the AVALLA language was introduced to write domain-specific scenarios in ASMs, and run them using AsmetaV [6]. Another ASM tool is ASM2C++ which translates ASMs to C++, and AVALLA scenarios to BDD code targeting the generated C++ code [4]. In contrast, our work does also not yet support natural language to write scenarios. Instead, the domain expert can create scenarios by interacting with the domain-specific VISB visualization. So, our base of communication is the VISB visualization, and the import/export of scenarios.

Documentation. PROB Jupyter [12] implements interaction with formal models (in B, Event-B, TLA+, etc.) in Jupyter notebooks via PROB. It also supports generating HTML, LaTeX, and PDF documents from the Jupyter notebooks. This way, it is also possible to validate requirements in PROB Jupyter, and to generate documentation with explanatory texts. However, PROB Jupyter does not yet support VISB domain-specific visualizations (only an older less flexible visualization technique [25]). In future, we would thus like to integrate VISB into [12], as an alternative to the static export in Sect. 3.

The LaTeX mode [22] of PROB can be used to produce LaTeX documents, and to generate documentation with explanatory texts, visualizations and tables. Again, it does not support VISB and domain-specific visualizations have to be created via LaTeX.

Visualizations. This work has already outlined how important (domain-specific) visualizations are to validate a formal model.

There are more visualization tools for the B method like BMotionWeb [18], BMotionStudio [19], AnimB[7], Brama [31], and the animation function [25] in PROB. A detailed comparison between these tools and VISB is described in [38]. In our approach, the domain expert does not need any expertise in dealing with formal models and tools. However, since the dynamic export is based on B2PROGRAM, only a subset of the B language is supported.

Stakeholders often describe state diagrams to formulate desired behavior patterns. State space projection was introduced by Ladenberger and Leuschel [21] to validate such diagrams. Our approach does not take state diagrams into account yet; this could be tackled in the future.

PVSio-Web [37] is a tool for visualizing PVS models and creating prototypes, especially human-machine interfaces. This enables the user to assemble an interactive visualization for the model. In our approach, VISB visualizations are created manually, i.e., by creating an SVG image in an editor such as Inkspace, and by writing the VISB glue file. There are also tools to create prototypes for VDM-SL models [27,28]. Similar to our work, those works also allow domain-specific visualization, animation, and recording scenarios. In addition to validation by users and domain experts, the VDM-SL tools also incorporate UI designers as stakeholders.

Simulators. JEB [26] supports animation, simulation and visualization by generating HTML with JavaScript from an Event-B model. The user can encode functions by hand to enable execution of complex models. To ensure the reliability of the simulated traces, JEB's approach introduced the notion of *fidelity*.

In our approach, it is also possible to write additional code by hand. Compared to JEB, B2PROGRAM supports importing/exporting of traces. JEB trans-

---

[7] http://wiki.event-b.org/index.php/AnimB.

lates Event-B models to JavaScript constructs which are then run by an *interpreter*. In contrast, B2PROGRAM *translates* B models nearly one-to-one to TypeScript classes.

Other techniques like co-simulation and timed probabilistic simulation are supported by tools such as INTO-CPS [33] and SIMB [36]. In PROB2-UI, SIMB can be used together with VISB. Simulation scenarios can thus be exported (cf. Sect. 3) to a domain expert. Another simulation tool is AsmetaS [10] which is part of the Asmeta toolset [11].

7   Conclusion and Future Work

In this work, we presented two solutions to improve the communication between modelers and domain experts by creating "interactive validation documents": (1) a (mostly) static export of a trace to an HTML file, (2) and a fully dynamic export of a classical B machine to an HTML document. While the static export works for all formalisms in PROB, the dynamic export only works for classical B machines supported by B2PROGRAM. The static export is suitable to analyse one scenario or trace, and allows the user to step through the saved trace and inspect the various states of the trace. In contrast, the dynamic export is suitable when domain experts have to animate traces, e.g., to modify existing traces, or to validate entire requirements.

Both approaches use domain-specific visualizations to help a domain expert reason about the formal model. For the dynamic export we extended B2PROGRAM to generate HTML and JavaScript code while incorporating VISB visualizations. This makes it possible to interact with the model and check its behavior without knowledge of the modeling language and its tools. Communication between modelers and domain experts is eased by features for importing and exporting scenarios. Overall, this work enables to involve domain experts in the development and validation process more actively. Those aspects have been demonstrated by two case studies: a light system model from the automotive domain, and a landing gear case study from the aerospace domain. Furthermore, we discussed the limitations of the dynamic export and analyzed the performance of the generated JavaScript from B2PROGRAM.

B2PROGRAM is available at:

https://github.com/favu100/b2program

Case studies are available at:

https://gitlab.cs.uni-duesseldorf.de/general/stups/visb-visualisation-
examples/-/tree/master/B2Program

In the future, we would like to allow writing additional text in natural language (e.g. requirement or explanatory text) for each executed operation of a trace. This would further ease communication between domain experts.

Acknowledgements. We would like to thank anonymous reviewers for their constructive feedback.

References

1. Abrial, J., Hoare, A.: The B-Book: Assigning Programs to Meanings. Cambridge University Press, Cambridge (2005)
2. Bagwell, P.: Ideal Hash Trees. Es Grands Champs, 1195 (2001)
3. Bendisposto, J., et al.: PROB2-UI: a java-based user interface for ProB. In: Lluch Lafuente, A., Mavridou, A. (eds.) FMICS 2021. LNCS, vol. 12863, pp. 193–201. Springer, Cham (2021). https://doi.org/10.1007/978-3-030-85248-1_12
4. Bonfanti, S., Gargantini, A., Mashkoor, A.: Design and validation of a C++ code generator from abstract state machines specifications. J. Softw. Evol. Process **32**(2), e2205 (2020)
5. Boniol, F., Wiels, V.: The landing gear system case study. In: Boniol, F., Wiels, V., Ait Ameur, Y., Schewe, K.-D. (eds.) ABZ 2014. CCIS, vol. 433, pp. 1–18. Springer, Cham (2014). https://doi.org/10.1007/978-3-319-07512-9_1
6. Carioni, A., Gargantini, A., Riccobene, E., Scandurra, P.: A scenario-based validation language for ASMs. In: Börger, E., Butler, M., Bowen, J.P., Boca, P. (eds.) ABZ 2008. LNCS, vol. 5238, pp. 71–84. Springer, Heidelberg (2008). https://doi.org/10.1007/978-3-540-87603-8_7
7. ClearSy. Atelier B, User and Reference Manuals. Aix-en-Provence, France (2016). http://www.atelierb.eu/
8. Fifarek, A.W., Wagner, L.G., Hoffman, J.A., Rodes, B.D., Aiello, M.A., Davis, J.A.: SpeAR v2.0: formalized past LTL specification and analysis of requirements. In: Barrett, C., Davies, M., Kahsai, T. (eds.) NFM 2017. LNCS, vol. 10227, pp. 420–426. Springer, Cham (2017). https://doi.org/10.1007/978-3-319-57288-8_30
9. Fischer, T., Dghyam, D.: Formal model validation through acceptance tests. In: Collart-Dutilleul, S., Lecomte, T., Romanovsky, A. (eds.) RSSRail 2019. LNCS, vol. 11495, pp. 159–169. Springer, Cham (2019). https://doi.org/10.1007/978-3-030-18744-6_10
10. Gargantini, A., Riccobene, E., Scandurra, P.: A metamodel-based simulator for ASMs. In: Proceedings ASM Workshop (2007)
11. Gargantini, A., Riccobene, E., Scandurra, P.: Model-driven language engineering: the ASMETA case study. In: Proceedings ICSEA, pp. 373–378 (2008)
12. Geleßus, D., Leuschel, M.: ProB and Jupyter for logic, set theory, theoretical computer science and formal methods. In: Raschke, A., Méry, D., Houdek, F. (eds.) ABZ 2020. LNCS, vol. 12071, pp. 248–254. Springer, Cham (2020). https://doi.org/10.1007/978-3-030-48077-6_19
13. Giannakopoulou, D., Pressburger, T., Mavridou, A., Schumann, J.: Generation of formal requirements from structured natural language. In: Madhavji, N., Pasquale, L., Ferrari, A., Gnesi, S. (eds.) REFSQ 2020. LNCS, vol. 12045, pp. 19–35. Springer, Cham (2020). https://doi.org/10.1007/978-3-030-44429-7_2
14. Giannakopoulou, D., Pressburger, T., Mavridou, A., Schumann, J.: Automated formalization of structured natural language requirements. Inf. Softw. Technol. **137**, 106590 (2021)
15. Hansen, D., et al.: Validation and real-life demonstration of ETCS hybrid level 3 principles using a formal B model. Int. J. Softw. Tools Technol. Transfer **22**(3), 315–332 (2020). https://doi.org/10.1007/s10009-020-00551-6
16. Houdek, F., Raschke, A.: Adaptive Exterior Light and Speed Control System (2019). https://abz2020.uni-ulm.de/case-study

17. Institute of Electrical and Electronics Engineers. IEEE Standard Computer Dictionary: A Compilation of IEEE Standard Computer Glossaries (1991)
18. Ladenberger, L.: Rapid creation of interactive formal prototypes for validating safety-critical systems. Ph.D. thesis, Universitäts-und Landesbibliothek der Heinrich-Heine-Universität Düsseldorf (2016)
19. Ladenberger, L., Bendisposto, J., Leuschel, M.: Visualising event-B models with B-motion studio. In: Alpuente, M., Cook, B., Joubert, C. (eds.) FMICS 2009. LNCS, vol. 5825, pp. 202–204. Springer, Heidelberg (2009). https://doi.org/10.1007/978-3-642-04570-7_17
20. Ladenberger, L., Hansen, D., Wiegard, H., Bendisposto, J., Leuschel, M.: Validation of the ABZ landing gear system using ProB. Int. J. Softw. Tools Technol. Transfer **19**(2), 187–203 (2015). https://doi.org/10.1007/s10009-015-0395-9
21. Ladenberger, L., Leuschel, M.: Mastering the visualization of larger state spaces with projection diagrams. In: Butler, M., Conchon, S., Zaïdi, F. (eds.) ICFEM 2015. LNCS, vol. 9407, pp. 153–169. Springer, Cham (2015). https://doi.org/10.1007/978-3-319-25423-4_10
22. Leuschel, M.: Formal model-based constraint solving and document generation. In: Ribeiro, L., Lecomte, T. (eds.) SBMF 2016. LNCS, vol. 10090, pp. 3–20. Springer, Cham (2016). https://doi.org/10.1007/978-3-319-49815-7_1
23. Leuschel, M., Butler, M.: ProB: a model checker for B. In: Araki, K., Gnesi, S., Mandrioli, D. (eds.) FME 2003. LNCS, vol. 2805, pp. 855–874. Springer, Heidelberg (2003). https://doi.org/10.1007/978-3-540-45236-2_46
24. Leuschel, M., Mutz, M., Werth, M.: Modelling and validating an automotive system in classical B and event-B. In: Raschke, A., Méry, D., Houdek, F. (eds.) ABZ 2020. LNCS, vol. 12071, pp. 335–350. Springer, Cham (2020). https://doi.org/10.1007/978-3-030-48077-6_27
25. Leuschel, M., Samia, M., Bendisposto, J.: Easy graphical animation and formula visualisation for teaching B. The B Method: from Research to Teaching, pp. 17–32 (2008)
26. Mashkoor, A., Yang, F., Jacquot, J.-P.: Refinement-based validation of event-B specifications. Softw. Syst. Model. **16**(3), 789–808 (2016). https://doi.org/10.1007/s10270-016-0514-4
27. Oda, T., Akari, K., Yamamoto, Y., Nakakoji, K., Chang, H.-M., Larsen, P.: Specifying abstract user interface in VDM-SL. In: Proceedings International Overture Workshop, pp. 5–20 (2021)
28. Oda, T., Yamamoto, Y., Nakakoji, K., Araki, K., Larsen, P.: VDM animation for a wider range of stakeholders. In: Proceedings Overture Workshop, pp. 18–32 (2015)
29. Parr, T.: StringTemplate Website (2013). http://www.stringtemplate.org/. Accessed 05 July 2022
30. Rivera, V., Cataño, N., Wahls, T., Rueda, C.: Code generation for event-B. STTT **19**(1), 31–52 (2017)
31. Servat, T.: BRAMA: a new graphic animation tool for B models. In: Julliand, J., Kouchnarenko, O. (eds.) B 2007. LNCS, vol. 4355, pp. 274–276. Springer, Heidelberg (2006). https://doi.org/10.1007/11955757_28
32. Snook, C., Hoang, T.S., Dghaym, D., Fathabadi, A.S., Butler, M.: Domain-specific scenarios for refinement-based methods. J. Syst. Architect. **112**, 101833 (2021)
33. Thule, C., Lausdahl, K., Gomes, C., Meisl, G., Larsen, P.G.: Maestro: the INTO-CPS co-simulation framework. Simul. Model. Pract. Theory **92**, 45–61 (2019)
34. Vu, F., Brandt, D., Leuschel, M.: Model checking B models via high-level code generation. In: Proceedings ICFEM (2022, to appear)

35. Vu, F., Hansen, D., Körner, P., Leuschel, M.: A multi-target code generator for high-level B. In: Ahrendt, W., Tapia Tarifa, S.L. (eds.) IFM 2019. LNCS, vol. 11918, pp. 456–473. Springer, Cham (2019). https://doi.org/10.1007/978-3-030-34968-4_25
36. Vu, F., Leuschel, M., Mashkoor, A.: Validation of formal models by timed probabilistic simulation. In: Raschke, A., Méry, D. (eds.) ABZ 2021. LNCS, vol. 12709, pp. 81–96. Springer, Cham (2021). https://doi.org/10.1007/978-3-030-77543-8_6
37. Watson, N., Reeves, S., Masci, P.: Integrating user design and formal models within PVSio-web. In: Proceedings Workshop Formal Integrated Development Environment, pp. 95–104 (2018)
38. Werth, M., Leuschel, M.: VisB: a lightweight tool to visualize formal models with SVG graphics. In: Raschke, A., Méry, D., Houdek, F. (eds.) ABZ 2020. LNCS, vol. 12071, pp. 260–265. Springer, Cham (2020). https://doi.org/10.1007/978-3-030-48077-6_21

Deductive Verification of Smart Contracts with Dafny

Franck Cassez$^{(\boxtimes)}$ ⓘ, Joanne Fuller, and Horacio Mijail Antón Quiles

ConsenSys, New York, USA
{franck.cassez,joanne.fuller,horacio.mijail}@consensys.net

Abstract. We present a methodology to develop verified smart contracts. We write smart contracts, their specifications and implementations in the verification-friendly language DAFNY. In our methodology the ability to write specifications, implementations and to reason about correctness is a primary concern. We propose a simple, concise yet powerful solution to reasoning about contracts that have *external calls*. This includes arbitrary re-entrancy which is a major source of bugs and attacks in smart contracts. Although we do not yet have a compiler from DAFNY to EVM bytecode, the results we obtain on the DAFNY code can reasonably be assumed to hold on Solidity code: the translation of the DAFNY code to Solidity is straightforward. As a result our approach can readily be used to develop and deploy safer contracts.

1 Introduction

The Ethereum network provides the infrastructure to implement a decentralised distributed ledger. At the core of the network is the Ethereum Virtual Machine [29] (EVM) which can execute programs written in EVM *bytecode*. This remarkable feature means that transactions that update the ledger are not limited to assets' transfers but may involve complex business logic that can be executed *programmatically* by *programs* called *smart contracts*.

Smart Contracts are Critical Systems. Smart contracts are programs and may contain bugs. For example, in some executions, a counter may over/underflow, an array dereference may be outside the range of the indices of the array. These runtime errors are vulnerabilities that can be exploited by malicious actors to attack the network: the result is usually a huge loss of assets, being either stolen or locked forever. There are several examples of smart contract vulnerabilities that have been exploited in the past: in 2016, a *re-entrance* vulnerability in the Decentralised Autonomous Organisation (DAO) smart contract was exploited to steal more than USD50 Million [13]. The total value netted from DeFi hacks in the first four months of 2022 [8], $1.57 billion, has already surpassed the amount netted in all of 2021, $1.55 billion.

Beyond runtime errors, some bugs may compromise the business logic of a contract: an implementation may contain subtle errors that make it deviate

ⓒ The Author(s), under exclusive license to Springer Nature Switzerland AG 2022
J. F. Groote and M. Huisman (Eds.): FMICS 2022, LNCS 13487, pp. 50–66, 2022.
https://doi.org/10.1007/978-3-031-15008-1_5

from the initial intended specifications (e.g., adding one to a counter instead of subtracting one).

The presence of bugs in smart contracts is exacerbated by the fact that the EVM bytecode of the contract is recorded in the immutable ledger and cannot be updated. The EVM bytecode of a contract is available in the ledger, and sometimes the corresponding source code (e.g., in Solidity [11], the most popular language to write smart contracts) is available too, although not stored in the ledger. Even if the source code is not available, the bytecode can be decompiled which makes it a target of choice for attackers. Overall smart contracts have all the features of safety critical systems and this calls for dedicated techniques and tools to ensure they are reliable and bug-free.

Smart Contracts are Hard to Verify. Ensuring that a smart contract is bug-free and correctly implements a given business logic is hard. Among the difficulties that software engineers face in the development process of smart contracts are:

- The most popular languages Solidity, Vyper [27] (and in the early development stage its offspring Fe [12]) to write smart contracts have cumbersome features. For instance there is a default *fallback* function that is executed when a contract is called to execute a function that is not in its interface. Some features like the composition of function modifiers have an ambiguous semantics [31] and developing a formal semantics of Solidity is still a challenge [19]. There are defensive mechanisms (reverting the effects of a transaction, enforce termination with gas consumption) that aim to provide some safety. However, these mechanisms neither prevent runtime errors nor guarantee functional correctness of a contract.
- Most of the languages (e.g., Solidity, Vyper for Ethereum) used to develop smart contracts are not *verification-friendly*. It is hard to express safety (and functional correctness properties) within the language itself. Proving properties of a contract usually requires learning another specification language to write specifications and then embed the source code into this specification language.
- Smart contracts operate in an *adversarial environment*. For instance, a contract can call other contracts that are untrusted, and that can even call back into the first contract. This can result in subtle vulnerabilities like *re-entrancy*, which are caused by other contracts.

Our Contribution. We present a methodology to develop verified smart contracts. First, we write smart contracts, their specifications and implementations in the verification-friendly language DAFNY. This is in contrast to most of the verification approaches for smart contracts that build on top of existing languages like Solidity or Vyper and require annotations or translations from one language to another. In our methodology the ability to write specifications, implementations and to reason about correctness is a primary concern. Second, we use a minimal number of contract-specific primitives: those offered at the EVM level. This has the advantage of reducing the complexity of compiling a high-level language like DAFNY to EVM bytecode. Third, we propose a simple, concise yet powerful solution to reasoning about contracts that have *external calls*. This includes arbitrary re-entrancy which is a major source of bugs and attacks in smart contracts. To summarise, our methodology comprises 3 main steps: 1) reason about the contract in isolation, *closed* contract, Sect. 2; 2) take into account possible exceptions, Sect. 3.1; 3) take into account arbitrary external calls, Sect. 3.2. Although we do not yet have a compiler from Dafny to EVM bytecode, the results we obtain on the DAFNY code can reasonably be assumed to hold on Solidity code: the translation of the DAFNY code in Solidity is straightforward. As a result our approach can readily be used to develop and deploy safer contracts.

Related Work. Due to the critical nature of smart contracts, there is a huge body of work and tools to test or verify them. Some of the related work targets highly critical contracts, like the deposit smart contracts [7,22,23], including the verification of the EVM bytecode.

More generally there are several techniques and tools[1] e.g., [2,3,9,14,15,30], for auditing and analysing smart contracts written in Solidity [11] or EVM bytecode, but they offer limited capabilities to verify complex functional requirements or do not take into account the possibility of re-entrant calls.

Most of the techniques [1,4,10,16,18,20,26,28] for the verification of smart contracts using high-level code implement a translation from Solidity (or Michelson for other chains) to some automated provers like Why3, F*, or proof assistants like Isabelle/HOL, Coq.

The work that is closest to our approach is [5]. In [5] a principled solution to check smart contracts with re-entrancy is proposed and based on instrumenting the code. Our solution (Sect. 3.2) is arguably simpler. Another difference is that [5] does not use the *gas* resource and is restricted to safety properties. Our approach includes the proof of termination using the fact that each computation has a bounded (though potentially arbitrary large) amount of resources. Modelling the gas consumption is instrumental in the solution we propose in Sect. 3.2 as it enables us to prove termination and to reason by well-founded induction on contracts with external calls.

2   Verification of Closed Smart Contracts

In this section, we introduce our methodology in the ideal case where the code of a smart contract is *closed*. By closed, we mean that there are no calls to functions outside (e.g., an external library or another smart contract) of the contract itself.

An Abstract View of the EVM. The Ethereum platform provides a global computer called the Ethereum Virtual Machine, EVM, to execute smart contracts.

In essence, smart contracts are similar to classes/objects in OO programming languages: they can be created/destructed, they have a non-volatile *state*, and they offer some *functions* (interface) to modify their state. Smart contracts are

---

[1] https://github.com/leonardoalt/ethereum_formal_verification_overview.

usually written in high-level languages like Solidity or Vyper and compiled into low-level EVM *bytecode*. The EVM bytecode of a contract is recorded in the ledger and is immutable. The state of the contract can be modified by executing some of its functions and successive states' changes are recorded in the ledger.

Transactions and Accounts. Participants in the Ethereum network interact by submitting *transactions*. Transactions can be simple ETH (Ethereum's native cryptocurrency) transfer requests or requests to execute some code in a smart contract. The initiator of a transaction must bound the resources they are willing to use by providing a maximum amount of *gas maxG*. In the EVM, each instruction consumes a given (positive) amount of gas. The execution of a transaction runs until it (normally) ends or until it runs out of gas. Before running a computation, the initiator agrees on a *gas price, gp*, i.e., how much one gas unit is worth in ETH. At the end of the computation, if there is gl gas units left,[2] the initiator is charged with $(maxG - gl) \times gp$ ETH. To implement this type of bookkeeping, the initiator must have an *account*, the *balance* of which is larger than the maximum fee of $maxG \times gp$ ETH, before executing the transaction.

There are two types of accounts in Ethereum: a *user* account which is associated with a physical owner; and a *contract* account which is associated with a piece of code stored in the ledger. Both have a *balance*, stored in the ledger, which is the amount of ETH associated with the account. An account is uniquely identified by its (160-bit) *address*.

Execution of a Transaction. The execution of a transaction involving a contract account can be thought of as a *message call*: an account m sends a message to a contract account c to execute one of its functions $f(\cdot)$ with parameters x; this call is denoted $c.f(x)$. The call can originate from a user account or from a contract account. When executing $c.f(x)$ some information about the caller m is available such has m's account's address and the maximum amount of gas m is willing to pay for the execution of $c.f(x)$. The caller m can also transfer some ETH to c at the beginning of the transaction. The general form of a transaction initiated by m and involving a contract c is written:

$$m \rightarrow v, g, c.f(x)$$

where m is the *initiator* of the transaction, v the *amount of ETH* to be transferred to c before executing $f(x)$, and g the *maximum amount of gas* m is willing to pay to execute $c.f(x)$. To reason about the correctness of smart contracts in a high-level language (not EVM bytecode), we use some features that are guided by the EVM semantics:

– the values of m, v, g in a transaction are fixed; this means that we can write a transaction as a standard method call of the form $c.f(x, msg, g)$ where $msg = (m, v)$ by just adding these values as (read-only) parameters to the original function f. We specify all the contracts' functions in this form $c.f(x, msg, g)$. In msg, m is the *message sender*, $msg.sender$, v the message value, $msg.value$.

---

[2] The EVM tracks the amount of gas left relative to the maximum.

– The only requirement on the gas consumption is that every function consumes at least one unit of gas, and similar for every iteration of a loop. We use the gas value to reason about termination, and we do not take into account the actual gas cost that only makes sense on the EVM bytecode.

Specification with Dafny. To mechanically and formally verify smart contracts, we use the verification-friendly language DAFNY [17]. DAFNY natively supports Hoare style specification in the form of pre- and post-conditions, as well as writing proofs as programs, and offers both imperative, object-oriented and functional programming styles. The DAFNY verification engine checks that the methods satisfy their pre- and post-conditions specifications and also checks for the runtime errors like over/underflows. The result of a verification can be either "no errors" – all the methods satisfy their specifications –, "possible violation" of a specification – this may come with a counter-example – or the verification can time out. The form of verification implemented in DAFNY is *deductive* as the verifier does not try to synthesise a proof but rather checks that a program adheres to its specification using the available hints. The hints can range from bounds on integer values to more complex lemmas. We refer the reader to [17] for a more detailed introduction to the language and its implementation.

To model the concepts (transaction, accounts) introduced so far, we provide some data types and an `Account` trait, Listing A.1. A trait is similar to an interface in Java. It can be mixed in a class or in another trait to add some specific capabilities. The trait `Account` provides two members: the balance of the account and its type[3] (contract or non-contract which is equivalent to user). For example, a user account can be created as an instance of the `UserAccount` class, line 16. A contract account is created by mixing in the `Account` trait and by setting the type of the contract accordingly: for instance, the `Token` contract, Listing A.2, mixes in `Account` providing the `balance` and `isContract` members. For high-level reasoning purposes it is enough to define a type `Address` as a synonym for `Account`.

Example: A Simplified Token Contract. We now show how to use our methodology to specify, implement and reason about a simple contract: a simplified `Token` contract. This contract implements a cryptocurrency: tokens can be minted and transferred between accounts. The contract's functionalities are:

– the contract's *creator* (an account) can mint new tokens at any time and immediately assign them to an account. This is provided by the `mint` function;
– tokens can be sent from an account `from` to another `to` provided the sender's (`from`) balance allows it. This is provided by the `transfer` function.

The complete DAFNY code (specification and implementation) for the `Token` contract is given in Listing A.2:

– the contract is written as a class and has a *constructor* that initialises the values of the state variables;

---

[3] In this paper we do not use any specific features related to the type of an account.

Listing A.1. Datatypes and Account Trait in DAFNY.

```
1   /** A message. */
2   datatype Msg = Msg(sender: Account, value: uint256)
3
4   type Address = Account
5
6   /** Provide an Account. */
7   trait Account {
8       /** Balance of the account. */
9       var balance : uint256
10
11      /** Type of account. */
12      const isContract: bool
13  }
14
15  /** A user account. */
16  class UserAccount extends Account {
17
18      constructor(initialBal: uint256)
19          ensures balance == initialBal
20      {
21          balance := initialBal;
22          isContract := false;
23      }
24  }
```

- each method has a *specification* in the standard form of predicates: the *pre-conditions*, `requires`, and the *post-condition*, `ensures`;
- the `Token` contract has a *global invariant*, `Ginv()`. The global invariant must be maintained by each method call. To ensure that this is the case, `Ginv()` is added to the pre- and post-conditions of each method[4] (inductive invariant);
- the contract is instrumented with *ghost* variables, and possibly ghost functions and proofs. Ghost members are only used in proofs and do not need to be executable. Moreover, a ghost variable cannot be used to determine the behaviour of non-ghost methods for example in the condition of an `if` statement;
- the *sum(m)* function is not provided but computes the *sum* of the *values* in the map *m*;
- each method consumes at least one unit of gas and returns the gas left after when it completes.

The `Token` contract has two non-volatile state variables: `minter` and `balances`. The `minter` is the creator of the instance of the contract (constructor) and is a `constant`, which enforces it can be written to only once. Initially no tokens have been minted and the map that records the balances (in `Token`, not ETH) is empty (line 20). In this specification the creator of the contract is free to deposit some ETH into the contract account. Note that we can also specify Solidity-like attributes: for instance, `payable` is a Solidity attribute that can be assigned to a function to allow a contract to receive ETH via a call to this function. If a function is not payable, ETH cannot be deposited in the contract via this function. In our setting we can simply add a pre-condition: `msg.value == 0` (Listing A.2, line 36).

---

[4] For the constructor it is only required to hold after the constructor code is executed.

The global invariant of the contract (line 9) states that the total amount of tokens is assigned to the accounts in `balances`. The ghost variable `totalAmount` keeps track of the number of minted tokens. The transfer method (line 32) requires that the source account is in the `balances` map whereas the target account may not be in yet. In the latter case it is added to the map. Note that the initiator must be the source account (`msg.sender == from`, line 36).

Verification of the Simplified Token Contract. The DAFNY verification engine can check whether implementations satisfy their pre-/post-conditions. In the case of the `Token` contract, DAFNY reports "no errors" which means that:

- there are no runtime errors in our program. For instance the two requirements `balances[from] >= amount` (line 34) and `balances[to] as nat + amount as nat <= MAX_UINT256` guarantee that the result of the operation is an `uint256` and there is no over/underflows at lines 50, 51. The update of a map m is written $m[k := v]$ and results in a map m' such that $m'[w] = m[w], k \neq w$ and $m'[k] = v$ (lines 50, 51, 72).
- The global invariant `GInv()` must be preserved by each method call: if it holds at the beginning of the execution of a method, it also holds at the end. This global invariant must also hold after the constructor has completed. If DAFNY confirms `GInv()` holds everywhere, we can conclude that `GInv()` holds after any finite number of calls to either `mint` or `transfer`.
- There are some other pre- and post-conditions that are in the specifications. For example, the `old` keyword refers to the value of a variable at the beginning of the method and line 41 states that the balance of the `from` account has been decreased by `amount`.

The specification of the `Token` contract presented in this section assumes the pre-conditions hold for each message (method) call. In practice, this has to be ensured at runtime: it is impossible to force an initiator to submit a transaction that satisfies the pre-conditions of a method. However, this is a reasonable assumption as in case the pre-conditions do not hold, we can simply abort the execution. This kind of behaviour is supported by the EVM semantics where it is possible to return a status of a computation and abort (similar to an exception) the execution of the function and *revert* its effects on the contract's state. Another more serious simplification of the `Token` contract is that there is no *external call* to another contract's method. It turns out that external calls can be problematic in smart contracts and are the source of several attacks.

Listing A.2. A Simple Token Contract in DAFNY.

```
1   class Token extends Account {
2
3       const minter: Address   // minter cannot be updated after creation
4       var balances : map<Address, uint256>
5
6       ghost var totalAmount: nat
7
8       /** Contract invariant. */
9       predicate GInv()
10          reads this`totalAmount, this`balances
11      {
12          totalAmount == sum(balances)
13      }
14
15      /** Initialise contract.  */
16      constructor(msg: Msg)
17          ensures GInv()
18          ensures balance == msg.value && minter == msg.sender
19      {
20          isContract, minter, balances, balance := true, msg.sender, map[], msg.value;
21          totalAmount := 0;
22      }
23
24      /**
25       *  @param  from    Source Address.
26       *  @param  to      Target Address.
27       *  @param  amount  The amount to be transfered from `from` to `to`.
28       *  @param  msg     The `msg` value.
29       *  @param  gas     The gas allocated to the execution.
30       *  @returns        The gas left after executing the call.
31       */
32      method transfer(from:Address,to:Address,
33          amount:uint256,msg:Msg,gas: nat) returns (g:nat)
34          requires from in balances && balances[from] >= amount && msg.sender == from
35          requires gas >= 1
36          requires msg.sender == from   && msg.value == 0;
37          requires to !in balances ||
38              balances[to] as nat + amount as nat <= MAX_UINT256
39          requires GInv()
40          ensures GInv()
41          ensures from in balances && balances[from] >= old(balances[from]) - amount
42          ensures to in balances
43          ensures to != from ==> balances[to] >= amount
44          decreases gas
45          modifies this
46      {
47          balance := balance + msg.value;
48          var newAmount: uint256 := balances[from] - amount ;
49          balances :=
50              balances[to := (if to in balances then balances[to] else 0) + amount];
51          balances := balances[from := newAmount];
52      }
53
54      /**
55       *  @param  to      Target Address.
56       *  @param  amount  The amount to receiving the newly minted tokens
57       *  @param  msg     The `msg` value.
58       *  @param  gas     The gas allocated to the execution.
59       *  @returns        The gas left after executing the call.
60       */
61      method mint(to:Address,amount: uint256,msg:Msg,gas:nat) returns (g:nat)
62          requires msg.sender == minter
63          requires gas >= 1
64          requires to !in balances ||
65              balances[to] as nat + amount as nat <= MAX_UINT256
66          requires GInv()
67          ensures totalAmount == old(totalAmount) + amount as nat
68          ensures GInv()
69          modifies this`balances, this`totalAmount
70      {
71          balances :=
72              balances[to := (if to in balances then balances[to] else 0) + amount];
73          // The total amount increases.
74          totalAmount := totalAmount + amount as nat;
75          g := gas - 1;
76      }
77  }
```

In the next section we show how to reason about smart contracts under adversarial conditions: exceptions and external calls.

3   Verification Under Adversarial Conditions

In this section we show how to take into account adversarial conditions: in the first section we describe how to move pre-conditions into runtime checks and enrich our specifications to precisely account for when a function call should revert. In the second part we propose a general mechanism to capture the possible adversarial effects of external calls.

3.1   Aborting a Computation

As mentioned before we cannot enforce the initiator of a transaction to satisfy any pre-conditions when calling a method in a smart contract. However, a simple way to handle exceptional cases is to explicitly check that some conditions are satisfied before executing the actual body of a method, and if it is not the case to abort the computation. In the EVM semantics this is known as a *revert* operation that restores the state of the contract before the transaction. The EVM has a special opcode, `Revert` to return the status of a failed computation.

In the previous section, we used pre-conditions to write the specification of the methods. We can automatically push these pre-conditions into runtime checks at the beginning of each method. To take into account the possibility of *exceptions* in a clean way, we lift the return values of each method to capture the status of a computation using a standard return generic type of the form `datatype Try<T> = Revert | Success(v: T)`. If a computation is successful, the value v of type T is returned and boxed in the `Success` constructor, otherwise `Revert` is returned.[5]

The implementation of the methods[6] `mint` and `transfer` can be lifted using the return `datatype Try<T>` as in Listing A.3, line 1. This datatype allows for the return of arbitrary values of type T and as a special case when no value is returned, we can set T = `Unit` the type inhabited by a single value.

The new code (Listing A.3) introduces the following features:

- the conditions under the first `if` statements of `mint` and `transfer` (respectively at lines 22 and 47) are the negation of the conjunction of all the pre-conditions that are in Listing A.2.
- The pre-condition `GInv()` remains in the code. It is not a runtime check but a property of the contract that has to be preserved. This invariant is not part of the executable code.
- In this example of a closed contract we can characterise exactly when the transaction should revert (`r.T?` is true if and only if r is of type T). For instance the post-condition at line 7 precisely defines the conditions under which the method should not abort.

---

[5] `Revert` is sometimes called `Failure` and can return a string error message.

[6] The constructor has no pre-condition, so we can assume it always succeeds.

– The post-conditions at lines 15 and 40 ensures that the state of the contract (`balances`) is unchanged.

DAFNY returns "no errors" for this program, and we can conclude that the global invariant is always satisfied after any number of calls to `mint` or `transfer`. The code for each method does not enforce any pre-condition on the caller and can be translated into runtime checks at the EVM bytecode level.

Listing A.3. The Token Contract with Revert.

```
1    datatype Try<T> = Revert() | Success(v: T)
2
3    method transfer(from:Address,to:Address,amount:uint256,msg:Msg,gas:nat)
4        returns (g: nat, r: Try<()>)
5
6        requires GInv()
7        ensures //  if r is of type Success
8            r.Success? <==>
9            (from in old(balances)
10           && old(balances[from]) >= amount
11           && msg.sender == from
12           && gas >= 1
13           && (to !in old(balances)||old(balances[to]) as nat + amount as nat<=MAX_UINT256))
14       /** State is unchanged on a revert. */
15       ensures r.Revert? ==> balances == old(balances)
16       ensures g == 0 || g <= gas - 1
17       ensures GInv()
18
19       decreases gas
20       modifies this
21   {
22       if !(from in balances && balances[from]>=amount && msg.sender==from && gas>=1
23           && (to !in balances || balances[to] as nat + amount as nat<=MAX_UINT256) ) {
24           return (if gas >= 1 then gas - 1 else 0), Revert();
25       }
26       var newAmount := balances[from] - amount;
27       balances := balances[to := (if to in balances then balances[to] else 0) + amount];
28       balances := balances[from := newAmount];
29       g, r := gas - 1, Success(());
30   }
31
32   method mint(to:Address,amount:uint256,msg:Msg,gas:nat) returns (g:nat,r: Try<()>)
33       requires GInv()
34       ensures r.Success? ==> totalAmount == old(totalAmount) + amount as nat
35       ensures r.Revert? <==>
36           !(msg.sender == minter && gas >= 1 &&
37               (to !in old(balances)||
38               old(balances[to]) as nat + amount as nat<=MAX_UINT256))
39       // state unchanged on a revert.
40       ensures r.Revert? ==> balances == old(balances)
41       ensures g == 0 || g <= gas - 1
42       ensures GInv()
43
44       modifies this`balances, this`totalAmount
45       decreases gas
46   {
47       if !(msg.sender == minter && gas >= 1 &&
48           (to !in balances || balances[to] as nat + amount as nat<=MAX_UINT256)) {
49           return (if gas >= 1 then gas - 1 else 0), Revert();
50       }
51       balances := balances[to := (if to in balances then balances[to] else 0) + amount];
52       // The total amount increases.
53       totalAmount := totalAmount + amount as nat;
54       g, r := gas - 1, Success(());
55   }
```

3.2 Reasoning with Arbitrary External Calls

We now turn our attention to smart contracts that have *external calls*. The semantics of the EVM imposes the following restrictions on the mutations of

Listing A.4. The Token Contract with a Notification.

```
method transfer(...) returns (g: nat, r: Try<()>)
...
{
    ...
    balances := balances[to := (if to in balances then balances[to] else 0) + amount];
    balances := balances[from := newAmount];
    //  External call to contract `to`.
    //  If we notify before updating balances, a re-entrant call may drain the contract
    //  of its tokens.
    g, status := to.notify(from, amount, gas - 1);
    ...
}
```

state variables for contracts: the state variables of a contract c can only be updated by a call to a method[7] in c. In other words another contract $c' \neq c$ cannot write the state variables of c.

Assume that when we transfer some tokens to a contract via the `transfer` method, we also *notify* the receiver. The corresponding new code for `transfer` is given in Listing A.4. If the method `notify` in contract `to` does not perform any external call itself, the segment `to.notify(·)` cannot modify the state variables of the `Token` contract, and the `Token` contract invariant `GInv()` is preserved. We may not have access to the code of `notify(·)` and may be unable to check whether this is the case.

If `notify` can call another contract it may result in unexpected consequences. For instance if the external call to the method `to.notify(·)` occurs before the update of `balances[from]`, `to.notify` may itself call (and collude with) `from` and call `from` to do the same transfer again. As a result many transfers will be performed (as long as some gas is left) and tokens will be *created* without a proper call to `mint`. The result is that the number of minted tokens does not correspond anymore to the number of tokens allocated to accounts, and the global invariant `Ginv()` does not hold anymore after `transfer`. This type of issue is commonly known as the *re-entrancy problem*. This vulnerability was exploited in the past in the so-called DAO-exploit [13].

There are several solutions to mitigate the re-entrancy problem. A simple solution is to require that calls to external contracts occur only as the last instruction in a method (Check-Effect-Interaction pattern [6]). This is a *syntactic sufficient condition* to ensure that every update on a contract's state occurs before any external calls. This enforces re-entrant calls to happen sequentially. A *semantic* approach for taking into external calls is proposed in [5] and rely on identifying segments of the code with external calls and adding some local variables to capture the effects of a call and reason about it.

We propose a similar but hopefully simpler technique[8] to model external calls and their effects. Similar to [5] we do not aim to identify re-entrant calls but we want to *include and model* the effect of possible external (including re-entrant) calls and check whether the contract invariant can be violated or not. For the

---

[7] We assume that all methods are *public*.

[8] It can be implemented directly in DAFNY with no need for extra devices.

sake of simplicity we describe our solution to this problem on the `to.notify(·)` example, Listing A.4, and make the following (EVM enforced) assumptions on `to.notify(·)`:

- it always terminates and returns the gas left and the status of the call (revert or success),
- it consumes at least one unit of gas,
- it may itself make arbitrary external calls including callbacks to `transfer` and `mint` in the `Token` contract. As a result there can be complex nested calls to `transfer` and `mint`.

Our solution abstracts the call to `to.notify(·)` into a generic `externalCall`. The new code for the `transfer` method is given in Listing A.5. We model the effect of the external call `to.notify(·)` (line 17) by a call to the `externalCall(·)` method.

The idea is that `externalCall(·)` is going to generate all possible re-entrant calls including nested calls to `transfer`. To do so, we introduce some *non-determinism* to allow an external call to callback `transfer` and `mint`. This occurs at lines 51 and 57. Note that the parameters (`from`, `to`, `amount`, `msg`) of the re-entrant calls are randomly chosen using the `havoc<T>()` method that returns an arbitrary value of type T.

The code of `externalCall` works as follows:

- non-deterministically pick k and use it to decide whether a re-entrant call occurs or not (lines 42–58). There are three options, and we use $k \mod 3$ to select among them. If $k \mod 3 = 0$ (and there is enough gas left), a re-entrant call to `transfer` occurs. If $k \mod 3 = 1$ a re-entrant call to `mint` occurs. Otherwise, ($k \mod 3 = 2$), no re-entrant call occurs.
- finally (lines 61–69), we non-deterministically pick a boolean variable b to decide whether a new external call occurs.

We do not provide a formal proof that this captures all the possible re-entrant calls[9], but rather illustrate that it models several cases. First, `externalCall` can simulate an arbitrary sequence `mint*` of calls to `mint`. This is obtained by selecting successive values of k such that $k \mod 3 = 1$ and then selecting $b = true$. For instance, the sequence of values $k = 1$, $b = true$, $k = 1$, $b = true$, $k = 2$, $b = false$ simulates two reentrant calls to `mint`, i.e., `mint.mint`. As the gas value is also a parameter of all the methods and can be arbitrarily large, this model can generate all the sequences of calls in `mint*`. Second, `externalCall` can also simulate nested `transfer/mint` calls. For instance, the sequence of values $k = 0$, $b = true$, $k = 1$, $b = false$, simulates two reentrant calls to `transfer` with a nested call to `mint`. Third, nested calls to `transfer` can also be generated by `externalCall`. The sequence of values $k = 0$, $b = true$, $k = 0$, $b = false$ simulates two nested re-entrant calls to `transfer`.

The re-entrant calls can be executed with arbitrary inputs and thus the input parameters are *havoced* i.e., non-deterministically chosen and `externalCall` can

---

[9] This is beyond the scope of this paper.

Listing A.5. The Token Contract with External Calls.

```
1   method transfer(from:Address,to:Address,amount:uint256,msg:Msg,gas:nat)
2     returns (g:nat,r:Try<()>)
3
4     ... // Ensures and requires same as Listing A.3
5   {
6     if !(from in balances && balances[from]>=amount && msg.sender==from && gas>=1
7        && (to !in balances || balances[to] as nat + amount as nat <= MAX_UINT256) ) {
8       return (if gas >= 1 then gas - 1 else 0), Revert();
9     }
10    var newAmount := balances[from] - amount;
11    balances := balances[to := (if to in balances then balances[to] else 0) + amount];
12    balances := balances[from := newAmount];
13    //  If we swap the line above and the externalCall,
14    //  we cannot prove invariance of GInv()
15    //  At this location GInv() must hold which puts a restriction
16    //  on where external call can occur.
17    var g1, r1 := externalCall(gas - 1);  // to.notify( from, amount );
18    assert g1 == 0 || g1 <= gas - 1;
19    //  We can choose to propagate or not the failure of external call.
20    //  Here choose not to.
21    g, r := (if g1 >= 1 then g1 - 1 else 0), Success(());
22  }
23
24  /**
25   * Simulate an external call with possible re-entrant calls.
26   *
27   * @param   gas The gas allocated to this call.
28   * @returns    The gas left after execution of the call and the status of the call.
29   *
30   * @note      The state variables of the contract can only be modified by
31   *            calls to mint and transfer.
32   */
33  method externalCall(gas: nat) returns (g: nat, r: Try<()>)
34    requires GInv()
35    ensures GInv()
36    ensures g == 0 || g <= gas - 1
37    modifies this
38    decreases gas
39  {
40    g := gas;
41    //  Havoc `k` to introduce non-determinism.
42    var k: nat := havoc();
43    //  Depending on the value of k % 3,
44    //  re-entrant call or not or another external call.
45    if k % 3 == 0 && g >= 1 {
46      //  re-entrant call to transfer.
47      var from: Address := havoc();
48      var to: Address := havoc();
49      var amount: uint256 := havoc();
50      var msg: Msg := havoc();
51      g, r := transfer(from, to, amount, msg, g - 1);
52    } else if k % 3 == 1 && g >= 1 {
53      //  re-entrant call to mint.
54      var to: Address := havoc();
55      var amount: uint256 := havoc();
56      var msg: Msg := havoc();
57      g, r := mint(to, amount, msg, g - 1);
58    }
59    //  k % 3 == 2, no re-entrant call.
60    //  Possible new external call
61    var b:bool := havoc();
62    if b && g >= 1 {
63      //  external call makes an external call.
64      g, r := externalCall(g - 1);
65    } else {
66      //  external call does not make another external call.
67      g := if gas >= 1 then gas - 1 else 0;
68      r := havoc();
69    }
70  }
71
72  /** Havoc a given type. */
73  method {:extern} havoc<T>() returns (a: T)
```

generate an arbitrary number of external and re-entrant calls including nested calls to `transfer` and `mint`.

The key ingredient that allows us to reason and prove correctness is the `gas` value. We require that `gas` strictly decreases (line 38) after each recursive call. This is stated in DAFNY with the `decreases` clause. DAFNY checks that the value of the `gas` parameter strictly decreases on mutually recursive calls.

Our objective is now to prove, using this model of external calls, that the global invariant `GInv()` of the contract is always satisfied. This seems to be a complex task as our model includes an arbitrary and unbounded number of possibly nested external calls. The result is a mutually recursive program: `transfer` can call `externalCall` and `externalCall` can call `transfer` or `externalCall`. However, the property that the `gas` value strictly decreases on every call enables us to reason by induction. As the gas decreases on each new call, the induction is well-founded. And DAFNY can indeed prove that the global invariant `GInv()` is preserved by all the methods including an arbitrary number of possibly re-entrant `externalCalls`. Our solution provides a way to model the effects of external calls abstractly but conservatively while still being able to prove properties in modular manner in an adversarial environment modelled by `externalCall`. Compared to other approaches we also guarantee termination because we take into account the minimum amount of gas that computations take.

Note that `externalCall` has the pre-condition `GInv()`. This means that in `transfer` the predicate `GInv()` must be true before the call to `externalCall`. This amounts to having restrictions on where external calls can occur. However, without any knowledge of what external calls can do, this seems to be a reasonable restriction. For instance, if the external call has a callback to `mint` we can only prove the preservation of the invariant `Ginv()` if it holds before the call to `mint`. Of course if we have more information about an external call, e.g., we know it does not call back, we can also take it into account with our model: we can adjust `externalCall` to reflect this knowledge.

In our example, if we swap the lines 12 and 17 (Listing A.5), DAFNY cannot verify that `GInv()` is preserved by `transfer`. The reason is that the invariant `Ginv()` does not hold before the external call.

To the best of our knowledge this solution is the first that does not require any specific reasoning device or extension to prove properties of smart contracts under adversarial conditions, but can be encoded directly in a verification-friendly language.

Running Dafny and Reproducing the Verification Results. The code used in this paper omits some functions and proofs hints (like `sum`) and may not be directly verifiable with DAFNY. The interested reader is invited to check out the code in the repository https://github.com/ConsenSys/dafny-sc-fmics to get the full version of our contracts. The repository contains the code of the `Token` contract, a simplified auction contract and instructions how to reproduce the DAFNY verification results.

The auction contract demonstrates that global invariants (`GInv()` in `Token`) are not limited to specifying *state* properties but can also capture two-state or multi-state properties. This can be achieved by adding ghost history variables using sequences. This type of specifications is expressive enough to encode some standard temporal logic properties on sequences of states of a contract, e.g., "Once the variable ended is set to true, it remains true for ever" in the simplified auction contract.

In our experiments, DAFNY can handle complex specifications and the contracts we have verified are checked with DAFNY within seconds on a standard laptop (MacBook Pro). The performance does not seem to be an issue at that stage, and if it would become an issue, there are several avenues to mitigate it: DAFNY supports modular verification, so we can break down our code into smaller methods; DAFNY has built-in strategies to manipulate the verification conditions and break them into simpler ones that can be checked independently.

4   Conclusion

We have proposed a methodology to model and reason about (Ethereum) smart contracts using the verification-friendly language DAFNY. The main features of our approach are: i) we encode the specifications and implementations of contracts directly in DAFNY with no need for any language extensions; ii) we take into account the possibility of *failures* and (arbitrary number of) *external calls*; iii) we specify the main properties of a contract using contract *global invariants* and prove these properties in a modular manner by a conservative abstraction of external calls with no need to know the code of externally called contracts.

To the best of our knowledge, our abstract model of the effect of external calls is new and the associated proof technique (mutually recursive method calls) is readily supported by DAFNY which makes it easy to implement.

We have tested our methodology on several contracts (e.g., Token, Simple Auction, Bank) and we believe that this technique can be used to verify larger contracts. Indeed, we can take advantage of the modular proof approach (based on pre- and post-conditions) supported by Dafny to design scalable proofs.

Our current work aims to automate the methodology we have presented by automatically generating the different versions of a given contract (closed, revert, external calls) from a simple source contract.

The approach we have presented is general and not exclusive to Dafny, and our methodology can be implemented within other verification-friendly languages like Why3 [20], Whiley [25], or proof assistants like Isabelle/HOL [21] or Coq [24].

References

1. Ahrendt, W., Bubel, R.: Functional verification of smart contracts via strong data integrity. In: Margaria, T., Steffen, B. (eds.) ISoLA 2020. LNCS, vol. 12478, pp. 9–24. Springer, Cham (2020). https://doi.org/10.1007/978-3-030-61467-6_2

2. Alt, L., Reitwiessner, C.: SMT-based verification of solidity smart contracts. In: Margaria, T., Steffen, B. (eds.) ISoLA 2018. LNCS, vol. 11247, pp. 376–388. Springer, Cham (2018). https://doi.org/10.1007/978-3-030-03427-6_28

3. Amani, S., Bégel, M., Bortin, M., Staples, M.: Towards verifying ethereum smart contract bytecode in Isabelle/HOL. In: Andronick, J., Felty, A.P. (eds.) 7th ACM SIGPLAN International Conference on Certified Programs and Proofs, CPP 2018, pp. 66–77. ACM (2018). https://doi.org/10.1145/3167084

4. Bhargavan, K., et al.: Formal verification of smart contracts. In: PLAS@CCS 2016. pp. 91–96. ACM (2016). https://doi.org/10.1145/2993600.2993611

5. Bräm, C., Eilers, M., Müller, P., Sierra, R., Summers, A.J.: Rich specifications for ethereum smart contract verification. Proc. ACM Program. Lang.5(OOPSLA), 1–30 (2021). https://doi.org/10.1145/3485523

6. Britten, D., Sjöberg, V., Reeves, S.: Using coq to enforce the checks-effects-interactions pattern in DeepSea smart contracts. In: Bernardo, B., Marmsoler, D. (eds.) 3rd International Workshop on Formal Methods for Blockchains, FMBC@CAV 2021. OASIcs, vol. 95, pp. 3:1–3:8. Schloss Dagstuhl - Leibniz-Zentrum für Informatik (2021). https://doi.org/10.4230/OASIcs.FMBC.2021.3

7. Cassez, F.: Verification of the Incremental Merkle Tree Algorithm with Dafny. In: Huisman, M., Păsăreanu, C., Zhan, N. (eds.) FM 2021. LNCS, vol. 13047, pp. 445–462. Springer, Cham (2021). https://doi.org/10.1007/978-3-030-90870-6_24

8. Choo, L.: Crypto is crumbling, and DeFi hacks are getting worse. https://www.protocol.com/fintech/defi-hacks-web3

9. ConsenSys Diligence: Mythx, https://mythx.io/

10. Dharanikota, S., Mukherjee, S., Bhardwaj, C., Rastogi, A., Lal, A.: Celestial: a smart contracts verification framework. In: Formal Methods in Computer Aided Design, FMCAD 2021, New Haven, CT, USA, pp. 133–142. IEEE (2021). https://doi.org/10.34727/2021/isbn.978-3-85448-046-4_22

11. Ethereum Foundation: Solidity documentation (2022). https://docs.soliditylang.org/en/v0.8.14/

12. Fe Team: Fe: an emerging smart contract language for the Ethereum blockchain (2022). https://github.com/ethereum/fe

13. Güçlütürk, O.G.: The DAO hack explained: unfortunate take-off of smart contracts (2018). https://ogucluturk.medium.com/the-dao-hack-explained-unfortunate-take-off-of-smart-contracts-2bd8c8db3562

14. Hajdu, Á., Jovanović, D.: SOLC-VERIFY: a modular verifier for solidity smart contracts. In: Chakraborty, S., Navas, J.A. (eds.) VSTTE 2019. LNCS, vol. 12031, pp. 161–179. Springer, Cham (2020). https://doi.org/10.1007/978-3-030-41600-3_11

15. Hajdu, Á., Jovanovic, D., Ciocarlie, G.F.: Formal specification and verification of Solidity contracts with events (short paper). In: Bernardo, B., Marmsoler, D. (eds.) 2nd Workshop on Formal Methods for Blockchains, FMBC@CAV 2020. OASIcs, vol. 84, pp. 2:1–2:9. Schloss Dagstuhl - Leibniz-Zentrum für Informatik (2020). https://doi.org/10.4230/OASIcs.FMBC.2020.2

16. da Horta, L.P.A., Reis, J.S., de Sousa, S.M., Pereira, M.: A tool for proving Michelson smart contracts in WHY3. In: IEEE International Conference on Blockchain, Blockchain 2020. Rhodes, Greece, pp. 409–414. IEEE (2020). https://doi.org/10.1109/Blockchain50366.2020.00059

17. Leino, K.R.M.: Accessible software verification with Dafny. IEEE Softw. **34**(6), 94–97 (2017). https://doi.org/10.1109/MS.2017.4121212

18. Marescotti, M., Otoni, R., Alt, L., Eugster, P., Hyvärinen, A.E.J., Sharygina, N.: Accurate smart contract verification through direct modelling. In: Margaria, T., Steffen, B. (eds.) ISoLA 2020. LNCS, vol. 12478, pp. 178–194. Springer, Cham (2020). https://doi.org/10.1007/978-3-030-61467-6_12
19. Marmsoler, D., Brucker, A.D.: A denotational semantics of solidity in isabelle/HOL. In: Calinescu, R., Păsăreanu, C.S. (eds.) SEFM 2021. LNCS, vol. 13085, pp. 403–422. Springer, Cham (2021). https://doi.org/10.1007/978-3-030-92124-8_23
20. Nehaï, Z., Bobot, F.: Deductive proof of industrial smart contracts using why3. In: Sekerinski, E., et al. (eds.) FM 2019. LNCS, vol. 12232, pp. 299–311. Springer, Cham (2020). https://doi.org/10.1007/978-3-030-54994-7_22
21. Nipkow, T., Paulson, L.C., Wenzel, M.: Isabelle/HOL — A Proof Assistant for Higher-Order Logic, LNCS, vol. 2283. Springer Heidelberg (2002). https://doi.org/10.1007/3-540-45949-9
22. Park, D., Zhang, Y.: Formal verification of the incremental Merkle tree algorithm (2020). https://github.com/runtimeverification/verified-smart-contracts/blob/master/deposit/formal-incremental-merkle-tree-algorithm.pdf
23. Park, D., Zhang, Y., Rosu, G.: End-to-end formal verification of ethereum 2.0 deposit smart contract. In: Lahiri, S.K., Wang, C. (eds.) CAV 2020. LNCS, vol. 12224, pp. 151–164. Springer, Cham (2020). https://doi.org/10.1007/978-3-030-53288-8_8
24. Paulin-Mohring, C.: Introduction to the coq proof-assistant for practical software verification. In: Meyer, B., Nordio, M. (eds.) LASER 2011. LNCS, vol. 7682, pp. 45–95. Springer, Heidelberg (2012). https://doi.org/10.1007/978-3-642-35746-6_3
25. Pearce, D.J., Utting, M., Groves, L.: An introduction to software verification with whiley. In: Bowen, J.P., Liu, Z., Zhang, Z. (eds.) SETSS 2018. LNCS, vol. 11430, pp. 1–37. Springer, Cham (2019). https://doi.org/10.1007/978-3-030-17601-3_1
26. Schiffl, J., Ahrendt, W., Beckert, B., Bubel, R.: Formal analysis of smart contracts: applying the KeY system. In: Ahrendt, W., Beckert, B., Bubel, R., Hähnle, R., Ulbrich, M. (eds.) Deductive Software Verification: Future Perspectives. LNCS, vol. 12345, pp. 204–218. Springer, Cham (2020). https://doi.org/10.1007/978-3-030-64354-6_8
27. Vyper Team: Documentation (2020). https://vyper.readthedocs.io/en/stable/
28. Wesley, S., Christakis, M., Navas, J.A., Trefler, R., Wüstholz, V., Gurfinkel, A.: Verifying SOLIDITY smart contracts via communication abstraction in SMARTACE. In: Finkbeiner, B., Wies, T. (eds.) VMCAI 2022. LNCS, vol. 13182, pp. 425–449. Springer, Cham (2022). https://doi.org/10.1007/978-3-030-94583-1_21
29. Wood, D.: Ethereum: a secure decentralised generalised transaction ledger (2022). https://ethereum.github.io/yellowpaper/paper.pdf
30. Wüstholz, V., Christakis, M.: Harvey: A Greybox Fuzzer for Smart Contracts, pp. 1398–1409. Association for Computing Machinery, New York (2020). https://doi.org/10.1145/3368089.3417064
31. Zakrzewski, J.: Towards verification of Ethereum smart contracts: a formalization of core of solidity. In: Piskac, R., Rümmer, P. (eds.) VSTTE 2018. LNCS, vol. 11294, pp. 229–247. Springer, Cham (2018). https://doi.org/10.1007/978-3-030-03592-1_13

Industrial Use Cases

Towards Reusable Formal Models
for Custom Real-Time Operating Systems

Julius Adelt$^{(\boxtimes)}$, Julian Gebker, and Paula Herber$^{(\boxtimes)}$

University of Münster, Einsteinstr. 62, 48149 Münster, Germany
{julius.adelt,paula.herber}@uni-muenster.de

Abstract. In embedded systems, the execution semantics of the real-time operating system (RTOS), which is responsible for scheduling and timely execution of concurrent processes, is crucial for the correctness of the overall system. However, existing approaches for the formal verification of embedded systems typically abstract from the RTOS completely, or provide a detailed and synthesizable formal model of the RTOS. While the former may lead to unsafe systems, the latter is not compatible with industrial design processes. In this paper, we present an approach for reusable abstract formal models that can be configured for custom RTOS. Our key idea is to formally capture common execution mechanisms of RTOS like preemptive scheduling and event synchronization abstractly in configurable timed automata models. These abstract formal models can be configured for a concrete custom RTOS, and they can be combined into a formal system model together with a concrete application. Our reusable models significantly reduce the manual effort of defining a formal model that captures concurrency and real-time behavior together with the functionality of an application. The resulting formal model enables analysis, verification, and graphical simulation. We validate our approach by formalizing and analyzing a rescue robot application running the custom open source RTOS EV3RT.

Keywords: Real-time Systems · Formal Verification · Reusability

1 Introduction

In the embedded systems industry, many companies use their own custom real-time operating system (RTOS). The RTOS schedules concurrent processes, takes care of process interactions and shared resources, and is thus crucial for the synchronization and timing behavior. To ensure the correctness of embedded systems, it is vital to correctly capture and analyze concurrency and time. Existing approaches for the formal verification of embedded systems, however, either abstract from the underlying RTOS completely (e.g. CPAchecker [6], Frama-C [9]) or they provide a fully formalized and verified RTOS (e.g. Sel4 [15]). While the former abstracts from the influence of the RTOS on concurrent, timing-dependent applications completely, the latter requires extremely high manual effort and expertise, as a new formalization is needed for each custom RTOS.

J. F. Groote and M. Huisman (Eds.): FMICS 2022, LNCS 13487, pp. 69–85, 2022.
https://doi.org/10.1007/978-3-031-15008-1_6

In this paper, we propose reusable abstract formal models that can be configured for custom RTOS. Our key idea is to formally capture common execution mechanisms of RTOS abstractly in configurable timed automata models. To achieve this, we abstractly formalize preemptive and non-preemptive execution, priority-based scheduling, general task management, event synchronizations, and sensor APIs. For a given custom RTOS, the designer can use our configurable timed automata models to build a formal model that defines the execution semantics of key RTOS components like the scheduler and tasks. Furthermore, if the designer defines a mapping from system calls to abstract execution mechanisms (e.g. task activations or event notifications), a given real-time application can be combined into a formal model together with the RTOS components. The resulting model captures the concurrent and real-time dependent behavior as well as the functionality of the application precisely, but abstracts from the implementation details of the custom RTOS. It can be analyzed and verified using existing tools for graphical simulation, formal verification, and timing analysis.

As a first step to validate the applicability of our approach, we have formalized and analyzed a search and rescue robot application running the custom open source RTOS EV3RT. To formalize this custom RTOS, we have configured our reusable abstract timed automata models with an appropriate scheduling strategy and mapped system calls to abstract execution mechanisms. We have manually translated the task implementations for our case study. The automation remains subject for future work. We have exploited UPPAAL's simulation and graphical animation of counter-examples to validate the system's functionality and the task interactions on the resulting formal model without executing it on the real robot hardware. For a simplified model, we have analyzed and verified crucial safety and timing properties using the UPPAAL model checker.

2   Preliminaries

In this section, we introduce preliminaries for the remainder of this paper, namely core components of real-time operating systems and UPPAAL timed automata.

2.1   Core Components of Real-Time Operating Systems

There exists a large variety of custom RTOS. However, many of them follow certain standards, like OSEK/VDX [17] (in the automotive domain) or TOPPERS [20]. These standards informally define kernel objects, e.g., tasks, events, and resources, and their interactions. In the following, we briefly introduce kernel objects that can commonly be found in any RTOS implementation.

Tasks. Tasks are typically the main execution unit in RTOS. While the instructions within each task are sequentially executed, tasks are concurrently started and may interleave each other. A key responsibility of an RTOS is to schedule tasks, i.e., to decide which task should be executed. To manage tasks and their states, many real-time systems use a task-control block (TCB) model. It is one of the most popular methods to manage different numbers of tasks and is compatible with any specific scheduling strategy. The TCB model specifies that each task of a given real-time system is linked with a data structure called task-control block containing at least a program counter, an identifier, register contents, a status (or state), and a priority if provided [16]. Most RTOS follow a task state scheme that is similar to the OSEK/VDX standard as shown in Fig. 1a [17]. Tasks typically start in a *suspended* state and become *ready* after activation. After system initialization, the task with the highest priority starts *running*. The running task may terminate its execution and become suspended again, it may wait for an event or a resource and become *waiting*, or it may be preempted by the scheduler if a task with a higher priority or some prioritized execution unit becomes ready. Tasks are released from a *waiting* state if, for example, a resource becomes available or an event occurs. Note that other RTOS standards use slightly different terms, e.g., *blocked* instead of *waiting* in TOPPERS compatible systems or *pending* instead of *ready* in VxWorks.

Handlers and Interrupt Subroutines. In addition to tasks, RTOS typically support prioritized execution units, e.g., interrupt subroutines or cyclic handlers. These prioritized execution units are typically not preemptable, i.e., they are executed from the beginning to the end whenever they become ready due to an external event (in case of interrupt subroutines) or the expiration of a periodic delay (in case of cyclic handlers). In this paper, we focus on cyclic handlers.

Events. In most embedded systems, tasks are either executed periodically (e.g., using cyclic handlers) or they are triggered by events. Most RTOS support events by providing mechanisms to *notify* an event, *wait* for an event and to *release* tasks that are waiting for an event. Often, bit patterns are used to wait for multiple events at the same time. Notifying tasks can then set bits that correspond to specific events within the bit pattern, while tasks that are waiting for one or more events define a corresponding bit mask on the bit pattern.

Scheduler. The scheduler is a system program within a real-time system specifying the execution order of execution units. In this paper, we assume a single processor system, so only one execution unit can be executed at a time. Schedulers can implement different scheduling strategies, for example, round-robin, first-come-first-served (FCFS), preemptive-priority or a mixture of these methods [16]. Most RTOS use preemptive and priority based scheduling.

2.2   Uppaal Timed Automata

Timed Automata [2] are a timed extension of the classical finite state automata. A notion of time is introduced by real-valued clocks, which are used in clock constraints to model time-dependent behavior. Concurrent processes are modelled by networks of timed automata, which are executed with interleaving semantics and synchronize on channels. Formally, the semantics of timed automata and networks of timed automata are given by [5] as follows:

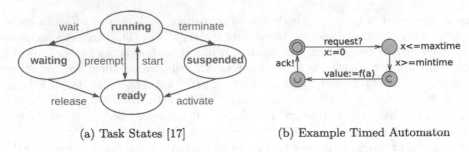

(a) Task States [17]   (b) Example Timed Automaton

Fig. 1. Task States and Timed Automata Example

Definition 1 (Operational Semantics of a Timed Automaton). *A timed automaton (TA) is a tuple (L, l_0, C, A, E, I), where*

- *L is a set of locations,*
- *$l_0 \in L$ is the initial location,*
- *C is a set of clock variables,*
- *A is a set of actions,*
- *$E \subseteq L \times A \times B(C) \times 2^C \times L$ is a set of edges, where $B(C)$ denotes a set of clock constraints*
- *$I : L \rightarrow B(C)$ assigns invariants to locations.*

We write $l \xrightarrow{a,g,r} l'$ for $(l, a, g, r, l') \in E$. The semantics of a TA is defined as a transition system $(S, s_0, \rightarrow)$, where $S \subseteq L \times \mathbb{R}_{\geq 0}^{|C|}$ is a set of states, $s_0 = (l_0, u_0)$ the initial state, and $\rightarrow \subseteq S \times (\mathbb{R}_{\geq 0} \cup A) \times S$ the transition relation. A clock valuation is a function $u : C \rightarrow \mathbb{R}_{\geq 0}$ that maps a non-negative real value to each clock, $u \in I$ denotes that a clock valuation satisfies an invariant, and $u' = [r \mapsto 0]u$ denotes a clock valuation where all clocks from the clock set r are reset to zero. A semantic step of a timed automaton can either be a time step (1) or a discrete transition (2) along an edge in the graphical representation:

(1) $(l, u) \xrightarrow{d} (l, u + d)$ iff $\forall d' : 0 \leq d' \leq d \Rightarrow u + d' \in I(l)$
(2) $(l, u) \xrightarrow{a} (l', u')$ iff $l \xrightarrow{a,g,r} l'$ such that $u \in g \wedge u' = [r \mapsto 0]u \wedge u' \in I(l')$

Definition 2 (Semantics of a Network of Timed Automata). *A network of timed automata (NTA) consists of n timed automata $\mathcal{A}_i = (L_i, l_{0,i}, C, A, E_i, I_i)$. The semantics of NTA is defined by a transition system $(S, s_0, \rightarrow)$. Each state $s \in S$ is a tuple $(\bar{l}, u)$, where $\bar{l}$ is a location vector and u is a clock valuation. $S = (L_1 \times \ldots \times L_n) \times \mathbb{R}_{\geq 0}^{|C|}$ denotes the set of states, $s_0 = (\bar{l}_0, u_0)$ the initial state, and $\rightarrow \subseteq S \times S$ the transition relation. Furthermore, τ denotes an internal action, $c!, c?$ sending resp. receiving an event on channel c, and g denotes a clock guard. $I(\bar{l})$ denotes the conjunction of all invariants $I_i(l_i)$. A semantic step can be either a time step (1), an independent step of a single automaton (2), or a synchronization between two automata (3):*

(1) $(\bar{l}, u) \rightarrow (\bar{l}, u + d)$ iff $\forall d' : 0 \leq d' \leq d \Rightarrow u + d' \in I(\bar{l})$

(2) $(\bar{l}, u) \to (\bar{l}[l_i'/l_i], u')$ iff $l_i \xrightarrow{\tau gr} l_i'$ such that $u \in g \wedge u' = [r \mapsto 0]u \wedge u' \in I(\bar{l}[l_i'/l_i])$

(3) $(\bar{l}, u) \to (\bar{l}[l_j'/l_j, l_i'/l_i], u')$ iff $l_i \xrightarrow{c?g_i,r_i} l_i' \wedge l_j \xrightarrow{c!g_j,r_j} l_j'$
   such that $u \in (g_i \wedge g_j) \wedge u' = [r_i \cup r_j \mapsto 0]u \wedge u' \in I(\bar{l}')$

UPPAAL [3–5] is a tool set for the modeling, simulation, animation and verification of NTA. The UPPAAL model checker enables the verification of temporal properties expressed in a subset of CTL. The simulator can be used to visualize counterexamples produced by the model checker. The UPPAAL modeling language extends TA by introducing bounded integer variables, C-like functions, binary and broadcast channels, and urgent and committed location. TA are modeled as a set of locations, connected by edges. Invariants can be assigned to locations and enforce that the location is left before they would be violated. Edges may be labeled with selections, guards, synchronizations and updates. Selections can be used to non-deterministically select a value from a given range. Updates are used to reset clocks and to manipulate the data space, where C is used as a host language. Processes synchronize by sending and receiving events through channels. Sending and receiving via a channel c is denoted by c! and c?, respectively. Binary channels are used to synchronize one sender with a single receiver. A synchronization pair is chosen non-deterministically if more than one is enabled. Broadcast channels are used to synchronize one sender with an arbitrary number of receivers. Urgent and committed locations are used to model locations where no time may pass. Leaving a committed location has priority over leaving non-committed locations.

An example UPPAAL TA is shown in Fig. 1b. The initial location is denoted by ⓞ, and request? and ack! (in light blue) denote synchronizations on channels. The clock variable x is first set to zero (in blue) and then used in two clock constraints: the invariant x <= maxtime (in pink) denotes that the corresponding location must be left before x becomes greater than maxtime, and the guard x >= mintime (in green) enables the corresponding edge at mintime. The value is computed using a C function f(a). The symbols ⓤ and ⓒ depict urgent and committed locations.

3 Related Work

There exists a variety of sophisticated verification tools for software verification, for example the CPAchecker [6], Frama-C [9], or VerCors [7]. These tools enable the automated or semi-automated formal verification of sequential or concurrent software. However, they abstract from the underlying RTOS as well as the timing behavior completely, yielding imprecise results if processes mainly interact via events or are heavily timing-dependant. Other approaches provide a complete formal RTOS model [15,18], derive an RTOS from a given formal model [19], or compile RTOS source code into an RTOS model to check conformance of a real-time operating system according to specific standards [8]. However, these approaches are not easily transferable to existing RTOS implementations.

There also exist several approaches to verify OSEK/VDX compliant systems. In [23], the authors present a TA model of a multitasking application running under a real-time operating system compliant with an OSEK/VDX standard. They have successfully verified timed and logical properties of the proposed model with the UPPAAL model checker. In particular, they demonstrate that the timing analysis is more precise than a classical scheduling theory. However, they solely consider non-preemptive scheduling, the model is not reusable for custom RTOS, and they do not provide reusable abstractions of general RTOS components. In [14], the authors present a CSP model of an OSEK/VDX RTOS kernel and verify various properties such as deadlock freedom. However, the application is not considered, and execution units with a higher precedence such as interrupt or cyclic handlers are disregarded. In [22], the authors present a formalization of the OSEK standard in Event-B and then verify RTOS implementations against the formalization. However, they again do not consider the application. In [10], the authors present an approach for the automatic verification of application-tailored OSEK kernels. Their key idea is to automatically compute an OS-application interaction graph from a given configuration and then to verify that it conforms to the standard. By generating the state transition graph statically, they avoid the state space explosion caused by thread interleaving. However, they disregard the concrete application and thus can neither verify properties of the application itself nor analyze its timing behavior. There exists a broad body of work for verifying schedulability using timed automata and extensions, e.g., [1, 12]. These approaches typically provide detailed models of scheduling strategies and tasks, but do not consider additional typical elements in RTOS, like events, or sensor information. Most closely related to our work are the approaches presented in [24–26]. There, the authors construct an abstract model of an OSEK/VDX RTOS kernel, combine it with a translation of a given application, and then verify the resulting overall model with an SMT-based approach in [25] and with the SPIN model checker in [24,26]. This work successfully demonstrates that real-time applications can be verified if the right abstractions are chosen. However, time and the inclusion of external information, like sensor data, is not considered. Most importantly, they also neither discuss possible generalizations nor the reusability of their formalization.

4 Reusable Formal Models for Custom RTOS

Our key idea to reduce the effort of the formalization of systems that use a custom RTOS is to provide reusable abstract models for standard RTOS concepts and components. To achieve this, we combine the abstract formal model of RTOS components with a transformation for application level implementations of tasks and handlers. The resulting overall formal model can be used to analyze concurrency, synchronization and timing behavior. Furthermore, it gives us access to existing analysis, verification, and simulation tools. Our overall approach is depicted in Fig. 2. The overarching goal is to analyze and verify *real time applications*. Those typically consist of (preemptable) *tasks* and (non-preemptable) *handlers*. The *real time application* is executed by a *custom RTOS*,

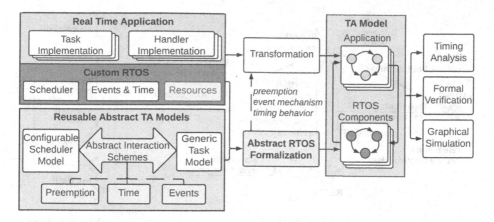

Fig. 2. Formalization with Reusable Abstract TA Models

which provides a *scheduler* and manages *events, time* and shared *resources*. To ease the formalization of systems that use a custom RTOS, we provide reusable abstract TA models of core RTOS components. Two key components are a *configurable scheduler model* and a *generic task model*. The *configurable scheduler model* provides a general scheme to schedule preemptive and non-preemptive execution units based on the task and handler information (e.g., identifier and priorities). It can be configured to a custom RTOS by implementing specific scheduling strategies. The *generic task model* provides a generic model for the state of a task, which is compatible with most RTOS implementations, including OSEK, TOPPERS, VxWorks, and FreeRTOS compliant implementations. Our reusable models define *abstract interaction schemes* for the interplay between RTOS components and the application, such as *preemption, time*, and *event* handling. By customizing our reusable abstract TA models for a given custom RTOS implementation, an *abstract RTOS formalization* can be derived, which formally models central RTOS components like the scheduler. For the analysis of a given real-time application, the abstract formal RTOS model is then combined with a formalization of the application itself. The application code, i.e., the implementation of tasks and handlers, can potentially be automatically transformed into TA representations using existing transformations [13]. Our reusable formal models of *abstract interaction schemes* provide the necessary extensions for the interactions with the formal RTOS model, i.e., a preemption scheme, an event mechanism that enables us to transform system calls like wait functions or event notifications, and timing behavior that is, for example, implemented using sleep functions. The resulting TA model can be used for *timing analysis, formal verification* and *graphical simulation*. In particular, the UPPAAL tool suite provides a powerful environment for graphical animation, simulation, model checking, and extensions for statistical model checking and test generation.

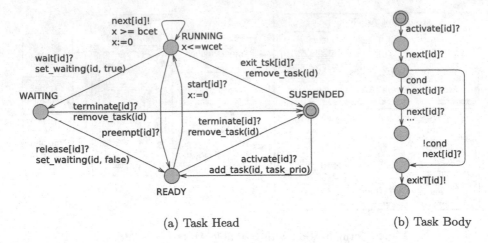

(a) Task Head   (b) Task Body

Fig. 3. Generic Task Model

In the following, we present our reusable TA models for tasks, cyclic handlers, events and timing behavior, and a configurable scheduler model. We briefly discuss how sensor inputs and communication can be abstractly modeled.

4.1 Formalization of Tasks

We model each task with two TA: one models the process states and controls the execution (*task head*), the other one contains the task implementation (*task body*). For the task head, we define a reusable TA template as shown in Fig. 3a. One location models each task state. We switch between these locations using synchronizations on channels. These channels are parameterized with the task *id*. This means that the task template needs to be included into a model only once and can be instantiated for all tasks. The task starts in the location *SUSPENDED*. It may be *activated* by the system initialization (which is also modeled as an automaton) at start-up or by other tasks. If a task is activated, its id and priority are inserted into the scheduler queue (*add_task()*). If the scheduler *starts* a task, a local clock x is reset to zero to model its execution time. In the *RUNNING* state, we continuously trigger statements of the task body with a *next* synchronization. The *next* synchronization controls the execution of the task body: within the body, each program statement is guarded with this synchronization, such that the next statement can only be executed if the task is still in its *RUNNING* state. In addition, we use the *next* synchronization to model real-time behavior. The next statement can only be executed if at least the best case execution time (*bcet*) has expired and must be executed at the latest when the worst-case execution time (*wcet*) elapses. The *bcet* and *wcet* can be provided as a global over-approximation of the execution times per statement for each task, or tailored to each statement by manipulating the global variables *bcet* and *wcet* at runtime. The execution of the task can be terminated by the task itself by

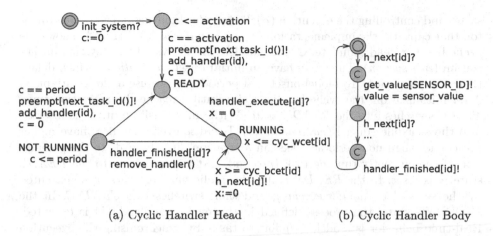

(a) Cyclic Handler Head   (b) Cyclic Handler Body

Fig. 4. Cyclic Handler Templates

calling a termination function, modeled as a synchronization on $exitT$. It is then removed from the scheduler queue and becomes *SUSPENDED*. If a task waits for an event, a resource, or a given amount of time by using some kind of wait or sleep function, the task switches from *RUNNING* to *WAITING*, and the task is set to waiting in its task control block. The task becomes *READY* again if it is *released* by the corresponding event, resource, or if the time expires. Finally, task preemption is modeled by a synchronization *preempt*, which is used by the scheduler to switch the currently active task from *RUNNING* to *READY* if a task with a higher priority becomes ready for execution. External events or cyclic handlers may also preempt the currently running task, as they have precedence over all tasks. Note that the task-specific variables *bcet* and *wcet* are bound to global variables in the system declaration. With that, they can be initialized and manipulated at runtime specifically for each task.

As the task body just contains sequentially executing statements, we assume that the function executed within the task can be transformed into an equivalent TA using existing method transformation techniques [13]. To model the interactions with the *task head*, we add the activation at the initial location as shown in Fig. 3b and guard each transition with a *next* synchronization to model the timing behavior and to ensure that execution only continues is the task is still running. The task may terminate by synchronizing on $exitT$.

By providing general formalizations for typical task states, best and worst case execution times, and preemption, our task templates are reusable for a large number of custom RTOS, including all that are OSEK/VDX compatible.

4.2 Formalization of Cyclic Handlers

As an illustrative example for the formalization of non-preemptable, prioritized handlers, we define reusable TA templates for cyclic handlers. Similar to tasks, we model cyclic handlers with two TA: a reusable TA template for modeling states and controlling the execution (*cyclic handler head*), and a second automaton that captures the implementation (*cyclic handler body*). Figure 4a shows the cyclic handler head template. Cyclic handlers are activated with system initialization (*init_system*). They may have an initial offset (*activation*), which delays their first execution. To model offset and periodicity, we use a clock variable c. After initialization, the cyclic handler waits until c reaches its activation time. Then it switches into the *READY* state. With this transition, its *id* is inserted into the scheduler queue (*add_handler()*). Because cyclic handlers have higher precedence than non-periodic tasks, an activation directly leads to the preemption of the currently running task (*preempt*). At the transition to the *READY* state, c is reset. In the *READY* state, the cyclic handler waits to be executed by the scheduler (*handler_execute*), and then switches to *RUNNING*. In the *RUNNING* state, the process defined in the cyclic handler body is executed. Real-time behavior is modeled similar to tasks by synchronising the execution of program statements with a *h_next* channel and an over-approximation of the execution times per statement with global worst-case (*h_wcet*) and best-case (*h_bcet*) execution times. Similar to the execution times of tasks, *h_wcet* and *h_bcet* can be manipulated at runtime for each handler. When the execution of the body finishes (*handler_finished*), the handler is removed from the scheduler queue (*remove_handler()*) and the state switches to the *NOT_RUNNING* state. When the *period* of the cyclic handler expires, the cyclic handler switches back to the *READY* state, c is reset, the handler is again added to the scheduler queue (*add_handler()*) and the currently running task is *preempted*.

The formalization of the cyclic handler body works similar to that of a task and is illustrated in Fig. 4b. Each program statement is synchronized with the head via the *h_next* channel. Both the scheduler and the handler head are informed about completion of the body's execution by a synchronization on the broadcast channel *handler_finished*.

4.3   Events and Timing Behavior

To support events, RTOS typically provide functions to set or notify events and to wait for events. We propose to translate these functions together with the task or handler body where they are called into the necessary updates and synchronizations as illustrated in Fig. 5. Triggering an event usually involves setting some bit pattern, as shown in Fig. 5a. Tasks that wait for an event switch into their *WAITING* state using a synchronization on an urgent broadcast channel *wait*, as shown in Fig. 5b. The *wait* signal is also sent to the scheduler to trigger rescheduling, as the currently running task is now blocked. To ensure that rescheduling is performed with priority, we send signals that trigger rescheduling from a committed location. Then, the task waits for a bit pattern (representing the occurrence of one or more events) specified with the wait function call. If the relevant events are set in the bit pattern, the task synchronizes on the urgent channel *release*, which results in switching from *WAITING* to *READY*. If the released task has a higher priority than the currently running task, the scheduler is informed that it might need to *reschedule* via an urgent broadcast

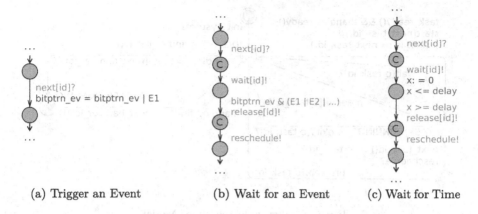

(a) Trigger an Event   (b) Wait for an Event   (c) Wait for Time

Fig. 5. Events and Timing Behavior

channel, which ensures that no time may pass. If the scheduler misses the signal *reschedule*, it is currently not running a task and will reschedule anyway.

The wait-release mechanism can also be used to model timing behavior. Most RTOS provide some kind of sleep function, which take a timing *delay* as parameter and switch the calling task to the *WAITING* state for the given amount of time. We can transform these kind of functions into a timed wait as shown in Fig. 5c. It uses the same sequence of *wait*, *release*, and *reschedule*, but now does not wait for an event but for the given *delay* by setting a local clock x to zero and then waiting until x is equal to the given *delay*.

4.1 Configurable Formal Scheduler Model

Figure 6 shows our TA template for a configurable scheduler. It is reusable for all custom RTOS that support separate execution modes for tasks and prioritized non-preemptive execution units such as interrupt subroutine or cyclic handlers. The scheduler manages task and handler information in separate queues, which can be used to determine whether some handler or task is ready for execution (*handler_ready()*, *task_ready()*), and to determine the handler or task with the highest priority (*next_handler_id()*, *next_task_id()*). The functions *next_handler_id()* and *next_task_id()* can be used to implement custom scheduling strategies that are compliant with the overall preemptive, priority-based execution scheme.

After system initialization, the scheduler first checks whether a handler is ready for execution. If this is the case, the handler with the highest priority (*next_handler_id()*) is activated by synchronizing on *handler_execute*. As handlers may not be preempted, the scheduler then just waits for the handler to signal termination via the *handler_finished* channel. If further handlers are ready for execution, they are then executed in the order of precedence provided by *next_handler_id()*. Only if no handler is ready anymore, tasks are executed. To this end, the scheduler activates the task with the highest priority via the

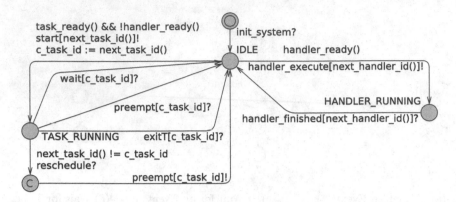

Fig. 6. Configurable Scheduler Model

channel *start* and stores its task id in the local variable *c_task_id*. While the task is running, it may voluntarily give up control by termination (*exitT*) or by waiting for an event or time (*wait*). In addition, it may be *preempted* by a handler becoming ready for execution, or by tasks with a higher priority. To capture the latter, we synchronize on *reschedule* whenever the task with the highest priority has changed. This may happen due to tasks waking up after a timed delay or due to an event notification. If this happens, we *preempt* the currently running task and reschedule. We use a committed location to ensure that preemption, which is considered to be essential for rescheduling, has priority over other enabled transitions (such that *reschedule* and *preempt* are always executed together).

4.5 Modeling Sensor Inputs and Communication

Processes can read in new sensor values during execution by synchronising on the *get_value* channel, as shown, for example, in the exemplary body of the cyclic handler in Fig. 4. To generate new sensor inputs, we propose the reusable TA model in Fig. 7. The template consists of a single location with a self-loop transition. If a process synchronizes via the *get_value* channel with the *SENSOR_ID* the variable for the *sensor_value* is updated with a non-deterministically chosen value from the sensor range (using a non-deterministic *selection* in UPPAAL).

More sophisticated external inputs, e.g., messages that are received via Bluetooth, can be explicitly modeled by providing the corresponding TA, e.g., an automaton that sends messages. The necessary blocking or non-blocking send and receive functions can be modeled using the wait pattern defined above, where a successful reception *releases* the receiving process for blocking calls.

5   Case Study: Search and Rescue Robots

To evaluate our approach, we have used our reusable formal models to abstractly capture the execution semantics of the custom RTOS EV3RT and manually

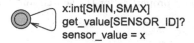

Fig. 7. Abstract Sensor Model

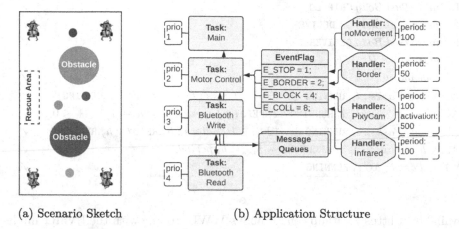

(a) Scenario Sketch   (b) Application Structure

Fig. 8. Search and Rescue Robot Application

translated an application that implements a search and rescue robot for LEGO Mindstorms into UPPAAL. EV3RT is a real-time operating system based software platform to develop real-time applications for the LEGO® Mindstorms EV3. It uses the TOPPERS/HRP2 kernel, which provides features such as preemptive multitasking and memory protection [11]. The kernel also offers kernel objects, such as tasks, cyclic handlers, eventflags and data queues to simplify the development of real-time applications [21].

The search and rescue robot application was developed as part of a student's project. Multiple EV3 robots are tasked with locating and evacuating objects out of a danger zone and into a rescue area. A server assigns search and evacuation routes to the robots. The robots communicate with the server via Bluetooth, detect obstacles with an infrared sensor, the border of the experiment table with a color sensor, and objects that should be evacuated with a pixy camera. The structure of the EV3RT application is shown in Fig. 8b. Each robot program consists of four tasks - a global main task, a motor control task and two tasks for reading and writing Bluetooth packages. Note that lower *prio* values indicate higher priorities. Three cyclic handlers periodically read from the color and infrared sensors and the pixy cam. Another cyclic handler periodically checks whether the robot is moving. An event flag is used to alert the motor control task to several events, namely that the robot stopped, that it has reached the map border or that the infrared sensor has detected a possible imminent collision.

With our reusable formal models, it was straight-forward to translate the rescue robot application into UPPAAL timed automata. The resulting model is

Table 1. Verified properties for the search and rescue robots.

Property	Result
E◊ $mainTaskBody$.GOAL_RECV	✓
E◊ $mainTaskBody$.GET_GOAL	✓
E◊ $mainTaskBody$.GRIPPED	✓
E◊ $mainTaskBody$.GO_DELIVER	✓
E◊ $mainTaskBody$.DELIVERED	✓
E◊ $status = S\_HOME$	✓
A□ ¬$deadlock$	✓
A□ ∀ $t_i \in Tasks : t_i$.RUNNING → ¬(∃ $t_j \in Tasks : t_i.id \neq t_j.id \wedge t_j$.RUNNING)	✓
A□ ∀ $t_i, t_j \in Tasks : t_i$.RUNNING ∧ t_j.READY ∧ $t_j.prio < t_i.prio$ → $t_j.c_{READY} \leq 0$	✓
A□ ∀ $t_i \in Tasks : t_i$.RUNNING → ¬(∃ $h_j \in Handlers : h_j$.READY ∨ h_j.RUNNING)	✓
A□ ∀ $h_i \in Handlers : h_i$.RUNNING → $h_i.c \leq h_i.period$	✓
∀ $t_i \in Tasks :$ A◊ t_i.RUNNING	✓

available at https://github.com/EmbSys-WWU. In line with the EV3RT implementation, we have configured our scheduler model such that only the task with the highest priority is executed and an FCFS strategy is chosen for equal priorities. We have transformed task and cyclic handler bodies manually to UPPAAL TA using our reusable formalization of activation, preemption, and wait function calls by mapping the general concepts to the EV3RT-specific system calls, e.g., `act_tsk()` to the channel *activate*, `exit_tsk()` to the channel *exitT*, `set_flg()` to a transition that sets the bit pattern of the given event, `wai_flg()` to the wait-release mechanism, `clr_flg()` to a transition that resets the bit pattern, and `ev3_infrared_sensor_get_distance()` to *get_value[IR_SENSOR]*. We have modeled sensor inputs with the sensor template shown in Fig. 7. We have abstracted from the server by manually defining a TA that generates Bluetooth messages. We have also abstracted from most functional variables, i.e., the position of the robot, the navigation and PID controller, and the specific sensor values. For the latter, we only distinguish two values for each sensor (i.e., obstacle/border/object detected or not detected). In summary, the resulting formal model abstracts from data, but precisely captures concurrency, synchronizations, timing, and the reaction to external events. These are typically particularly hard to test and debug, while many errors arise from faulty task integration, misunderstandings of the scheduling semantics, and timing issues.

With the formal TA model, we were able to simulate possible sequences of events and actions, without the necessity to execute the software on the real hardware, which is very tedious, error-prone, and time consuming. In contrast to the real execution, which is not only slow but also very difficult to debug, we were able to manually trace possible executions and interleavings between tasks and handlers, with timing and state information. The graphical animation proved to be extremely helpful for this manual validation process.

We have used the UPPAAL model checker to verify the reachability properties shown in the upper part of Table 1, namely that the possible sequences of events and actions include sequences where the robot receives a goal, moves to the goal, grips an object, delivers it to the rescue zone, completes the delivery, and returns to its home position. Although our formal model abstracts from most data variables, it contains the process interactions and their (approximate) timing. Thus, the state space is too large to be fully explored. Still, to validate our formal model of the scheduler and process and handler interactions, we have built a simplified model where no messages are sent to the system (i.e., the Bluetooth message generator is switched off). For this simplified model, we have verified the safety properties shown in lower part of Table 1. These show that the scheduler behaves as intended, i.e. that it never deadlocks, that only one task is running at a time, that tasks are executed according to their priorities, that only one handler is running at a time, that cyclic handlers are always executed within the specified cycle, and that all tasks are eventually executed.

6 Conclusion

In this paper, we have presented an approach to reduce the manual effort for the formalization of real-time applications that are developed with custom RTOS. Our key idea is to provide reusable formal models and abstractions. We have presented TA templates that provide a configurable scheduler model, a generic task model that can control the execution of preemptable tasks, and a cyclic handler model that periodically executes non-preemptable handlers. Other handlers (e.g. interrupt handlers) can analogously be modeled by replacing the periodic trigger with an external event. In addition, we provide reusable formalizations of typical interaction schemes, in particular the notification of events, waiting for events, and waiting for time. For a given custom RTOS, the reusable models can be configured such that key RTOS components can be transformed into an abstract formal model. For a given real-time application, those can then be combined into a formal system model by transforming task and handler implementations with the help of the reusable formalizations of typical interaction schemes (e.g., for wait and sleep function calls). The resulting overall model can be analyzed, formally verified, and graphically simulated using the UPPAAL tool suite.

As a first step to validate the applicability of our approach, we have configured our reusable formal models for the custom open source RTOS EV3RT and then manually translated a search & rescue robot implementation into a formal UPPAAL TA model. We have used the resulting formal model to manually analyze the concurrency and real-time behavior, and to automatically verify a number of crucial properties for a simplified system that abstracts from data. In particular, the manual analysis within the animated simulation as well as the graphical animation of counter-examples have proven to be extremely helpful, as the execution on the real hardware is error-prone, time consuming and concurrency and synchronization issues are very hard to debug. The properties we have verified with the UPPAAL model checker on the abstract system are crucial for correct concurrent and timed behavior.

In future work, we plan to validate our approach with other custom RTOS. Furthermore, we plan to automate the transformation process by providing a transformation engine that should be configurable for various custom RTOS.

References

1. Abdeddaïm, Y., Maler, O.: Preemptive job-shop scheduling using stopwatch automata. In: Katoen, J.-P., Stevens, P. (eds.) TACAS 2002. LNCS, vol. 2280, pp. 113–126. Springer, Heidelberg (2002). https://doi.org/10.1007/3-540-46002-0_9
2. Alur, R., Dill, D.L.: A theory of timed automata. Theoret. Comput. Sci. **126**, 183–235 (1994)
3. Behrmann, G., David, A., Larsen, K.G.: A tutorial on UPPAAL. In: Bernardo, M., Corradini, F. (eds.) SFM-RT 2004. LNCS, vol. 3185, pp. 200–236. Springer, Heidelberg (2004). https://doi.org/10.1007/978-3-540-30080-9_7
4. Bengtsson, J., Larsen, K., Larsson, F., Pettersson, P., Yi, W.: UPPAAL — a tool suite for automatic verification of real-time systems. In: Alur, R., Henzinger, T.A., Sontag, E.D. (eds.) HS 1995. LNCS, vol. 1066, pp. 232–243. Springer, Heidelberg (1996). https://doi.org/10.1007/BFb0020949
5. Bengtsson, J., Yi, W.: Timed automata: semantics, algorithms and tools. In: Desel, J., Reisig, W., Rozenberg, G. (eds.) ACPN 2003. LNCS, vol. 3098, pp. 87–124. Springer, Heidelberg (2004). https://doi.org/10.1007/978-3-540-27755-2_3
6. Beyer, D., Keremoglu, M.E.: CPAchecker: a tool for configurable software verification. In: Gopalakrishnan, G., Qadeer, S. (eds.) CAV 2011. LNCS, vol. 6806, pp. 184–190. Springer, Heidelberg (2011). https://doi.org/10.1007/978-3-642-22110-1_16
7. Blom, S., Darabi, S., Huisman, M., Oortwijn, W.: The VerCors tool set: verification of parallel and concurrent software. In: Polikarpova, N., Schneider, S. (eds.) IFM 2017. LNCS, vol. 10510, pp. 102–110. Springer, Cham (2017). https://doi.org/10.1007/978-3-319-66845-1_7
8. Béchennec, J.L., Roux, O.H., Tigori, T.: Formal model-based conformance verification of an OSEK/VDX compliant RTOS. In: 2018 5th International Conference on Control, Decision and Information Technologies (CoDIT), pp. 628–634 (2018). https://doi.org/10.1109/CoDIT.2018.8394813
9. Cuoq, P., Kirchner, F., Kosmatov, N., Prevosto, V., Signoles, J., Yakobowski, B.: Frama-C. In: Eleftherakis, G., Hinchey, M., Holcombe, M. (eds.) SEFM 2012. LNCS, vol. 7504, pp. 233–247. Springer, Heidelberg (2012). https://doi.org/10.1007/978-3-642-33826-7_16
10. Deifel, H.P., Göttlinger, M., Milius, S., Schröder, L., Dietrich, C., Lohmann, D.: Automatic verification of application-tailored OSEK kernels. In: IEEE (2017)
11. EV3RT Project: EV3RT (2019). https://ev3rt-git.github.io/about/
12. Han, P., Zhai, Z., Nielsen, B., Nyman, U.: Model-based optimization of ARINC-653 partition scheduling. Int. J. Softw. Tools Technol. Transf. **23**(5), 721–740 (2021)
13. Herber, P., Fellmuth, J., Glesner, S.: Model checking systemc designs using timed automata. In: IEEE/ACM/IFIP International Conference on Hardware/Software Codesign and System Synthesis, CODES+ISSS 2008, pp. 131–136. ACM (2008). https://doi.org/10.1145/1450135.1450166

14. Huang, Y., Zhao, Y., Zhu, L., Li, Q., Zhu, H., Shi, J.: Modeling and verifying the code-level OSEK/VDX operating system with CSP. In: 2011 Fifth International Conference on Theoretical Aspects of Software Engineering, pp. 142–149. IEEE (2011)
15. Klein, G., et al.: sel4: formal verification of an OS kernel. In: ACM SIGOPS 22nd Symposium on Operating Systems Principles, SOSP 2009. ACM (2009). https://doi.org/10.1145/1629575.1629596
16. Laplante, P.A., et al.: Real-Time Systems Design And Analysis. Wiley, New York (2004)
17. OSEK: ISO 17356–3:2005 Road vehicles - Open interface for embedded automotive applications - Part 3: OSEK/VDX Operating System (OS). International Organization for Standardization (2005)
18. Shi, J., He, J., Zhu, H., Fang, H., Huang, Y., Zhang, X.: ORIENTAIS: Formal verified OSEK/VDX real-time operating system. In: 2012 IEEE 17th International Conference on Engineering of Complex Computer Systems. pp. 293–301. IEEE (2012)
19. Tigori, K.T.G., Béchennec, J.L., Faucou, S., Roux, O.H.: Formal model-based synthesis of application-specific static rtos. ACM Trans. Embed. Comput. Syst. **16**(4), 1–25 (017). https://doi.org/10.1145/3015777
20. TOPPERS Project: Toyohashi open platform for embedded real-time systems. https://www.toppers.jp/en/project.html
21. TRON: μITRON4.0 Specification (2007). https://www.tron.org/wp-content/themes/dp-magjam/pdf/specifications/en_US/TEF024-S001-04.03.00_en.pdf. Accessed 02 Sep 2021
22. Vu, D.H., Chiba, Y., Yatake, K., Aoki, T.: Verifying OSEK/VDX OS design using its formal specification. In: 2016 10th International Symposium on Theoretical Aspects of Software Engineering (TASE), pp. 81–88. IEEE (2016)
23. Waszniowski, L., Hanzálek, Z.: Formal verification of multitasking applications based on timed automata model. Real-Time Syst. **38**(1), 39–65 (2008)
24. Zhang, H., Aoki, T., Chiba, Y.: Verifying OSEK/VDX applications: a sequentialization-based model checking approach. IEICE Trans. Inf. Sys. **98**(10), 1765–1776 (2015)
25. Zhang, H., Aoki, T., Lin, H.H., Zhang, M., Chiba, Y., Yatake, K.: SMT-based bounded model checking for OSEK/VDX applications. In: 2013 20th Asia-Pacific Software Engineering Conference (APSEC), vol. 1, pp. 307–314. IEEE (2013)
26. Zhang, H., Li, G., Cheng, Z., Xue, J.: Verifying OSEK/VDX automotive applications: a spin-based model checking approach. Softw. Test. Verif. Reliab. **28**(3), e1662 (2018)

Formal Verification of an Industrial UML-like Model using mCRL2

Anna Stramaglia(✉) and Jeroen J. A. Keiren

Eindhoven University of Technology, Eindhoven, The Netherlands
{a.stramaglia,j.j.a.keiren}@tue.nl

Abstract. Low-code development platforms are gaining popularity. Essentially, such platforms allow to shift from coding to graphical modeling, helping to improve quality and reduce development time. The Cordis SUITE is a low-code development platform that adopts the Unified Modeling Language (UML) to design complex machine-control applications. In this paper we introduce Cordis models and their semantics. To enable formal verification, we define an automatic translation of Cordis models to the process algebraic specification language mCRL2. As a proof of concept, we describe requirements of the control software of an industrial cylinder model developed by Cordis, and show how these can be verified using model checking. We show that our verification approach is effective to uncover subtle issues in the industrial model and its implementation.

1 Introduction

Abstract models are commonly used during the design phase of software. For example, class diagrams are used to describe the structure of a software system, and behavioral models describe the possible executions. Model checking can be used to verify that such behavioral models satisfy their requirements. While model checking is a promising technique, its industrial applications are still limited. There are several reasons for this. Among others, it is considered tedious to create a detailed behavioral model prior to implementing the system. Furthermore, model checking tools primarily use low-level, academic languages that require specific expertise not typically acquired by engineers in industry.

Low-code development platforms (LCDPs) [20] are gaining popularity. Such platforms focus on increasing the level of abstraction of software development, shifting from coding to graphical modeling, and generating code from these low-code models. LCDPs allow addressing both issues described above. First of all, the detailed behavioral model is now created during specification of the system. Second, if their semantics are well-understood, the models can be automatically translated to the languages used by state-of-the-art model checkers.

The Cordis SUITE[1] is an LCDP for machine-control applications, based on graphic Model-Driven Software Engineering. Its development environment is the Cordis Modeler, which uses Altova UModel[2] as front-end for drawing the models.

---

[1] https://www.cordis-suite.com.
[2] https://www.altova.com.

© The Author(s), under exclusive license to Springer Nature Switzerland AG 2022
J. F. Groote and M. Huisman (Eds.): FMICS 2022, LNCS 13487, pp. 86–102, 2022.
https://doi.org/10.1007/978-3-031-15008-1_7

Cordis models are described in a rich language that uses an extension of UML [16] class diagrams and state machine diagrams for describing the static structure and behavior, respectively. Additionally, it includes a large fragment of Structured Text [12]. Source code for Programmable Logic Controllers (PLCs) or the .NET platform can be generated directly from the models. Hence, the resulting implementation is consistent with the corresponding Cordis model. Cordis, the company developing this LCDP, has shown an interest in extending the Cordis SUITE with model checking capabilities.

Our contributions are as follows. We describe the structure and semantics of Cordis models, and automatically translate these to mCRL2 [9] to enable model checking. The use of mCRL2 is motivated by the availability of its tool set [2] with powerful verification tools such as simulation, model checking and the verification of first-order modal μ-calculus formulae [8]. We illustrate the feasibility of modeling and verification of Cordis models using a pneumatic *cylinder*. We specify, informally and formally, two typical requirements of the cylinder and verify whether they are satisfied by the model. One of the requirements is not satisfied by the cylinder model. We analyze its counterexample and identify a subtle issue in the model. The issue is reproducible in the implementation. A fix of the issue, now distributed by Cordis, is described and verified.

Related Work. A large amount of work has been done in the application of formal verification to industrial domains. Most of this work focuses on specific domains, such as railway infrastructure management [1,10,21] and medical applications [13,17,22]. Closer to our research are works on modeling and verification of control software, such as CERN's FSM language [11], which uses a strict hierarchical architecture of finite state machines for a specific machine control application, and OIL, developed and used by Canon Production Printing, which has a strong focus on separation of concerns [3].

Modeling languages such as SysML and UML can be used to model systems from any domain. The verification of state machine diagrams in these languages has been studied extensively, see, e.g., [1,6,14,15,19,23,24]. UML state machine diagrams are, e.g., transformed to Petri nets [15]. Others transform various UML behavioral diagrams into a single transition system for the model checker NuSMV [5]. The work closest to ours focuses on the verification of SysML state machines in the railway industrial domain [1]. Like in our work, state machines are assigned a formal semantics, and translated to mCRL2 for formal verification. Their semantics and execution model focuses on distributed execution of state machines communicating via queues, whereas our work focuses on a strictly sequential execution with communication via shared variables.

Outline. In Sect. 2 we introduce Cordis models. The cylinder model is described in Sect. 3. In Sect. 4 we describe the mCRL2 specification of Cordis models, the requirements of the cylinder model, and the results of its verification. Discussion and conclusions are presented in Sect. 5 and Sect. 6, respectively.

2 Cordis Models

The Cordis SUITE is a collection of tools for developing, testing and deploying system control software, with a focus on machine control. We consider three of these tools. The *Cordis Modeler* is an LCDP for creating machine-control applications. It uses an extension of the Unified Modeling Language (UML) such that every Cordis model describes the structure and behavior of a *machine* using class diagrams and state machine diagrams, respectively. Additionally, it can check for design errors, and generate source code for Programmable Logic Controllers (PLCs) or the .NET platform. The *Cordis Machine Control Server (MCS)* loads model information from the modeler, and connects to the PLC in order to exchange state information and data with the running system. The *Cordis Machine Control Dashboard (MCD)* is a Human-Machine Interface used to show live system data and live state machine diagrams when the PLC is running, providing real-time and historical information about the execution.

2.1 Class Diagrams

In this paper we illustrate the syntax and semantics of Cordis models, and their verification, using the concrete example of a pneumatic cylinder. The *static structure* of a Cordis model is described by its class diagram. The class diagram of the pneumatic cylinder is described in Example 1. Pneumatic cylinders are commonly used in factory automation systems for clamping, ejecting and lifting, and in industrial processes for materials handling and packaging. A pneumatic cylinder consists of a cylinder barrel with a piston that moves back and forth by means of compressed air controlled by electrically controlled valves.

Example 1. The cylinder we consider moves the piston between the *zero position* (completely retracted) and the *end position* (extended). Its class diagram consists of a single class, shown in Fig. 1. Classes can be tagged with stereotypes <<Machine>> and <<MachinePart>>, respectively, denoting the machine controlled by the system and a component of it. For the sake of simplicity, we consider the cylinder in isolation, but it typically is a machine part in a larger machine. A class

Fig. 1. Cylinder class

has *properties*, variables stored in the class, and *operations*, both tagged with Cordis-specific stereotypes describing their role in the system.

Stereotypes <<Input>> and <<Output>> describe variables used to interface with the environment, typically the hardware. Inputs iZeroPosSensor and iEndPosSensor detect whether the cylinder is at its zero or end position, respectively. The outputs oValveMoveToZeroPos and oValveMoveToEndPos are used to actuate the valves. Stereotypes <<InputSignal>> and <<OutputSignal >> are used to define shared variables to communicate between objects within the model, input signals are read by the cylinder and output signals are written by the cylinder. Stereotypes such as <<Observer>>, <<Var>>, <<Setting>> and <<Message>> are less important for the verification and ignored in this paper, see [25] for a more detailed explanation. Class operations, with stereotype <<Cmd>>, are commands issued (asynchronously) to the class, by the environment or another component. Commands TOGGLE, MOVE_TO_ZERO_POSITION, MOVE_TO_END_POSITION, and EmergencyStop are self-explanatory. Command CONDITIONING can be used to force (re)initialization of the cylinder.

2.2   State Machine Diagrams

Structure. The behavior of an object is defined using a hierarchy of state machine diagrams. Cordis state machine diagrams are similar to those defined in standard UML [16], with some Cordis specific details.

At the highest level, a state machine diagram consists of *top-level state machines*. A (top-level) state machine consists of a hierarchy of states and pseudo-states, whose types are mostly taken from standard UML, connected by transitions. A state can be a reference to a *subdiagram* or to a *substatemachine*. The key difference between these is whether they are executed as part of the diagram that references it (subdiagram) or separately (substatemachine). When a transition to a substatemachine is taken, control is transferred to the substatemachine.

Transitions have a *source* and *target* state, and can optionally be labeled by *guards* and *actions*. For a transition without guard, the guard is assumed to be *true* if the source of the transition is an initial state or an exit node, or the target of the transition is a choice node. If the source is a choice node, the empty guard is treated as *else*. Otherwise, the empty guard is assumed to be *false*.

Example 2. Consider the top-level state machine Main of the cylinder from our running example, shown in Fig. 2. From the initial state of Main, denoted by •, substatemachine Disabled is reached. This substatemachine has a number of states used to model different ways out of it (see Figs. 4 and 5). For instance, if Disabled determines that the cylinder is in its zero position it reaches state CondInZero, hence, guard [State(Disabled.Conditioning.CondInZero)] evaluates to *true* and state machine Main takes the transition to In_Zero_Pos.

Cordis models can contain *prestates* and *poststates* to model behavior that must be executed every time an object is allowed to execute a step, regardless of its current state. Pre- and poststates can either appear inside a state machine,

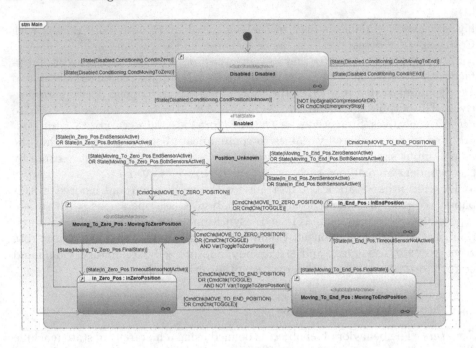

Fig. 2. State machine `Main`.

or at the top-level of the state machine diagram. The behavior of multiple pre- and poststates is always combined into a single pre- or poststate by taking the sequential composition of all pre- and poststates in a predefined order.

The poststate of the cylinder model updates output signals `oInEndPosition`, `oInZeroPosition` and `oEnabled` to reflect the cylinder's current position.

Semantics. Cordis models are executed using a cyclic execution model. In each cycle all objects execute in a predetermined order defined in the class diagram.

The order of execution within an object is depicted as an activity diagram in Fig. 3a. First the *inputs* are read. This essentially caches the current values of the inputs, input signals and the currently active command in local variables. To facilitate reasoning about the behavior of subsystems in isolation during verification, we also consider input signals and commands as free variables. Second, the (combined) prestate of the object is executed. If a new command was sent to the object, the *guard condition* is evaluated to determine whether the command can be accepted. If the guard condition is true, the *command action* is executed, otherwise the *reject action* is executed; these are defined in Structured Text by the user. The *command ready condition* determines whether, at the end of the current cycle, the command has been fully processed and can be removed from the interface. If this condition is false, the command will remain on the interface; if it is not overwritten by a new command, in the next cycle only the command ready condition is reevaluated. Since a single command can be evaluated per

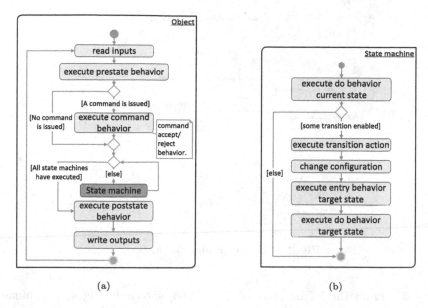

Fig. 3. Order of execution of (a) one object, and (b) a state machine within the object.

cycle, if a new command is issued it overwrites the previous one. After the command has executed, all state machines in the object execute in a predetermined order, in turns. Finally, the poststate is executed and the outputs are written.

Figure 3b depicts the execution of a single state machine. First, the do behavior of the current active state is executed. Second, if a transition is enabled in the current configuration, one such transition is executed. If multiple transitions are enabled, one is selected as follows: if the source state of one enabled transition contains the source state of another enabled transition, the transition from the outermost state is executed; transitions to other states take priority over self-loop transitions; otherwise the first transition from a predetermined order is executed.[3] If a transition was executed, the current state is changed and the behavior of the transition and the entry behavior of the target state are executed. If no transition is executed, the current state is unchanged.

3   Cylinder

We now describe the behavior of the cylinder model introduced in Sect. 2.

State machine Main, in Example 2, refers to substatemachines Disabled, MovingToZeroPosition, MovingToEndPosition, and it contains subdiagrams InZeroPosition and InEndPosition. We next elaborate on the details relevant for the verification, described in Sect. 4.2. For a full model description, see [25].

---

[3] Currently, the implementation chooses the order of creation.

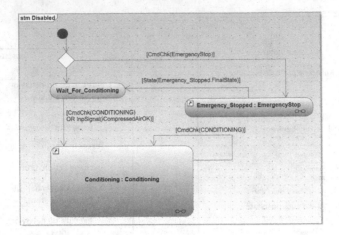

Fig. 4. Substatemachine `Disabled`

Disabled. From the initial state of `Disabled`, shown in Fig. 4, if command `EmergencyStop` was accepted, the system moves to subdiagram `Emergency Stop`, otherwise the system moves directly to `Wait_For_Conditioning`. Subdiagram `Conditioning` of `Disabled`, shown in Fig. 5, determines, based on the current values of the input signals, inputs and outputs, which state in `Main` reflects the current situation of the cylinder using a cascade of choice nodes. The cascade of choice nodes can be interpreted as an **if ... else if ... else** ... conditional. The states without outgoing transitions are used from state machine `Main` to determine the appropriate exit from `Disabled`.

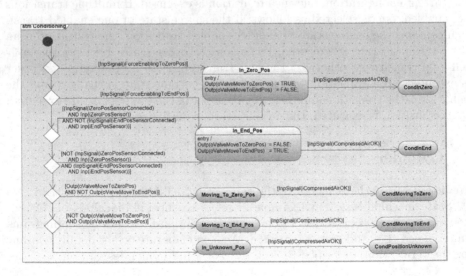

Fig. 5. State machine diagram `Conditioning`

MovingToZero- MovingToEndPosition and InZero- InEndPosition. The two substatemachines `MovingToEndPosition` and `MovingToZeroPosition` are symmetric, and describe the behavior of the cylinder when it is moving to the end position or to the zero position, respectively. Subdiagrams `InEndPosition` and `InZeroPosition` are also symmetric, and describe the behavior of the cylinder when it is completely extended or retracted, respectively.

4 Model Checking Cordis Models Using mCRL2

We enable formal verification of Cordis models through an automatic translation of the Cordis semantics to the modeling language mCRL2 [9]. The language is based on process algebra with data. Its associated tool set [2] can be used for modeling, validating and verifying systems. Although mCRL2 allows specifying communicating, parallel processes, the formalization of the semantics of Cordis models we present in this work only uses sequential processes. In the following subsections we describe our translation to mCRL2, see Sect. 4.1, and the formalization of a number of properties, see Sect. 4.2. We again use the model of a pneumatic cylinder (see Example 1) as a running example.

4.1 Translation to mCRL2

The mCRL2 specification of Cordis models consists of a sequence of several processes that model the behavior of the system. Essentially, each execution step shown in Fig. 3 is represented by a process in the mCRL2 specification.

The basic building block in a process is an action, such as a, b, that can be parameterized with data, e.g., `a(0)`, `b(false)`. When p and q are processes, the sequential composition `p.q` denotes the process in which first p is executed and upon termination, q is executed. The alternative composition, or choice, `p + q` denotes that either p or q is executed. Recursive processes can be defined by writing process equations of the form `P = q`, where P is the name of the process, and q is a process expression in which named processes are referred to.

In the mCRL2 specification of Cordis models, all processes are parameterized with the current configuration of the system, i.e., the current states of all state machines, and the current values of all class properties and operations. In what follows we sometimes omit (part of) the parameters, and write ... instead. Each state machine in the model is identified uniquely by a nonnegative index.

Example 3. For the cylinder example discussed in this paper, the process describing the top-level of the system is as follows.

```
P_main(state_machine: Nat, s1: List(State), ..., cmd2: Command, cmd2_ready: Bool,
       cmd2_accepted: Bool, behaviors: List(Int), ...,
       M2'ToggleToZeroPosition: Bool, M2'iZeroPosSensor: Bool,
       M2'iEndPosSensor: Bool, M2'oValveMoveToZeroPos: Bool,
       M2'oValveMoveToEndPos: Bool, M2'iCompressedAirOK: Bool,
       M2'iZeroPosSensorConnected: Bool, M2'iEndPosSensorConnected: Bool,
       M2'iResetOutputsOnEStop: Bool, M2'iForceEnablingToZeroPos: Bool,
       M2'iForceEnablingToEndPos: Bool, M2'oInZeroPosition: Bool,
       M2'oInEndPosition: Bool, M2'oEnabled: Bool, ...) = P_set_inputs();
```

The parameter state_machine tracks the state machine that is currently executing. The current configuration of the system is tracked by, for every top-level state machine, a list of states s1, containing the currently active states. States are defined using **sort** State = **struct** State_(state:*Nat*, entry: *List*(behavior), cont:*List*(behavior)) that is, unique identifier, state, and entry and continuous behavior, entry and cont. For every machinepart, indexed by an integer i, the command currently on the interface (along with some additional information) is kept in cmdi. Also class properties are stored as parameters. The machinepart Cylinder has index 2 and, e.g., input iEndPosSensor is stored as M2'iEndPosSensor, where M2 refers to machinepart 2.

We next focus on the most relevant parts of the mCRL2 specification following the Cordis semantics execution. See [25] for a more detailed description.

At the beginning of each cycle, the values of the inputs are received by the system. As the inputs are not controlled by the system, we model these by receiving arbitrary values of the domain of the inputs.

Example 4. For the cylinder model this is formalized as follows.

```
P_set_inputs(..., M2'iZeroPosSensor: Bool, M2'iEndPosSensor: Bool, ...) =
    sum M2'iZeroPosSensor', M2'iEndPosSensor': Bool
    . inputs(M2'iZeroPosSensor', M2'iEndPosSensor')
. P_set_free_input_signals(M2'iZeroPosSensor = M2'iZeroPosSensor',
                           M2'iEndPosSensor = M2'iEndPosSensor');
```

In this equation P_set_inputs is a parameterized process which represents the reception of the <<Input>> parameters. The *sum* denotes a generalized alternative composition that generates the choice between all four combinations of the input parameters. Subsequently, P_set_free_input_signals is called, where the new values of the inputs are assigned to the process parameters.

The process P_set_free_input_signals is similar to P_set_inputs, it allows setting arbitrary values to the input signals. This process in turn calls P_set_free_commands, which cycles through all machineparts to model commands that are issued by the environment. Issuing commands is modeled by a non-deterministic choice over all commands of the machinepart. Commands are indexed by an integer i. If no new command is issued this is indicated by action no_freecmd. If command i is issued this is indicated by action freecmd(i).

Once all external inputs to the system have been established, the cyclic execution of machineparts is performed. In the case of the cylinder, only machinepart 2 needs to execute. First, the prestate is executed (which is empty in case of the cylinder). Subsequently, the command on the interface is executed.

Example 5. In the cylinder model, command MOVE_TO_ZERO_POSITION has index 6, and it is executed using the following code.

```
P_command_6(..., s1: List(State), ..., cmd2: Command,
            cmd2_ready: Bool, cmd2_accepted: Bool, ...) =
  (isCommand2_MOVE_TO_ZERO_POSITION(cmd2) && !cmd2_accepted)
    -> command(6, true)
      . P_command_6_exec(behaviors = accept(cmd2), cmd2_accepted = true,
               cmd2_ready = S79 in s1 || S103 in s1 || S89 in s1 || S93 in s1)
 + (isCommand2_MOVE_TO_ZERO_POSITION(cmd2) && cmd2_accepted)
    -> chk_ready . P_statemachines_M2(cmd2_ready = ...);
```

When a command is issued, cmd2_accepted is currently false. If the command guard evaluates to true, the second argument of the action command is *true*; otherwise it is set to *false*. If the command is accepted, the command accept behavior is listed for execution, indicated by behaviors = accept(cmd2); if the command is rejected, reject(cmd2) is assigned instead. If the command was accepted in a previous cycle, cmd2_accepted is true, and action chk_ready is reported. In both cases, the command ready condition is evaluated in the assignment to cmd2_ready. Here it is true if the state machine is currently in one of four states. If the command was just accepted, the corresponding behavior is executed in P_command_6_exec, otherwise no transition behavior is executed.

Subsequently, the state machines execute. There is a separate process for each top-level state machine. In the cylinder, the corresponding process for Main is P_statemachines_S1. This cycles through all state machines in order, and allows each state machine to take a transition. Transitions are defined by **sort** Transition = **struct** Transition_(source:List(State), dest: List(State), behavior:List(behavior)), that is, its source states, its target states, and the behavior to execute if it is taken. The state machine process offers a non-deterministic choice over all transitions in the state machines.

Example 6. We give an example of one transition in the process of the cylinder. The other transitions are similar.

```
P_transitions_S1(state_machine: Nat, s1: List(State),...) =
  ...
+ (state_machine == 1 && (head(source(t100)) in s1)
    && (!M2'iCompressedAirOK || isCommand2_EmergencyStop(cmd2) && cmd2_accepted))
  -> trans(100)
  .P_execute_behaviors_S1(behaviors = behavior(t100) ++ entry(head(dest(t100))),
             s1 = dest(t100) ++ remove_prefix(s1, rhead(source(t100))), ...)
+ ...
```

In this excerpt, t100 refers to the transition with source state Main.Enabled and target state Main.Disabled.InitialState in Fig. 2, guarded by [NOT InpSignal(iCompressedAirOK) OR CmdChk(EmergencyStop)].

The summand consists of a guard which says that state machine Main is executing, i.e., state_machine == 1, and source state Main.Enabled is part of the current configuration, i.e., (head(source(t100)) in s1). Furthermore, it checks if command EmergencyStop was accepted using isCommand2_Emergency Stop(cmd2) && cmd2_accepted.[4] In case the condition is satisfied, the action trans(100) is executed and P_execute_behaviors_S1 is called in order to execute the behaviors labelling the transition (if any), behavior(t100), as well as the entry behavior of the target state, entry(head(dest(t100))). The next state that is reached in the state machine is dest(t100) ++ remove_prefix (s1, rhead(source(t100))), where dest(t100) is the configuration reached after taking t100, and remove_prefix(s1, rhead(source (t100))) removes all the states that are left by taking t100 from the configuration. Following the priority rules, transitions that have lower priority include the negation of the guards of all transitions with higher priority in their condition.

---

[4] Note that in mCRL2, && (conjunction) binds stronger than || (disjunction).

After all state machines have executed one transition and the corresponding behavior, the poststate is executed. A pre- or poststate consists of Structured Text code that is translated to a sequence of mCRL2 processes. The poststate execution amounts to executing the corresponding processes.

For the poststate of the cylinder, this is modeled as follows.

```
P_poststate_M2(..., behaviors: List(Int), ...) =
  (behaviors == []) -> post_done.P_remove_command_M2()
+ (behaviors != [] && head(behaviors) == 3)
  -> post(3).P_3(behaviors = tail(behaviors));
```

In `P_3` the process parameters are updated, reflecting the poststate assignments.

After this, `P_poststate_M2` is reentered and transition `post_done` is taken, and if a command was on the interface and the command ready condition was true, it is removed from the interface and the process parameters for it are reset to their default value. Execution subsequently repeats from the beginning.

4.2 Formal Verification of Requirements

One of the primary goals of formalizing Cordis models using mCRL2 is to enable the formal verification of requirements. In this section, we first describe the requirements. Subsequently we discuss their formalization.

Requirements. In total, we have formulated 12 requirements for the cylinder, and formalized and verified them. Due to space limitations, in this section we describe one safety requirement and one liveness requirement. For details of the remaining requirements the reader is referred to [25].

The requirements we consider are the following two:

1. Invariantly, if one of the output signals `oInEndPosition` or `oInZeroPosition` is *true*, also output signal `oEnabled` is *true*.
2. Whenever output signal `oEnabled` is *false* and input signal `iCompressed-AirOK` is *true*, inevitably output signal `oEnabled` becomes *true* unless command `CONDITIONING` is accepted.

Formalization of Requirements Using the Modal μ-calculus. We describe requirements using the first order modal μ-calculus [8]. This is a very expressive temporal logic that extends the μ-calculus with data.

In general, the requirements we are interested in refer to the interfaces of the machine parts, that is, their inputs, input signals, commands, output signals, and outputs. The first three are set explicitly in the translation. The output signals and outputs are only available implicitly, thus, in order to expose their values, we have extended the translation with self-loops. For this, we use actions such as `state_M2'oInEndPosition(true)`, where `state` indicates this is a stateloop, `M2` refers to the machinepart, `oInEndPosition` is the name of the output, and *true* is its current value. Similarly, we expose the current state of the system.

This is used to formalize the first requirement as follows.

```
[true*](<state_M2'oInEndPosition(true)||state_M2'oInZeroPosition(true)>true
      => <state_M2'oEnabled(true)>true)
```

This formula should be read as follows. First, [true*] represents all sequences consisting of zero or more actions. After each such sequence the remainder of the formula should hold. For the remainder, note that formula <a>true holds in every state with an outgoing a transition. If we write the action formula a || b inside a modality, this matches the set of actions containing a, b; essentially, || here denotes the union of the sets of action represented by a and b, which are the singleton sets containing a and b, respectively. Hence, <state_M2'oInEndPosition (true)||state_M2'oInZeroPosition(true)>true holds in every state that has an outgoing transition labeled state_M2'oInEndPosition(true) or state_M2'oInZeroPosition(true). In each such state, the formula requires that also <state_M2'oEnabled(true)>true holds, i.e., the state has an outgoing transition labeled state_M2'oEnabled(true). We refer to [9] for a more extensive introduction to the first order μ-calculus.

The second requirement is formalized as follows.

```
nu X(enabled: Bool = false, compressedAirOk: Bool = false) .
 (forall e: Bool . <state_M2'oEnabled(e)>true =>
   ((forall c: Bool . [exists a2, a3, a4, a5, a6: Bool .
      free_input_signals(c, a2, a3, a4, a5, a6)]X(e,c)) &&
    [!exists a1, a2, a3, a4, a5, a6: Bool .
      free_input_signals(a1, a2, a3, a4, a5, a6)]X(e,compressedAirOk))) &&
 (forall e: Bool . [state_M2'oEnabled(e)]false =>
   ((forall c: Bool . [exists a2, a3, a4, a5, a6: Bool .
      free_input_signals(c, a2, a3, a4, a5, a6)]X(enabled,c)) &&
    [!exists a1, a2, a3, a4, a5, a6: Bool .
      free_input_signals(a1, a2, a3, a4, a5, a6)]X(enabled,compressedAirOk))) &&
 (val(!enabled && compressedAirOk) =>
   mu X . [!((exists a2, a3, a4, a5, a6: Bool .
              free_input_signals(false, a2, a3, a4, a5, a6)) ||
             command(9, true) ||
            (exists b: Bool . state_M2'oValveMoveToZeroPos(b) ||
                             state_M2'oValveMoveToEndPos(b) ||
                             state_M2'oInZeroPosition(b) ||
                             state_M2'oInEndPosition(b) ||
                             state_M2'oEnabled(b)) ||
           (exists i: Nat, l: List(Nat) . states(i, l))
      )]X || <state_M2'oEnabled(true)>true)
```

This formula uses a greatest fixed point (nu) and a least fixed point (mu). The greatest fixed point is parameterized by two Boolean variables, enabled and compressedAirOk, that keep track of whether oEnabled or iCompressedAir Ok have become *true*, respectively. In order to keep track of these values, we distinguish two cases. If a transition state_M2'oEnabled(e) is enabled, denoted by *forall* e: *Bool*. <state_M2'oEnabled(e)>true, we check if an action free_input_signals is enabled. If so, we determine the value assigned to iCompressedAirOk using *forall* c: *Bool* . [exists a2, a3, a4, a5, a6: *Bool* .free_input_signals(c, a2, a3, a4, a5, a6)]X(e,c)). We use *exists* inside the modality to represent generalised union, and match any value for the rest of the input signals. We update enabled to the value observed by the self-loop, and compressedAirOk to the value set in free_input_signals. If free_input_signals is not enabled, only compressedAirOk is updated. The case where state_M2'oEnabled(e) is not enabled is handled in a similar way.

Now, if enabled is *false*, and compressedAirOk is *true*, the least fixed point subformula needs to hold. To interpret this formula, we first note that formula mu Y . [!a]Y || <b>*true* captures that inevitably a state is reached where a b transition is enabled, unless an a transition happens. So, in principle, the following formula denotes that, as long as iCompressedAirOk does not become *false*, represented by the first argument to free_input_signals, and command CONDITIONING is not accepted, represented by command(9, *true*), then we inevitably end up in a state where oEnabled is *true*.

```
mu Y . [!((exists a2, a3, a4, a5, a6: Bool .
             free_input_signals(false, a2, a3, a4, a5, a6)) ||
          command(9, true))]Y ||
       <state_M2'oEnabled(true)>true)
```

However, as we extended the model with self-loops, by taking such self-loops we trivially end up in an infinite sequence on which no state where oEnabled holds is reached. We therefore need to exclude paths through these self-loops.[5]

4.3 Results

We have verified the two properties from Sect. 4.2, as well as 10 additional requirements. For our experiments we have used Cordis Modeler version 3.14.1630. 7156 and mCRL2 tool set Release 202106.0. The cylinder model described and studied in this paper is relatively simple, its state space after reduction has 3049 states and 18736 transitions. This is reflected by the verification time: each of the properties can be verified in less than 5 s. Property 2 is *false*, and all of the other requirements are satisfied by the model. In case a property does not hold, the mCRL2 tool set offers a subset of the labeled transition system that underlies the cylinder specification as a counterexample that contains sufficient information to prove that the property is violated [26]. In the next section, we discuss the counterexample to property 2 in detail.

5   Discussion

The counterexample of requirement 2 has 39 states and 39 transitions. It is a transitions sequence that leads to a cycle on which iCompressedAirOK remains *true* and command CONDITIONING is never accepted, but oEnabled remains *false*, shown in Fig. 6. The counterexample follows the execution model of Sect. 2.2. In each cycle the state machines are executed in the predetermined order: Main, MovingToZeroPosition, MovingToEndPosition and Disabled.

For the sake of readability, in Fig. 6, the actions which are not essential to describe the trace are labeled with τ; a sequence of τ transitions is denoted by a dotted arrow labeled τ. We denote *true* and *false* as tt and ff, respectively.

---

[5] We here rely on the fact that the additional information is only exposed through self-loop transitions. This avoids the need for introducing an additional greatest fixed point.

The execution starts from the state with an unlabeled arrow pointing to it; in the first cycle, state Main.Disabled.Wait_For_Conditioning is reached via *trans(207)*. In the second cycle, iCompressedAirOK is set to *true*, command CONDITIONING is accepted, indicated by *command(9, tt)*, and, with *trans(174)* state Main.Disabled.Conditioning.InitialState is reached.

The third cycle starts in the loop, moving in counterclockwise direction. In this cycle (and subsequent) iCompressedAirOK remains *true*, no new command is issued, but action *chk_ready* expresses that command CONDITIONING is still on the interface. It follows that the self-transition in Fig. 4, *trans(175)*, from state Main.Disabled.Conditioning to state Main.Disabled.Conditioning.InitialState, is taken. Subsequent cycles behave identically and state Main.Disabled.Conditioning.InitialState is infinitely often re-entered.

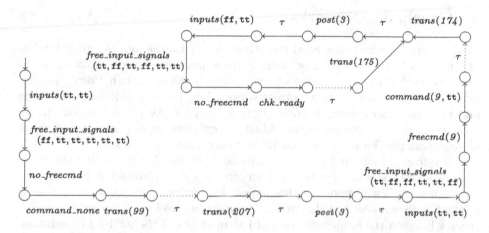

Fig. 6. Counterexample found verifying property 2

Reproducing the Counterexample. By loading the executing PLC code in the debugger provided by the PLC vendor and stepping through it, we can reproduce the exact behavior of the counterexample. This increases the confidence in the correctness of the translation to mCRL2, and proves that the counterexample contains ample information to be efficiently reproduced in the running system.

Root Cause Analysis and Solution. The system is able to loop in the self-transition from and to subdiagram Conditioning, in Fig. 4, because of two reasons: (1) in Cordis models, the outermost enabled transition gets priority over more deeply nested transitions, this is inherited from the semantics; and (2) the command continuously remains active on the interface. We focus our analysis on the latter. Command CONDITIONING has guard condition State(Main.Disabled), command ready condition NOT State(Main.Disabled), and no accept and reject actions. Thus, command CONDITIONING is accepted if the system currently is in state machine Disabled, and the command is ready if the system leaves Disabled. In the counterexample, when command CONDITIONING is accepted, we are in state machine Disabled, the command ready condition is *false*, and the self-loop on Conditioning has higher priority than the transitions in Fig. 5.

Based on the analysis, we observe that command CONDITIONING behaves like a trigger that always remains high. The solution to avoid this behavior is to modify the command ready condition from NOT State(Main.Disabled) to *true*. This way, the command will only act as one single trigger to enter state machine conditioning: when issued and accepted, command CONDITIONING stays active on the interface for exactly one cycle. The change does not affect the relevant behavior of the cylinder model. Changing the cylinder model accordingly, and re-verifying the requirements shows that also requirement 2 holds.

6   Concluding Remarks

In this paper we have discussed the semantics of Cordis models, an extension of standard UML used for modeling complex machine-control applications, in order to enable the verification of these models. Even though Cordis models are not primarily designed for formal verification, we were able to characterize and implement an automatic translation to mCRL2. As a proof of concept we have verified the behavior of an industrial cylinder model against a number of requirements. Furthermore, we have shown that the verification process is effective to find bugs, and that these can be reproduced in the actual system.

There are some aspects to the formalization and verification process that we do not explicitly report in this paper. In particular, using earlier versions of the Cordis modeler and the mCRL2 translation, we have uncovered inconsistencies between the implementation of the models and the mCRL2 translation. Addressing those has resulted in modifications to both the semantics in the Cordis modeler and the mCRL2 translation. In order to understand and debug such issues, both having clear counterexamples in mCRL2, and the ability to step through the PLC code using a debugger have proven indispensable.

Future Work. Cordis models of complete industrial systems usually consist of multiple interacting objects. To this end, the translator from Cordis models to mCRL2 has been extended to deal with multiple component systems. We are currently expanding our work to deal with such complex models. In particular, we are investigating the use of symbolic model checking techniques [4] to deal with large state spaces. Furthermore, compositional model checking [18] could help in the verification of large models by incrementally generating state spaces of subsystems, reducing them, and combining them into larger subsystems, prior to verification. We are investigating improvements to static analysis tools to optimize mCRL2 models [7], and static analysis techniques such as dead variable analysis for Cordis models, reducing state space sizes. Finally, in our collaboration with Cordis, we are integrating model checking into the Cordis SUITE.

Acknowledgements. This work was supported partially by the MACHINAIDE project (ITEA3, No. 18030) and through EU regional development funding in the context of the OP-Zuid program (No. 02541). We thank Wieger Wesselink and Yousra Hafidi for contributions to the development of the mCRL2 translation, and Cordis Automation B.V. for their feedback on earlier versions of this paper.

References

1. Bouwman, M., Luttik, B., van der Wal, D.: A formalisation of SysML state machines in mCRL2. In: Peters, K., Willemse, T.A.C. (eds.) FORTE 2021. LNCS, vol. 12719, pp. 42–59. Springer, Cham (2021). https://doi.org/10.1007/978-3-030-78089-0_3
2. Bunte, O., et al.: The mCRL2 toolset for analysing concurrent systems. In: Vojnar, T., Zhang, L. (eds.) TACAS 2019. LNCS, vol. 11428, pp. 21–39. Springer, Cham (2019). https://doi.org/10.1007/978-3-030-17465-1_2
3. Bunte, O., Gool, L.C.M., Willemse, T.A.C.: Formal verification of OIL component specifications using mCRL2. In: ter Beek, M.H., Ničković, D. (eds.) FMICS 2020. LNCS, vol. 12327, pp. 231–251. Springer, Cham (2020). https://doi.org/10.1007/978-3-030-58298-2_10
4. Burch, J.R., Clarke, E.M., McMillan, K.L., Dill, D.L., Hwang, L.J.: Symbolic model checking: 10^{20} states and beyond. Inf. Comput. **98**(2), 142–170 (1992). https://doi.org/10.1016/0890-5401(92)90017-A
5. Cimatti, A., et al.: NuSMV 2: an OpenSource tool for symbolic model checking. In: Brinksma, E., Larsen, K.G. (eds.) CAV 2002. LNCS, vol. 2404, pp. 359–364. Springer, Heidelberg (2002). https://doi.org/10.1007/3-540-45657-0_29
6. Dubrovin, J., Junttila, T.: Symbolic model checking of hierarchical UML state machines. In: 2008 8th International Conference on Application of Concurrency to System Design, pp. 108–117. ISSN: 1550–4808 (2008). https://doi.org/10.1109/ACSD.2008.4574602
7. Groote, J.F., Lisser, B.: Computer assisted manipulation of algebraic process specifications. ACM SIGPLAN Notices **37**(12), 98–107 (2002). https://doi.org/10.1145/636517.636531
8. Groote, J.F., Mateescu, R.: Verification of temporal properties of processes in a setting with data. In: Haeberer, A.M. (ed.) AMAST 1999. LNCS, vol. 1548, pp. 74–90. Springer, Heidelberg (1998). https://doi.org/10.1007/3-540-49253-4_8
9. Groote, J.F., Mousavi, M.R.: Modeling and Analysis of Communicating Systems. MIT Press, Cambridge (2014). https://mitpress.mit.edu/books/modeling-and-analysis-communicating-systems
10. Hansen, H.H., Ketema, J., Luttik, B., Mousavi, M.R., van de Pol, J.: Towards model checking executable UML specifications in mCRL2. Innov. Syst. Softw. Eng. **6**(1–2), 83–90 (2010). https://doi.org/10.1007/s11334-009-0116-1
11. Hwong, Y.L., Keiren, J.J.A., Kusters, V.J.J., Leemans, S., Willemse, T.A.C.: Formalising and analysing the control software of the compact muon solenoid experiment at the large hadron collider. Sci. Comput. Program. **78**(12), 2435–2452 (2013). https://doi.org/10.1016/j.scico.2012.11.009
12. John, K.H., Tiegelkamp, M.: The programming languages of IEC 61131-3. In: John, K.H., Tiegelkamp, M. (eds.) IEC 61131-3: Programming Industrial Automation Systems: Concepts and Programming Languages, Requirements for Programming Systems, Decision-Making Aids, pp. 99–205. Springer, Heidelberg (2010). https://doi.org/10.1007/978-3-642-12015-2_4

13. Keiren, J.J.A., Klabbers, M.D.: Modelling and verifying IEEE Std. 11073–20601 session setup using mCRL2. Electron. Commun. EASST **53** (2013). https://doi.org/10.14279/tuj.eceasst.53.793

14. Liu, S., et al.: A formal semantics for complete UML state machines with communications. In: Johnsen, E.B., Petre, L. (eds.) IFM 2013. LNCS, vol. 7940, pp. 331–346. Springer, Heidelberg (2013). https://doi.org/10.1007/978-3-642-38613-8_23

15. Lyazidi, A., Mouline, S.: Formal verification of UML state machine diagrams using petri nets. In: Atig, M.F., Schwarzmann, A.A. (eds.) NETYS 2019. LNCS, vol. 11704, pp. 67–74. Springer, Cham (2019). https://doi.org/10.1007/978-3-030-31277-0_5

16. Object Management Group: OMG Unified Modelling Language (UML). Technical report Version 2.5.1 (2017). https://www.omg.org/spec/UML/2.5.1/PDF

17. Pore, A., et al.: Safe reinforcement learning using formal verification for tissue retraction in autonomous robotic-assisted surgery. In: 2021 IEEE/RSJ IROS, pp. 4025–4031 (2021). https://doi.org/10.1109/IROS51168.2021.9636175. ISSN: 2153-0866

18. de Putter, S., Wijs, A.: Compositional model checking is lively. In: Proença, J., Lumpe, M. (eds.) FACS 2017. LNCS, vol. 10487, pp. 117–136. Springer, Cham (2017). https://doi.org/10.1007/978-3-319-68034-7_7

19. Rodríguez, R.J., Fredlund, L.Å., Herranz, Á., Mariño, J.: Execution and verification of UML state machines with erlang. In: Giannakopoulou, D., Salaün, G. (eds.) SEFM 2014. LNCS, vol. 8702, pp. 284–289. Springer, Cham (2014). https://doi.org/10.1007/978-3-319-10431-7_22

20. Sahay, A., Indamutsa, A., Ruscio, D.D., Pierantonio, A.: Supporting the understanding and comparison of low-code development platforms. In: 2020 46th Euromicro Conference on SEAA, pp. 171–178 (2020). https://doi.org/10.1109/SEAA51224.2020.00036

21. Salunkhe, S., Berglehner, R., Rasheeq, A.: Automatic transformation of SysML model to event-B model for railway CCS application. In: Raschke, A., Méry, D. (eds.) Rigorous State-Based Methods. LNCS, vol. 12709, pp. 143–149. Springer, Cham (2021). https://doi.org/10.1007/978-3-030-77543-8_14

22. Santone, A., et al.: Radiomic features for prostate cancer grade detection through formal verification. La radiologia medica **126**(5), 688–697 (2021). https://doi.org/10.1007/s11547-020-01314-8

23. Santos, L.B.R., Júnior, V.A.S., Vijaykumar, N.L.: Transformation of UML behavioral diagrams to support software model checking. In: FESCA 2014. EPTCS, vol. 147, pp. 133–142 (2014). https://doi.org/10.4204/EPTCS.147.10, arXiv: 1404.0855

24. Schäfer, T., Knapp, A., Merz, S.: Model checking UML state machines and collaborations. ENTCS **55**(3), 357–369 (2001). https://doi.org/10.1016/S1571-0661(04)00262-2

25. Stramaglia, A., Keiren, J.J.A.: Formal verification of an industrial UML-like model using mCRL2 (extended version) (2022). arXiv: 2205.08146

26. Wesselink, W., Willemse, T.A.C.: Evidence extraction from parameterised Boolean equation systems. In: Benzmüller, C., Otten, J. (eds.) proceedings of ARQNL 2018 affiliated with IJCAR 2018, Oxford, UK, 18 July 2018. CEUR, vol. 2095, pp. 86–100. CEUR-WS.org (2018). http://ceur-ws.org/Vol-2095/paper6.pdf

Chemical Case Studies in KeYmaera X

Rose Bohrer[✉][ID]

Worcester Polytechnic Institute, Worcester, MA 01609, USA
rbohrer@wpi.edu

Abstract. Safety-critical chemical processes are well-studied in the formal methods literature, including hybrid systems models which combine discrete and continuous dynamics. This paper is the first to use a theorem-prover to verify hybrid chemical models: the KeYmaera X prover for differential dynamic logic. KeYmaera X provides parametric results that hold for a whole range of parameter values, non-linear physical dynamics, and a small trusted computing base.

We tell a general story about KeYmaera X: recent advances in automated reasoning about safety and liveness for differential equations have enabled elegant proofs about reaction dynamics.

Keywords: Hybrid Systems · Theorem Proving · Chemical Reactor

1 Introduction

Classical results on safe and optimal control [18] of chemical reactions [40] are the conceptual foundation for industrial chemical processes. Formal methods for chemical reactors are well-studied [4,20,25,30,36], but even textbook cases [18] lack *high fidelity* models (e.g., nonlinear dynamics and wide ranges of parameter values). We study textbook cases; these inform the study of practical cases.

We study (1) model-predictive control of an irreversible reaction (Sect. 3.1) and (2) an uncontrolled reversible reaction (Sect. 3.2) in KeYmaera X [16], a theorem-prover for *differential dynamic logic* (dL) [34]. See Sect. 4 for tradeoffs.

Both reactions contain challenges suitable as verification benchmarks: (1) nonlinear dynamics interacting with model-predictive controllers, and (2) theorems that test current tools' abilities regarding asymptotic properties, e.g., stability [27] or persistence [39]. Though reaction (2) is continuous, continuous reasoning is essential to hybrid. We find that new stability [41], variant [41], and Darboux polynomial [35] tools in KeYmaera X simplify our proofs.

2 Background

In KeYmaera X, correctness properties are stated and proved in *differential dynamic logic* (dL) [34], where hybrid systems are written in *hybrid program* notation. We discuss dL, then KeYmaera X usage.

© The Author(s), under exclusive license to Springer Nature Switzerland AG 2022
J. F. Groote and M. Huisman (Eds.): FMICS 2022, LNCS 13487, pp. 103–120, 2022.
https://doi.org/10.1007/978-3-031-15008-1_8

2.1 Differential Dynamic Logic

We introduce dL syntax and semantics; see literature [34] for details. Semantics are state-based: state ω maps variables x to real numbers $\omega(x) : \mathbb{R}$. The syntax consists of terms (with a numeric meaning in each state), hybrid programs (which nondeterministically change the state when run), and formulas (which are true or false in each state). Terms are real-valued polynomials. Hybrid programs and formulas may contain each other. We use standard notation, e.g., $B ::= C \mid D$ means every B is either a C or a D.

Definition 1 (Hybrid Programs). *Hybrid programs α, β are defined by:*

$$\alpha, \beta ::= \ ?P \mid x := e \mid \{x' = f(x)\&Q\} \mid \alpha \cup \beta \mid \alpha; \beta \mid \alpha^*$$

Hybrid programs are defined by their *runs*: from a starting state, what final states are reachable? Hybrid programs can have one run (deterministic), many runs (nondeterministic), or zero runs (early termination). Programs $?P$ and $\{x' = f\&Q\}$ contain formulas P and Q; see Definition 2 for more about formulas.

The test program $?P$ never modifies the state; if formula P is true, then $?P$ ends in the current state, but if P is false, then $?P$ has no final states, representing execution failure. Deterministic assignment $x := e$ updates the state by storing the current value of term e in variable x. Ordinary differential equation systems (ODEs) are the defining feature of hybrid programs: ODEs composed with discrete operations model hybrid systems. ODE $\{x' = f(x)\&Q\}$ evolves in continuous time with $x' = f(x)$, where $f(x)$ is a term. The duration of evolution is nondeterministic. If an *evolution domain constraint* Q is provided, Q is tested continuously, and evolution must stop before Q ever becomes false. Choices $\alpha \cup \beta$ nondeterministically run *either* α *or* β, as opposed to running both. Composition $\alpha; \beta$ runs α, then β in the resulting state(s). Duration of loops α^* is nondeterministically-chosen but finite: zero, one, or many repetitions can occur. We also use if$(P)\{\alpha\}$else$\{\beta\}$, which reduces to choices and tests.

Definition 2 (Formulas). *There are many formulas P, Q in dL. We only use:*

$$P, Q ::= \cdots \mid e \geq \tilde{e} \mid \neg P \mid P \wedge Q \mid P \rightarrow Q \mid [\alpha]P \mid \langle\alpha\rangle P$$

Formulas represent true/false questions about the state ω. Comparison $e \geq \tilde{e}$ is true whenever the value of e is at least that of $\tilde{e}$ in a given state. All other comparisons $e > \tilde{e}, e = \tilde{e}, e \neq \tilde{e}, e \leq \tilde{e}, e < \tilde{e}$ are definable using $e \geq \tilde{e}$ and other logical connectives, so we use them freely. Negation $\neg P$ is true when P is false. Conjunction $P \wedge Q$ is true when both P and Q are. Implication $P \rightarrow Q$ is true when P's truth would imply Q's truth.

The defining formulas of dL, $[\alpha]P$ and $\langle\alpha\rangle P$, are respectively true in state ω if *every* or *some* run of α starting from state ω ends in a state where P is true. For many programs α, including all in this paper, *all runs* equates to *all time*.

KeYmaera X proves truth in *every state*, called *validity*.

We use standard notation for axioms and proof rules. Each rule has a horizontal line and means: if all *premise* formulas above the line are valid, so is the *conclusion* formula below. Rules can use *schema variables* (e.g., P, α) for arbitrary programs or formulas, respectively. For example, the loop rule

$$\text{LOOP} \; \frac{P \to J \quad J \to [\alpha]J \quad J \to Q}{P \to [\alpha^*]Q}$$

means for all P, Q, J, α that if premises $P \to J$, $J \to [\alpha]J$, and $J \to Q$ are all valid, so is $P \to [\alpha^*]Q$. Formula J is *proved* true for all iterations, thus we call J the *loop invariant*. This *proven* loop invariant should not be confused with use of the word *invariant* in hybrid automata to mean an *assumed* constraint on ODE evolution. We call such constraints *evolution domain constraints*.

2.2 KeYmaera X

We discuss the KeYmaera X [28] user interface (Fig. 1). KeYmaera X is an interactive, tactical prover: users interactively pick proof techniques at each step. Each technique is implemented as a *tactic* [15] program. Tactics range from propositional rules (e.g., conjunction and implication) to complex search procedures. The *default* (`auto`) procedure tries many methods, solving many simple problems automatically. User effort varies much between proofs. We will discuss how automation reduces effort. Tactics help with rigor: complex methods reduce to simple, trusted steps.

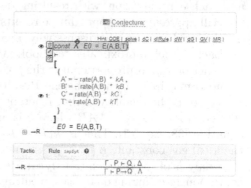

Fig. 1. KeYmaera X. Clicking highlighted symbol does a step. Last rule is shown at bottom. Top shows suggestions.

3 Results

We contribute case studies on two classic kinds of chemical reactions. The first is an irreversible reaction in a well-mixed adiabatic batch reactor. The second case study is a reversible reaction between two compounds, i.e., where the output can react again and form the input. We chose these examples because they are classic [38]. Both case studies emphasize recent advances in KeYmaera X proof automation, which simplified proofs. Where limitations remain, we discuss them.

3.1 Controlled Irreversible Reactions

We formalize a classic scenario: an irreversible, exothermic reaction in an adiabatic, well-mixed batch reactor. *Irreversible* [38, §2.1] means the reaction is one-way: outputs do not react to create inputs. *Adiabatic* [38, §2.14] means heat does not leave or enter the reactor. *Well-mixed* [38, §2.12] means the reaction occurs evenly in space throughout the reactor. In this basic synthesis reaction, two (first-order) reactants react to form a third, plus heat ($A + B \longrightarrow C + heat$).

The case study contains four models, each with proof. The first shows conservation of energy, validating that adiabatic reactors are closed systems. The remaining three models add a model-predictive bang-bang controller [18], which predicts future behavior according to the model, then applies an all-or-nothing control action. It is proved that the control ensures a safety property: overheating is prevented. We use this standard control approach in order to focus on the continuous reaction dynamics. The driving difference between the last three models is their increasingly complex reaction dynamics, which mandate increasingly complex controls and proofs. In the second model, the reaction rate is constant. In the third model, the rate is linear in temperature, thus exponential in time. In the final model, the rate is proportional to the product of temperature and each concentration, with resulting dynamics beyond a simple exponential, yet still approximate. Approximate results are the best that can be expected for non-linear dynamics. We discuss why, including verification challenges.

Each model approximates textbook [38, Eq. 2.93] reaction dynamics, where the reaction *rate* is proportional to the product of concentrations of each reactant A and B multiplied by a coefficient. Recall that the *concentration* of a reactant in a mixture is the quantity of that reactant per unit quantity of the mixture. The rate equation is $rate = kAB$ where k is an exponential given by the Arrhenius equation [38, Eq. 5.1]. That is, $k(T) = k_0 e^{-E/RT}$ where T is temperature, R is the ideal gas constant, E is the reaction's activation energy and k_0 a constant.

Analysis of the reaction rate dynamics is nontrivial: *rate* is a product of three continuously-changing quantities, resulting in a non-linear ODE. Moreover, $k(T)$ is exponential in T, resulting in a *non-polynomial* ODE. KeYmaera X handles non-linear ODEs well, but is restricted to polynomial ODEs, as is standard. We thus reach our first limitation: to ensure a polynomial ODE, we approximate the temperature dependence as linear. This assumption is reasonable because polynomial ODEs are a standard assumption, and our nonlinear dynamics are still more precise than prior models [20,25,30,36,45]. Our second limitation is that the reactants are first-order, so their influence on rate is linear. We do so because such reactions are common and lead to elegant equations. KeYmaera X supports polynomials of any degree, so we expect the approach to work for higher-order reactions, so long as the order is fixed. Limitations aside, the results are fully parametric, e.g., the results can be applied to *any* first-order reactants in *any* amount by plugging in new coefficients and concentrations.

Energy Conservation. The basic dL model for energy conservation is presented in Fig. 2. Energy conservation is interesting in its own right, because it implies the system is closed. This helps support our claim that the model is *adiabatic*: heat energy does not leave nor enter. The variables A, B, and C stand for the current concentration of each reactant present in the reactor.

$E \equiv KE + U \quad U \equiv \min(A/k_A, B/k_B) \, k_T \quad KE \equiv T \quad rate \equiv T_s \, A_0 \, B_0 \, k_{ra} + k_{rb}$

$const \equiv k_{ra} > 0 \wedge k_{rb} \geq 0 \wedge k_A > 0 \wedge k_B > 0 \wedge k_C > 0 \wedge k_T > 0$

$ode \equiv \{A' = -rate \, k_A, B' = -rate \, k_B, C' = rate \, k_C, T' = rate \, k_T\}$

$(P \rightarrow [\alpha]Q) \equiv (const \wedge E_0 = E \rightarrow [ode]E_0 = E)$

Fig. 2. Conservation-of-energy for uncontrolled irreversible reaction, constant heating

Reactor temperature is written T. In our analysis, we decompose energy into kinetic (heat) and potential (chemical) energy: $E \equiv KE + U$. Potential energy $U \equiv \min(A/k_A, B/k_B) \, k_T$ is the product of the amount (concentration) of C remaining to be produced (the reaction ends when either A or B is exhausted) with the heat released per unit amount (C). That is, we model C as if it possesses no potential energy, since we are interested only in energies relevant to the current reaction. We model the reaction rate as $T_s \, A_0 \, B_0 \, k_{ra} + k_{rb}$, which makes two intentional simplifications. First, we use approximate *current* concentrations A, B with *initial* concentrations A_0, B_0. Secondly, we simplify the temperature factor to T_s, which is a *constant* even as temperature T changes, thus the influence of heat is *static* throughout the reaction. We determine the reaction rate as a product of the concentration factor and temperature factor. For generality, the coefficients k_{ra}, k_{rb} let the rate be any *linear function of* the product. Formula const specifies signs of constants.

The ode indicates that all concentrations A, B, C and the reactor temperature T all change proportional to the reaction rate; A and B are lost as C and heat are gained. Coefficients k_A, k_B, k_C, k_T indicate the rates at which each changes, which may depend respectively on the stoichiometric coefficients of the reaction or how strongly exothermic it is.

Finally, the theorem statement $(P \rightarrow [\alpha]Q)$ states that under the simple constant assumptions, energy is conserved because at all times the current energy E remains equal to its initial value E_0. We now describe the KeYmaera X proof.

Proof. The default proof procedure of KeYmaera X (Sect. 2.2) proves the theorem automatically with *differential invariants* [34, Lem. 11.3], demonstrating the capabilities of this standard dL rule. We present the (relevant case of the) *differential invariant* [34, Lem. 11.3] rule

$$DI \quad \frac{Q \rightarrow [x' := f(x)](e)' = (\tilde{e})'}{e = \tilde{e} \rightarrow [\{x' = f(x) \& Q\}]e = \tilde{e}}$$

which shows $e = \tilde{e}$ is true throughout an ODE if it holds initially and differentials are equal throughout. We prove $E_0 = E$ thus: E_0 is constant, so proving $E' = 0$ throughout suffices. Expanding the definition of E yields $(E)' = (T + \min(A/k_A, B/k_B) \, k_T)' = rate \, k_T + \min((A)'/k_A, (B)'/k_B) \, k_T = rate \, k_T + \min(-rate \, k_A/k_A, -rate \, k_B/k_B) \, k_T = rate \, k_T + \min(-rate, -rate) \, k_T = (rate - rate) \, k_T = 0$. Due to KeYmaera X's automation, the entire proof is automatic.

On-Off Reactions. This model keeps the basic heating dynamics but adds bang-bang control. Figure 3 describes the model in full. Parts unchanged from Fig. 2 are grayed out to aid comparison. The impact of this theorem is that the reactor is provably safe under idealistic assumptions, i.e., when concentrations and temperatures change very little or have little impact on reaction rate.

$$\text{rate} \equiv T_s\,A_0\,B_0\,k_{ra} + k_{rb}$$

$$\text{const} \equiv k_{ra} > 0 \wedge k_{rb} \geq 0 \wedge k_A > 0 \wedge k_B > 0 \wedge k_C > 0 \wedge k_T > 0 \wedge T > 0 \wedge \epsilon > 0$$

$$\text{ctrl} \equiv \{\text{if}(T_{max} - T \leq \epsilon\,\text{rate}\,k_R)\{\text{isOn} := 0\}\text{else}\{\text{isOn} := 1\}\}; t := 0$$

$$\text{ode} \equiv \{A' = \text{isOn} \cdot -\text{rate}\,k_A, B' = \text{isOn} \cdot -\text{rate}\,k_B, C' = \text{isOn} \cdot \text{rate}\,k_C,$$
$$T' = \text{isOn} \cdot \text{rate}\,k_T, t' = 1 \wedge t \leq \epsilon \wedge A \geq 0 \wedge B \geq 0 \wedge C \geq 0\}$$

$$(P \rightarrow [\alpha]Q) \equiv (\text{const} \wedge T \leq T_{max} \rightarrow [\{\text{ctrl}; \text{ode}\}^*]T \leq T_{max})$$

Fig. 3. Safety for irreversible reaction with bang-bang control, constant heating

The greatest change is the addition of a *time-triggered* controller: the system now repeats in a loop, with the controller guaranteed to run at least every $\epsilon > 0$ time units. The controller (ctrl) is *model-predictive* because it *predicts* whether it would be dangerous to keep the reaction running for ϵ time: if the remaining temperature buffer $T_{max} - T$ is no more than the temperature change that could occur after reacting for time ϵ, it would be unsafe to keep reacting. If so, the reaction shuts off (isOn := 0), else it turns on (isOn := 1). Note isOn is an *indicator variable*; its only possible values are 0 and 1. Specifically, the controller linearly predicts the maximum temperature change as $\epsilon\,\text{rate}\,k_R$ and shuts off if the safe temperature would be exceeded. Importantly, this approach predicts unsafe events before they occur and shuts off before the damage is done. Either way, the timer t is reset to 0.

The ode is updated so that each reaction equation is multiplied by isOn, causing no physical changes to occur when the reactor is turned off. This model is best-suited for situations where it is possible to quickly halt a reaction. The ode gains an *evolution domain constraint*, which serves to restrict its duration of evolution: an ODE may evolve only while the constraint remains true. Our constraint serves two purposes. Firstly, $t \leq \epsilon$ implements time-triggering: if each iteration takes at most ϵ time, there is at most ϵ delay between control cycles. Secondly, the constraints $A \geq 0 \wedge B \geq 0 \wedge C \geq 0$ model the assumption of nonnegative concentrations. For example, the reaction ends if A or B reach zero.

Finally, the updated theorem statement $(P \rightarrow [\alpha]Q)$ is now a safety statement, stating that the reactor never exceeds its maximum safe temperature.

Proof. As the model now contains a loop, the proof uses *loop invariant* reasoning in addition to *differential invariant reasoning*, both distinct concepts from *evolution domain constraints*. We prove that the safety condition $T \leq T_{max}$ is a *loop invariant*, meaning it holds before and after every loop repetition. We use the standard loop rule from Sect. 2.1.

Already, a lemma arises in the ODE proof. Certain *differential invariant* proofs can only succeed by first proving lemmas, called *differential cut* formulas, which are then available as assumptions in the invariant proof. Specifically, we prove the cut $T_{max} - T > (\epsilon - t)$ rate k_T, meaning the remaining safe temperature gap exceeds the projected temperature change during the remaining time. The cut proves automatically by the differential invariant rule, from which the loop invariant, then safety condition, follow by automatic proof.

Fixed Exponents. For the next model, the first fundamental change is that we update the definition of rate to use the current temperature, so that the reaction rate evolves exponentially over time. Because dynamic reaction rates are an increase in complexity, we simplify other aspects of the reaction rate formula by dropping k_{ra} and k_{rb}. The remaining changes follow from that one: amts is a helper definition for definitions such as $taylor^+(x, t)$, which is an upper bound on temperature over time, constructed as a Taylor series approximation. Taylor series bring a fundamentally new proof approach for more complicated dynamics: exponential dynamics need approximations in dL. Taylor series are a flexible approximation: if precision were unsatisfactory, the degree could be increased. However, this Taylor bound is only provably an upper bound on a limited time interval which happens to be $1/(2\,\text{amts})$, which we thus take as our upper limit on ϵ. In practice, we hypothesize that the time limit is artificial: time could be expressed in any desired units, increasing the interval. The constants are updated to include assumptions on initial values of amounts and the controller is updated to use the Taylor approximation. The ode is updated to explicitly assume nonnegative temperature, which is a safe assumption since our goal is to avoid high, not low, temperatures. This new result shows safety with idealized modeling of concentrations under more realistic *heating* assumptions (Fig. 4).

---

rate $\equiv$ T A_0 B_0 $\epsilon \equiv 1/(2\,\text{amts})$ amts $\equiv k_T A_0 B_0$ $taylor^+(x, t) \equiv (1 + 2\,t\,\text{amts})\,x$

const $\equiv k_A > 0 \wedge k_B > 0 \wedge k_C > 0 \wedge k_T > 0 \wedge \epsilon > 0 \wedge A_0 \geq 0 \wedge B_0 \geq 0$

ctrl $\equiv \{$if$(T_{max} \leq taylor^+(T, \epsilon))\{$isOn $:= 0\}$else$\{$isOn $:= 1\}\}; t := 0$

ode $\equiv \{A' = $ isOn $\cdot$ $-$rate k_A, $B' = $ isOn $\cdot$ $-$rate k_B, $C' = $ isOn $\cdot$ rate k_C,

   $T' = $ isOn $\cdot$ rate k_T, $t' = 1 \wedge t \leq \epsilon \wedge A \geq 0 \wedge B \geq 0 \wedge C \geq 0 \wedge T \geq 0\}$

$(P \to [\alpha]Q) \equiv ($const$\wedge T > 0 \wedge T \leq T_{max} \wedge A = A_0 \wedge B = B_0 \to [\{$ctrl; ode$\}^*]T \leq T_{max})$

Fig. 4. Safety for irreversible reaction with bang-bang control, fixed-exponent heating

---

Proof. The loop invariant is unchanged. We add several differential cuts; order matters since each one can serve as an assumption in following proofs: i) $t \geq 0$ just means time is nonnegative, ii) $A_0 B_0 T k_T \geq 0$ ensures forward (or 0) reaction rate, and iii) $taylor^+(T_{old}, t) - T \geq 0$ bounds temperature T above with $taylor^+()$ in terms of old temperature T_{old}. The final cut requires advanced proof techniques because term $taylor^+(T_{old}, t) - T$ decreases; differential invariants alone are provably [32, Thm 6.1] insufficient for such terms. KeYmaera X can solve this goal with the following high-level rule that uses Darboux polynomial (inequality) reasoning [35, Corr. 3.2]:

$$\text{DBX}_{\succcurlyeq} \quad \frac{Q \rightarrow (p)' \geq g\,p}{p \succcurlyeq 0 \rightarrow [\{x' = f(x)\&Q\}]p \succcurlyeq 0}$$

Here, both instances of $\succcurlyeq$ are replaced uniformly with one of $>$ or $\geq$. Note $(e)'$ is shorthand for the *Lie derivative* of p, with all variables of form x' replaced by their corresponding $f(x)$. The polynomial p is called a *Darboux* polynomial if the premise holds, then polynomial g is called its *cofactor*. It is natural to ask what power is gained by the addition of this proof rule. Certainly, it is stronger than differential invariant reasoning (which would require $Q \rightarrow (p)' \geq 0$) because $g\,p$ is allowed to be negative. Yet its full usefulness goes deeper, as the rule serves as a basis for differential radical invariant reasoning which is provably complete for semianalytic invariants [35, Thm. 4.5], a large class of invariants.

KeYmaera X's built-in invariant generator can search for Darboux polynomials, but it did not find a suitable polynomial for our example, so we found one manually by algebra. Using the definition of the ODE, we solved for a polynomial that satisfies the proof goal, in this case: $g \equiv A_0\,B_0\,k_T$. After choosing a suitable Darboux polynomial, the remaining proof goals completed using KeYmaera X's default proof method. Further applications of Taylor approximations are discussed in Sect. 4.

Dynamic Exponents. Even our final controlled model (Fig. 5) makes some important simplifying assumptions. Note that our model makes the impact of temperature on reaction rate a linear one, whereas the true Arrhenius equation [38, Eq. 5.1] implies an exponential effect on reaction rate. Linear functions can locally approximate exponential ones, but exponentials remain of future interest. Despite these limitations, the final model is important because it shows safety with both nontrivial heating *and* concentration dynamics.

The core change in the final model is a more advanced reaction rate dynamics, where the reaction rate dynamically changes in response to the concentration of each reactant. Definitions amts and ϵ are updated for the same reason. The timestep ϵ now changes dynamically: as the reaction proceeds, the acceptable delay *increases*, thus becoming easier to satisfy. It simplifies the analysis to have ϵ change only at each loop iteration rather than continuously, so we introduce variables A_1, B_1 to stand for the values of A, B at the *start* of each ODE evolution. The changes to the model are modest, but the dynamic changes are notable: the reaction rate is now a product of three changing variables, no longer an exponential with a fixed base. Likewise, additional proof steps will be required to account for changing concentrations, but the core proof approach is unchanged.

Proof. In this proof, the reaction rate changes as the concentration of each reactant changes, so we strengthen the loop invariant to capture the status of the reactant concentrations: $0 \leq T \wedge T \leq T_{max} \wedge A \leq A_0 \wedge B \leq B_0$. The differential

rate ≡ T A B $\epsilon \equiv 1/(2\,A_1\,B_1\,k_T)$ amts ≡ A B k_T
const ≡ $k_A > 0 \wedge k_B > 0 \wedge k_C > 0 \wedge k_T > 0 \wedge \epsilon > 0 \wedge A_0 \geq 0 \wedge B_0 \geq 0$
ctrl ≡ {if($T_{max} \leq$ taylor$^+$(T,ϵ)){isOn := 0}else{isOn := 1}}; $t := 0; A_1 := A; B_1 := B$
ode ≡ {A′ = isOn · −rate k_A, B′ = isOn · −rate k_B, C′ = isOn · rate k_C,
        T′ = isOn · rate $k_T, t' = 1 \wedge t \leq \epsilon \wedge A \geq 0 \wedge B \geq 0 \wedge C \geq 0 \wedge T \geq 0$}
$(P \to [\alpha]Q) \equiv ($const$\wedge$T $> 0\wedge$T $\leq$ T$_{max}\wedge$A $= A_0\wedge$B $= B_0 \to [\{$ctrl; ode$\}^*]$T $\leq$ T$_{max})$

Fig. 5. Safety for irreversible reaction with bang-bang control, advanced heating

cuts are similar to before, with an additional lemma that the concentrations of the first two reactants do not increase: $A \leq A_1 \wedge A_1 \leq A_0 \wedge B \leq B_1 \wedge B_1 \leq B_0$. The differential cut for the Taylor series is unchanged, and the same Darboux polynomial $g \equiv A_0\,B_0\,k_T$ suffices.

3.2 Uncontrolled Reversible Reactions

We study reversible reactions. We consider a textbook scenario where two reactants A and B can each react to form the other $(A \rightleftharpoons B)$. To our knowledge, we provide the first computer-checked proofs for the asymptotic behavior of this classic, widely-used textbook scenario. Specifically, our final model shows *persistence* [39], a relative of stability: the system eventually gets arbitrarily close to its equilibrium state, then stays close forever. We build up to this result with lemmas: the system is always moving (nonstrictly) toward equilibrium and can arbitrarily approach equilibrium in finite, bounded time. To complete the story, we show that although the equilibrium can always be arbitrarily approximated, it can never be reached exactly.

Pure Reactant Decreases. We consider a scenario starting with pure reactant A, which then becomes a mixture. We show the current amount of A never exceeds the initial amount, which is intuitive by conservation of mass. The lemma might be of practical use directly, e.g., to verify that a container never overflows, but we mainly use it as a lemma for persistence. Here, the two reactants are named A and B, with initial values $A = A_0 > 0$ and $B = 0$. Reactants A and B are engaged in a *reversible reaction* where A converts to B at forward rate k_F and B converts to A at reverse rate k_R. It is well-known [38, Ch. 3] that the system asymptotically approaches an equilibrium state, called a *dynamic equilibrium*,

ode ≡ {A′ = −A k_F + B k_R, B′ = A k_F − B k_R}
const ≡ $A_0 > 0 \wedge k_R > 0 \wedge k_F > 0$
$(P \to [\alpha]Q) \equiv ($const $\wedge$ A $= A_0 \wedge$ B $= 0 \to [$ode$]$A $\leq A_0)$

Fig. 6. Concentration of A is nonincreasing during reversible reaction.

in which the forward and reverse reactions perfectly cancel out. We define ode using a classic textbook model of a reversible reaction, which does not model heat: the reaction rates are based solely on concentrations and constants.

Proof. This proof completes automatically: the automatic prover successfully reasons by differential invariant.

Equilibrium Avoidance. We show that the amounts of the reactants never exactly reach the equilibrium. Though not directly used in the persistence proof, we prove this because it is a fundamental property in its own right which tacitly influences how a chemical plant is designed and operated. An operator would never wait for perfect equilibrium to occur, only for the system to get *close* to equilibrium, because perfect equilibrium (provably) never occurs.

The initial condition and ODE are unchanged, only the postcondition changes, which mandates a new proof approach. To state the new postcondition, we define the amounts of A present at the equilibrium ($\tilde{A}$). The above definition of $\tilde{A}$ can be found by solving for equilibrium ($A' = 0 \wedge B' = 0$) in ode subject to conservation of mass ($A + B = A_0$) (Fig. 7).

$$\text{ode} \equiv \{A' = -A\,k_F + B\,k_R, B' = A\,k_F - B\,k_R\}$$
$$\text{const} \equiv A_0 > 0 \wedge k_R > 0 \wedge k_F > 0 \qquad \tilde{A} \equiv A_0\,(k_R/(k_F + k_R))$$
$$(P \rightarrow [\alpha]Q) \equiv (\text{const} \wedge A = A_0 \wedge B = 0 \rightarrow [\text{ode}]A \neq \tilde{A})$$

Fig. 7. Equilibrium is never reached during reversible reaction.

Proof. A simple change in postcondition creates a major increase in proof complexity, because we now wish to show a lower bound instead of an upper bound. We use multiple differential cuts, one of which uses Darboux reasoning.

- $A - A_0\,(k_R/(k_F + k_R)) > 0$ means A's rate of change is always in the direction of the equilibrium
- $A + B = A_0$ is conservation of mass
- $A > 0 \wedge B \geq 0$ means we never have a negative amount of either reactant, the first being positive. This requires a Darboux argument with polynomial $-(k_F + k_R)$ because the amount of the first reactant does decrease with time.

Once these cuts have been proven, automation suffices to finish the proof.

Equilibrium Approach. We show that we get arbitrarily close to the equilibrium, given sufficient time. For every positive epsilon ($\epsilon > 0$), there exists a time when we get that close to the equilibrium. The assumption changes slightly; the theorem statement changes more: we prove a *diamond* modality $\langle \text{ode}\rangle A \leq \tilde{A} + \epsilon$ because we want to show we *eventually* approach the equilibrium. The practical impact of this result is that if an engineer desires an almost-perfect equilibrium, that can be attained, but the cost is time.

$\mathsf{const} \equiv \mathsf{A_0} > 0 \wedge \mathsf{k_R} > 0 \wedge \mathsf{k_F} > 0 \wedge \epsilon > 0$

$\mathsf{ode} \equiv \{\mathsf{A}' = -\mathsf{A}\,\mathsf{k_F} + \mathsf{B}\,\mathsf{k_R}, \mathsf{B}' = \mathsf{A}\,\mathsf{k_F} - \mathsf{B}\,\mathsf{k_R}\} \qquad \tilde{A} \equiv \mathsf{A_0}\,(\mathsf{k_R}/(\mathsf{k_F} + \mathsf{k_R}))$

$(P \rightarrow \langle \alpha \rangle Q) \equiv (\mathsf{const} \wedge \mathsf{A} = \mathsf{A_0} \wedge \mathsf{B} = 0 \rightarrow \langle \mathsf{ode} \rangle \mathsf{A} \leq \tilde{A} + \epsilon)$

Fig. 8. Equilibrium is approached during reversible reaction.

Proof. Previous proofs highlighted advances in proof automation for box properties of ODEs; this proof relies on advances in proof automation for diamond properties of ODEs. The *differential variant* rule is the diamond counterpart to *differential invariant* reasoning for box properties. The *differential variant* principle [41, Corr. 24] says: if a progress bound $d > 0$ on derivative $(p)'$ holds everywhere outside the goal region ($\neg(p \succcurlyeq 0)$), then we reach the goal eventually:

$$\mathrm{DV} \succcurlyeq \frac{\exists d > 0\, \forall x (\neg(p \succcurlyeq 0) \rightarrow (p)' \geq d)}{\langle \{x' = f(x)\} \rangle p \succcurlyeq 0}$$

where $\succcurlyeq$ stands uniformly for either $>$ or $\geq$, where d is a fresh variable, and where $x' = f(x)$ provably has a global solution (i.e., for all time). In the premise, $(p)'$ is shorthand for the *Lie derivative* of p, with all variables of form x' replaced by their corresponding $f(x)$.

The key insight behind our proof is that the rate of progress is proportional to our current displacement from the equilibrium. Since we seek to get the displacement within some ϵ, we can assume without loss of generality that the current displacement is at least ϵ, giving a bound d on the progress rate: $d = \epsilon\,(\mathsf{k_F} + \mathsf{k_R})$. This progress rate also confirms standard intuitions about the system dynamics: higher rates of progress are made when far away from the equilibrium and when reaction rates are high.

Persistence. Persistence means there exists a point after which we forever remain within ϵ of the equilibrium. Persistence is of practical importance because it shows both that the system can get arbitrarily close to equilibrium *and* that the system stays that way *indefinitely*. In short, this result is important from a control perspective because it shows the system is well-controlled, even without a controller. As a theorem-proving case study, persistence is an excellent comprehensive test case because it combines boxes and diamonds. Only the theorem statement need be updated; all other definitions are unchanged (Fig. 9):

$\mathsf{const} \equiv \mathsf{A_0} > 0 \wedge \mathsf{k_R} > 0 \wedge \mathsf{k_F} > 0 \wedge \epsilon > 0$

$\mathsf{ode} \equiv \{\mathsf{A}' = -\mathsf{A}\,\mathsf{k_F} + \mathsf{B}\,\mathsf{k_R}, \mathsf{B}' = \mathsf{A}\,\mathsf{k_F} - \mathsf{B}\,\mathsf{k_R}\} \qquad \tilde{A} \equiv \mathsf{A_0}\,(\mathsf{k_R}/(\mathsf{k_F} + \mathsf{k_R}))$

$(P \rightarrow \langle \alpha \rangle Q) \equiv (\mathsf{const} \wedge \mathsf{A} = \mathsf{A_0} \wedge \mathsf{B} = 0 \rightarrow \langle \mathsf{ode} \rangle [\mathsf{ode}] \mathsf{A} \leq \tilde{A} + \epsilon)$

Fig. 9. Reversible reaction is persistent.

Proof. We combine proof techniques, first showing we eventually approach the equilibrium (variant reasoning, as in Fig. 8), then showing the concentration of A stays near the equilibrium (invariant reasoning, as in Fig. 6).

A major strength of logic is *compositionality*: complex proofs are but combinations of simple parts. For example, our dL proof of form $pre \to \langle \alpha \rangle [\alpha] P$ (call this formula D for short) can be divided into a variant proof and invariant proof, respectively proofs of some formulas of form $B \equiv pre \to \langle \alpha \rangle A$ and $C \equiv const \land A \to [\alpha] P$ for some A. At a high level, KeYmaera X lived up to its compositionality promise, but at a low level, there is always room for improvement. The differential variant rule only allows inequalities as postconditions, but C expects $const \land A$. We bridge this gap using the mond rule and Kd2 axiom:

$$\text{KD2 } [\alpha]P \to \langle \alpha \rangle Q \to \langle \alpha \rangle (P \land Q) \qquad \text{MOND } \frac{P \vdash Q}{\langle \alpha \rangle P \vdash \langle \alpha \rangle Q}$$

Invariants prove C. Applying mond on C yields $\langle \alpha \rangle (const \land A) \to \langle \alpha \rangle [\alpha] P$. Prove the left side by Kd2. Its first premise holds by vacuity because const is constant; its second is by lemma B, which holds by a variant argument. The result is D, as desired.

Lessons for KeYmaera X Development. To our knowledge, the limitation to inequalities in differential variants is not fundamental, but incidental to KeYmaera X's implementation. We recommend that the developers relax this limitation. More generally, we found ourselves manually proving properties of the form $const \to \langle \alpha \rangle const$ where α does not modify free variables of *const*. Such formulas only hold when α has a run (i.e., $\langle \alpha \rangle true$ holds), thus are nontrivial to automate, yet still deserve attention because they are common. The mond rule and Kd2 axiom were key to our proof, but are only visible on the UI when the user searches for them by name. We recommend that the developers provide visibility, either through the UI or through example proofs.

Tactics in KeYmaera X seek to enable concise proof scripts, so it is desirable to automate counting the size of proof scripts and underlying proof terms. To our knowledge, KeYmaera X's current support for size counting is experimental. We recommend that the developers promote size counting to a stable feature. Our proof scripts ranged from 3 to 41 proof steps, and experience suggests that a tactic-free proof would likely be much longer. This is consistent with results from the literature, where tens of lines of tactics may correspond to $>200,000$ steps [8, §4.1]. Our slowest proof completed in 8 s on a modern workstation. Model complexity and proof-checking time were not directly related: some simple models ran slower than complex ones because simple models support the highest level of automation, but highly-automated proofs check more slowly than highly-interactive proofs.

In short, theorem-proving case studies are not only important because they demonstrate the benefits of new automation, but because they discover directions for future development.

4   Related Work

Related work includes hybrid systems verification, reactor design, and reaction kinetics. We begin with theorem-proving approaches to verification, specifically.

Hybrid Systems Theorem Proving. Specialized *hybrid systems* provers [16,44] provide a high degree of generality (parametricity, nonlinearity, unbounded time) and rigor, while making efforts to mitigate the high degree of user effort typical of theorem-proving. For example, generality in our case study means many different reactions and reactors are supported by modifying parameter values, with no new proof effort. Rigor is not merely of theoretical interest: in many hybrid systems reasoning techniques which do not share our rigorous logical foundations, many soundness edge cases have recently been identified [41, Tab. 1]. Soundness violations are unacceptable in verification.

We use the KeYmaera X [16] prover for its exceptional rigor: its axioms have been proved sound in a theorem-prover [7] and it soundly derives its advanced proof methods [35] [41, Tab. 1] from sound axioms.

Hybrid Hoare Logic (HHL) [22,44] is another notable hybrid systems logic; an HHL case study similar to ours could be interesting future work. HHL Prover and KeYmaera X both base their ODE invariant automation on the same core algorithm [23], so this aspect of automation is likely comparable in both.

Other Logical Approaches. We are aware of only one prior logical proof [45] of a chemical process with nontrivial hybrid dynamics. Unlike ours, it is not in a theorem-prover and does not address persistence nor reactions, but rather a mixing process. General-purpose theorem-provers [1,12,26,37] have formalized hybrid systems, including stability [26,37], but not applied them to reactions.

Reachability. Model-checkers using reachability analysis [2,9,11,14] are hybrid theorem-provers' main competitors. They increase automation, but have restrictions in generality. We discuss this tradeoff, which led us to use theorem-proving.

Foremost, KeYmaera X supports persistence. To our knowledge, persistence is not among the specific classes (e.g., safety and reach-avoid correctness) of properties supported in any model-checker. Logic allows mixing existential and universal properties freely, supporting broad classes of properties.

Secondly, model-checkers use *compact* regions, i.e., variables have finite bounds. In contrast, KeYmaera X allows non-compact *parametric* results. This enables arbitrarily large reaction and heating rates, timesteps, and tank capacities.

Thirdly, we use multi-affine ODEs. Many model-checkers support multi-affine ODEs [2,5,9,11], but struggle with scalability, compared to affine systems [3,14]. Our small-scale results potentially enable future scalability: multi-affine component-based proofs scale to hundreds of variables [6], an order of magnitude beyond nonlinear ODE benchmarks [5,9,11].

Theorem-provers benefit from strong correctness arguments. KeYmaera X's trusted computing base is an order of magnitude smaller than self-reported counts of popular model-checkers [16] and its axioms have a machine-checked soundness proof [7]. Correctness is not merely a theoretical concern. Soundness bugs in Flow* and dReach have been identified post-release [31]. Predecessors of techniques used in this paper had known soundness bugs [41, Table 1]. The model-checking community has acknowledged these concerns. Ariadne developers [10] have specifically cited the correctness benefits of theorem-proving for reachability. Developers of SpaceEx, PHAVer, HyTech, Lyse, and VNODE-LP [13,29] have cited implementation correctness concerns for reachability analysis. KeYmaera X is typically preferred over paper proofs, because paper proofs would employ invariant and variant techniques with comparable complexity to our own, but sacrifice automatic detection of proof errors, which are common.

Theorem-proving's downside is the requirement for interactive proofs by users. Automation discussed herein only assists, not eliminates, interaction. In contrast, push-button automation is common for model-checkers. Due to these nontrivial tradeoffs, both theorem-proving and model-checking remain essential.

Stability and Persistence. Hybrid system stability is well-studied both inside [26, 37,42] and outside [21,24,27] theorem-provers, with persistence also studied [39]. Lyapunov functions have shown stability of a chemical reaction on paper, but not in a prover [19]. Stability and its relatives in KeYmaera X specifically are a new topic [42]; ours is the first application-focused study in KeYmaera X.

Chemical Engineering. The chemical engineering results we formalized are classical; our innovation is the rigor and generality (parametricity, non-linearity) with which we formalize them in KeYmaera X. Standard textbooks provided kinetics for well-mixed adiabatic batch reactors [38, Eq. 2.93], uncontrolled reversible reactions [38, Ch. 3], and the Arrhenius equation [38, Eq. 5.1]. Standard control theory textbooks introduce model-predictive control and bang-bang control [18].

Although basic models of reactors are widely-used in formal methods, ours is the first in a theorem-prover. It additionally overcomes others' limitations:

– Previous chemical proofs ignored persistence and reactors [45]
– Optimal scheduling [36] and safety proofs [25] only used state machines
– A verified plant design used simple piecewise-constant dynamics [20]
– CEGAR verification of tanks [30] ignored reactors

Industrial usage of formal methods typically prioritizes optimal control and optimization of plant configuration, accepts approximations as a tradeoff for nonlinearity, and cites scalability to networks of reactions and changes in parameter values as common issues [43]. This paper provides a parametric model that supports nonlinear dynamics through approximation, and formally proves the approximation correct against nonlinear dynamics. Because dL is amenable to constrained optimization for control [17] and efficient verification of compound systems by decomposition into reusable components [6], it is expected that the dL-based approach can be extended to overcome the aforementioned industrial challenges in future work. If successful, the benefits to the chemical industry would include increased confidence in software correctness and potential improvements in scalability and efficiency of parameter changes, when designing plants and controllers. Maximal realism would require direct access to industrial designs, but our proofs already demonstrate that improvements in ODE realism can often be accommodated with modest changes to invariants. For models beyond ODEs, such as PDE models of non-uniform heat transfer, differential games can be explored because they can express Hamilton-Jacobi-like PDEs [33]. Though industrial users do not frequently cite concerns regarding formalization of correctness proofs [43], they still stand to benefit from such guarantees because constructing chemical plants is expensive, making design mistakes costly.

5 Conclusion

We used the KeYmaera X theorem prover for differential dynamic logic to formalize two case studies: a batch reactor and a reversible reaction, each of which consisted of four models and their proofs. This work served two purposes:

– To our knowledge, we provided the first proof in a theorem prover of these classic chemical engineering results.
– We demonstrated how recent advances in KeYmaera X's automation, such as its implementation of invariant checking, Darboux reasoning, and differential variants, contribute to the proofs.

There are two directions of future work which could promote industrial impact. A component-based approach could compose the models and proofs for individual reactions into complete reaction networks or chemical plants. Previous proofs suggest a component-based approach could scale to hundreds of variables [6], indicating potential to improve upon the scalability of competing approaches [43]. Secondly, a black-box approach [8] incorporating constrained optimization [17] could make our work useful for realistic industrial controllers, which may involve components too complex for current white-box verification techniques. Our model could be used at runtime to check whether a complex controller's control decision is within a safe range; if not, our simple controller can be used as a safe fallback.

Acknowledgements. We thank the reviewers and Yong Kiam Tan for careful readings and feedback. We thank Therese Smith, Andrew Teixeira, and Grier Wallace for helpful discussions.

References

1. Ábrahám-Mumm, E., Steffen, M., Hannemann, U.: Verification of hybrid systems: formalization and proof rules in PVS. In: ICECCS. IEEE (2001)
2. Althoff, M., Grebenyuk, D., Kochdumper, N.: Implementation of Taylor models in CORA 2018. In: ARCH. EPiC Series in Computing, vol. 54. EasyChair (2018)
3. Bak, S., Tran, H., Johnson, T.T.: Numerical verification of affine systems with up to a billion dimensions. In: HSCC. ACM (2019)

4. Bauer, N., Kowalewski, S., Sand, G., Löhl, T.: A case study: multi product batch plant for the demonstration of control and scheduling problems. In: ADPM (2000)
5. Benvenuti, L., Bresolin, D., Collins, P., Ferrari, A., Geretti, L., Villa, T.: Assume-guarantee verification of nonlinear hybrid systems with ARIADNE. Intl. J. Robust Nonlinear Control 24(4), 699–724 (2014)
6. Bohrer, R., Luo, A., Chuang, X.A., Platzer, A.: CoasterX: a case study in component-driven hybrid systems proof automation. In: ADHS. Elsevier (2018)
7. Bohrer, R., Rahli, V., Vukotic, I., Völp, M., Platzer, A.: Formally verified differential dynamic logic. In: CPP. ACM (2017)
8. Bohrer, R., Tan, Y.K., Mitsch, S., Myreen, M.O., Platzer, A.: VeriPhy: verified controller executables from verified cyber-physical system models. In: PLDI. ACM (2018)
9. Chen, X., Ábrahám, E., Sankaranarayanan, S.: Flow*: an analyzer for non-linear hybrid systems. In: Sharygina, N., Veith, H. (eds.) CAV 2013. LNCS, vol. 8044, pp. 258–263. Springer, Heidelberg (2013). https://doi.org/10.1007/978-3-642-39799-8_18
10. Collins, P., Niqui, M., Revol, N.: A Taylor function calculus for hybrid system analysis: validation in Coq. In: NSV (2010)
11. Duggirala, P.S., Potok, M., Mitra, S., Viswanathan, M.: C2E2: a tool for verifying annotated hybrid systems. In: HSCC. ACM (2015)
12. Dupont, G., Ameur, Y.A., Singh, N.K., Pantel, M.: Event-B hybridation: a proof and refinement-based framework for modelling hybrid systems. ACM Trans. Embed. Comput. Syst. 20(4), 1–37 (2021)
13. Frehse, G., Giacobbe, M., Henzinger, T.A.: Space-time interpolants. In: Chockler, H., Weissenbacher, G. (eds.) CAV 2018. LNCS, vol. 10981, pp. 468–486. Springer, Cham (2018). https://doi.org/10.1007/978-3-319-96145-3_25
14. Frehse, G., et al.: SpaceEx: scalable verification of hybrid systems. In: Gopalakrishnan, G., Qadeer, S. (eds.) CAV 2011. LNCS, vol. 6806, pp. 379–395. Springer, Heidelberg (2011). https://doi.org/10.1007/978-3-642-22110-1_30
15. Fulton, N., Mitsch, S., Bohrer, B., Platzer, A.: Bellerophon: tactical theorem proving for hybrid systems. In: Ayala-Rincón, M., Muñoz, C.A. (eds.) ITP 2017. LNCS, vol. 10499, pp. 207–224. Springer, Cham (2017). https://doi.org/10.1007/978-3-319-66107-0_14
16. Fulton, N., Mitsch, S., Quesel, J.-D., Völp, M., Platzer, A.: KeYmaera X: an axiomatic tactical theorem prover for hybrid systems. In: Felty, A.P., Middeldorp, A. (eds.) CADE 2015. LNCS (LNAI), vol. 9195, pp. 527–538. Springer, Cham (2015). https://doi.org/10.1007/978-3-319-21401-6_36
17. Fulton, N., Platzer, A.: Verifiably safe off-model reinforcement learning. In: Vojnar, T., Zhang, L. (eds.) TACAS 2019. LNCS, vol. 11427, pp. 413–430. Springer, Cham (2019). https://doi.org/10.1007/978-3-030-17462-0_28
18. Glad, T., Ljung, L.: Control Theory. CRC Press, Boca Raton (2018)
19. Hangos, K.M.: Engineering model reduction and entropy-based Lyapunov functions in chemical reaction kinetics. Entropy 12(4), 772–797 (2010)
20. Hassapis, G., Kotini, I., Doulgeri, Z.: Validation of a SFC software specification by using hybrid automata. IFAC Proc. 31(15), 107–112 (1998)
21. Koutsoukos, X.D., He, K.X., Lemmon, M.D., Antsaklis, P.J.: Timed Petri nets in hybrid systems: stability and supervisory control. Discrete Event Dyn. Syst. 8, 137–173 (1998). https://doi.org/10.1023/A:1008293802713
22. Liu, J., et al.: A calculus for hybrid CSP. In: Ueda, K. (ed.) APLAS 2010. LNCS, vol. 6461, pp. 1–15. Springer, Heidelberg (2010). https://doi.org/10.1007/978-3-642-17164-2_1

23. Liu, J., Zhan, N., Zhao, H.: Computing semi-algebraic invariants for polynomial dynamical systems. In: EMSOFT. ACM (2011)
24. Lozano, R., Fantoni, I., Block, D.J.: Stabilization of the inverted pendulum around its homoclinic orbit. Syst. Control Lett. **40**(3), 197–204 (2000)
25. Lukoschus, B.: Compositional verification of industrial control systems: methods and case studies. Ph.D. thesis, Christian-Albrechts Universität Kiel (2004)
26. Mitra, S., Chandy, K.M.: A formalized theory for verifying stability and convergence of automata in PVS. In: Mohamed, O.A., Muñoz, C., Tahar, S. (eds.) TPHOLs 2008. LNCS, vol. 5170, pp. 230–245. Springer, Heidelberg (2008). https://doi.org/10.1007/978-3-540-71067-7_20
27. Mitra, S., Liberzon, D.: Stability of hybrid automata with average dwell time: an invariant approach. In: CDC. IEEE (2004)
28. Mitsch, S., Platzer, A.: The KeYmaera X proof IDE: concepts on usability in hybrid systems theorem proving. In: FIDE. EPTCS, vol. 240 (2016)
29. Nedialkov, N.S.: Implementing a rigorous ODE solver through literate programming. In: Rauh, A., Auer, E. (eds.) Modeling, Design, and Simulation of Systems with Uncertainties. MATHENGIN, vol. 3, pp. 3–19. Springer, Heidelberg (2011). https://doi.org/10.1007/978-3-642-15956-5_1
30. Nellen, J., Ábrahám, E., Wolters, B.: A CEGAR tool for the reachability analysis of PLC-controlled plants using hybrid automata. In: Bouabana-Tebibel, T., Rubin, S.H. (eds.) Formalisms for Reuse and Systems Integration. AISC, vol. 346, pp. 55–78. Springer, Cham (2015). https://doi.org/10.1007/978-3-319-16577-6_3
31. Nguyen, L.V., Schilling, C., Bogomolov, S., Johnson, T.T.: Runtime verification for hybrid analysis tools. In: Bartocci, E., Majumdar, R. (eds.) RV 2015. LNCS, vol. 9333, pp. 281–286. Springer, Cham (2015). https://doi.org/10.1007/978-3-319-23820-3_19
32. Platzer, A.: The structure of differential invariants and differential cut elimination. Log. Meth. Comput. Sci. (2012)
33. Platzer, A.: Differential hybrid games. ACM Trans. Comput. Log. **18**(3), 1–44 (2017)
34. Platzer, A.: Logical Foundations of Cyber-Physical Systems. Springer, Cham (2018). https://doi.org/10.1007/978-3-319-63588-0
35. Platzer, A., Tan, Y.K.: Differential equation invariance axiomatization. J. ACM **67**(1), 1–66 (2020)
36. Potočnik, B., Bemporad, A., Torrisi, F.D., Mušič, G., Zupančič, B.: Hybrid modelling and optimal control of a multiproduct batch plant. Control. Eng. Pract. **12**(9), 1127–1137 (2004)
37. Rouhling, D.: A formal proof in Coq of a control function for the inverted pendulum. In: CPP. ACM (2018)
38. Schmidt, L.D.: The Engineering of Chemical Reactions. Oxford University Press, Oxford (1998)
39. Sogokon, A., Jackson, P.B., Johnson, T.T.: Verifying safety and persistence properties of hybrid systems using flowpipes and continuous invariants. In: Barrett, C., Davies, M., Kahsai, T. (eds.) NFM 2017. LNCS, vol. 10227, pp. 194–211. Springer, Cham (2017). https://doi.org/10.1007/978-3-319-57288-8_14
40. Stephanopoulos, G.: Chemical Process Control: An Introduction to Theory and Practice. Prentice-Hall, Hoboken (1984)
41. Tan, Y.K., Platzer, A.: An axiomatic approach to existence and liveness for differential equations. Formal Aspects Comput. **33**, 461–518 (2021). https://doi.org/10.1007/s00165-020-00525-0

42. Tan, Y.K., Platzer, A.: Deductive stability proofs for ordinary differential equations. In: TACAS 2021. LNCS, vol. 12652, pp. 181–199. Springer, Cham (2021). https://doi.org/10.1007/978-3-030-72013-1_10
43. Tsay, C., Pattison, R.C., Piana, M.R., Baldea, M.: A survey of optimal process design capabilities and practices in the chemical and petrochemical industries. Comput. Chem. Eng. **112**, 180–189 (2018)
44. Wang, S., Zhan, N., Zou, L.: An improved HHL prover: an interactive theorem prover for hybrid systems. In: Butler, M., Conchon, S., Zaïdi, F. (eds.) ICFEM 2015. LNCS, vol. 9407, pp. 382–399. Springer, Cham (2015). https://doi.org/10.1007/978-3-319-25423-4_25
45. Qiwen, X., Weidong, H.: Hierarchical design of a chemical concentration control system. In: Alur, R., Henzinger, T.A., Sontag, E.D. (eds.) HS 1995. LNCS, vol. 1066, pp. 270–281. Springer, Heidelberg (1996). https://doi.org/10.1007/BFb0020952

Analysing Capacity Bottlenecks in Rail Infrastructure by Episode Mining

Philipp Berger[1] , Wiebke Lenze[2] , Thomas Noll[1(✉)] , Simon Schotten[3],
Thorsten Büker[3], Mario Fietze[4], and Bastian Kogel[2]

[1] Software Modeling and Verification Group, RWTH Aachen University,
Aachen, Germany
{Berger,Noll}@cs.rwth-aachen.de
[2] Institute of Transport Science, RWTH Aachen University, Aachen, Germany
{Lenze,Kogel}@via.rwth-aachen.de
[3] quattron management consulting GmbH, Aachen, Germany
{Simon.Schotten,Thorsten.Bueker}@quattron.com
[4] German Centre for Rail Traffic Research, Dresden, Germany
FietzeM@dzsf.bund.de

Abstract. We introduce a methodology to identify and analyse capacity bottlenecks in railway networks. It is based on operational data that has been recorded in real operation. In a first step, network areas that exhibit frequent and significant train delays are determined. Next, the actual causes of such delays are investigated by analysing interdependences between train runs and by distinguishing between primary and secondary delays. This is achieved by employing episode mining techniques to enable the systematic identification of temporal patterns that occur frequently in the data about train runs.

Keywords: Train delays · Capacity bottlenecks · Episode mining

1   Introduction

Since most rail networks are already heavily utilised in many sections, further increase in passenger and freight transportation will raise the infrastructure usage and the number of bottlenecks even more. These challenges need to be addressed by, e.g., using the existing infrastructure more efficiently and expanding the network appropriately. That is why knowledge about the location of the most critical areas of the network and the related causes of delays is essential.

To gain such knowledge, the German Centre for Rail Traffic Research[1] has commissioned a project to identify, analyse and dissolve such bottlenecks automatically. This paper concentrates on the second step, presenting the methods developed to investigate the propagation of delays.

---

[1] https://www.dzsf.bund.de/.

Funded by the German Centre for Rail Traffic Research.

J. F. Groote and M. Huisman (Eds.): FMICS 2022, LNCS 13487, pp. 121–133, 2022.
https://doi.org/10.1007/978-3-031-15008-1_9

Our approach is based on historical railway traffic data, which records trains moving in the railway system in real operation over longer periods of time. The aim is to identify the actual causes of disruptions by identifying interdependences between (delayed) train runs, with the goal of distinguishing primary and secondary delays. To this aim, we employ episode mining [6], a data-driven technique which enables the analysis of temporal patterns that frequently occur in a given time-stamped event sequence.

The remainder of this paper is organised as follows. We continue in Sect. 2 with giving an overview of related work. In Sect. 3, we describe the systematic evaluation of operational data of train runs with the goal of identifying capacity bottlenecks, which are locations (i.e., stations or sections) of the network where trains frequently suffer an increase in delay. The most critical bottlenecks are then analysed using the episode mining methods as explained in Sect. 4. The outcome of this evaluation is described in Sect. 5, and the paper ends with some conclusions in Sect. 6.

2   Related Work

The application of data and process mining methods to real railway traffic data seems a natural choice. Surprisingly, comparatively few research efforts have been undertaken to develop appropriate techniques. The work that is presumably closest to ours is described in [1], where also a mining algorithm for frequent episodes is employed to analyse knock-on delays in the Belgian railway system. However, Cule et al. only consider trains passing a single spatial reference point, which does not allow to investigate the propagation of delays over larger parts of the network.

The problem of automatically identifying systematic dependences between train delays is also addressed in [2]. Flier et al. develop efficient algorithms to detect two of the most important types of dependences in real-world railway delay data, namely dependences due to resource conflicts and due to maintained connections. Once such dependences are found in the input data, they are more closely examined by statistical methods in a subsequent step.

Another application of (process) mining techniques, but with a different objective, is presented in [5]. The work by Mannhardt et al. is based on railway traffic control logs that register precise information about the actual scheduling of trains at a station. Process mining is used with this data to investigate the quality of ad-hoc decisions that are taken by railway dispatchers in reaction to unplanned events. This allows to explore and to evaluate scheduling strategies for dealing with unexpected disruptions.

Yet another application is the exploratory analysis of train re-routings in Belgium based on discovered process models [3]. The method developed by Janssenswillen et al. is able to identify areas in the railway network where trains have a higher tendency to diverge from their actually allocated route, which provides a starting point to improve the planning of capacity usage.

3 Identification of Capacity Bottlenecks

As relevant background information for the episode mining technique developed in the following, this section summarises the method to identify capacity bottlenecks which has been elaborated in [4] and [8].

3.1 Method

Bottlenecks are identified based on delay information of trains. Our method counts the occurrence of delays at one location ("delay event") and weights delay increases based on a train's initial delay. An emergence of a delay for a punctual train is weighted higher compared to already heavily delayed trains. Delays are classified using six categories as shown in Fig. 1.

Fig. 1. Delay categories defined by delay times (in seconds) [4]

Due to different category widths, delay increases lead to category changes more or less quickly. Such category changes are counted in order to identify bottlenecks. To avoid delays to be balanced by delay reductions of other trains, only changes into higher categories are considered. Moreover, changes from category 0 to category 1 represent changes for premature trains that do not cause bottlenecks and are therefore not included. Trains with delays in category 5 highly deviate from their scheduled time slot, which also makes them unsuitable for the identification of bottlenecks. The delay increases and category changes that are measured can be weighted, with more category changes entailing higher weights. We recommend weighting them according to generally accepted priorities of the affected train type, assigning e.g. high weighting factors to long-distance passenger trains. Details can be found in [4].

3.2 Results

Using the method presented, bottlenecks and their severity are calculated for an investigation area such as (a part of) a rail network. We have applied the method to the German rail network, which consists of about 10 000 locations. With its 40 000 train runs per day, the total amount of measured events is about 900 000 for both arrivals and departures per day (not every location is served every day, for example access points for industry). Since there is a regular major change of the timetable in December and since different timetables are employed at weekends, all business days between January 2nd and November 30th of a year are considered, resulting in a total amount of measured events of more than 410 million.

The method's result is a list of railway lines and stations sorted by their significance concerning the network's performance. Lines and stations with highest significance are identified as bottlenecks. Such bottlenecks are characterised by large delay increases and delay propagations.

4 Analysing Delay Propagations

The approach described in the following is based on the list of (critical) bottlenecks as determined in Sect. 3, together with the relevant input data.

4.1 Goals and Overview

Our goal is to identify the actual causes of delays by analysing interdependences between train runs and by distinguishing between primary and secondary delays. The former refer to delays that are not caused by interaction with other trains but are due to disruptions such as technical malfunctions or additional time required by passengers for changing trains. The latter result from other trains being delayed. Possible reasons are the blocking of a railway section by another train or a connecting train having to wait for another train. Thus, secondary delays are delays that are propagated between train runs. In order to enable the development of approaches to resolve bottlenecks, primary delays will be categorised in a later phase of the project to distinguish between technical and organisational causes. This, however, is mostly manual work which is outside the scope of this paper.

Obviously, the problem to be solved requires the systematic analysis of temporal patterns that occur frequently in the data about train runs. To this aim, we employ a technique called *episode mining* that supports such tasks and that has successfully been applied to similar problems before [1]. In a nutshell, episodes represent summary information about temporal constellations that often occur in (time-stamped) input event data. In our setting, they are employed to answer the following central question: *Which trains are frequently together delayed?* Episode mining algorithms are based on certain numeric parameters that serve to give quantitative characterisations of the following aspects:

- What does *delayed* mean?
  We introduce a parameter D which specifies the *minimal delay* that is considered to be critical. Episode mining only takes those train runs into account whose delay in the considered network location is at least D. A typical value is $D = 3$ min.
- What does *together* mean?
  We introduce a parameter W which specifies the *length of the sliding window* that is moved stepwise over the (temporally ordered) input event data. Thus, a common appearance of two or more train runs is only considered to be temporally connected (and thus included in an episode) when they occur within the temporal distance as specified by W. A typical value is $W = 30$ min.

– What does *frequently* mean?
We introduce a parameter T which specifies the *frequency threshold* as an absolute value. It allows to distinguish between sporadic and statistically significant temporal patterns by defining the minimal number of occurrences of an episode in the input data. In other words, after the actual mining phase an episode is disregarded if its occurrence frequency is below T.

In contrast to the first two parameters, the interpretation of T is context specific. It depends on both the length of the event sampling period and the window parameter W. This is due to the fact that the length W of the sliding window has strong impact on both the size and the frequency of matching episodes. On the one side, enlarging W means that (also) larger episodes are found since more train runs are considered to be in temporal connection. On the other side, this also increases the occurrence frequency of episodes: As the window is moved stepwise over the input data, two or more train runs whose temporal distance falls below W are considered multiple times. More precisely, the smaller the distance in relation to W, the stronger the episode frequency is increased. A concrete example illustrating these connections will follow later.

4.2 Episode Mining

We will now explain the episode mining technique in detail, providing both formalisations and illustrative examples. Let us start with the formal definition of episodes.

Definition 1 (Episode)

– *Let E be a non-empty, finite set of* events.
– *An* event occurrence $(e, t) \in E \times \mathbb{N}$ *consists of an event $e \in E$ and a time stamp $t \in \mathbb{N}$.*
– *An* episode *is a partial order $P = (E, \rightarrow)$, i.e., $\rightarrow \subseteq E \times E$ is reflexive, transitive and anti-symmetric. The size of P is given by $|E|$, i.e., the number of events.*
– *An episode $P_1 = (E_1, \rightarrow_1)$ is called a* sub-episode *of another episode $P_2 = (E_2, \rightarrow_2)$ if $E_1 \subseteq E_2$ and $\rightarrow_1 \subseteq \rightarrow_2$. Correspondingly, P_2 is called a* super-episode *of P_1 in this case. This relation is denoted by $P_1 \preceq P_2$.*

In this paper, episodes are usually represented by directed acyclic graphs (DAGs) whose vertices correspond to events and where the transitive closure of the edges determines the ordering relation. Note that the distinction between sub- and super-episodes refers to the level of *preciseness* of episodes: If $P_1 \preceq P_2$ and $P_1 \neq P_2$, then P_2 contains more events or temporally orders more events than P_1, which actually means that P_2 gives more precise information about a temporal pattern than P_1.

Example 1. In our application, events correspond to train runs that are delayed in a certain network location, and time stamps indicate the time of arrival (or departure). Figure 2 shows (the DAG representation of) an example episode. It can be interpreted as follows:

- Trains 1, 5, 7, 12 and 42 are "often" delayed together.
- In "many" cases, train 1 arrives before 5 and 42 as well as both 5 and 42 before 12.
- No (frequent) order occurs neither between trains 5 and 42 nor between 7 and other trains.

As we will see in the following, these qualitative descriptions are made precise by means of the numeric parameters that have been introduced before.

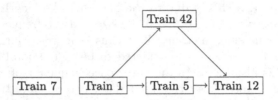

Fig. 2. An episode showing frequently occurring temporal orders between trains

The episode mining algorithm that is employed in our analysis is described in [9]. It operates on sequences of event occurrences (i.e., time-stamped events). As seen in the previous example, in our setting an event corresponds to the arrival (or departure) of a train with a delay of at least D at a certain network bottleneck (identified as described in Sect. 3). To derive the corresponding episode information, a sliding window of length W is moved stepwise over the input sequence, and the corresponding episode information is collected. The following definition states which episodes are recorded for the events in the currently considered section of the input data stream.

Definition 2 (Matching episode)

- Let $((e_1, t_1), \ldots, (e_n, t_n)) \in (E \times \mathbb{N})^*$ be an ordered sequence of time-stamped events, i.e., $e_i \neq e_j$ for $i \neq j$ and $t_1 < \ldots < t_n$.
- A section of duration W is a sub-sequence $S = ((e_k, t_k), \ldots, (e_l, t_l))$ such that $t_l - t_k \leq W$ and ($l = n$ or else $t_{l+1} - t_k > W$).
- Let $P = (\{e_k, \ldots, e_l\}, \rightarrow)$ be the corresponding (maximal) episode, that is, $e_i \rightarrow e_j$ iff $i \leq j$. Then every sub-episode of P (including P itself) matches S.

As we will see later, during episode mining it is important that not only maximal matching episodes but also their (proper) sub-episodes are taken into account. This is due to the fact that when moving the sliding window over the input sequence, the number of matching occurrences of each episode (the so-called *support value*) is computed, and all episodes with differing support values will be taken into account.

Let us illustrate the computation of support values by means of a toy example. A detailed explanation of the algorithm can be found in [9]. As explained before, it operates on a sequence of time-stamped events which is obtained from the data base of train runs by applying the following input transformation:

1. remove all runs with delay $< D$,
2. filter to the network location of interest, and
3. project to the time of arrival (TOA) and the train identifier.

Example 2. Let us assume that the input transformation yields the sequence of train arrivals shown in Fig. 3a, which are aggregated into three lines A, B, and C. Observe that it consists of three temporally contiguous blocks (TOA 12:00–12:02, 12:20–12:22, 12:30–12:32) with larger gaps in between. Performing an episode analysis with a window size of $W = 2\,\text{min}$ (and a step size of 1 min) yields the result given in Fig. 3b.[2]

Here, episodes 1–3 match all three blocks (and thus have a support value of 3), whereas 4 and 5 match the first and the third block and 6 and 7 only the second block.

TOA	Train
12:00	A
12:01	B
12:02	C
12:20	A
12:21	C
12:22	B
12:30	A
12:31	B
12:32	C

(a) Input sequence

No.	Episode	Support
1	(A, B, C)	3
2	(A → B, C)	3
3	(A → C, B)	3
4	(A, B → C)	2
5	(A → B → C)	2
6	(A, C → B)	1
7	(A → C → B)	1

(b) Resulting episodes

Fig. 3. Episode analysis

Obviously, the analysis is quite complex as the number of (possible) episodes increases exponentially with the number of events. Therefore, an important goal is to reduce the number of results as much as possible. The first step is to remove episodes that are redundant in the sense that they are accompanied by a proper super-episode with the same support value. In this case, the sub-episode can be removed without any loss of information as the super-episode is, on the one hand, more precise and, on the other hand, covers all situations matched by the sub-episode (as their support values coincide). The following definition introduces the notion of closedness to characterise non-redundant episodes.

Definition 3 (Closed episode). *Let* $\{P_1, \ldots, P_n\}$ *be a set of episodes with support values* $s : \{P_1, \ldots, P_n\} \to \mathbb{N}$. *For* $i \in \{1, \ldots, n\}$, P_i *is called* closed *if there exists no* $j \in \{1, \ldots, n\} \setminus \{i\}$ *such that* $P_i \preceq P_j$ *and* $s(P_i) = s(P_j)$.

---

[2] Actually, the analysis also returns sub-episodes of smaller size, e.g., when the sliding window overlaps with the beginning or the end of a block. We omit those for simplicity.

Example 3. With regard to the previous example, we make the following observations:

- (A, B, C) is a proper sub-episode of all other episodes. Since, e.g., $(A \rightarrow B, C)$ has the same support, episode 1 is not closed.
- $(A \rightarrow B, C)$ and $(A \rightarrow C, B)$ only have $(A \rightarrow B \rightarrow C)$ and $(A \rightarrow C \rightarrow B)$, respectively, as proper super-episodes, which both have less support. Therefore, episodes 2 and 3 are closed.
- $(A, B \rightarrow C)$ and $(A, C \rightarrow B)$ respectively have $(A \rightarrow B \rightarrow C)$ and $(A \rightarrow C \rightarrow B)$ as proper super-episodes with the same support. Therefore, episodes 4 and 6 are not closed.
- $(A \rightarrow B \rightarrow C)$ and $(A \rightarrow C \rightarrow B)$ have no proper super-episode, making episodes 5 and 7 closed by definition.

As an intermediate result, we obtain a list of closed episodes together with their frequency distribution (support). In the next step, we filter out "outliers" by applying the threshold parameter T.

Example 4. By imposing threshold parameter $T = 3$ on the four closed episodes found in the previous example, we obtain only those closed episodes that match every block, which are $(A \rightarrow B, C)$ and $(A \rightarrow C, B)$. This result can be interpreted as follows:

- Trains A, B and C are frequently delayed together.
- Train A always arrives before both B and C (since otherwise also (A, B, C) were a closed episode).
- Train A (locally) causes the delay (since A is never preceded by any other train).

While the meaning of the delay parameter D and of the window size parameter W are directly understandable, the interpretation of the threshold parameter T is less intuitive and more context dependent. Its definition depends on both W and on the sampling period that is chosen for the input and yields an absolute value. The following example might illustrate this: Let us assume for a window size $W = 1800\,\text{s}$ and a step size of $1\,\text{s}$ that train B arrives $50\,\text{s}$ after train A. This single instance already yields a support of $1800 - 50 = 1750$ for (sub-)episode $(A \rightarrow B)$. This value gets closer to 1800 if the distance between the trains decreases. On the other hand, increasing the distance reduces the support. In the extreme case, it becomes one if window size and distance coincide (as demonstrated in Example 2). In other words, the support value correlates with the temporal vicinity of (delayed) trains, which is clearly a desirable effect. Thus, if an overall support of, say, 40 000 was computed by episode mining and if both trains run once per day, then we can deduce that this arrival pattern occurred on at least $\lceil \frac{40\,000}{1800} \rceil = 23$ days. A reasonable choice of the threshold parameter T has to take all this context information into account.

4.3 Algorithm and Implementation

As explained before, the principle of episode mining is to move a sliding window over the event data of a network location and to count the temporal patterns as they are matched. However, since the number of possible sub-episodes increases exponentially with the number of train runs occurring in the window, this simple approach does not scale. Instead, the algorithm employed in our project, which is described in [9], picks up the idea of operating on closed episodes, as described in the previous subsection. However, as we have also seen, it is not possible to define a unique episode closure based on support values because an episode may have several closed super-episodes.

To tackle this problem, so-called strict episodes are introduced, which enable a unique definition of a closure operator. After efficiently computing strict closed episodes, the closed episodes that we are actually interested in can be obtained by means of a post-processing step. This algorithm has been implemented by N. Tatti in the open-source Closed Episodes Miner tool, which is available online[3] and whose code is used in our implementation.

4.4 Adaptations

In order to take the special needs of our railway project into account, the generic episode mining algorithm needs to be adapted. Since we wanted to avoid any modification of the complex implementation itself, we enriched it by additional data pre- and post-processing steps. These are briefly described in the following.

- Restriction to *total* (i.e., linearly ordered) episodes: The mining algorithm described in the previous section identifies both total and non-total episodes. For the purpose of bottleneck analysis, however, the former are better suited as they allow to directly identify chains of dependences. Therefore, in the current version of our analysis, we simply remove all non-total episodes from the result. Note, however, that this does not mean that delayed trains are always ordered in the same way. If they occur in varying orders on several days, corresponding total episodes with different support values are generated.
- Restriction to episodes in which the subsequent trains suffer an *increase in delay* in the respective location: As explained before, our analyses only considers trains whose delay exceeds a predefined delay threshold D. In order to distinguish between primary and secondary delays, it is necessary to identify the first location where two (or more) trains interact. This means that two (or more) delayed trains following each other should not be captured at every location of their common route but only at the position where the delay is actually propagated. Therefore as an additional restriction we require that all trains in an episode except for the first one suffer an increase in delay of at least 30 s, which turned out to be a reasonable choice of this threshold parameter.

---

[3] https://version.helsinki.fi/dacs/2010-closed-episodes-miner.

Unfortunately, this additional restriction cannot be directly configured in the mining algorithm. Instead, all events that satisfy the delay-increase requirement are duplicated and are marked in a way which allows to filter redundant events after the mining phase.

Moreover, the following optimisations are applied in order to reduce the number of events that can occur in the sliding window. This is particularly necessary for locations that are heavily charged, resulting in temporally dense event streams.

- *Arrival* vs. *departure* times: Since delay propagations can occur both in the inflow and outflow of a network location, both arrival and departure times need to be considered in the analysis. This means that episodes can indicate all four possible combinations of dependences between arrivals and departures. In particular, they can be recorded between arrival and departure of the same train. Such dependences, however, are irrelevant and are therefore ignored.

  Moreover, the following pre-processing steps are applied to further reduce the number of time-stamped events to be considered:
  - If the difference between two time stamps of the same train is below a certain threshold (here: 15 s), both are combined into one event, which removed roughly 33% of events. This, in particular, applies to a non-stopping transit of a train.
  - If two time stamps of the same train directly follow each other without intervening time stamps of other trains, they are combined into one event if their distance does not exceed a threshold of 5 min, which removes roughly 15% of events.

  Both threshold values turned out to yield a good compromise between the reduction effect on the one hand and the precision of analysis on the other hand.
- Independent investigation of *driving directions* for train stops (i.e., non-crossing locations): In stopping points without switches, conflicts can only occur between trains passing into the same direction. Opposite directions can therefore be evaluated independently of each other.
- Exclusion of *suburban trains*: In major train stations, suburban trains are excluded from the analysis. On the one hand, this is necessary since otherwise the amount of input data exceeds our computation capacities. On the other hand, suburban trains are usually running on separate tracks in major stations such that interactions between suburban and other kinds of trains are limited.
- Evaluation of *train lines*: In situations where trains are operated in regular intervals, interactions cannot only be identified between train runs but also between train lines (cf. Example 2). Aggregating runs into lines has the positive effect of increasing the number of related events, which facilitates the identification of temporal patterns in the overall data. However, the assignment of train lines to train numbers is non-trivial as they are not properly documented in the input data, and as they can change over the year. Even worse, line numbers for freight trains are not at all schematised but vary daily.

To meet these challenges, different methods are applied to introduce line identifiers for passenger and freight trains. The former are based on the target arrival and departure times of trains, assuming one-hour intervals as the prevalent scheduling schema. To deal with the latter, the identification of lines is based on train paths, that is, predefined slots in the scheduling schema that are allocated to freight trains.

5 Evaluation Results

In this project, episode mining techniques have proven to be useful for analysing the propagation of delays in railway networks. They allow to derive interactions between train runs by observing temporal patterns between time-stamped events without requiring detailed knowledge about the technical infrastructure at the considered location. Thus they yield results that can hardly be achieved on a network-wide scale using other (non-automated) methods. More concretely, running episode mining on a data set with approx. 10 000 locations and altogether 93 million events (remaining after filtering a total amount of 410 million events by the mentioned criteria) roughly takes 6 h.

It also turned out, however, that the interpretation of pattern frequencies, i.e., support values for episodes, is not straightforward. For example, with a non-optimised scheduling of trains using a large signal headway, support values are typically lower than after optimisation, even if the same delay times are propagated. This is due to the fact that in the optimised case, trains follow each other in shorter distances, leading to more frequent occurrences of episodes in the sliding window. Similar observations apply to the comparison of different locations in the network.

To facilitate the interpretation of analysis results, diagrams such as the one shown in Fig. 4 can be helpful. It has been produced using the OpenTimeTable Tool [7] and illustrates the propagation of a delay between two trains (1 followed by 2) running from station A (left) to B (right). The vertical axis represents time (progressing downwards), while the horizontal axis gives the position of a train at the respective point in time. The planned scheduling of train 1 and 2 according to the timetable is indicated in green and blue thin solid lines, respectively. The green bars visualise a number of actual runs over a longer period of time, with the corresponding medians given by dashed lines. The increasing gap between the solid and the dashed lines indicates the progressive deviation of both trains from their planned schedule The diagram thus clearly demonstrates that the increasing delay of the first train also causes the second train to gain delays.

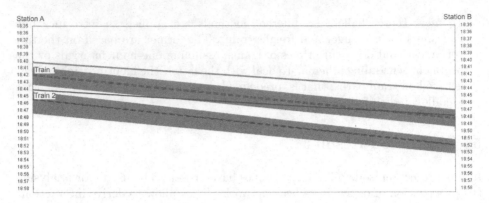

Fig. 4. Visualisation of a delay propagation between two trains (vertical axis: time, horizontal axis: position) (Color figure online)

6   Conclusions and Outlook

In this paper, we investigated systematic methods to identify and, in particular, to analyse capacity bottlenecks in railway networks. The approach that we applied in the latter step is based on episode mining, a data-driven technique which enables the systematic analysis of temporal patterns that occur frequently in time-stamped event data. In our setting, this provides systematic information about train runs that have been recorded in real operation, especially in network locations that have earlier been classified as capacity bottlenecks. By analysing interdependences between such train runs, episode mining allows to distinguish between primary and secondary delays.

Current project work concentrates on appropriate approaches to resolve bottlenecks. To this aim, primary delays will be categorised to distinguish between technical and organisational causes. Even though some statistical data about such causes is available from the operational data base, additional manual effort will be required to obtain a consistent classification. Finally, the overall method will be implemented by means of a prototypical software tool.

References

1. Cule, B., Goethals, B., Tassenoy, S., Verboven, S.: Mining train delays. In: Gama, J., Bradley, E., Hollmén, J. (eds.) IDA 2011. LNCS, vol. 7014, pp. 113–124. Springer, Heidelberg (2011). https://doi.org/10.1007/978-3-642-24800-9_13
2. Flier, H., Gelashvili, R., Graffagnino, T., Nunkesser, M.: Mining railway delay dependencies in large-scale real-world delay data. In: Ahuja, R.K., Möhring, R.H., Zaroliagis, C.D. (eds.) Robust and Online Large-Scale Optimization. LNCS, vol. 5868, pp. 354–368. Springer, Heidelberg (2009). https://doi.org/10.1007/978-3-642-05465-5_15
3. Janssenswillen, G., Depaire, B., Verboven, S.: Detecting train reroutings with process mining. EURO J. Transp. Logist. **7**(1), 1–24 (2017). https://doi.org/10.1007/s13676-017-0105-8

4. Lenze, W., et al.: Identification of bottlenecks in rail infrastructure. Accepted for Presentation at 5th International Conference on Railway Technology (RAILWAYS 2022). https://www.railwaysconference.com
5. Mannhardt, F., Landmark, A.D.: Mining railway traffic control logs. Transp. Res. Procedia **37**, 227–234 (2019). https://doi.org/10.1016/j.trpro.2018.12.187
6. Mannila, H., Toivonen, H., Inkeri Verkamo, A.: Discovery of frequent episodes in event sequences. Data Min. Knowl. Discov. **1**, 259–289 (1997). https://doi.org/10.1023/A:1009748302351
7. Nash, A., Ullius, M.: Optimizing railway timetables with OpenTimeTable. In: Computers in Railways IX, pp. 637–646. WIT Press (2004). https://www.witpress.com/elibrary/wit-transactions-on-the-built-environment/74/12093
8. Schotten, S., et al.: Einblick DZSF-Projekt Identifikation von Kapazitätsengpässen. Eisenbahntechnische Rundschau **5**, 2–6 (2022)
9. Tatti, N., Cule, B.: Mining closed strict episodes. Data Min. Knowl. Discov. **25**, 34–66 (2012). https://doi.org/10.1007/s10618-011-0232-z

Testing and Monitoring

Test Suite Augmentation for Reconfigurable PLC Software in the Internet of Production

Marco Grochowski$^{(\boxtimes)}$ ⓘ, Marcus Völker ⓘ, and Stefan Kowalewski ⓘ

Embedded Software, RWTH Aachen University, Aachen, Germany
{grochowski,voelker,kowalewski}@embedded.rwth-aachen.de

Abstract. Regression testing is an established technique used to attest the correctness of reconfigurations to PLC software. After such a reconfiguration, a test suite might not be adequate to ensure the absence of regressions, requiring the derivation of new test cases to uncover potential regressions. This paper presents a combination of state-of-the-art symbolic execution algorithms for test suite augmentation, an indispensable part of regression testing. Test generation is guided towards the changed behavior using a technique known as four-way forking. The old and new PLC software are executed in the same symbolic execution instance to account for the effects of the reconfiguration and increase the chances of generating difference-revealing test cases. The prototypical implementation is evaluated using domain-specific benchmarks such as the PLCopen Safety library and the Pick and Place Unit, exposing the limitations in applicability and effectiveness of the used techniques for safeguarding PLC software subject to frequent reconfigurations as found in cyber-physical production systems.

Keywords: Regression testing · Test suite augmentation · Symbolic execution · Programmable logic controllers · Internet of Production

1 Introduction

Transformability, a property resulting from the flexibility and mechanical reconfigurability of a cyber-physical production system (CPPS), is one of the primary enablers to cope with changing intrinsic and extrinsic demands and is a necessary prerequisite to guarantee the ability to compete with other companies [9]. An overview of the life cycle and value chain of a CPPS is given in Fig. 1. In contrast to a conventional production system, a CPPS is subject to a high degree of reconfigurability during its life cycle. This highly agile manufacturing paradigm leads to an increase in complexity as the insights gained during production turns into data that controls the production process. Due to the heterogeneity and emergent behavior of CPPS, unwanted regressions might accompany those reconfigurations and take their toll on the functional safety and reliability of software components [6]. In the context of static reconfigurations where the entire CPPS

© The Author(s), under exclusive license to Springer Nature Switzerland AG 2022
J. F. Groote and M. Huisman (Eds.): FMICS 2022, LNCS 13487, pp. 137–154, 2022.
https://doi.org/10.1007/978-3-031-15008-1_10

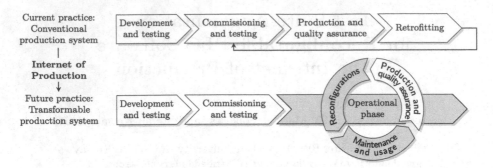

Fig. 1. Juxtaposition of the life cycle and value chain of cyber-physical production systems (Figure adapted from illustration in [19]).

is stopped and analyzed during maintenance, short downtimes are crucial, and we argue that lightweight verification techniques such as testing are suitable to assess the CPPS's correctness quickly. Consequently, the goal is to reduce the lead-time after a reconfiguration to the CPPS has occurred by reducing the time it takes to test the reconfigured programmable logic controller's (PLC) software throughout the ramp-up phase during maintenance as depicted in Fig. 1.

Regression Testing. Regarding the reconfigurations to PLC software, they manifest themselves in the form of the addition of new functionality, the modification of already existing functionality, or the removal of functionality, which most often also requires adaptations to the test suite. As the manual creation of difference-revealing test cases requires enormous effort and expertise, automated techniques are desirable. One prominent set of such automated techniques that tackles test suite maintenance is termed regression testing. Figure 2 illustrates the process of regression testing and test suite augmentation after a syntactic reconfiguration. Consider the test suite T_{all}^P for a PLC program P before a reconfiguration with which the reconfigured PLC program P' should be tested. There are two primary reasons why re-executing the whole test suite is infeasible. The first one is that the test suite might be too large and require too much time while not focusing on the parts of the software affected by the reconfiguration. The other aspect is that the test suite might not even test the changed behavior of P'. In this sense, test suite augmentation is necessary and an important complementary technique to traditional regression testing techniques [21,23]. Dealing with reconfigurations to the PLC software and its effect on the test suite is a two-step approach during test suite maintenance. First, one has to assess if the test suite T_{all}^P is still *adequate* enough for testing P'. Standard measures for adequacy are whether the test suite is homogeneous with regards to the program paths, for instance, line or branch coverage. Nonetheless, one has to keep in mind that coverage alone does not quantify the capability of a test suite to reveal regressions. If the test suite is not homogeneous with regards to the failure [20], i.e., it structurally covers the reconfigured program path but does not propagate a divergence to the output, it will not reveal the regression after a faulty syntactic

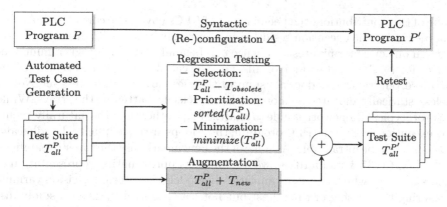

Fig. 2. Application of regression testing techniques and test suite augmentation after a syntactic reconfiguration.

reconfiguration. Second, the reconfigurations in P' need to be identified, and the test case generation algorithm has to be guided to cover the potentially reconfigured behavior. As regressions are only observable for inputs that expose a behavioral difference, we use a concept coined as four-way forking [10] to guide the test case generation into parts of the software affected by a reconfiguration. As the identification of the reconfiguration is a challenging problem, we resort to manual software annotations to explicitly denote the reconfigured parts from one version to another.

Syntactic Reconfiguration. The syntactic reconfiguration mentioned in Fig. 2 follows the concept presented in [10], where a change(old,new) macro was used to characterize the effect of the reconfiguration. The first argument of this macro represents the expression from the PLC software before the reconfiguration, and the second argument represents the expression of the PLC software after the reconfiguration. As a result, the manifestation of reconfigurations to PLC software stated earlier, i.e., the addition of new functionality, e.g., adding an extra assignment $x :=$ change$(x, 1)$;, the modification of already existing functionality, e.g., changing the right-hand side of an assignment $x := y +$ change$(1, 2)$;, or the deletion of functionality, e.g. removal of straightline code if(change(true, false)) ... code ... can be expressed succinctly with the change(old,new) macro. This way of annotating the expressions of reconfigured parts of the software has a significant benefit as it keeps the correspondence between both versions intact and was therefore chosen for analyzing the semantic effects of the implication introduced by the reconfigurations.

1.1 Limitations and Contributions

A premise resulting from the introduction is the existence of syntactically change-annotated PLC programs given as input to our framework. To further narrow the scope of this contribution, the peculiarities of PLCs have to be considered. A PLC is subject to cyclic execution resulting in non-termination. Still, every execution through one cycle terminates and hence can be analyzed. The programming languages for PLCs forbid recursive calls, i.e., the call-flow graph is acyclic [8]. Furthermore, our framework does not support the use of arrays or pointers yet. Nevertheless, statically allocated memory can be modeled by flattening the arrays. While the prototypical framework is able to analyze loops other than the naturally occurring execution cycle of the PLC program, these loops are not explicitly handled and analysis might be intractable. As some of the benchmarks use the timer capabilities of the IEC 61131-3 standard [8], we use an over-approximating representation of timers from [1], which non-deterministically models the internal decision variable measuring the passing of time. Last but not least, control tasks are usually distributed in the context of Industry 4.0, yet most often still coordinated centrally. Instead of having a single PLC that controls the various actuators in the CPPS, multiple PLCs exist, one for each control task and one overarching, coordinating PLC. Despite that, we model the distributed control task as one, compositional, *classic* PLC program, in which the other control tasks are incorporated as function blocks and executed on one single PLC controller (cf. Sect. 4). This neglects the influences of different times and latencies introduced due to the communication between each controlling PLC. We assume that the sequential modeling using a single PLC is a feasible abstraction of several distributed PLCs running in parallel, realizing the same control task, because the business logic is implemented by a single, coordinating PLC, which processes the messages of the other distributed PLCs sequentially in all circumstances. To this end,

- we improve the scalability of an existing Dynamic Symbolic Execution (DSE) algorithm for PLC software,
- we evaluate the feasibility of DSE and the concept of four-way forking for test suite augmentation of reconfigured PLC software on benchmarks of varying difficulty and compare it to previous results.

2   Related Work

Symbolic execution is one of the primary techniques for software testing and resulted in the development of numerous language-agnostic analysis tools in the past [3]. Previous work has investigated the applicability of DSE in test suite generation for PLC software [4]. The results were promising but have not been applied to tackle the problem of test suite augmentation after a reconfiguration. In contrast to [4], the concolic and compositional DART algorithm, also known as SMART [5], explores the program execution tree depth-first on a per path basis allowing for the use of summaries. However, we currently refrain from summarization due to our conflicting merging strategy. An approach that aids regression testing with static change-impact analysis is called directed incremental SE (DiSE) [22]. The rationale behind this is that static analysis avoids the problems of undecidability of whether there exists an input that is difference-revealing against the reconfigured program by over-approximating the semantic properties using syntactic dependencies such as control- and data dependencies.

The results from the static analysis are used to guide symbolic execution by exploring only paths that can reach parts of the software affected by the reconfiguration. This approach, however, has two severe disadvantages. We argue that these *slices* give only conservative estimates and are often too imprecise, reducing opportunities for information reuse from the prior analysis of the reconfigured PLC software. Furthermore, DiSE only explores one execution path through the impacted parts of the software, and besides reachability, there is no guidance in the direction of real divergences. This lead us to the choice of Shadow Symbolic Execution (SSE) [10] for test suite augmentation. SSE uses a seeded exploration with a test case that touches the presumable *patch*, or in our terminology, the reconfiguration. The novelty of SSE is that it executes the old (presumed buggy) and new (presumed patched) program within the same SE instance. Therefore, it allows the algorithm not to re-execute potentially expensive path prefixes, which provides several opportunities to prune and prioritize paths and simplify constraints. Despite this, the reconfigurations are touched by a test case that dictates the context in which the potential reconfiguration is reached and hence limits the generalization. Furthermore, both programs need to be merged into a change-annotated, unified version.

Verification and Testing in the PLC Domain. Regarding the safeguarding of reconfigurations in the PLC domain several techniques on various levels have emerged in the past years. TESTIAS [24] is a tool for model-based verification of reconfigurations to distributed automation systems. It works on a higher level than PLC software, i.e., trying to prove the correctness of a reconfiguration affecting the functional perspective of services in a CPPS. Prioritization for regression testing of reconfigured PLC software with regards to system tests was evaluated in [17]. It optimizes the regression testing process of CPPS after a reconfiguration, however, it is unable to generate difference-revealing test cases. Another interesting approach poses the modular regression verification of the VERIFAPS library which was successfully applied to the Pick and Place Unit (PPU) case study in [18]. Modular regression verification requires the specification of relational regression verification contracts allowing for the decomposition of the verification task resulting in efficient solving, yet being far from a push-button technology.

3 Methodology

An overview of our prototypical test suite augmentation (TSA) framework is given in Fig. 3 and explained throughout this section. TSA can be considered as a development time technique, in which the developer manually annotates the desired changes and is able to assess their implications on the observable behavior of the PLC software. The input to the program analysis framework is a manually change-annotated PLC program in structured text (ST), one of the five IEC 61131 programming languages [8], using the change(old,new) annotation macro introduced in Sect. 1. Before going in-depth with the core TSA algorithm, we briefly describe our intermediate representation of the PLC software.

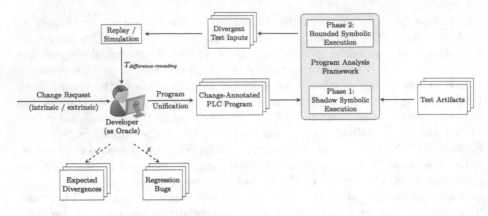

Fig. 3. Overview of the prototypical TSA framework.

3.1 Intermediate Representation

A PLC program can consist of several program organization units (POUs), which provide an interface definition of the input, local, and output variables, and a body containing the actual instructions that operate on this interface. The IEC 61131 standard [8] distinguishes between three types of POUs, namely functions, function blocks, and programs. A program represents the main entry, whereas function blocks and functions represent stateful and stateless procedures, respectively. At cycle entry, new input values are read from the environment and written to the input variables. During the execution of the cycle, the program operates on a copy of these input variables and internal state variables. The state variables also comprise output variables written to the PLC's output at the cycle exit. While new values are assigned to input variables in each cycle, the internal state variables retain their values. During the parsing and compiling of the input program, function blocks are lowered to *regular* procedures operating on references of their variables. As a result, parameterized calls to function blocks are modeled as parameterless calls preceded and succeeded by a sequence of input and output assignments in the respective caller, which do not modify the state explicitly but rather transfer the flow of control between procedures. For this purpose, we have chosen a goto-based intermediate representation (IR) to represent a subset of the ST language [8] in form of a so-called control-flow graph (CFG) [2]. We model the PLC program as a pair $P = (G, \mathcal{G})$, where $G \in \mathcal{G}$ is the CFG of the program POU, and $\mathcal{G}$ is a set of CFGs representing nested function blocks occurring in the program. The instructions supported by this IR are defined over variables $x \in \mathbf{X}$, Boolean and arithmetic expressions e as usual

$$I ::= \mathbf{assign}(x, e) \mid \mathbf{ite}(e, \mathbf{goto}\ b_{\ell_1}, \mathbf{goto}\ b_{\ell_2}) \mid \mathbf{call}\ G' \mid \mathbf{return} \mid \mathbf{cycle}\ .$$

Unlike in typical goto-based IRs, we introduced a **cycle** instruction, explicitly denoting the end of the execution cycle. Given the terminology, we will dive into the baseline symbolic execution framework used for generating the test cases which is reused during the application of SSE.

3.2   Bounded Symbolic Execution

Our implementation of the Bounded Symbolic Execution (BSE) for TSA is composed of three components: an execution context, an executor, and an exploration strategy. An execution context $q = (c, \ell, f, \rho, \sigma, \pi)$ consists of a cycle c, a label ℓ referring to a vertex b_ℓ of a CFG G, a frame stack f, a concrete store ρ, which associates variables with concrete values, a symbolic store σ, which associates variables with symbolic values, and a path constraint π. The frame stack f holds triples $(G_{callee}, scope, \ell_{caller})$, where G_{callee} denotes the CFG of the callee, $scope$ is the scope in which the call occurred, and ℓ_{caller} denotes the intra-procedural label of the caller at which the execution should resume after returning from the callee. The BSE algorithm is given in Algorithm 1 and explained in the following. It is also commonly known as compositional SE in literature [3] augmented with parameterizable local and global termination criterias.

Exploration Strategy.   We decided for a cycle-based, depth-first exploration strategy similar to [4] with parameterizable timeout, coverage, and cycle bounds. As the cyclic execution of PLC programs significantly increases the computation time of symbolic execution, we adjusted the termination criteria in line 2 to consider a configurable cycle exploration bound. The priority queue $\mathcal{Q}$ is sorted heuristically by prioritizing execution contexts with a lower cycle count, resulting in the exploration of all feasible execution paths through one execution cycle before continuing with the next cycle. Furthermore, candidate execution contexts with a deeper path length and a concretely executable store are prioritized over execution contexts with a shallower path length. This enables the depth-first exploration to simulate a breadth-first exploration through one cycle and generates concise test cases with no unnecessary executed cycles. When encountering the end of the cycle during execution (cf. line 25), the cycle counter is increased and new concrete input valuations and fresh symbolic variables are derived.

Assignments, Branches and Calls.   The semantic effects of the instructions on the respective stores are captured via an evaluation function eval. For an assignment **assign**(x, e), the concrete and symbolic store are updated via $\rho \leftarrow \rho[x \mapsto \mathrm{eval}_\rho(e)]$ and $\sigma[x \mapsto \mathrm{eval}_\sigma(e)]$, respectively, as illustrated in line 10. The bracket notation [] denotes the usual replacement for the specified variable in the store. Whenever an **ite**$(e, \mathbf{goto}\,\ell_1, \mathbf{goto}\,\ell_2)$ instruction is encountered, the path constraint is updated symbolically depending on the result of the branch expressions concrete evaluation (cf. line 12). In case the expression evaluates to true, execution is continued in the positive branch and a test case is derived if this label is yet uncovered. We also check if the other path is feasible under the current path constraint and fork the execution context with the concrete valuation of the model (cf. lines 15–19). As mentioned in the beginning of Sect. 3.1, call and return effects are lowered to input and output assignments during compilation. Therefore, the **call** and **return** instruction modify the frame stack and update the control-flow accordingly.

Algorithm 1: Bounded Symbolic Execution

Input   : Program $P = (G, \mathcal{G})$, CFG $G = (\mathbf{X}, \mathbf{X}_{in}, (B, E), b_{\ell_e}, b_{\ell_x})$
Output   : Test Suite T

1   $\mathcal{Q} \leftarrow \{(0, \ell_e, \emptyset, \rho_{\ell_e}, \sigma_{\ell_e}, true)\}$; $\mathcal{M} \leftarrow \emptyset$
2   **while** $(\mathcal{Q} \neq \emptyset \vee \mathcal{M} \neq \emptyset) \wedge \neg\texttt{terminationCriteriaMet}$ **do**
3   **if** $\mathcal{Q} = \emptyset$ **then** $\mathcal{Q}$.push(merge($\mathcal{M}$))
4     $q \leftarrow (c, \ell, f, \rho, \sigma, \pi) \leftarrow \mathcal{Q}$.pop()
5   **if** reachedMergePoint(q) **then**
6       $\mathcal{M}$.push(q)
7   **else**
8   **switch** instructionAt(ℓ) **do**
9   **case** assign(x, e) **do**
10          $\mathcal{Q}$.push($(c, \ell+1, f, \rho[x \mapsto \texttt{eval}_\rho(e)], \sigma[x \mapsto \texttt{eval}_\sigma(e)], \pi)$)
11   **case** ite(e, **goto** ℓ_1, **goto** ℓ_2) **do**
12   **if** $\texttt{eval}_\rho(e)$ **then**
13            $q_1 \leftarrow (c, \ell_1, f, \rho_1, \sigma_1, \pi \wedge \texttt{eval}_\sigma(e))$; $\mathcal{Q}$.push(q_1)
14   **if** $\neg$covered(ℓ_1) **then** T.deriveTestCase(q_1)
15   **if** tryFork($\pi \wedge \texttt{eval}_\sigma(\neg e)$) **then**
16              $\rho_2 \leftarrow \texttt{model}(\pi \wedge \texttt{eval}_\sigma(\neg e))$
17              $q_2 \leftarrow (c, \ell_2, f, \rho_2, \sigma, \pi \wedge \texttt{eval}_\sigma(\neg e))$; $\mathcal{Q}$.push(q_2)
18   **if** $\neg$covered(ℓ_2) **then** T.deriveTestCase(q_2)
19   **end**
20   **else**   `// analogous, omitted for brevity`
21   **case** call G' **do**
22   f.push(G', getScope(G), ℓ_{G_r}); $\mathcal{Q}$.push($(c, \ell_{G'_e}, f, \rho, \sigma, \pi)$)
23   **case** return **do**
24          $(\_, \_, \ell_{G_r}) \leftarrow f$.pop(); $\mathcal{Q}$.push($(c, \ell_{G_r}, f, \rho, \sigma, \pi)$)
25   **case** cycle **do**
26          $\mathcal{Q}$.push($(c+1, \ell_e, f, \rho[x \in \mathbf{X}_{in} \mid x \mapsto \texttt{random}()]$,
                               $\sigma[x \in \mathbf{X}_{in} \mid x \mapsto x_{fresh}], \pi)$)
27   **end**
28   **end**
29 **end**
30 **return** T

Merge Strategy. Execution contexts are merged at all possible points where the control-flow joins with respect to realizable paths as opposed to merging at the cycle end as in [4]. During execution, we check whether the current context reached an interprocedural realizable merge point (cf. line 5) and add it to the merge queue $\mathcal{M}$ for further processing.

Unreachable Branches. The detection of unreachable branches is an essential task to avoid the encoding of infeasible paths when applying symbolic execution. As our static analysis (SA) is currently not capable of abstract interpretation, we leveraged the algorithms from CRAB[1] to build a value set analysis calculating the

---

[1] https://github.com/seahorn/crab.

possible values for each variable at each label of our CFGs. Using this information, we can statically deduce whether a branch is reachable or not. While being a powerful tool it is apparent that the SA of CRAB is not tailored to the domain of PLC software. To express our IR in a form such that CRAB is able to analyze it, it passes several code transformation pipelines including basic block encoding, three-address code, call-transformation and static single assignment which severely bloats up the CFG representation. In order to get precise information the expensive boxes domain was chosen [7]. The boxes domain is sensitive to the number of "splits" on each variable which come, among other things, from joins and Boolean operations. Unfortunately, the benchmarks in Sect. 4 "split" a lot due to the cyclic dependency between variables and the state-machine like behavior. Therefore, to still be able to reuse at least some information from the SA, we decided for a trade-off between precision and run time by tuning the behavior of the boxes domain to convexify after a certain amount of disjunctions resulting in imprecise but still usable results.

3.3 Shadow Symbolic Execution

Intuitively, two things are needed for TSA after a reconfiguration: (1) the test cases must reach potentially affected areas along different, relevant paths (specific chains of data- and control-dependencies), and (2) test cases must account for the state of the PLC software and the effects of the reconfigurations, i.e., be difference-revealing. An interesting research question in this context is whether the concept of four-way forking stemming from the SSE [10] algorithm is applicable to the PLC domain using the change(old, new) macros (cf. Sect. 1) to apply TSA for reconfigurable PLC software. In general, it can be intractable, because outputs are potentially difference-revealing after k cycles (depending on the internal state) and hence the analysis runs out of memory before the difference is reached. In general, deriving difference-revealing test cases in the style of SSE [10] is a two-step application of SE algorithms (cf. Fig. 3) and is presented in detail in Algorithm 2. In line 1 of Algorithm 2 the test suite of the version before the reconfiguration is reused and executed on the change-annotated PLC program to determine which test cases "touch" the change. Prior to execution, in case the interface has changed due to the

---

Algorithm 2: Test Suite Augmentation using SSE [10]

> **Input**   : Program $P = (G, \mathcal{G})$, CFG $G = (\mathbf{X}, \mathbf{X}_{in}, (B, E), b_{\ell_e}, b_{\ell_x})$, Test Suite
> $\mathcal{T}$
>
> **Output** : Difference revealing test cases $T_{difference\text{-}revealing}$

1 $T_{change\text{-}traversing} \leftarrow$ collectChangeTraversingTestCases$(G, \mathcal{T})$
2 **foreach** $t \in T_{change\text{-}traversing}$ **do**   // Phase 1 – SSE
3 $\quad \{(q_0, t'_0), \ldots, (q_m, t'_m)\} := \mathcal{Q}_{divergent}.$push$($findDivergentContexts$(t))$
4 **end**
5 **foreach** $(q, t') \in \mathcal{Q}_{divergent}$ **do**   // Phase 2 – BSE
6 $\quad T_{divergent}.$push$($performBoundedExecution$(q, t'))$
7 **end**
8 $T_{difference\text{-}revealing} \leftarrow$ checkForOutputDifferences$(T_{divergent})$

reconfiguration, the test case does not contain valuations for all variables. Therefore, we augment the test case with additional valuations using the 0-default initialization for *BOOL* and *INT* as defined in IEC61131-3, *false* and 0, respectively. Each executed test case is further augmented with additional information such as the execution history and state valuations reaching the end of the cycles of the old program version. As a test case can "touch" multiple change-annotated labels, we consider only the test cases that cover as much information as possible with regards to the respective change-annotated label. This reduces the amount of test cases needed for consideration in the first phase without losing expressiveness, as test cases spanning along multiple cycles with the same prefix are prioritized. When functionality is added depending on newly introduced input variables, the prior test suite is unable to cover these labels, hence we keep track of labels that were change-annotated but not "touched" by any test case.

Finding Divergent Contexts. Before continuing with the explanation of Algorithm 2, we present how divergent contexts are found during symbolic execution. Algorithm 3 uses the concept of four-way forking to determine whether the execution of a test case leads to potential divergent behavior or not. It is driven by the concrete input valuations of the corresponding test case (cf. line 1) and the augmented BSE is concolically executed on a per cycle basis using a single execution context, hence no merging. In general, the algorithm is similar to the one presented in Algorithm 1. We adapted the handling of branches to support the four-way forking and introduced additional data structures for storing the shadow expressions in the context, here hidden behind the concrete and symbolic store. As change annotations may occur in any instruction (or expression) we use the notion of symbolic change shadows and check whether such a change shadow influences the behavior of the current execution path. In case a branch is encountered during the concolic execution of the test case, we recursively check if the expression contains a symbolic change *shadow* (cf. line 7). If the current branch expression contains no shadow expression, we continue the execution as illustrated in Algorithm 1 in the lines 12–20. In case the branch expression contains a shadow expression, it might lead to divergent behavior. In order to check whether the current test case takes different paths in the old and the new version of the code, we first evaluate it under the concrete store of the divergent context resolving all shadow expressions (cf. line 8). If the valuations of the expression in the old and the new context do not coincide, the test case exposes truly divergent behavior which might trigger difference-revealing outputs. At this point, the execution stops and the divergent context is added to the queue to be explored in the second phase. If the valuations are equal, there still might be potential divergent behavior. First, we encode the expression using the old and the new symbolic valuations and then check in lines 14–17 whether potential divergent behavior exists. For this purpose, we explore subsequently whether there exist concrete valuations that may diverge and derive a test case as a witness. The forked divergent context is added to the divergent context queue and the execution continues with either following the true or the false branch trying to propagate the execution context to a deeper nested potentially divergent

---

Algorithm 3: findDivergentContexts – BSE with four-way forking [10]

Input : CFG $G = (\mathbf{X}, \mathbf{X}_{in}, (B, E), b_{\ell_e}, b_{\ell_x})$, Test Case t

Output : Divergent Contexts $\mathcal{Q}_{divergent}$

```
 1 foreach c_t ∈ t do
 2 │   q ← (c, ℓ, f, ρ_input^{c_t}, σ, π)
 3 │   while c = c_t do
 4 │   │   switch instructionAt(ℓ) do
 5 │   │   │               // other cases analogous to BSE, omitted for brevity
 6 │   │   │   case ite(e, goto ℓ_1, goto ℓ_2) do
 7 │   │   │   │   if containsShadowExpression(eval_σ(e)) then
 8 │   │   │   │   │   (v_old, v_new) ← eval_ρ^{shadow}(e)
 9 │   │   │   │   │   if v_old ≠ v_new then                    // divergent behavior
10 │   │   │   │   │   │   Q_divergent.push((q, t))
11 │   │   │   │   │   │   return Q_divergent
12 │   │   │   │   │   else                        // potential divergent behavior
13 │   │   │   │   │   │   (φ_old, φ_new) ← eval_σ^{shadow}(e)
14 │   │   │   │   │   │   if tryDivergentFork(π ∧ ¬φ_old ∧ φ_new) then
15 │   │   │   │   │   │   │   Q_divergent.push((q_forked, deriveTestCase(q_forked)))
16 │   │   │   │   │   │   end
17 │   │   │   │   │   │   if tryDivergentFork(π ∧ φ_old ∧ ¬φ_new) then
18 │   │   │   │   │   │   │   Q_divergent.push((q_forked, deriveTestCase(q_forked)))
19 │   │   │   │   │   │   end
20 │   │   │   │   │   │   if v_old then
21 │   │   │   │   │   │   │   q ← (c, ℓ_1, f, ρ, σ, π ∧ φ_old ∧ φ_new);
22 │   │   │   │   │   │   else
23 │   │   │   │   │   │   │   q ← (c, ℓ_2, f, ρ, σ, π ∧ ¬φ_old ∧ ¬φ_new);
24 │   │   │   │   │   │   end
25 │   │   │   │   end
26 │   │   │   else                        // analogous to BSE, omitted for brevity
27 │   │   end
28 │   end
29 end
30 end
31 return Q_divergent
```

---

context. On termination, i.e., either when a divergent context is found or when all the concrete input valuations for each cycle of this test case have been executed, the algorithm returns the set of divergent contexts and continues with the next test case.

Propagating Divergent Contexts. The second phase of Algorithm 2 performs a seeded BSE (cf. Algorithm 1) for each found divergent context in the first phase. The divergent context and test case passed as parameters in line 6 represent either a diverging concrete execution or were generated because of a potential, possible divergence at the four-way fork in the first phase. This phase runs until the termination criteria is met and tries to generate as many test cases as possible. These test cases cover paths originating from a divergence and hence may expose differences in the outputs between the old and the new version of the reconfigured PLC program. In line 8 of Algorithm 2 the derived divergent test cases are checked for output differences. The execution of modified instructions does not mean that they are necessarily difference-revealing because the subdomains do not need to be homogeneous with regards to the failure [20]. Hence to determine whether a test case exposes an externally observable difference, the outputs on the test case in the new version are compared to the outputs on the test case in the old version. If the outputs differ on a per cycle basis, the test case is added to the set of difference-revealing test cases and requires further examination by the developer.

4   Evaluation

The evaluation was conducted on an Intel(R) Core(TM) i5-6600K CPU @ 3.50 GHz desktop with 16 GB of RAM running openSUSE Leap 15.3. For SMT-solving, we utilized the high-performance automated theorem prover Z3 by Microsoft [13]. The benchmarks evaluated with ARCADE.PLC were also run with the same evaluation setup. The code of our contribution and the corresponding benchmarks are available for download at https://github.com/embedded-software-laboratory/TSA-FMICS22.

In the following, we first present the achieved performance improvements for the BSE as our TSA implementation heavily relies on it before presenting the results of the TSA algorithm on a few selected benchmarks.

PLCopen Safety Suite. The benchmark consists of a set of safety-related PLC programs provided by the PLCopen organization [15]. The results are listed in Table 1 and show for each evaluated function block the lines of code (LOC), the coverage values as well as the runtimes of the implementation of a merge-based test generation algorithm in ARCADE.PLC [4] in comparison to the results of our contribution. Because both tools use different IRs, the number of reachable branches is omitted. The timeout (TO) was set to 10 min. For the detection of unreachable branches, ARCADE.PLC uses a values-set analysis, however, we did not add the time to the results. Instead, we ran both programs with this additional pre-computed information to only focus on the performance of the DSE algorithms. The SA_{manual} refers to the use of CRAB and manual annotation for truly unreachable branches which were over-approximated due to the convexification of the disjunctions (cf. Sect. 3). As far as the function blocks are concerned, both approaches perform equally well. As all blocks follow the same general structure, the LOC can be seen as a reference for giving a rough estimate on what one would expect time wise from the analysis. A significant difference between both approaches is the amount of test cases generated. While ARCADE.PLC generates concise test cases for every branch, our contribution tries to avoid redundancies due to shorter test cases being included in longer test cases, hence generating less test cases overall. This is neither a benefit nor a disadvantage and could be obtained by a static postprocessing on the test suite generated by ARCADE.PLC. Do note that ARCADE.PLC does not dump any test cases in case it runs into a TO due to a technical limitation. The programs on the bottom half are bigger in the sense that they are composed of multiple function blocks from the top with additional logic and were analyzed without manual SA annotation. As more and more calling contexts are available it becomes apparent that delaying the merging until the end of the cycle performs way worse than merging on all realizable paths when the opportunity emerges. Most notably, the performance degenerates on blocks which make heavy use of timer and edge trigger function blocks because only specific paths can reach deeper behavior.

Table 1. Comparison of branch coverage and runtimes for the test generation of the PLCopen Safety library, ordered alphabetically.

Function Block / Program	LOC	ARCADE.PLC + SA			Contribution + SA$_{manual}$		
		cov. [%]	T [#]	time [s]	cov. [%]	T [#]	time [s]
Antivalent	136	100	61	0.74	100	23	0.37
EDM	229	100	134	5.22	100	62	3.49
Emergency_Stop	127	100	66	0.45	100	27	0.33
Enable_Switch	133	100	71	1.13	100	32	1.28
Equivalent	133	100	62	0.86	100	26	0.59
ESPE	127	100	66	0.42	100	27	0.31
Guard_Locking	148	100	80	1.01	100	37	0.87
Guard_Monitoring	174	100	82	1.45	100	34	1.12
Mode_Selector	239	100	70	5.20	100	30	1.08
Muting_Seq	262	97.5	-	TO	100	53	49.6
Out_Control	121	100	67	0.77	100	31	0.61
Safe_Stop	157	100	73	3.52	100	32	0.59
Safely_Limit_Speed	175	100	91	9.90	100	41	1.38
Safety_Request	191	100	88	1.29	100	40	1.01
Testable_Safety_Sensor	291	100	147	16.93	100	68	17.08
Two_Hand_Control_Type_II	126	100	83	0.85	100	38	0.73
Two_Hand_Control_Type_III	184	100	107	1.63	100	46	0.95
DiagnosticsConcept	537	65.49	-	TO	91.00	104	TO
Muting	1119	51.24	-	TO	80.23	196	TO
SafeMotion	1061	38.15	-	TO	73.71	156	TO
SafeMotionIO	811	53.50	-	TO	71.65	106	TO
TwoHandControl	608	58.79	-	TO	86.34	131	TO

Pick and Place Unit (PPU). The benchmark consists of a total of 15 scenarios for the PPU of an open-source bench-scale manufacturing system[2]. While it is

[2] https://www.mw.tum.de/ais/forschung/demonstratoren/ppu/.

limited in size and complexity, this trade-off between problem complexity and evaluation effort does not harm the expressiveness of the benchmark. In this evaluation, we focused on the first four scenarios and translated them from their PLCopen XML representation to ST using the VERIFAPS library[3]. The Scenario_0 consists of a stack, crane and a ramp of which the latter is only mechanical. The reconfiguration Scenario_{0 → 1} aims to increase the ramp's capacity. This reconfiguration does not affect the software as the ramp is a purely mechanical component. As a response to changing customer requirements, the reconfiguration Scenario_{0 → 2} enables the PPU to handle both plastic and metallic workpieces. For this purpose, an induction sensor is introduced which changes the output behavior of the stack component. The behavior of the crane is untouched. The third reconfiguration Scenario_{2 → 3} introduces the stamping functionality of metallic workpieces. This impacts the behavior of the crane as workpieces need to be stamped before being transported to the ramp. The results of the test suite generation using BSE without SA results are shown in Table 2. The PPU has more complex behavior in comparison to the PLCopen safety suite, which is also reflected in the required time/termination criteria for the test case generation. A comparison with ARCADE.PLC was omitted as it was not able to analyze the benchmarks.

Table 2. Results of the test suite generation using BSE for selected PPU scenarios.

PPU Scenario	LOC	cov. [%]	T [#]	time [s]	cycle [#]
Scenario_0	412	88.97	45	169.82	25
Scenario_1	412	88.97	45	170.12	25
Scenario_2	459	89.61	55	274.19	25
Scenario_3	768	91.67	102	1198.08	25

Table 3 shows the results of the TSA for the manually change-annotated reconfigured PLC programs.

Table 3. Results of the TSA using Algorithm 2 for selected reconfiguration scenarios of the PPU.

PPU Evolution	ℓ_{ca} [#]/ ℓ_u [#]	T_{ca} [#]	Phase 1		Phase 2		T_{diff} [#]
			Q_{div} [#]	t [s]	T_{div} [#]	t [s]	
Scenario_{0 → 1}	0/0	0	0	0	0	0	0
Scenario_{0 → 2}	12/1	45	2	1.77	52	54.99	23
Scenario_{2 → 3}	50/21	55	21	19.49	1269	3423.94	1269

---

[3] https://github.com/VerifAPS/verifaps-lib.

The first column of Table 3 denotes the analyzed reconfiguration scenario. The second column contrasts how many change-annotated labels ℓ_{ca} in the reconfigured program exists and how many of those change-annotated labels remain untouched ℓ_u by the test suite of the prior version. This ratio gives an estimate on how suited the previous test suite is to find divergences. The third column denotes the number of test cases T_{ca} in the previous test suite which exercise any number of change-annotated labels ℓ_{ca} in the change-annotated PLC program. One has to keep in mind that the generated test cases are succinct with regards to the required number of cycles to reach a specific branch (in case of branch coverage). Due to the cyclic nature of the PLC software, test cases which cover deeper nested branches, i.e., branches reachable after a certain amount of cycles, can share a partial prefix with test cases covering already some of the branches on these paths. This is a natural limitation of the SSE approach for cyclic programs resulting in an increased analysis time for phase 1 and phase 2. The fourth column denotes the number of derived divergent contexts and the time it took to complete phase 1 for each representative test case. The fifth column denotes the number of divergent test cases generated from propagating the divergent contextes during BSE using the corresponding triggering test cases as a seed for the concolic execution and the time it took to complete phase 2. The sixth column denotes the number of difference-revealing test cases found by checking the observable behavior of the old and the new version of the program on the divergent test cases.

5 Conclusion

The state of the art for TSA is dominated by DSE techniques [3]. We implemented a baseline BSE improving scalability issues prevalent in prior work [4] due to infrequent merging and inefficient storing of the execution contexts. On top of this baseline, we implemented the concept of four-way forking from SSE [10] and evaluated the feasibility of this technique on a manually instrumented *regression* benchmark. The number of untouched change-annotated labels in the benchmark of Table 3 show the limitation of the SSE approach when trying to analyze reconfigurations that introduce new functionality and modify the interfaces of the POUs. As SSE is driven by concrete inputs from an existing test suite, hitting a change is trivially necessary to exercise it. This also means that important divergences can be missed as it strongly depends on the quality of the initial inputs. There has been work that investigated a full exploration of the four-way fork, not only to a predefined bound, but the experiments have shown that it is intractable in general [14] – it does not scale well. Another downside of the SSE approach in the domain of PLC software lies in the search for additional divergent behaviors. Starting a BSE run from the divergence in the new version leads to the coverage of locations that would have been covered with a more succinct prefix. Due to the cyclic nature, the path prefix of the divergence prevents the coverage of the prior branches – however, it is undecidable in general whether this is redundant or not as it would require a procedure to check before the execution, whether that path is difference-revealing or not.

To conclude, SSE can be used to generate difference-revealing test cases that are suitable for augmentation of the test suite after a reconfiguration. However, it certainly requires further techniques to reduce the amount of generated difference-revealing test cases to benefit the developer during reconfiguration.

Outlook. In future work, we would like to improve our baseline BSE and evaluate more sophisticated merging strategies [16] or the incorporation of incremental solving [12]. While merging may prevent an exponential growth of symbolic execution contexts and can boost the efficiency [11], the reuse of summaries alleviates the analysis by not doing redundant work for paths through the program we have already seen during execution [12]. However, summarization and merging are conflicting techniques as checking whether a summary is applicable or not is based on concrete values, a piece of information we would lose through a merge. It remains unclear how to benefit the most from merging and summarization.

Acknowledgements. Funded by the Deutsche Forschungsgemeinschaft (DFG, German Research Foundation) under Germany's Excellence Strategy – EXC-2023 Internet of Production – 390621612.

References

1. Adiego, B.F., Darvas, D., Viñuela, E.B., Tournier, J.C., Suárez, V.M.G., Blech, J.O.: Modelling and formal verification of timing aspects in large plc programs. IFAC Proc. **47**(3), 3333–3339 (2014). https://doi.org/10.3182/20140824-6-ZA-1003.01279. 19th IFAC World Congress
2. Allen, F.E.: Control flow analysis. In: Northcote, R.S. (ed.) Proceedings of a Symposium on Compiler Optimization, Urbana-Champaign, Illinois, USA, 27–28 July 1970, pp. 1–19. ACM (1970). https://doi.org/10.1145/800028.808479
3. Baldoni, R., Coppa, E., D'Elia, D.C., Demetrescu, C., Finocchi, I.: A survey of symbolic execution techniques. ACM Comput. Surv. **51**(3), 50:1-50:39 (2018). https://doi.org/10.1145/3182657
4. Bohlender, D., Simon, H., Friedrich, N., Kowalewski, S., Hauck-Stattelmann, S.: Concolic test generation for PLC programs using coverage metrics. In: Cassandras, C.G., Giua, A., Li, Z. (eds.) 13th International Workshop on Discrete Event Systems, WODES 2016, Xi'an, China, 30 May – 1 June 2016, pp. 432–437. IEEE (2016). https://doi.org/10.1109/WODES.2016.7497884
5. Godefroid, P.: Compositional dynamic test generation. In: Hofmann, M., Felleisen, M. (eds.) Proceedings of the 34th ACM SIGPLAN-SIGACT Symposium on Principles of Programming Languages, POPL 2007, Nice, France, 17–19 January 2007, pp. 47–54. ACM (2007). https://doi.org/10.1145/1190216.1190226
6. Grochowski, M., et al.: Formale methoden für rekonfigurierbare cyber-physische systeme in der produktion. at-Automatisierungstechnik **68**(1), 3–14 (2020). https://doi.org/10.1515/auto-2019-0115
7. Gurfinkel, A., Chaki, S.: BOXES: a symbolic abstract domain of boxes. In: Cousot, R., Martel, M. (eds.) SAS 2010. LNCS, vol. 6337, pp. 287–303. Springer, Heidelberg (2010). https://doi.org/10.1007/978-3-642-15769-1_18

8. International Electrotechnical Commission: IEC 61131-3:2013 Programmable controllers - Part 3: Programming languages. IEC International Standard IEC 61131-3:2013 (2013). https://webstore.iec.ch/publication/4552
9. Jeschke, S., Brecher, C., Song, H., Rawat, D.B. (eds.): Industrial Internet of Things. SSWT, Springer, Cham (2017). https://doi.org/10.1007/978-3-319-42559-7
10. Kuchta, T., Palikareva, H., Cadar, C.: Shadow symbolic execution for testing software patches. ACM Trans. Softw. Eng. Methodol. **27**(3), 10:1-10:32 (2018). https://doi.org/10.1145/3208952
11. Kuznetsov, V., Kinder, J., Bucur, S., Candea, G.: Efficient state merging in symbolic execution. In: Proceedings of the 33rd ACM SIGPLAN Conference on Programming Language Design and Implementation, PLDI 2012, pp. 193–204. Association for Computing Machinery, New York (2012). https://doi.org/10.1145/2254064.2254088
12. Lin, Y., Miller, T., Søndergaard, H.: Compositional symbolic execution: Incremental solving revisited. In: Potanin, A., Murphy, G.C., Reeves, S., Dietrich, J. (eds.) 23rd Asia-Pacific Software Engineering Conference, APSEC 2016, Hamilton, New Zealand, 6–9 December 2016, pp. 273–280. IEEE Computer Society (2016). https://doi.org/10.1109/APSEC.2016.046
13. de Moura, L., Bjørner, N.: Z3: an efficient SMT solver. In: Ramakrishnan, C.R., Rehof, J. (eds.) TACAS 2008. LNCS, vol. 4963, pp. 337–340. Springer, Heidelberg (2008). https://doi.org/10.1007/978-3-540-78800-3_24
14. Noller, Y., Nguyen, H.L., Tang, M., Kehrer, T., Grunske, L.: Complete shadow symbolic execution with java pathfinder. ACM SIGSOFT Softw. Eng. Notes **44**(4), 15–16 (2019). https://doi.org/10.1145/3364452.33644558
15. PLCopen - Technical Committee 5: Safety software, technical specification, part 1: Concepts and function blocks. Technical report, PLCopen (2020). https://plcopen.org/system/files/downloads/plcopen_safety_part_1_version_2.01.pdf
16. Sen, K., Necula, G., Gong, L., Choi, W.: MultiSE: multi-path symbolic execution using value summaries. In: Proceedings of the 2015 10th Joint Meeting on Foundations of Software Engineering, ESEC/FSE 2015, pp. 842–853. Association for Computing Machinery, New York (2015). https://doi.org/10.1145/2786805.2786830
17. Ulewicz, S., Vogel-Heuser, B.: Industrially applicable system regression test prioritization in production automation. IEEE Trans Autom. Sci. Eng. **15**(4), 1839–1851 (2018). https://doi.org/10.1109/TASE.2018.2810280
18. Weigl, A., Ulbrich, M., Lentzsch, D.: Modular regression verification for reactive systems. In: Margaria, T., Steffen, B. (eds.) ISoLA 2020, Part II. LNCS, vol. 12477, pp. 25–43. Springer, Cham (2020). https://doi.org/10.1007/978-3-030-61470-6_3
19. Weyrich, M., Zeller, A.: Testen von industrie-4.0-systemen - wie vernetzte systeme und industrie 4.0 unser verständnis von systemtest und qualitätssicherung ändern (2016). https://www.ias.uni-stuttgart.de/dokumente/vortraege/2016-01-26_Industrie40_Duesseldorf_v12final.pdf
20. Weyuker, E.J., Jeng, B.: Analyzing partition testing strategies. IEEE Trans. Softw. Eng. **17**(7), 703–711 (1991). https://doi.org/10.1109/32.83906
21. Xu, Z., Kim, Y., Kim, M., Cohen, M.B., Rothermel, G.: Directed test suite augmentation: an empirical investigation. Softw. Test. Verif. Reliab. **25**(2), 77–114 (2015). https://doi.org/10.1002/stvr.1562
22. Yang, G., Person, S., Rungta, N., Khurshid, S.: Directed incremental symbolic execution. ACM Trans. Softw. Eng. Methodol. **24**(1), 3:1-3:42 (2014). https://doi.org/10.1145/2629536

23. Yoo, S., Harman, M.: Regression testing minimization, selection and prioritization: a survey. Softw. Test. Verif. Reliab. **22**(2), 67–120 (2012). https://doi.org/10.1002/stv.430
24. Zeller, A., Jazdi, N., Weyrich, M.: Functional verification of distributed automation systems. Int. J. Adv. Manufact. Technol. **105**(9), 3991–4004 (2019). https://doi.org/10.1007/s00170-019-03791-2

Monitoring of Spatio-Temporal Properties with Nonlinear SAT Solvers

André de Matos Pedro[1]([✉]) [iD], Tomás Silva[1,2], Tiago Sequeira[1],
João Lourenço[2], João Costa Seco[2], and Carla Ferreira[2]

[1] VORTEX-CoLab, Vila Nova de Gaia, Portugal
andre.pedro@vortex-colab.com
[2] NOVA-LINCS, NOVA University Lisbon, Lisbon, Portugal

Abstract. The automotive industry is increasingly dependent on computing systems with variable levels of critical requirements. The verification and validation methods for these systems are now leveraging complex AI methods, for which the decision algorithms introduce non-determinism, especially in autonomous driving. This paper presents a runtime verification technique agnostic to the target system, which focuses on monitoring spatio-temporal properties that abstract the evolution of objects' behavior in their spatial and temporal flow. First, a formalization of three known traffic rules (from the Vienna convention on road traffic) is presented, where a spatio-temporal logic fragment is used. Then, these logical expressions are translated to a monitoring model written in the first-order logic, where they will be processed by a non-linear satisfiability solver. Finally, the translation allows the solver to check the validity of the encoded properties according to an instance of a specific traffic scenario (a trace). The results obtained from our tool that automatically generates a monitor from a formula show that our approach is feasible for online monitoring in a real-world environment.

1 Introduction

Autonomous Driving System (ADS) is a field of study that belongs to the Cyber-Physical Systems (CPSs) domain, partially seen as safety-critical systems due to the high impact that a hazard can have [27]. Correctness and validation of an ADS are crucial, as any error or malfunction of the system may lead to loss of life, environmental damage, or financial impact on trust and reputation [22]. Challenges on the verification and validation methodologies for these systems are being introduced by sub-symbolic AI methods, for which the decision algorithms are known to introduce non-determinism [2,6,7,15].

Runtime Verification (RV) is a lightweight verification method commonly used in safety-critical systems [16,19,30] performed during runtime, which offers the possibility to act whenever a fault is observed. In RV, a formal requirement is used to automatically generate a monitor that checks if the target system is compliant with it. In this paper, we are interested in formally representing how ADSs interact with the environment, hence, we use Linear Temporal Logic

J. F. Groote and M. Huisman (Eds.): FMICS 2022, LNCS 13487, pp. 155–171, 2022.
https://doi.org/10.1007/978-3-031-15008-1_11

(LTL), a tool widely used in RV [16], to describe the evolution over time, and Modal Metric Spaces (MS), which allows us to formally reason about the surrounding space of the system [18]. By combining these two logical frameworks, we enable a full description of the ADS in space at all time instants.

The traffic safety rules that driving systems, and more specifically ADS, are subjected to, usually specify temporal and spatial features. The spatio-temporal languages (e.g., [12,14,20]) provide the adequate formalization and fulfillment of the ADS requirements [24], which are specified over time and space. In the present work, we consider the safety requirements of an ADS to be expressed by sets of spatial constraints along a discrete linear time frame.

This paper proposes an RV approach that can deal with different autonomous systems and focus on the monitoring of their spatio-temporal properties. These properties are safety requirements that represent road safety constraints over objects that are specified by their distances or topological relations. From a macro perspective, Fig. 1 schematizes our architecture, where the relations between simulator, monitor and vehicle can be seen. The simulator implements the scenario described using ASAM standard [11] and the Ego vehicle implements the set of requirements. Then the Monitor Block that runs a solver checks whether the requirement is met and draws a verdict. Step 1 starts with the formalization of the requirements. From a micro perspective, the verification of a *LTL combined with a fragment of MS* (LTL × MS) [12] formula consists on the construction of a monitoring model and a decision procedure. Given a trace (step 4) that comes from the ADS, the decision procedure inside the Monitor Block answers whether a trace satisfies the monitoring model (step 5) and draws a verdict (step 6). As shown in Fig. 1, the scenario (step 3) and the corresponding formalized traffic rules (step 2) are given as input to the Translation and Model Construction, where the translation to a set of *first order language of the real numbers* (FOL$_\mathbb{R}$) constraints is done. This engine creates a monitoring model in FOL$_\mathbb{R}$, which is interpreted by the non-linear satisfiability solver that is provided by the SMT solver Z3 [8] and runs inside the Monitor Block. Parallel to the monitoring model, a trace at runtime feeds the Monitor Block, and a Trace Encoder is provided to encode it to FOL$_\mathbb{R}$. So, the monitor block can produce a verdict based on a trace that came from the ADS, a scenario, and a requirement.

Problem Statement. Consider monitoring the behaviour of an ADS, while driving at an urban intersection, that must comply with road safety rules defined by the international Vienna convention [24]. The present work focuses on presenting a logic fragment, expressive enough to describe a specific set of road traffic rules. Thanks to this fragment we were able to build an inline monitor that verifies if these legal requirements [24] are being met. In simple terms the road safety requirement '*the car shall stop when it reaches a stop sign and then carries on when the path is clear*' is a spatio-temporal property. When encoded as a FOL$_\mathbb{R}$ formula, nonlinear SAT solvers are able to verify its satisfiability.

Paper Contributions. First, we present a formalization of three traffic rules, taken from the Vienna convention [24] using LTL × MS, and applied to the

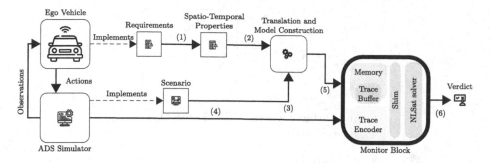

Fig. 1. Ego vehicle spatio-temporal monitoring architecture.

context of these three traffic rules, the construction of the traffic T-shaped junction scenario. Second, we encoded these rules written in LTL × MS and our scenario in FOL$_\mathbb{R}$, the language interpretable by the SMT solver Z3 [8]. Then, to encapsulate the encoding, our tool automatically generates runtime monitor blocks that can verify whether the requirements check in the simulated environment. Finally, we show evidence of the feasibility and scalability of online monitoring.

Paper Structure. Section 2 introduces some important concepts and definitions of the LTL × MS language. Section 3 presents the formalization of three road traffic rules in terms of LTL × MS and a T-shaped traffic junction, where the aforementioned rules are applicable. Moreover, the scenario is abstracted to FOL$_\mathbb{R}$ and the trace is introduced as well as its encoding to FOL$_\mathbb{R}$. Section 4 introduces the monitor generation approach, while Sect. 5 shows the feasibility of the monitor approach. Finally, Sects. 6 and 7 present the related work and draw conclusions and directions for future work, respectively.

2 Preliminaries

The combination of temporal logic with spatial logic has been exhaustively explored [1,12,13,23]. LTL is a propositional discrete linear temporal logic, adequate for model checking of reactive systems and RV [19]. The time flow in LTL is a set of points that are strictly ordered by the precedence relation < [10], and is restricted to the usage of propositions and how they are sequenced. Furthermore, LTL has the temporal operators 'Until', $\alpha \mathbf{U} \omega$—α has to hold until ω becomes true—and 'Since', $\alpha \mathbf{S} \omega$—α has been true since ω was true.

Regarding the spatial logic, Kuts et al. [18] introduced MS, which includes the bounded distance operators: $\exists^{=a}$, $\exists^{<a}$, $\exists^{>a}$, and $\exists^{\leq b}_{>a}$. As an example, Fig. 2 gives a visual description of $\exists^{\leq a} p_1$ and $\exists^{\leq a} (p_1 \sqcap p_2)$ in a metric space, where p_1, p_2 are spatial variables, expanded by a units. Wolter and Zakharyaschev [33] presented a restricted version named MS$^{\leq,<}$ that just considers the operators $\exists^{\leq,<}$. Marco et al. [1, p. 545] showed that the satisfiability and the computational complexity of the combination of LTL with MS$^{\leq}$ is decidable. However, despite the expressiveness of LTL × MS, decision procedures for spatio-temporal

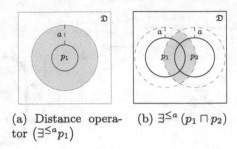

(a) Distance opera- (b) $\exists^{\leq a}\,(p_1 \sqcap p_2)$
tor $(\exists^{\leq a} p_1)$

Fig. 2. Examples of distance term operators on a metric space $\mathfrak{D}$.

languages are scarce [14]. As far as we know, in this paper we introduce the first decision procedure for LTL $\times$ MS.

Definition 1 (LTL $\times$ MS - Syntax). *The terms and formulas are inductively defined by*

$$\varrho :: = p \mid \overline{\varrho} \mid \varrho_1 \sqcap \varrho_2 \mid \varrho_1 \sqcup \varrho_2 \mid \exists^{\leq a} \varrho \mid \varrho_1 \mathfrak{U} \varrho_2 \qquad \text{(terms)}$$
$$\varphi :: = \varrho_1 \sqsubseteq \varrho_2 \mid \neg\varphi \mid \varphi_1 \wedge \varphi_2 \mid \varphi_1 \vee \varphi_2 \mid \varphi_1 \, \mathcal{U} \, \varphi_2 \mid \varphi_1 \, \mathcal{S} \, \varphi_2, \quad \text{(formulas)}$$

where $p \in \mathfrak{P}$ is a spatial variable (or proposition), a is a rational number (distance), and $\mathfrak{P}$ a nonempty set of variables. $\mathfrak{U}$ and $\mathcal{U}$ stand for the binary operator 'Until' for terms and formulas, respectively. While $\mathcal{S}$ is the 'Since' operator. Moreover, ρ is denoted as an instance of ϱ and ϕ as an instance of φ.

Definition 2 (LTL $\times$ MS - Terms Semantics). *A metric temporal model is a pair of the form $\mathfrak{M} = (\mathfrak{D}, \mathfrak{N})$ [1], where $\mathfrak{D} = (\Delta, d)$ is a metric space, Δ represents a nonempty set of points that reproduce the entire universe, d is a function of the form $\Delta \times \Delta$ describing the distance between every two points in Δ, satisfying the axioms identity of indiscernibles, symmetry and triangle inequality [17]. The valuation $\mathfrak{N}$ is a map associating each spatial variable p and time instant n to a set $\mathfrak{N}(p, n) \subseteq \Delta$. The valuation can be inductively extended to arbitrary LTL $\times$ MS terms such as*

$$\mathfrak{N}(\overline{\varrho}, n) \quad = \Delta - \mathfrak{N}(\varrho, n),$$
$$\mathfrak{N}(\varrho_1 \sqcap \varrho_2, n) \;= \mathfrak{N}(\varrho_1, n) \cap \mathfrak{N}(\varrho_2, n),$$
$$\mathfrak{N}(\exists^{\leq a} \varrho, n) \quad = \{x \in \Delta \mid \text{there exists a } y \in \mathfrak{N}(\varrho, n) \text{ such that } d(x,y) \leq a\},$$

$$\mathfrak{N}(\varrho_1 \mathfrak{U} \varrho_2, n) \;= \bigcup_{m > n} \left(\mathfrak{N}(\varrho_2, m) \cap \bigcap_{k \in \,]n, m[} \mathfrak{N}(\varrho_1, k) \right)$$

The shorthands 'Eventually' $\diamondsuit$, 'Always' $\boxdot$, and 'Next' $\odot$ are defined using $\mathfrak{U}$, $\diamondsuit \varrho \equiv \top \mathfrak{U} \varrho$, $\boxdot \varrho \equiv \overline{\diamondsuit \overline{\varrho}}$, and $\odot \varrho \equiv \bot \mathfrak{U} \varrho$, where $\top$ and $\bot$ denote the universe and the empty set. $\odot$ is the next operator and its semantics is $\mathfrak{N}(\odot, n) = \mathfrak{N}(\varrho, n+1)$, while $\diamondsuit$ stands for the eventually operator with $\mathfrak{N}(\diamondsuit, n) = \bigcup_{m > n} \mathfrak{N}(\varrho, m)$, and $\boxdot$ means the always operator where $\mathfrak{N}(\boxdot, n) = \bigcap_{m > n} \mathfrak{N}(\varrho, m)$.

Definition 3 (LTL × MS - Formulas Semantics [12]). *An LTL × MS formula φ is said satisfiable if there exists a model $\mathfrak{M}$ such that $(\mathfrak{M}, n) \models \varphi$ for some time point $n \in \mathbb{N}$. $\mathfrak{M}$ is equipped with the following properties*

$$(\mathfrak{M}, n) \models \varrho_1 \sqsubseteq \varrho_2 \quad \textit{iff} \quad \mathfrak{N}(\varrho_1, n) \subseteq \mathfrak{N}(\varrho_2, n),$$

$$(\mathfrak{M}, n) \models \neg\varphi \quad \textit{iff} \quad (\mathfrak{M}, n) \not\models \varphi,$$

$$(\mathfrak{M}, n) \models \varphi_1 \wedge \varphi_2 \quad \textit{iff} \quad (\mathfrak{M}, n) \models \varphi_1 \quad \text{and} \quad (\mathfrak{M}, n) \models \varphi_2,$$

$$(\mathfrak{M}, n) \models \varphi_1 \, \mathcal{U} \, \varphi_2 \quad \textit{iff} \quad \text{there is a } m > n \text{ such that } (\mathfrak{M}, m) \models \varphi_2 \text{ and}$$
$$(\mathfrak{M}, k) \models \varphi_1 \text{ for all } k \in (n, m),$$

$$(\mathfrak{M}, n) \models \varphi_1 \, \mathcal{S} \, \varphi_2 \quad \textit{iff} \quad \text{there is a } m < n \text{ such that } (\mathfrak{M}, m) \models \varphi_2 \textit{ and}$$
$$(\mathfrak{M}, k) \models \varphi_1 \text{ for all } k \in (n, m).$$

Regarding temporal modalities, $\Diamond$ stands for 'Eventually', $\Box$ for 'Always' and $\bigcirc$ for 'Next', which can be defined using $\mathcal{U}$: $\Diamond\varphi \equiv \top \mathcal{U} \varphi$, $\Box\varphi \equiv \neg\Diamond\neg\varphi$ and $\bigcirc\varphi \equiv \bot \mathcal{U} \varphi$. When talking about past, the connectors are defined in an analogous way using $\mathcal{S}$. Thus, $\Diamondblack\varphi \equiv \top \mathcal{S} \varphi$ for 'Once', $\boxminus\varphi \equiv \neg\Diamondblack\neg\varphi$ for 'Historically' and $\ominus\varphi \equiv \bot \mathcal{S} \varphi$ for 'Yesterday'. Note that the traditional universal modalities $\forall$ and $\exists$ are expressible in our language. $\forall\varrho$ can be seen as an abbreviation for $\top \sqsubseteq \varrho$ and $\exists\varrho$ for $\neg(\varrho \sqsubseteq \bot)$. Along our work we will use the symbol := to denote 'is defined'. Also, to construct complex formulas we introduce four spatial patterns over terms ρ_1, ρ_2, where the atomic formula $\varrho_1 = \varrho_2$ stands for $(\varrho_1 \sqsubseteq \varrho_2) \wedge (\varrho_2 \sqsubseteq \varrho_1)$, as follows:

$$\text{DC}(\rho_1, \rho_2) \quad := \quad \rho_1 \sqcap \rho_2 = \bot, \text{ (disconnected)}$$

$$\text{EQ}(\rho_1, \rho_2) \quad := \quad (\rho_1 \sqsubseteq \rho_2) \wedge (\rho_2 \sqsubseteq \rho_1), \text{ (equally connected)}$$

$$\text{O}(\rho_1, \rho_2) \quad := \quad \neg(\text{DC}(\rho_1, \rho_2)) \wedge \neg(\rho_1 \sqsubseteq \rho_2) \wedge \neg(\rho_2 \sqsubseteq \rho_1), \text{ (overlapped)}$$

$$\text{I}(\rho_1, \rho_2) \quad := \quad (\rho_1 \sqsubseteq \rho_2) \wedge \neg(\rho_2 \sqsubseteq \rho_1). \text{ (included)}$$

Encoding Language FOL$_\mathbb{R}$

The FOL$_\mathbb{R}$ denotes the first-order logic defined over the structure $(\mathbb{R}, <, +, \times, 1, 0)$ that consists of the set of all well-formed sentences of first-order logic that involve quantifiers and logical combinations of polynomial expressions over real variables. The first-order language FOL$_\mathbb{R}$ forms the set $\mathbb{L}$, and $\mathbb{P}$ means the set of real variables in FOL$_\mathbb{R}$.

3   Running Example

The concrete traffic scenario studied throughout this work is depicted in Fig. 3a. It consists of a T-shaped junction where the vehicle **C**, from a one-way road, approaches the intersection where faces a stop sign in order to enter a bi-directional road. In this road there is a tram going one way in its rails named as *Tram* and a car going the other way identified as **C'**. In the junction of these roads there is a box junction that, according to the Vienna convention on road

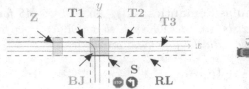 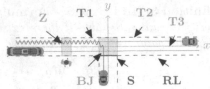

(a) Model with all reference trajectories and without actors.

(b) Unsatisfiable model with actors and the oscillating Ego vehicle trajectory.

Fig. 3. Running Example: An urban T-shaped junction scenario.

traffic, is an area where it is prohibited to stop. In addition, there is a pedestrian zebra crossing in the bi-directional road. It is also possible to see three different solid lines noted as **T1** (red), **T2** (orange), and **T3** (green) that represent the reference trajectories the vehicles may take in this specific use case.

The goal of this running example is to provide validation for complex Ego vehicles. To this end, we start by introducing the formalization of the traffic rules in LTL × MS, the encoding of the traffic scenario, and later the trace definition and encoding. Note that a scenario describes static objects while a trace describes dynamic objects that live within a scenario. Objects are entities such as pedestrians, cyclists, vehicles, trajectories, or horizontal/vertical traffic signs (e.g., crosswalk, stop sign).

Informally, an Ego vehicle shall follow a reference trajectory when at a cross region with a safety-margin of at least one meter. In LTL × MS, we write

$$\Box\Big(\mathsf{O}\,(\mathbf{T1}, \exists^{\leq 1}\mathbf{C})\Big),\tag{1}$$

where **T1** corresponds to the reference trajectory, and **C** to the Ego vehicle. The model in Fig. 3b does not satisfy (1) since the oscillation of the Ego vehicle along the reference trajectory **T1** is above the accepted threshold of one meter.

3.1 Formalization of Road Traffic Rules with LTL × MS

According to the Vienna convention [24], road traffic rules describe the way in which pedestrians and vehicles should behave in a street environment. Without loss of generality, we identify three specific rules of interest to describe in LTL × MS language. These rules translate general autonomous driving system safety requirements to check a given scenario.

Rule 1 (vehicle safety-margin). *To simplify the presentation, this rule is divided into two parts: (a) a vehicle should maintain a safety-margin relative to the walkways (based on article 13 [24]) while following its trajectory, and (b) a vehicle should maintain a safety-margin from the vehicle in front of it. In LTL × MS, the (a) part of this rule can be described by*

$$\neg\Diamond\Big(\mathsf{O}\,(\mathbf{RL}, \exists^{\leq 1}\mathbf{C})\Big),\tag{2}$$

where **RL** *means the road limits. Informally, it reads as the vehicle* **C** *should maintain a safety-margin of at least one meter ($\exists^{\leq 1}\mathbf{C}$) between the car and the road limit, while following its predefined trajectory. Moreover (2) can be written in terms of temporal connectors and predicates, by expanding* $\lozenge$ *and* $\square$*, we arrive to the following expression:*

$$\neg\left[\top\,\mathcal{U}\left(\neg(\mathbf{RL}\sqcap(\exists^{\leq 1}\mathbf{C})=\bot)\wedge\neg(\mathbf{RL}\sqsubseteq\exists^{\leq 1}\mathbf{C})\wedge\neg((\exists^{\leq 1}\mathbf{C})\sqsubseteq\mathbf{RL})\right)\right]. \quad (3)$$

The safety-margin (b) of at least two meters between two vehicles, can be expressed as:

$$\neg\lozenge\left(0\,(\exists^{\leq 2}\mathbf{C}',\exists^{\leq 2}\mathbf{C})\right), \quad (4)$$

where **C'** *corresponds to an external car. The overall rule is the conjunction of formulas (2) and (4). The second term of the conjunction is transformed in*

$$\neg\left[\top\,\mathcal{U}\left(\neg(\exists^{\leq 2}\mathbf{C}'\sqcap\exists^{\leq 2}\mathbf{C}=\bot)\wedge\neg(\exists^{\leq 2}\mathbf{C}'\sqsubseteq\exists^{\leq 2}\mathbf{C})\wedge\neg(\exists^{\leq 2}\mathbf{C}\sqsubseteq\exists^{\leq 2}\mathbf{C}')\right)\right].$$
$$\quad (5)$$

Rule 2 (stop-on-forbidden areas). *A vehicle should not stop on top of (a) a box junction, based on the Portuguese road marks M17b and article 18 of the Vienna convention; (b) a crosswalk, based on article 23 al.3 [24]; (c) tram rails, based on article 23 al.3 [24].*

Regarding part (a), it is mandatory that a vehicle must never stop on top of a box junction, that is, from instant n, when the vehicle overlaps the delimited region, at $n+1$ it cannot be in the exact same position as it was in the previous moment. Writing in LTL $\times$ MS we have:

$$\square\left(\mathtt{I}\,(\mathbf{C},\mathbf{BJ})\vee 0\,(\mathbf{C},\mathbf{BJ})\rightarrow\neg\mathtt{EQ}\,(\mathbf{C},\odot\mathbf{C})\right), \quad (6)$$

where **BJ** *corresponds to the box junction. The previous implication is extended by using the logical equivalence $\varphi_1\rightarrow\varphi_2\equiv\neg\varphi_1\vee\varphi_2$. First we expand $\odot$ and $\square$ operators,*

$$\top\,\mathcal{U}\left[\neg\left(\mathtt{I}\,(\mathbf{C},\mathbf{BJ})\vee 0\,(\mathbf{C},\mathbf{BJ})\right)\vee\neg\mathtt{EQ}\,(\mathbf{C},\bot\mathcal{U}\mathbf{C})\right],$$

then the predicates 0, EQ *and* I,

$$\top\,\mathcal{U}\left[\left((\neg(\mathbf{C}\sqsubseteq\mathbf{BJ})\vee\mathbf{BJ}\sqsubseteq\mathbf{C})\wedge((\mathbf{C}\sqcap\mathbf{BJ}=\bot)\vee\mathbf{C}\sqsubseteq\mathbf{BJ}\vee\mathbf{BJ}\sqsubseteq\mathbf{C})\right)\right.$$
$$\left.\vee\neg(\mathbf{C}\sqsubseteq\bot\mathcal{U}\mathbf{C}\wedge\bot\mathcal{U}\mathbf{C}\sqsubseteq\mathbf{C})\right]. \quad (7)$$

This rule is now ready for the monitor generation. Parts (b) and (c) have an analogous encoding but with crosswalk and tramway regions, respectively.

Rule 3 (stop-sign). *According to the road traffic laws, a vehicle shall stop at a stop sign within a maximum distance of one meter. In LTL $\times$ MS, this rule can be described in a compact form by*

$$\square\left[\left(0\,(\mathbf{S},\exists^{\leq 1}\mathbf{C})\wedge\neg\lozenge\mathtt{EQ}\,(\mathbf{C},\odot\mathbf{C})\right)\rightarrow\lozenge\left(\mathtt{EQ}\,(\mathbf{C},\odot\mathbf{C})\wedge\mathtt{DC}\,(\mathbf{S},\lozenge\mathbf{C})\right)\right], \quad (8)$$

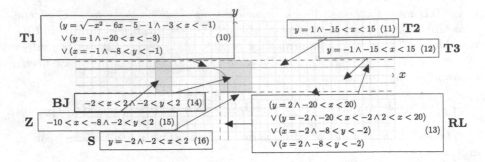

Fig. 4. Scenario encoding as spatial variables **T1**, **T2**, **T3**, **RL**, **BJ**, **Z** and **SL**.

where **S** *is the location of the stop sign. Starting by the expansion of* $\odot$, $\diamondsuit$, $\Diamond$, $\diamondsuit$, *0, EQ, DC, and* $\square$ *operators, we have*

$$
\top\,\mathcal{U}\left[\left(\mathbf{S}\sqcap\exists^{\leq 1}\mathbf{C}=\bot\right)\vee\neg\left(\mathbf{S}\sqsubseteq\exists^{\leq 1}\mathbf{C}\right)\vee\neg\left(\exists^{\leq 1}\mathbf{C}\sqsubseteq\mathbf{S}\right)\right.
$$

$$
\vee\left(\top\,\mathcal{S}\left(\mathbf{C}\sqsubseteq(\bot\,\mathcal{U}\,\mathbf{C})\wedge(\bot\,\mathcal{U}\,\mathbf{C})\sqsubseteq\mathbf{C}\right)\right)
$$

$$
\left.\vee\left(\top\,\mathcal{U}\left((\mathbf{C}\sqsubseteq(\bot\,\mathcal{U}\,\mathbf{C})\wedge(\bot\,\mathcal{U}\,\mathbf{C})\sqsubseteq\mathbf{C})\wedge(\mathbf{S}\sqcap(\top\,\mathcal{U}\,\mathbf{C})=\bot)\right)\right)\right]. \quad (9)
$$

The derived expressions (3), (5), (7) and (9) of the three considered rules are ready to be used as input to the monitor generation algorithm presented later. Let us proceed with the scenario and trace encoding of our running example.

3.2   Scenario and Trace Encoding (Static and Dynamic Objects)

Figure 4 shows the encoding for each static object present in the model of Fig. 3b, which is based on region restrictions represented as inequalities. The trajectories and road limits are described by line segments which can be expressed as sets of linear and non-linear polynomials. The box junction and the crosswalk are defined by bounding boxes.

The objects present in our running example are divided into two categories: static objects, as road limits, crosswalk, box junction, etc.; and objects that can behave dynamically over time, such as vehicles, trams or pedestrians. For these latter elements, there is a need of a continuous trace to keep track of their position at every time step. At all instants, the trace is sent from the simulator in the form of a tree data structure, and it is translated into formulas written in $FOL_{\mathbb{R}}$ (see Fig. 4). In practice, the scenario and trace are transformed in such way that a satisfiability solver can interpret them. Let us turn our attention to trace definition and encoding.

Definition 4 (Infinite Trace). *An infinite trace forms the set* $A^{\mathbb{N}_0}=\{\sigma:\mathbb{N}_0\mapsto A\}$, *where* $(\sigma_0,\sigma_1,\sigma_2,\dots)$ *defines a sequence of symbols.*

For the sake of simplicity, we will use the function $add : \mathbb{S} \times \mathbb{L} \mapsto \mathbb{B}$ to add constraints to the set h (hash map), and $find : \mathbb{S} \mapsto \mathbb{L}$ to return the constraint with a given index (string). These functions are not effect-free. Also, the $next :$ $A^{N_0} \mapsto A^{N_0}$ function over the sequence of symbols with type A^{N_0} is defined by $next\ ((Cons(h,t)) := t()$, and $now : A^{N_0} \mapsto A$ by $now(Cons(h,t)) := h$. These functions get the next sequence of symbols and the current symbol in the sequence, respectively. An A symbol has a list of objects, and set $A_{[O]}$ is a list of A_O objects (see the JSON trace in Fig. 5). For the sake of simplicity, we also define the dual of "next" as $prev : A^{N_0} \mapsto A^{N_0}$.

In general terms, the trace encoding consists on the construction of the function $eval : \mathfrak{P} \mapsto \mathbb{L}$ that is defined by $eval(p) := find\ p$, which evaluates a spatial variable to an expression in $FOL_{\mathbb{R}}$. To encode a symbol from a trace, we have to pick the symbol from the trace and produce the set of inequality constraints that defines their objects. Figure 5 presents the definition of the enc function and other auxiliary functions, where the enc function gets as input a symbol and produces the constraints with an index to the set h. Also, the function $encode$ constructs the set of constraints for a given finite trace. To encode infinite traces, we have to infinitely iterate over trace symbols and produce the inequalities in an incremental way. Instead of defining a new encoding function, we make use of the $next$ and $prev$ functions in the next section.

Without loss of generality, let us see a circle as a ball, and a bounding box as a rectangle or square in the two-dimensional Euclidean space. Note that other geometric shapes can be translated but are out of the scope of our running example. The $obj : id \mapsto \mathbb{L}$ function generates the objects as constraints defining circles and bounding boxes with free variables, and $id \in \{\texttt{circle}, \texttt{bbox}\}$. It defines, as follows:

$$obj(s) := \begin{cases} (\texttt{x4} - \texttt{x1})^2 + (\texttt{x5} - \texttt{x2})^2 < \texttt{x3}^2, & \text{if } s = \texttt{circle} \\ (\texttt{x1} - \texttt{x3}/2) \leq \texttt{x5} \wedge \texttt{x5} \leq (\texttt{x1} + \texttt{x3}/2) \wedge \\ (\texttt{x2} - \texttt{x4}/2) \leq \texttt{x6} \wedge \texttt{x6} \leq (\texttt{x2} + \texttt{x4}/2), & \text{if } s = \texttt{bbox} \end{cases}$$

Let us now see how the resultant expressions can use the variables binder $\texttt{let}$. The evaluation of the expression $\texttt{let}\ ((\texttt{x1}\ 1)\ (\texttt{x2}\ 2)\ (\texttt{x3}\ 3)).\ obj\ \texttt{circle}$ results in $(\texttt{x1} - 1)^2 + (\texttt{x2} - 2)^2 < 3^2$, where $\texttt{x1}$ and $\texttt{x2}$ are the remaining free variables. Then, we can bind these variables with a quantifier such as $\forall x, y.\ \texttt{let}\ (\texttt{x1}\ 1)\ (\texttt{x2}\ 2)\ (\texttt{x3}\ 3).\ obj(\texttt{circle})$, where $(1, 2)$ is the center point of the circle, and 3 the radius. This will be the way we replace free variables.

4 Monitoring Model Construction

As input our algorithm receives an LTL $\times$ MS property that represents a requirement under analysis and produces a model in $FOL_{\mathbb{R}}$. Every term $\rho \in \mathfrak{T}$ (the set of all words of ϱ) is translated by the recursive function $\mathbf{conv}_{\varrho} : \mathfrak{T} \mapsto \mathbb{L}$ into $FOL_{\mathbb{R}}$ (see Fig. 6). The $dist : \mathbb{R} \times \mathfrak{T} \mapsto \mathbb{L}$ function applies the Property 1 that says that any formula containing distance operators has an equivalent formula where the distance operators are just applied to the propositions.

$c : A \mapsto A_{[O]}$

$c(s) := s.objects$

$enc : A_{[O]} \mapsto \mathbb{B}$

$enc(l) := if \ l = empty \ then \ true$

$\quad else \ enco(hd(l)) \ \textbf{and} \ enc(tl(l))$

$enco : A_O \mapsto \mathbb{B}$

$enco(o) := if \ s.type = circle \ then$

$\quad add(o.id, \textbf{let} \ (\textbf{x1} \ o.x) \ (\textbf{x2} \ o.y)$

$\quad\quad (\textbf{x3} \ o.radius). \ obj(\textbf{circle}))$

$\quad else \ (if \ s.type = bbox \ then$

$\quad\quad add(o.id, \textbf{let} \ (\textbf{x1} \ o.x) \ (\textbf{x2} \ o.y)$

$\quad\quad (\textbf{x3} \ o.width) \ (\textbf{x4} \ o.height).$

$\quad\quad obj(\textbf{bbox})) \ else \ false \ )$

$encode : A^{\mathbb{N}_0} \times \mathbb{N}_{>0} \mapsto \mathbb{L}$

$encode(t, n) := if \ n > 0 \ then$

$\quad enc(c(now(t))) \ \textbf{and}$

$\quad encode(next(t), n - 1) \ else \ true$

```
{
  "trace": [
    {
      "symbolid": "1",
      "ts": "00:00:01",
      "objects": [
        {
          "id": 1,
          "position": {
            "x": 0.5,
            "y": -0.5
          },
          "region": {
            "type": "circle",
            "radius": 0.5
          }
        },
        ... ]
    },
    ... ]
}
```

(a) Definition of the function *encode* and its auxiliar functions.

(b) Trace with one circular object with center $(0.5, -0, 5)$ and radius 0.5.

Fig. 5. Functional definition and example of a trace in JSON format.

Property 1 (Distance Operator). Let ρ be a term, V the set of free variables in ρ, and e a rational number. For any ρ and e, the distance operator $\exists^{\leq e}\rho$ has an equivalent expression with every free variable $a \in V$ such that $\exists^{\leq e}a$.

The $next_\rho : \mathfrak{T} \mapsto \mathbb{L}$ function also has a similar property to distance operators but instead of distance it assigns to each proposition the successor (a nested of next operators just on propositions). To conclude $\textbf{conv}_\rho$ conversion function over terms, the $unfold : \mathfrak{T} \times \mathfrak{T} \mapsto \mathbb{L}$ function generates a bounded instance of the infinite sequence

$$\bigvee_{i=1}^{n} \left[\bigwedge_{j=1}^{i} \left(\underbrace{\odot \ldots \odot}_{j \text{ times}} \rho_1 \right) \wedge \underbrace{\odot \ldots \odot}_{j \text{ times}} \rho_2 \right],$$

where $\rho_1, \rho_2 \in \varrho$ are the input terms. Let us now move our attention to formulas.

Every formula ϕ in $\mathfrak{F}$ (the set of all words of φ) is translated by the function $\textbf{conv}_\varphi : \mathfrak{F} \mapsto \mathbb{L}$ (again in Fig. 6). The expression $\forall(x, y, \cdot).(\textbf{conv}_\varrho(\rho_1) \rightarrow \textbf{conv}_\varrho(\rho_2))$ binds all the remaining free variables of the resulting expression in FOL$_\mathbb{R}$. For instance, $\forall(x, y).x < y$. The function $next_\varphi : \mathfrak{F} \mapsto \mathbb{L}$ generates

$$\mathbf{conv}_\varrho(\rho) := \begin{cases} eval(p), & \text{if } \rho = p \\ \neg\mathbf{conv}_\varrho(\rho), & \text{if } \rho = \bar{\rho} \\ \mathbf{conv}_\varrho(\rho_1) \wedge \mathbf{conv}_\varrho(\rho_2), & \text{if } \rho = \rho_1 \sqcap \rho_2 \\ \mathbf{conv}_\varrho(\rho_1) \vee \mathbf{conv}_\varrho(\rho_2), & \text{if } \rho = \rho_1 \sqcup \rho_2 \\ dist(e, \mathbf{conv}_\varrho(\rho)), & \text{if } \rho = \exists^{\leq e} \rho \\ next_\varrho(\mathbf{conv}_\varrho(\rho)), & \text{if } \rho = \perp\mathcal{U}\rho \\ \mathbf{conv}_\varrho(unfold(\rho_1, \rho_2)), & \text{if } \rho = \rho_1\mathcal{U}\rho_2, \end{cases}$$

$$\mathbf{conv}_\varphi(\phi) := \begin{cases} \forall(x, y, \cdot).(\mathbf{conv}_\varrho(\rho_1) \to \mathbf{conv}_\varrho(\rho_2)), & \text{if } \phi = \rho_1 \sqsubseteq \rho_2 \\ \neg(\mathbf{conv}_\varphi(\phi)), & \text{if } \phi = \neg\rho \\ \mathbf{conv}_\varphi(\phi_1) \wedge \mathbf{conv}_\varphi(\phi_2), & \text{if } \phi = \phi_1 \wedge \phi_2 \\ \mathbf{conv}_\varphi(\phi_1) \vee \mathbf{conv}_\varphi(\phi_2), & \text{if } \phi = \phi_1 \vee \phi_2 \\ next_\varphi(\mathbf{conv}_\varphi(\phi)), & \text{if } \phi = false\,\mathcal{U}\,\phi \\ \mathbf{conv}_\varphi(unfold_\mathcal{U}(\phi_1, \phi_2)), & \text{if } \phi = \phi_1\,\mathcal{U}\,\phi_2 \\ previous_\varphi(\mathbf{conv}_\varphi(\phi)), & \text{if } \phi = false\,\mathcal{S}\,\phi \\ \mathbf{conv}_\varphi(unfold_\mathcal{S}(\phi_1, \phi_2)), & \text{if } \phi = \phi_1\,\mathcal{S}\,\phi_2 \end{cases}$$

Fig. 6. Conversion functions $\mathbf{conv}_\varrho(\rho)$ and $\mathbf{conv}_\varphi(\phi)$.

formula ϕ from the next instance, while $previous_\varphi : \mathfrak{F} \mapsto \mathbb{L}$ generates formula ϕ from the previous instance. Function $unfold_X : \mathfrak{F} \times \mathfrak{F} \mapsto \mathbb{L}$ generates a bounded instance of the infinite sequence

$$\bigvee_{i=1}^{n}\left[\bigwedge_{j=1}^{i}\left(\underbrace{X \ldots X}_{j \text{ times}}\rho_1\right) \wedge \underbrace{X \ldots X}_{j \text{ times}}\rho_2\right]$$

where $\phi_1, \phi_2 \in \varphi$ are the input formulas. Funtion $unfold_\mathcal{U} : \mathfrak{F} \times \mathfrak{F} \mapsto \mathbb{L}$ is defined by $unfold_X$ when $X = \bigcirc$, while $unfold_\mathcal{S} : \mathfrak{F} \times \mathfrak{F} \mapsto \mathbb{L}$ by $unfold_X$ when $X = \ominus$.

Trace Inlining. Since formulas and terms converts into incomplete $\text{FOL}_\mathbb{R}$ expressions, the formalization of the trace completes the encoding. The trace encoding consists essentially on the construction of the function $eval$ that has ben already defined. This function replaces spatial variables with expressions in $\text{FOL}_\mathbb{R}$. Note that the trace is a valuation and assigns constraints to the expressions in $\text{FOL}_\mathbb{R}$. $encode$ has been already defined while $inline : \mathbb{L} \times \mathbb{L} \mapsto \mathbb{L}$ includes the trace in the monitoring model. Note that this inlining is a binding of every free variable of $\mathbf{conv}_\varphi(\phi)$ in $encode(trc, n)$. The first argument receives the monitoring model, and the second argument receives the mapping of the spatial variables to the constraints in $\text{FOL}_\mathbb{R}$ (given by the hash map). Let trc be a trace of length n, and ϕ a formula in LTL $\times$ MS.. The inlining is defined by

$$inline(\mathbf{conv}_\varphi(\phi), encode(trc, n)).$$

The process concludes by inlining the finite trace in the monitoring model.

Partial Incremental Evaluation – Without Unfolding Temporal Operators. To improve algorithm efficiency, scalability, and support infinite traces we decided to construct a modified version of the previous algorithm without using the unfolding of temporal operators (functions $\mathcal{U}$ and $\mathcal{S}$). We perform this on the assumption that temporal terms are bounded. The temporal part is then processed incrementally using incremental evaluation (push and pop operators) on the non-linear satisfiability solver. The s acts as a state such as true t, false f or unknown u. For this evaluation, we consider the known temporal patterns

$$\Box\hat{\phi}, \Diamond\hat{\phi}, \Box\left(\hat{\phi}_1 \rightarrow \Diamond\hat{\phi}_2\right), \Box\left(\hat{\phi}_1 \rightarrow \neg\Diamond\hat{\phi}_2\right), \Diamond\left(\hat{\phi}_1 \wedge \Box\hat{\phi}_2\right), \text{ and } \Diamond\left(\hat{\phi}_1 \wedge \Diamond\neg\hat{\phi}_2\right).$$

Past temporal operators are unrolled for infinite traces and incrementally evaluated for infinite traces (unknown last element). The $eval_i(\Box\phi)$ has the truth value *false* or *unknown*, while $eval_i(\Diamond\phi)$ has the truth value *true* or *unknown*, and $eval_i(\Box(\phi_1 \rightarrow \Diamond\phi_2))$ has the same truth value of $eval_i(\Box\phi)$.

One could expect to construct the function $eval_i(\phi, \Sigma, s)$ defined by

$$\begin{cases} solve\left(conv_\varphi^i(\phi), enc(\Sigma)\right) & \text{if } \phi = \hat{\phi} \\ and\left[eval_i\left(\hat{\phi}_1, \Sigma, s\right), eval_i\left(\phi_1, \Sigma, s\right)\right] & \text{if } \phi = \hat{\phi}_1 \wedge \phi_1 \\ implies\left[eval_i\left(\phi_1, \Sigma, s\right), eval_i\left(\phi_2, \Sigma, s\right)\right] & \text{if } \phi = \phi_1 \rightarrow \phi_2 \\ ite\left[s = u, eval_i\left(\phi, next(\Sigma), c_\top\left(s, eval_i(\phi_1, next(\Sigma), u)\right)\right), f\right] & \text{if } \phi = \Box\phi_1 \\ ite\left[s = u, eval_i\left(\phi, next(\Sigma), c_\bot\left(s, eval_i(\phi_1, next(\Sigma), u)\right)\right), t\right] & \text{if } \phi = \Diamond\phi_1 \\ ite\left[s = u, eval_i\left(\phi, prev(\Sigma), c_\bot\left(s, eval_i(\phi_1, prev(\Sigma), u)\right)\right), t\right] & \text{if } \phi = \Diamondblack\phi_1 \end{cases}$$

where $\phi \in \varphi$ a formula, $\hat{\phi}$ a formula without temporal operators, Σ is a infinite trace with $next, prev$ operators, and $s \in \mathfrak{S}$ a symbol. $\mathfrak{S}$ denotes the set $\{t, f, u\}$, $ite : \{t, f\} \times \{t, f\} \times \{t, f\} \mapsto \{t, f\}$ defines the if-then-else function, $and : \{t, f\} \times \{t, f\} \mapsto \{t, f\}$ implements the conjunction, $implies : \{t, f\} \times \{t, f\} \mapsto \{t, f\}$ implements the implication, $c_\top : \mathfrak{S} \times \{t, f\} \mapsto \mathfrak{S}$ converts the pair (u, f) to f and u otherwise, and $c_\bot : \mathfrak{S} \times \{t, f\} \mapsto \mathfrak{S}$ converts the pair (u, t) to t and u otherwise.

Property 2 (Spatial Isolation on ϱ terms). A spatial variable $a \in \mathfrak{P}$ is free of modifiers for any term.

From Property 2, terms have no free variables and no assumptions have to be given for the incremental evaluation, the reason why it simplifies *implies* and *and* functions in the incremental evaluation function $eval_i$. A spatial variable maintains its form regardless of where it is evaluated. Function $solve : \mathbb{L} \times \mathbb{L} \mapsto \{t, f\}$ solves an expression in $FOL_\mathbb{R}$ assuming another expression in $FOL_\mathbb{R}$. Note that $\bigcirc$ temporal operator vanish and is not incrementally evaluated.

Table 1. Table displaying the evaluation results. The first column indicates the considered rules. The last two columns, unroll and incremental methods, show the time (in seconds) and the memory (in Megabytes) used by the solver, the overall runtime the monitor takes to execute (RT) and frames per second (FPS).

	Rule($\|\varrho\|, \|\varphi\|$)	$\Sigma(\|\Sigma\|)$	Unroll Solver Time	Mem	RT	FPS	Incremental Solver Time	Mem	RT	FPS
Empirical	1.a (2,2)	e1(13)	1.14	4.49	1.19	5.58	0.26	2.87	0.42	19.12
	1.a (2,2)	e2(13)	0.07	4.05	0.13	65	0.03	2.86	0.04	185.71
	1.b (1,1)	e3(13)	0.02	3.03	0.05	185.71	0.12	2.75	0.26	34.21
	1.b (1,1)	e4(13)	0.05	3.06	0.09	92.86	0.08	2.45	0.17	56
	2.a (1,3)	e5(13)	0.18	3.53	0.23	31.71	0.17	2.83	0.33	26
	2.a (1,3)	e6(13)	0.16	3.51	0.21	35.14	0.09	2.85	0.17	53.85
	2.b (1,3)	e7(13)	0.25	3.53	0.29	24.07	0.17	2.80	0.34	27.45
	3. (3,6)	e8(14)	0.50	6.98	1.05	9.03	0.07	5.40	0.26	39.39
	3. (3,6)	e9(13)	1.29	7.06	1.71	4.33	0.10	5.45	0.28	36.84
	3. (3,6)	e10(15)	1.11	7.45	1.64	5.45	0.11	5.44	0.46	22.81
	Average		0.48	4.67	0.66	**45.9**	0.12	3.57	0.27	**50.1**
Simulator	1.a (2,2)	s1(243)	73.82	18.48	74.29	1.64	2.38	2.91	3.18	43.71
	1.a (2,2)	s2(157)	0.34	5.78	0.46	196.25	0.79	2.89	1.08	83.96
	1.a (2,2)	s3(146)	0.28	6.37	0.44	202.78	0.51	2.89	0.74	116.8
	1.b (1,1)	s1(243)	0.15	5.14	0.45	405	0.70	2.79	1.52	109.46
	1.b (1,1)	s4(311)	0.40	5.19	0.64	299.04	0.97	2.85	1.75	114.34
	2.a (1,3)	s1(243)	6.73	7.95	7.09	17.58	1.19	2.86	2.07	74.54
	2.a (1,3)	s5(369)	12.99	7.66	13.72	13.82	2.37	2.90	3.96	58.29
	2.a (1,3)	s6(198)	8.11	7.83	8.69	11.79	0.46	2.85	0.80	157.14
	3. (3,6)	s4(311)	396.40	110.23	413.11	0.38	10.83	7.80	23.71	9
	3. (3,6)	s5(369)	951.87	117.48	1029.76	0.19	9.90	8.31	27.27	9.93
	3. (3,6)	s6(198)	1044.16	124.92	1090.95	0.09	12.25	8.52	26.57	5.1
	Average		226.84	37.91	239.96	**104.4**	3.85	4.32	8.42	**71.1**

5 Empirical Evaluation

The monitor runs in parallel to the ADS under test having no direct impact on the system itself, as seen in Fig. 1. The system evolves around the simulation of a specific scenario, that feeds ADS with its observations. The system reacts to observation and produces actions for the agents running on the simulator in an endless loop. The monitor receives the observations from the simulator as a trace to check a property and generates a verdict indicating if its satisfied.

The traces and scenario were evaluated on a i5-8365U CPU running Linux 5.10.11. Traces are provided by a simulated T-shaped junction scenario in the CARLA 0.9.13 autonomous driving simulator [9]. Scalability is an aspect to keep in mind since the size of a trace matters for monitoring performance, therefore, we test each property with different trace sizes to understand how different methods perform. When performing the empirical evaluation (hand-built sample traces to validate the tool – e1–e10), the Unroll method is slower than the Incremental method in average, with exception of rule 1.b, where the Unroll is slightly better, with a higher memory consumption (see Table 1). However, the biggest difference are the rules 1.a and 3, where the Incremental method is clearly better than the Unroll. These rules impact the highest average in the time (0.48 s) and memory spent (4.67 MB) by the solver, as well as the RT (0.66 s) and low FPS values (45.9) of the Unroll, in comparison with the Incremental method.

The behavior described previously also applies when it comes to the Simulator evaluation (traces got from simulation environment – s1–s6). Yet, the differences are more pronounced. In the worst case scenario (rule 3), the time spent by the solver in the Unroll method is approximately 85 times slower than the solver in Incremental method, 1044.16 s and 12.25 s, respectively. Moreover, the memory usage is considerably higher in Unroll (in average 37.91 MB) than in Incremental (in average 4.32 MB) method.

When observing the average value of the incremental method (higher than 60), this value means that our approach is able to comfortably work with modern cameras with an acquisition rate of 60 Hz. ADSs cameras have lower framerates. Our performance measurements are also prone to different resolutions as our approach does not depend of the size of the image matrix. To summarize, the data displayed in Table 1 shows a clear advantage of Incremental over Unroll method. The tool and documentation for artifact evaluation can be found in https://github.com/anmaped/stem-binaries.git.

6   Related Work

When talking about autonomous vehicles, these systems are subjected to the local traffic laws and is a crucial problem to solve, as pointed out by Henry Prakken [26]. He studied if the Dutch traffic law, with its exceptions, conflicts, and commonsense knowledge, can be implemented in fully autonomous vehicles and present three approaches to design AVs in compliance with traffic rules. Cristian-Ioan Vasile et al. [32] formalized a minimum-violation plan of an AV by using a fragment of LTL. Moreover, they used the logic fragment to specify the behavior and incorporate it in the motion planner algorithm.

Alternatively, the AV as a system ideally has to self-check whether the autonomous part obeys the traffic rules. Based on signal temporal logic (STL), Nikos Aréchiga [4] proposed a step forward in this direction. He enabled the automatic synthesis of runtime monitors, similar to what we presented in this work, but without considering space as a first-class citizen. Also, he defined a set of contracts to ensure that the overall system will not have collisions if followed by all traffic participants. Cardoso et al. [7] suggests verification by contracts as a powerful tool to handle complex systems such as AVs.

Similar to our work, Xu and Li [34] introduced a spatial logic to check collision avoidance properties. They do not consider the evolution in time of the traffic junction with its actors and do not produce any verdict. Another work that resembles ours is [29], where they encode STL to a mixed-integer programming solver, allowing the monitoring of AV failures in an urban scenario in real-time. In our work, we encode our LTL $\times$ MS expression to $FOL_\mathbb{R}$ as well, but traffic rules are not formalized in STL as we do with our temporal language.

Several works focus on the formalization of traffic rules. For example, [5] uses Defeasible Deontic Logic to handle exceptions and resolve conflicts in overtaking Australian traffic rules. In terms of temporal logic, the research presented in [3,21,28], addressed several traffic scenarios, such as highways and junctions. Schwammberger and Alves [31] proposed a spatio-temporal language similar to the one in our work to formalize three road crossing rules in the UK and emphasizes the need for a Digital Highway Code for AVs, but the decision procedure is missing. Pek *et al.* [25] writes overtaking rules as non-linear arithmetic expressions and uses real-world data and simulations to validate their method.

7 Conclusion and Future Work

Even with smarter techniques, unfolding the $\mathcal{U}$ and $\mathcal{S}$ operators is computationally expensive and proves infeasible in practical terms. Incremental evaluation of infinite traces at run-time reduces the burden of checking spatial constraints, since unbounded time is a bottleneck when solving time constraints with a satisfiability solver. In our approach, the temporal sequences are checked partially at runtime and the spatial part using exclusively the satisfiability solver.

Our empirical evaluation shows good evidence of the scalability of our incremental evaluation method by running symbols of arbitrary sequences with more 70 symbols or 'frames' per second. To emphasize it, a conventional CPU (one core) could monitor a trace from a camera with a total acquisition rate greater than 60 Hz which we tested by setting up our running example on the CARLA autonomous driving simulator. Our approach also takes advantage of multiple cores as we could split the objects in the environment into different instances, the Ego vehicle and the surrounding objects.

One way to optimize our tool, is to configure the solver to use the most suitable tactic, tailoring it even more for the models we intend to verify. Another way, is to increase the number of surrounding objects and use predictive distance-based techniques based on geometric projections to allow the monitor to skip symbols of a sequence and decrease CPU utilization.

Acknowledgments. This work was partially supported by the European Regional Development Fund (ERDF) through the Competitiveness and Internationalization Operational Program (COMPETE 2020) of Portugal 2020 [Project STEROID with number 069989 (POCI-01-0247-FEDER-069989)]. This work was also partially supported by FCT/MCTES grant UIDB/04516/2020.

References

1. Aiello, M., Pratt-Hartmann, I., van Benthem, J.: Handbook of Spatial Logics. Springer, Dordrecht (2007). https://doi.org/10.1007/978-1-4020-5587-4

2. Akintunde, M.E., Botoeva, E., Kouvaros, P., Lomuscio, A.: Formal verification of neural agents in non-deterministic environments. Auton. Agents Multi-Agent Syst. **36**(1), 1–36 (2021). https://doi.org/10.1007/s10458-021-09529-3

3. Alves, G.V., Dennis, L.A., Fisher, M.: A double-level model checking approach for an agent-based autonomous vehicle and road junction regulations. J. Sens. Actuator Netw. **10**(3), 41 (2021)

4. Aréchiga, N.: Specifying safety of autonomous vehicles in signal temporal logic. In: 2019 IEEE Intelligent Vehicles Symposium, IV 2019, Paris, France, 9–12 June 2019, pp. 58–63. IEEE (2019)

5. Bhuiyan, H., Governatori, G., Bond, A., Demmel, S., Badiul Islam, M., Rakotonirainy, A.: Traffic rules encoding using defeasible deontic logic. In: JURIX 2020, Brno, Czech Republic, December 2020, volume 334 of Frontiers in Artificial Intelligence and Applications, pp. 3–12. IOS Press (2020)

6. Borg, M., et al.: Safely entering the deep: a review of verification and validation for machine learning and a challenge elicitation in the automotive industry. J. Autom. Softw. Eng **1**, 12 (2018)

7. Cardoso, R., et al.: A review of verification and validation for space autonomous systems. Curr. Robot. Rep. **2**, 09 (2021)

8. de Moura, L., Bjørner, N.: Z3: an efficient SMT solver. In: Ramakrishnan, C.R., Rehof, J. (eds.) TACAS 2008. LNCS, vol. 4963, pp. 337–340. Springer, Heidelberg (2008). https://doi.org/10.1007/978-3-540-78800-3_24

9. Dosovitskiy, A., Ros, G., Codevilla, F., López, A.M., Koltun, V.: CARLA: an open urban driving simulator. In: CoRL 2017, Mountain View, California, USA, November 2017, Proceedings, volume 78 of Machine Learning Research, pp. 1–16. PMLR (2017)

10. Allen Emerson, E.: Temporal and modal logic. In: van Leeuwen, J. (ed.) Handbook of Theoretical Computer Science, Volume B: Formal Models and Semantics, pp. 995–1072. Elsevier and MIT Press, London (1990)

11. Association for Standardisation of Automation and Measuring Systems. https://www.asam.net/standards/. Accessed 11 Apr 2022

12. Gabelaia, D., Kontchakov, R., Kurucz, A., Wolter, F., Zakharyaschev, M.: Combining spatial and temporal logics: expressiveness vs. complexity. J. Artif. Intell. Res. **23**, 167–243 (2005)

13. Gerevini, A., Nebel, B.: Qualitative spatio-temporal reasoning with RCC-8 and Allen's interval calculus: computational complexity. In: ECAI'2002, Lyon, France, July 2002. Proceedings, pp. 312–316. IOS Press (2002)

14. Haghighi, I., Jones, A., Kong, Z., Bartocci, E., Grosu, R., Belta, C.: SpaTeLl: a novel spatial-temporal logic and its applications to networked systems: a novel spatial-temporal logic and its applications to networked systems. In: HSCC 2015, Seattle, WA, USA, April 2015. Proceedings, pp. 189–198. ACM (2015)

15. Huang, X., et al.: A survey of safety and trustworthiness of deep neural networks: verification, testing, adversarial attack and defence, and interpretability. Comput. Sci. Rev. **37**, 100270 (2020)

16. Kane, A.: Runtime monitoring for safety-critical embedded systems. Ph.D. thesis, Carnegie Mellon University, Pittsburgh (2015)

17. Kurucz, A., Wolter, F., Zakharyaschev, M.: Modal logics for metric spaces: open problems. In: We Will Show Them! Essays in Honour of Dov Gabbay, Vol. 2, pp. 193–108. College Publications (2005)

18. Kutz, O., Wolter, F., Sturm, H., Suzuki, N.-Y., Zakharyaschev, M.: Logics of metric spaces. ACM Trans. Com. Log. **4**(2), 260–294 (2003)

19. Leucker, M., Schallhart, C.: A brief account of runtime verification. J. Logic Algebraic Program. **78**(5), 293–303 (2009)
20. Li, T., STSL: a novel spatio-temporal specification language for cyber-physical systems. In: QRS 2020, pp. 309–319. IEEE (2020)
21. Maierhofer, S., Rettinger, A., Charlotte Mayer, E., Althoff, M.: Formalization of interstate traffic rules in temporal logic. In: 2020 IEEE Intelligent Vehicles Symposium (IV), pp. 752–759. IEEE (2020)
22. Mehmed, A.: Runtime monitoring for safe automated driving systems. Ph.D. thesis, Mälardalen University (2020)
23. Muller, P.: A qualitative theory of motion based on spatio-temporal primitives. In: KR1998, Trento, June 1998, pp. 131–143. Morgan Kaufmann (1998)
24. United Nations. Vienna convention on road traffic (1968). https://unece.org/DAM/trans/conventn/Conv_road_traffic_EN.pdf. Accessed 11 Apr 2022
25. Pek, C., Zahn, P., Althoff, M.: Verifying the safety of lane change maneuvers of self-driving vehicles based on formalized traffic rules. In: 2017 IEEE Intelligent Vehicles Symposium (IV), pp. 1477–1483 (2017)
26. Prakken, H.: On the problem of making autonomous vehicles conform to traffic law. Artif. Intell. Law **25**(3), 341–363 (2017). https://doi.org/10.1007/s10506-017-9210-0
27. Riedmaier, S., Ponn, T., Ludwig, D., Schick, B., Diermeyer, F.: Survey on scenario-based safety assessment of automated vehicles. IEEE Access **8**, 87456–87477 (2020)
28. Rizald, A., et al.: Formalising and monitoring traffic rules for autonomous vehicles in Isabelle/HOL. In: Polikarpova, N., Schneider, S. (eds.) IFM 2017. LNCS, vol. 10510, pp. 50–66. Springer, Cham (2017). https://doi.org/10.1007/978-3-319-66845-1_4
29. Sahin, Y.M., Quirynen, R., Di Cairano, S.: Autonomous vehicle decision-making and monitoring based on signal temporal logic and mixed-integer programming. In: 2020 American Control Conference (ACC), pp. 454–459 (2020)
30. Sánchez, C., et al.: A survey of challenges for runtime verification from advanced application domains (beyond software). Formal Methods Syst. Des. **54**, 279–335 (2019). https://doi.org/10.1007/s10703-019-00337-w
31. Schwammberger, M., Alves, G.V.: Extending urban multi-lane spatial logic to formalise road junction rules. In: FMAS 2021, Virtual, October 2021. Proceedings, volume 348 of EPTCS, pp. 1–19 (2021)
32. Vasile, C.-I., Tumova, J., Karaman, S., Belta, C., Rus, D.: Minimum-violation scLTL motion planning for mobility-on-demand. In: ICRA 2017, pp. 1481–1488 (2017)
33. Wolter, F., Zakharyaschev, M.: Reasoning about distances. In: Gottlob, G., Walsh, T. (eds.) IJCAI 2003, Acapulco, Mexico, 9–15 August 2003. Proceedings, pp. 1275–1282. Morgan Kaufmann (2003)
34. Xu, B., Li, Q.: A spatial logic for modeling and verification of collision-free control of vehicles. In: ICECCS 2016, Dubai, United Arab Emirates, November 2016. Proceedings, pp. 33–42. IEEE Computer Society (2016)

Model-Based Testing of Internet of Things Protocols

Xavier Manuel van Dommelen[1,2(✉)] [iD], Machiel van der Bijl[2],
and Andy Pimentel[1]

[1] University of Amsterdam, Amsterdam, The Netherlands
xavier_vd@outlook.com
[2] Axini, Amsterdam, The Netherlands
https://www.axini.com

Abstract. Internet of Things (IoT) is a popular term to describe systems/devices that connect and interact with each other through a network, e.g., the Internet. These devices communicate with each other via a communication protocol, such as Zigbee or Bluetooth Low Energy (BLE), the subject of this paper. Communication protocols are notoriously hard to implement correctly and a large set of test-cases is needed to check for conformance to the standard. Many of us have encountered communication problems in practice, such as random mobile phone disconnects, difficulty obtaining a Bluetooth connection, etc. In this paper, we research the application of industry strength Model-Based Testing (MBT) within the IoT domain. This technique contributes to higher quality specifications and more efficient and more thorough conformance testing. We show how we can model part of the BLE protocol specification using the Axini Modeling Platform (AMP). Based on the model, AMP is then able to automatically test the conformance of a BLE device. With this approach, we found specification flaws in the official BLE specifications as well as conformance errors on a certified BLE system.

Keywords: Model-Based Testing · Internet of Things ·
Communication Protocol · Bluetooth Low Energy · Embedded Systems

1 Introduction

The term *Internet of Things (IoT)* has become well known. IoT generally refers to everyday objects that have obtained the ability to connect and interact with each other through a network [33]. Over the years, the number of these IoT devices has grown tremendously, reaching an approximate amount of 9.9 billion devices in 2021 [17]. Along with this growth, new IoT devices are being developed that often implement the same widely accepted communication protocols [2]. Examples are Bluetooth Low Energy [6] and Zigbee [11]. It is important that these protocols are implemented correctly. When the implementations deviate from the specification, the functionality to interact with other systems using the same communication protocol could be affected.

© The Author(s), under exclusive license to Springer Nature Switzerland AG 2022
J. F. Groote and M. Huisman (Eds.): FMICS 2022, LNCS 13487, pp. 172–189, 2022.
https://doi.org/10.1007/978-3-031-15008-1_12

Currently, manufacturers face several challenges that prevent them from extensively testing the communication protocols in their IoT devices [7]. For this reason, research has started looking into different testing approaches to overcome these challenges. One of these approaches is *Model-Based Testing (MBT)* [8].

Research on MBT for IoT protocol testing looks mainly into proof of concepts and investigates individual challenges [1,16,29]. As a result, it is difficult to evaluate to what extent MBT is capable of resolving the problems in this domain. Such an evaluation is needed to compare testing approaches to determine which one is the most optimal, in particular in an industrial setting. For this reason, our research tries to investigate which challenges industrial strength model-based testing is able to resolve and what other influences this approach brings.

1.1 Related Work

IoT can be seen as cyber physical systems. Model-based testing is an interesting technique that has shown its merits in modeling and testing cyber physical systems [30,31].

Our work focuses on testing protocol conformance through MBT on IoT systems, but there is related work that researches other aspects. The work of Yoneyama et al. [34] uses MBT to test the robustness of the COAP protocol by modeling network faults. Additionally, the work of Aziz et al. [3] demonstrates that by formally modeling the MQ Telemetry Transport protocol, an IoT protocol, and analyzing the result, they can evaluate the correctness of the protocol. These papers differ from our work by concentrating on testing the protocol itself instead of testing the conformance of the implemented protocol. Malik et al. [22] use MBT as a tool to demonstrate that we can automatically test IoT protocols on systems remotely. In their work, they briefly describe why they make use of MBT but their main topic is the framework for remotely testing IoT systems and their protocols. The case study of Tappler et al. [29] shows how models for a model-based testing approach can be automatically created through active automated learning. Furthermore, this work demonstrates that by using their automatically generated models they are capable of finding implementation mistakes that go against the MQTT communication protocol specifications. Ahmad et al. [1] investigate the possibility to use a model-based testing approach to test IoT systems in their entirety. In addition to just testing the system, they discuss a framework that enables sharing models between developers as a service. While the focus of these papers is to obtain a proof of concept with a specific goal in mind, our work differs by highlighting the implications of using MBT in the IoT domain in an industrial setting.

Finally, the work of Inçki et al. [16] presents a model-based testing implementation in which they could perform interoperability tests to evaluate the IoT communication protocol COAP. However, they do not present any experiments that make use of their presented approach. Consequently, we are not able to evaluate the benefits or disadvantages of using MBT in contrast to our work. Furthermore, they do not give an in-depth explanation and reflection on the implications of using model-based testing.

1.2   Contributions

Our research focuses on the application of MBT with a commercial tool on a non-trivial part of the industrial BLE protocol. We describe which implications MBT could have on the IoT protocol testing domain based on practical experience. Furthermore, we discuss how the specifications of a widely used IoT communication protocol, Bluetooth Low Energy, can be translated into a formal model. Based on this experience, we discuss which obstacles are likely to be encountered and how they can be overcome when translating an IoT protocal. In this process, we highlight several flaws in the official Bluetooth Low Energy specifications version 4.2 [6], showing that MBT is a method to improve specifications. Finally, by applying our proof of concept to test a certified BLE system, we show that certain assumptions about MBT also hold in practice. And we find implementation errors in the process.

2   Preliminaries

2.1   Internet of Things

IoT refers to everyday objects that have obtained the ability to connect and interact with each other through a network [33]. According to Elnashar [10], the challenges related to IoT fall into two categories: challenges relating to unlicensed networks that aim for short-range communication and challenges relating to cellular licensed networks.

This document focuses on the short-range communication category, because this category contains significantly more manufacturers [10,15,26]. This means that to ensure interoperability between IoT systems more parties require a sufficient testing environment. Additionally, IoT systems from this category generally use the same communication protocols [2,32]. As a result, a generic testing environment becomes more important since this would benefit all the different manufacturers.

One of the popular communication protocols in the IoT domain is the Bluetooth Low Energy (BLE) protocol [2]. This protocol is known for its low power consumption, low setup time, and supporting star network topology with unlimited number of nodes. BLE systems can receive a certificate indicating that their system conforms to the BLE specifications when they pass a list of unit tests defined by the organisation behind BLE, Bluetooth SIG[1].

2.2   Model-Based Testing

Software testing verifies that a software system implements its requirements. Such a verification can be done in four steps [18,20,30]: specification interpretation, test creation, test execution, and test result evaluation. Model-Based Testing (MBT) is a method that can automate all of these steps except for the

---

[1] https://www.bluetooth.com/.

specification interpretation step by using a formal model defining the require-
ments/specifications [8,31]. The model describes the behavior of the System
Under Test (SUT) in terms of how the inputs and outputs of the SUT relate,
and uses this formal definition to generate and execute test cases to evaluate the
correctness of the SUT. A testing environment using MBT generally requires
three key technologies [8]: Modeling Language, Test Generation, and a Supporting Infrastructure. Figure 1 gives an overview of the components which we
discuss below.

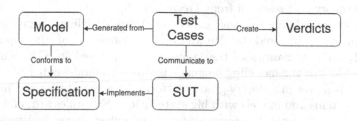

Fig. 1. Model-Based Testing pipeline [18]

Modeling Formalism. There are several modeling formalisms that can be
used in MBT [31], for example Finite State Machine (FSM), Labeled Transition System (LTS) [30], Unified Modeling Language (UML) [4], and Symbolic
Transition System (STS) [12]. FSMs and LTSs are often used for MBT [31]. To
describe a SUT using an LTS, a set of states and transitions are defined. The
transitions are used to reflect the correct behavior between the different states
in which the SUT could be. Finally, a Symbolic Transition System (STS) is an
extension to an LTS that introduces the concept of data to the models. This
addition of data is relevant since it allows us to prevent a state-space explosion
when dealing with data structures [12].

Test Case Generation. Based on a formal model an algorithm can generate
test cases automatically. Using this approach, a large number of test cases can be
generated. Due to time-constraints it is not always possible to execute all of these
test cases, therefore we need *test criteria* [24,27] to limit the number of generated
tests. Test cases consist of two ingredients: *stimuli* which represents inputs to
the SUT and a set of allowed *responses* which represent possible outputs from
the SUT. Once a test case is generated, stimuli will be passed on to the SUT
and observed outputs are presented to the testing environment. The MBT tool
checks if the observed responses are defined in the model. If this is the case,
the test case will pass otherwise it will fail. For the assignment of verdicts a
correctness notion between the model and the SUT, a so called conformance
relation, is important. The conformance relation that we use is the *input-output
conformance, IOCO* theory [30] which also uses STSs [13].

In order to automatically execute test cases we need some supporting infrastructure. The connection to the SUT is often implementation specific, in our case BLE. The connection to the MBT tooling is often standardized.

2.3   Axini Modeling Platform (AMP)

For our research we use the Axini Modeling Platform. Axini is a product company that specializes in modeling and model-based testing. AMP is an industry strength MBT tool that is used in Finance, Rail and High-tech. It is based on the IOCO theory and research from Tretmans [30].

AMP uses a modeling language called the Axini Modeling Language (AML). This language is inspired by ProMeLa, the language of the Spin model checker [21]. The semantics of the language is expressed in STS. The reason we choose AMP is: the modeling language is suited to model cyber physical systems, AMP is a proven industry grade platform (10+ years) that can handle big industrial systems and models with big state spaces. Examples are safety-critical rail systems, pension and insurance systems and cyber-physical systems.

3   MBT in the Context of IoT

3.1   IoT Testing Challenges

Looking at existing literature, we see that one of the overarching challenges for the industry to make fully conformant BLE devices, is that it costs too many resources to obtain and maintain an extensive test-suite [7,19,23,29]. First, the protocols from this domain change regularly [19,28]. As a result, testing environments need to be updated frequently and thus require significant maintenance [35]. Another obstacle is the large number of test cases necessary to test for conformance. IoT protocols, such as BLE, contain a wide range of different potential configurations. Optimally, a tester would test all combinations to test for conformance. However, with conventional manual methods, this becomes too expensive [7,19]. Finally, the quickly changing protocols also require backwards compatibility. Manufacturers are required to test against systems implementing older supported protocol versions.

3.2   Positioning MBT in IoT

MBT holds several benefits over traditional testing techniques. One benefit is that the resulting testing environment can quickly respond to changing specifications [24,31]. Changes made within the model are easier to maintain than manually changing individual low-level test cases when requirements change. Because frequently changing specifications are a problem, MBT would give a benefit over traditional testing methods that do not use an abstract representation within this domain.

Another benefit is that MBT results in arguably better tests compared to the manually created tests [5,31]. Pretschner [25] presents this with a different angle.

He mentions that the resulting tests cases are not necessarily of higher quality but that the higher quantity is the cause for a better testing environment. This higher number of test cases results in a higher coverage. In the IoT context, because it is difficult to obtain high coverage, this is a desired trait. MBT makes this possible through its high level of automation.

For MBT to reach this high level of automation, a model is required before testing can begin. The creation of such models is a non-trivial process, resulting in an additional potentially time-consuming step [5,9,24]. Consequently, it potentially takes longer before testing can begin compared to other methods that do not require this step. The modeling step also brings benefits. Because a modeler needs to critically think about the specifications for the creation of the model, this increases the chance of finding specification flaws [24,31]. This is specifically relevant in the IoT domain, where different manufacturers all need to follow the same specifications. Additionally, because manufacturers need to follow the same specifications, one model should suffice to supply every manufacturer with an extensive testing environment.

Based on the literature, we believe that MBT can form a solution to overcome the problems in the IoT testing domain if the previously discussed assumptions hold.

4   The AMP MBT Environment to Test BLE IoT Systems

To evaluate the assumptions from the previous section we require an MBT environment that can test the conformance of BLE devices. In this section, we discuss our design decisions, experience, and findings when implementing such an environment on the AMP platform.

4.1   SUT

For our experiment, we decided to model and test systems that implement the BLE specifications version 4.2 [6] from the official Bluetooth organization: Bluetooth SIG[2]. This version was chosen because a system running this version was easily accessible for experiments. Based on our experience we believe that the resulting process would be similar to other protocol versions.

One can access a Bluetooth Controller's capabilities through the Host Controller Interface (HCI) [6]. This interface functions as an API to perform specific actions on the different lower-level software layers on a Bluetooth system. We use this to test the conformance of the BLE protocol on a system.

The specifications of BLE describe the protocol using different *layers*. Each of these layers has its requirements and provides specific functionality. For the scope of our research, we decided to model the Link Layer. This layer describes the steps that two systems implementing the BLE protocol should take to obtain and sustain a connection. If a manufacturer makes a mistake in the implementation of this layer, it can directly influence the interoperability. Because interoperability is an important factor for IoT systems, we decided to model this specific layer.

---

[2] https://www.bluetooth.com/.

178   X. M. van Dommelen et al.

4.2 Model Creation

We will use a representation of the Link Layer's behavior, see Fig. 2, to highlight
which parts we implemented within our model. The states within this figure that
are accessible within our model are marked green.

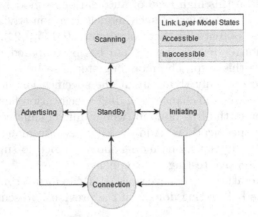

Fig. 2. State diagram of the Link Layer state machine on the Low Energy Controller
according to the Bluetooth Core Specification version 4.2 [6] (Color figure online)

Due to time constraints, we decided not to model the *Connection* state,
marked orange. Being able to also test this behavior would extend our work
such that we could also directly evaluate interoperability between systems. We
leave this to future work. Given the experience with the scale of models in AMP
we do not expect any problems with such an extension. Finally, a full version of
our obtained model can be requested by contacting Axini.

Model Overview. For the creation of our model, we used the state machine
from Fig. 2 as our starting point. We decided to use the same states within our
model and search through the specifications to look for the corresponding HCI
commands for the basic transitions.

Using the HCI command descriptions as a foundation, we concluded that the
following HCI commands would be most applicable to reflect the state transitions:

- HCI_LE_Set_Advertise_Enable. Handles the transitions between the *StandBy*
  and *Advertising* state.
- HCI_LE_Set_Scan_Enable. Handles the transitions between the *StandBy* and
  Scan state.
- HCI_LE_Create_Connection. Handles the transition from the *StandBy* to the
  Initiating State.
- HCI_LE_Create_Connection_Cancel. Handles the transition from the *Initiating* state to the *StandBy* state.

To model the different configurations, we selected the configuration options for the *Scanning* and *Advertising* state. The model represents this using transitions that go towards the same state after successfully changing the state configurations. The HCI commands that resemble these transitions are:

- HCI_LE_Set_Advertising_Parameters
- HCI_LE_Set_Scan_Parameters

4.3   AML Model Example

Given the scope of this paper it goes too far to introduce the entire AML modeling language. Instead we treat a part of the model and we show a part of the visualization of the model. The visualization is shown in Fig. 3. The model uses similar states as the state machine from the BLE specification in Fig. 2: Scanning, Advertising, Standby, Initiating.

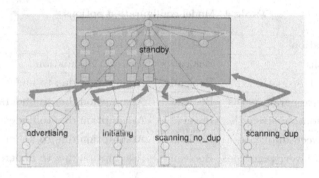

Fig. 3. AMP model visualization State diagram of the Link Layer

To give the reader some idea of what AML looks like, we discuss a simplified model in which we can successfully enable advertising following the BLE protocol. This model is shown in Listing 1.1.

Listing 1.1. AML model example

```
process ('main') {
    stimulus 'hci_le_set_advertise_enable',
        'advertising_enable' => : integer
    response 'status', 'code' => : integer

    state 'standbyState'
        receive 'hci_le_set_advertise_enable',
            constraint: 'advertising_enable==1'
        send 'status', constraint: 'code==1'
        goto: 'advertiseState'
    ...
}
```

In this model we define a process named 'main'. This process has one interface with one stimulus (input) 'hci_le_set_advertise_enable' and one response (output) 'status'; both have an integer parameter. The process shows a *state* with two actions: after the SUT receives a *hci_le_set_advertise_enable* stimulus with the *advertising_enable* parameter set to 1 it should give a *status* response back with a value of 1. The test case will continue from the *advertiseState* and pick a new action to test. For these tests, the stimulus parameters are solved with a constraint solver. We use constraints to define more complex input domains to model the other commands and different scenarios.

Model Configurations. In addition to the model that reflects BLE specifications, we added several model configuration options. A tester can use these configurations to manage to what extent the model is used during the generation of test cases. A list of supported configuration options is shown in Table 1.

Table 1. Model configuration options

ID	Configuration	Data Type	Motivation
1	error_paths	Boolean	Scenario Simulation
2	error_self_loop_paths	Boolean	Assumption due to underspecification
3	error_future_param_paths	Boolean	Assumption due to underspecification
4	error_validation_strength	Integer	Assumption due to underspecification
5	scan_between_duplicates	Boolean	Assumption due to underspecification
6	force_link_layer_transitions	Boolean	Assumption due to underspecification

- Configuration 1 allows one to trigger transitions that would result in an error code.
- Configuration 2 allows one to trigger transitions that could change the state but instead would result in the same state.
- Configuration 3 allows to trigger transitions that would result in an error because parameter values would be used that are reserved for future usage.
- Configuration 4 accepts five different strength values:
  - With strength 0 all error codes are allowed when an error code is expected.
  - With strength 1, only the error codes that are specifically mentioned in the specifications need to correspond to any of the expected errors if multiple errors could be thrown. Otherwise all error codes are accepted.
  - With strength 2 we have the same situation as with strength 1 however we apply our assumption on which error has a precedence when multiple errors could be thrown thus only allowing only one error code.
  - When strength 3 we only accept one or more of the expected errors. There is no precedence check.
  - Finally, with strength 4 we only accept the error codes with the highest precedence according to our assumptions.

- Configuration 5 allows one to trigger transitions that would move between the two possible scanning states in which *Filter_Duplicates* is enabled or disabled.
- Configuration 6 allows one to trigger transitions that would check if transitions that would not be possible according to the link layer specification result in the correct error code.

Motivation. While investigating the BLE specifications for the model, we found several topics that contained underspecifications. As a result, a developer can have different interpretations of what a *correct* BLE implementation would be. For these topics, we made assumptions about what the correct behavior of the protocol should be. However, it is also possible that a tester disagrees with our design. To compensate, we added configuration flags that allow a tester to configure the model such that test cases related to these assumptions will not get generated.

Findings. During the development of the model, we encountered several obstacles. The first obstacle is related to finding a point from which a tester can start modeling using the BLE specifications. The extensive specifications make it difficult to find a starting point. However, after finding this point, the remaining modeling process became straightforward. Additionally, the creation of the model became a time-consuming process because of the complexity of the BLE protocol. The protocol defines actions that contain many rules and can be different based on the system's state. Doing this correctly requires a tester to fully understand the specifications and reflect this flawlessly in a model resulting in a time-consuming process. These findings support the assumption that the modeling step is a time-consuming process. The authors think this could be significantly reduced if a BLE expert is available during the modeling process. Preferably the modeling takes place during the specification process.

After performing the modeling step, we see that the model is not our only result. During the process, we also discovered several flaws in the official BLE specifications. Most of these flaws are related to underspecification, but we also found a place where the specifications were contradicting. As a result, our experience confirms the assumption that we can find specification flaws during the modeling step and use this as a method to refine the specifications.

Limitations. We mentioned earlier that we use HCI commands to interact with a BLE system. These commands require two types of parameters. The first type contains parameters that together define which command should be running: OpCode Group Field, Opcode Command Field, and the expected resulting event code. We decided to separate these parameters from our model and put them as constants in our adapter. As a result, we limited the model to a static set of HCI commands that it can simulate. The second type contains parameters that define the configuration for an HCI function. According to the specifications, these parameters have a maximum memory size. We also followed this limitation in our model, but as a consequence, we are unable to test outside this memory range.

Finally, some HCI commands we simulate can generate additional event codes in the background. In our model, we only simulate the response code behavior, but for future work, we recommend also taking these event codes into account.

4.4   Adapter

As discussed in the background, the purpose of the adapter is to handle the communication between the SUT and the testing environment, AMP. Additionally, the adapter contains the translation logic from model labels into SUT actions and vice versa. This translation was straightforward to implement because our model follows the BLE specifications. However, we found that programming the communication with the HCI layer is a rather tedious task. The reason for this is that the documentation about programming on the HCI layer is scarce [14]. Consequently, the adapter step, which is supposed to be relatively small compared to modeling, became a more time-consuming process than expected. In the end, we decided to go with a Python implementation for the adapter. This adapter uses the PyBluez library[3] to communicate with the HCI of a BLE system.

5   Testing BLE Using AMP

By using AMP with the described model and adapter from Sect. 4, we can test any BLE system that implements BLE version 4.2. In this section, we describe how we test such a system, an *Intel Dual Band Wireless-AC 8265 [Bluetooth adapter]*. This SUT has received a certificate[4] from the official Bluetooth SIG organization indicating that they have correctly implemented BLE version 4.2.

To evaluate our approach and the SUT, we perform two experiments. The first experiment tests if we can find conformance errors using the platform. The second experiment looks into our found underspecifications that can potentially lead to implementation assumptions.

5.1   Assumption

A fundamental assumption we make for our experiments is that the test platform does not contain errors. In other words, we assume that the model, adapter, and testing environment (AMP) are all implemented correctly. Using this assumption, we can conclude that the found mistakes are caused by the SUT and not by potential flaws in one of these components. Our thorough analysis of the findings support this assumption.

---

[3] https://github.com/pybluez/pybluez.
[4] https://launchstudio.bluetooth.com/ListingDetails/3524.

5.2 Test Generation Configurations

Using our model-based testing platform, we can generate test cases to test a given SUT. The size of the test cases are configured by the tester and influence how much of the model can be traversed during one test-case. Additionally, a tester can set the number of test cases that during a test run are generated. Similar to the first configuration, this configuration influences the test coverage that can be obtained.

For our experiments, we wanted to obtain a model coverage of 100% to at least test each transition once. Through manual experiments, we found that this coverage can be achieved within a test case by setting the size to 30. Additionally, we decided to set the number of test cases that are generated during one test run to 20. We found this number to be enough for our goal to demonstrate that we can find conformance errors.

5.3 Conformance Experiment

In this experiment, we test the SUT using the previously discussed test generation configurations. Additionally, in Sect. 4.3, we discussed model configurations to enable and disable some of our assumptions regarding what the correct implementation should be. Because we do not want to leave room for discussion after we would find a conformance mistake, we decided to disable all configurations regarding assumptions.

Results. Running the testing environment with the previously described configurations, we obtain the results that are displayed in Fig. 4.

The results from Fig. 4 show us that we can obtain a Transition Coverage of 100%. Furthermore, the results show us that we can automatically find 19 test cases where the SUT does not conform to our model. If we would categorize our failed test cases based on which behavior deviates from the specifications, we obtain the categorization as shown in Table 2.

Table 2. Overview of the failed test cases and their cause using results from the *Conformance Experiment*

Test-case ID	State	Label	Expected	Output
2,4,5,7,15,17,18,20	Scan	setAdvertisingParams	0	18 (invalid parameters)
3,11,13,14	StandBy	setScanParams	0	18 (invalid parameters)
8,19	StandBy	createConnection	0	18 (invalid parameters)
9,12	StandBy	setAdvertisingParams	0	18 (invalid parameters)
10	Advertise	setScanParams	0	18 (invalid parameters)
16	StandBy	createConnection	0	13 (limited resources)

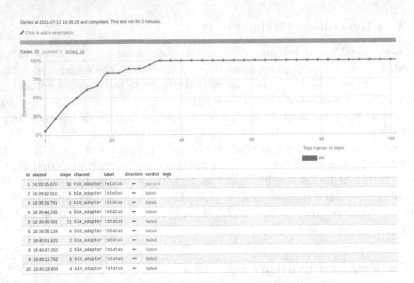

Fig. 4. Screenshot of AMP showing a partial overview of the resulting test cases and their evaluations using the configurations as discussed for the *Conformance Experiment*

This overview shows that we can find 6 different conformance mistakes based on the specifications. Furthermore, we see that most failed cases are caused by inaccurate error responses when using valid parameters.

Nonetheless, some of these error categories may be caused by the same underlying problem. As a result, this overview might show more errors than the SUT contains. However, the fact remains that we can find conformance flaws in a certified BLE system by applying a state-of-the-art MBT tool.

5.4   Model Assumption Experiment

For this experiment, we want to investigate our found underspecifications. By running our testing environment, while enforcing all of our assumptions through the model configurations, we can investigate if the SUT's implementation is different from our definition of a *correct* implementation. If we find implementation differences, we can confirm that manufacturers have different interpretations of what the correct behavior is when following the BLE specifications. Such findings can support the idea that our found underspecifications are a problem.

Results. Running the testing environment using our enforced assumptions on the SUT resulted in the test-run overview shown in Fig. 5.

First, these results show that enforcing our assumption configurations results in a Transition Coverage of 59.49%. Consequently, our test run does not cover the entire model. However, within this test run, we can still find behavior on the SUT that deviates from our assumptions. Table 3 shows an overview of the related conformance errors.

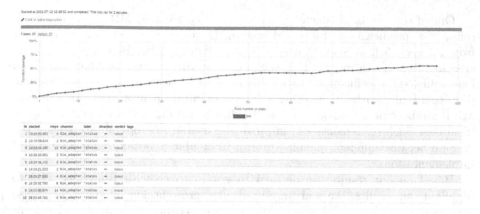

Fig. 5. Screenshot of AMP showing a partial overview of the resulting test cases and their evaluations using the configurations as discussed for the *Model Assumption Experiment*

Table 3. Categorised implementation errors related to different underspecification assumptions using the configurations as discussed for the *Model Assumption Experiment*

Assumption Configuration	Number of Failed Test Case(s)
error_self_loop_paths	6
error_future_param_paths	13
error_validation_strength	0
scan_between_duplicates	1
force_link_layer_transitions	0

Based on this categorization, we can confirm that the SUT behaves differently regarding three of our specification assumptions. As a result, our approach can highlight three topics within the specification that could lead to different implementations due to underspecification.

6 Discussion

The *conformance* experiment from Subsect. 5.3 shows us that we can find conformance flaws in a certified BLE system. This suggests that MBT can test more thoroughly than the testing environment that was used for the BLE certification of the SUT. This means that MBT can assist in obtaining more extensive testing environments and thus can assist in improving conformance and finally interoperability on IoT systems. Additionally, because our experiment showed that we can test BLE systems, a similar approach can be used to also test other communication protocols within the IoT domain.

One of the potential benefits discussed in Sect. 3 is that MBT can be used to refine the specifications of a tested system. During the *assumption* experiment from Subsect. 5.4, we show that specification flaws can be discovered during the creation step of the model. This suggests that the assumption that MBT can help refine the specifications also holds for BLE. Consequently, we can assume that this will also hold for other IoT communication protocols. As a result, MBT can become a method to refine the different communication protocol specifications. Such refinements will improve the overall interoperability within the domain because different manufacturers will be able to obtain more conformant implementations.

Based on our results, we decided to get in touch with Bluetooth SIG to highlight our results. We sent an e-mail after crosschecking if these flaws also remained in the latest, 5.2, specifications. As of writing this paper, we have not received a response.

Furthermore, we discussed our approach and findings with the creator of Bluetooth, Dr. Ir. Jaap C. Haartsen. In this meeting, he highlighted the current problems in the IoT Bluetooth domain. He mentioned that interoperability with machines from other manufacturers is a challenge for IoT manufacturers. In this context, it would be interesting to extend our work to the higher software layers that apply the BLE protocol.

7 Conclusion

It is crucial for IoT systems that the communications protocols such as BLE conform to the protocol's specifications. In our research, we have shown that manufacturers struggle to obtain testing environments that can test the specification conformance of their systems. Our experiments confirmed this by demonstrating that we can find conformance flaws in a certified BLE system using our proposed MBT environment. Additionally, we showed that we can find weaknesses in the official BLE specification by using MBT. Correcting these flaws will allow different manufacturers to create implementations that are more conformant and thus will assist in ensuring interoperability. Finally, based on these findings, we believe that MBT can be a solution within the IoT protocol testing domain using existing MBT tools such as AMP.

7.1 Future Work

Our work focuses on researching the possibilities of MBT to test IoT protocols. However, our research does not perform a comparison study with other testing methods for this domain. The next step would be to compare this method to other testing methods and discuss what method would be the most optimal for this domain. Another direction that research could look into is testing the interoperability between IoT systems. This direction would be interesting because our work assumes that conformance errors will result in interoperability issues but does not test it directly. Finally, because our testing environment was able to find conformance errors on a certified BLE system, it becomes interesting to research if such errors also occur on more systems in the market.

References

1. Ahmad, A., Bouquet, F., Fourneret, E., Le Gall, F., Legeard, B.: Model-based testing as a service for IoT platforms. In: Margaria, T., Steffen, B. (eds.) ISoLA 2016. LNCS, vol. 9953, pp. 727–742. Springer, Cham (2016). https://doi.org/10. 1007/978-3-319-47169-3_55

2. Al-Sarawi, S., Anbar, M., Alieyan, K., Alzubaidi, M.: Internet of things (IoT) communication protocols. In: 2017 8th International Conference on Information Technology (ICIT), pp. 685–690. IEEE (2017)

3. Aziz, B.: A formal model and analysis of an IoT protocol. Ad Hoc Netw. **36**, 49–57 (2016)

4. Bernard, E., et al.: Model-based testing from UML models. INFORMATIK 2006-Informatik für Menschen-Band 2, Beiträge der 36. Jahrestagung der Gesellschaft für Informatik eV (GI) (2006)

5. Binder, R.V., Legeard, B., Kramer, A.: Model-based testing: where does it stand? Commun. ACM **58**(2), 52–56 (2015)

6. Bluetooth SIG: Core specification 4.2 (2014). https://www.bluetooth.com/ specifications/specs/core-specification-4-2/. Accessed 28 June 2021

7. Bures, M., Cerny, T., Ahmed, B.S.: Internet of things: current challenges in the quality assurance and testing methods. In: Kim, K.J., Baek, N. (eds.) ICISA 2018. LNEE, vol. 514, pp. 625–634. Springer, Singapore (2019). https://doi.org/10.1007/ 978-981-13-1056-0_61

8. Dalal, S.R., et al.: Model-based testing in practice. In: Proceedings of the 21st International Conference on Software Engineering, pp. 285–294 (1999)

9. Dias Neto, A.C., Subramanyan, R., Vieira, M., Travassos, G.H.: A survey on model-based testing approaches: a systematic review. In: Proceedings of the 1st ACM International Workshop on Empirical Assessment of Software Engineering Languages and Technologies: Held in Conjunction with the 22nd IEEE/ACM International Conference on Automated Software Engineering (ASE) 2007, pp. 31–36 (2007)

10. Elnashar, A.: IoT evolution towards a super-connected world. arXiv preprint arXiv:1907.02589 (2019)

11. Ergen, S.C.: ZigBee/IEEE 802.15.4 summary. UC Berkeley, 10 September 2004

12. Frantzen, L., Tretmans, J., Willemse, T.A.C.: Test generation based on symbolic specifications. In: Grabowski, J., Nielsen, B. (eds.) FATES 2004. LNCS, vol. 3395, pp. 1–15. Springer, Heidelberg (2005). https://doi.org/10.1007/978-3-540-31848-4_1

13. Frantzen, L., Tretmans, J., Willemse, T.A.C.: A symbolic framework for model-based testing. In: Havelund, K., Núñez, M., Roşu, G., Wolff, B. (eds.) FATES/RV -2006. LNCS, vol. 4262, pp. 40–54. Springer, Heidelberg (2006). https://doi.org/ 10.1007/11940197_3

14. Huang, A.S., Rudolph, L.: Bluetooth Essentials for Programmers. Cambridge University Press, Cambridge (2007)

15. Hwang, J., Aziz, A., Sung, N., Ahmad, A., Le Gall, F., Song, J.: AUTOCON-IoT: automated and scalable online conformance testing for IoT applications. IEEE Access **8**, 43111–43121 (2020)
16. Incki, K., Ari, I.: Observing interoperability of IoT systems through model-based testing. In: Fortino, G., et al. (eds.) InterIoT/SaSeIoT -2017. LNICST, vol. 242, pp. 60–66. Springer, Cham (2018). https://doi.org/10.1007/978-3-319-93797-7_8
17. Statista Inc.: Internet of things (IoT) active device connections installed base worldwide from 2015 to 2025* (2020). https://www.statista.com/statistics/1101442/iot-number-of-connected-devices-worldwide/
18. Janssen, S.: Transforming source code into symbolic transition systems for practical model-based testing (2017)
19. Kim, H., et al.: IoT-TaaS: towards a prospective IoT testing framework. IEEE Access **6**, 15480–15493 (2018)
20. Koopman, P., Alimarine, A., Tretmans, J., Plasmeijer, R.: GAST: generic automated software testing. In: Peña, R., Arts, T. (eds.) IFL 2002. LNCS, vol. 2670, pp. 84–100. Springer, Heidelberg (2003). https://doi.org/10.1007/3-540-44854-3_6
21. Krichen, M., Tripakis, S.: Black-box conformance testing for real-time systems. In: Graf, S., Mounier, L. (eds.) SPIN 2004. LNCS, vol. 2989, pp. 109–126. Springer, Heidelberg (2004). https://doi.org/10.1007/978-3-540-24732-6_8
22. Malik, B.H., et al.: IoT testing-as-a-service: a new dimension of automation. Int. J. Adv. Comput. Sci. Appl. **10**(5) (2019)
23. Marinissen, E.J., et al.: IoT: source of test challenges. In: 2016 21th IEEE European Test Symposium (ETS), pp. 1–10. IEEE (2016)
24. Pretschner, A.: Model-based testing in practice. In: Fitzgerald, J., Hayes, I.J., Tarlecki, A. (eds.) FM 2005. LNCS, vol. 3582, pp. 537–541. Springer, Heidelberg (2005). https://doi.org/10.1007/11526841_37
25. Pretschner, A., et al.: One evaluation of model-based testing and its automation. In: Proceedings of the 27th International Conference on Software Engineering, pp. 392–401 (2005)
26. Saleem, J., Hammoudeh, M., Raza, U., Adebisi, B., Ande, R.: IoT standardisation: challenges, perspectives and solution. In: Proceedings of the 2nd International Conference on Future Networks and Distributed Systems, pp. 1–9 (2018)
27. Schieferdecker, I.: Model-based testing. IEEE Softw. **29**(1), 14 (2012)
28. Taivalsaari, A., Mikkonen, T.: A roadmap to the programmable world: software challenges in the IoT era. IEEE Softw. **34**(1), 72–80 (2017)
29. Tappler, M., Aichernig, B.K., Bloem, R.: Model-based testing IoT communication via active automata learning. In: 2017 IEEE International Conference on Software Testing, Verification and Validation (ICST), pp. 276–287. IEEE (2017)
30. Tretmans, J.: Model based testing with labelled transition systems. In: Hierons, R.M., Bowen, J.P., Harman, M. (eds.) Formal Methods and Testing. LNCS, vol. 4949, pp. 1–38. Springer, Heidelberg (2008). https://doi.org/10.1007/978-3-540-78917-8_1
31. Utting, M., Pretschner, A., Legeard, B.: A taxonomy of model-based testing approaches. Softw. Test. Verif. Reliab. **22**(5), 297–312 (2012)
32. Vorakulpipat, C., Rattanalerdnusorn, E., Thaenkaew, P., Hai, H.D.: Recent challenges, trends, and concerns related to IoT security: an evolutionary study. In: 2018 20th International Conference on Advanced Communication Technology (ICACT), pp. 405–410. IEEE (2018)
33. Xia, F., Yang, L.T., Wang, L., Vinel, A.: Internet of things. Int. J. Commun. Syst. **25**(9), 1101 (2012)

34. Yoneyama, J., Artho, C., Tanabe, Y., Hagiya, M.: Model-based network fault injection for IoT protocols. In: Proceedings of the 14th International Conference on Evaluation of Novel Approaches to Software Engineering, pp. 201–209. SCITEPRESS-Science and Technology Publications, Lda (2019)
35. Ziegler, S., Fdida, S., Viho, C., Watteyne, T.: F-interop – online platform of interoperability and performance tests for the internet of things. In: Mitton, N., Chaouchi, H., Noel, T., Watteyne, T., Gabillon, A., Capolsini, P. (eds.) InterIoT/SaSeIoT - 2016. LNICST, vol. 190, pp. 49–55. Springer, Cham (2017). https://doi.org/10.1007/978-3-319-52727-7_7

Methodology

Formally Verifying Decompositions of Stochastic Specifications

Anton Hampus[1]([⊠])[iD] and Mattias Nyberg[1,2]([⊠])

[1] KTH Royal Institute of Technology, Stockholm, Sweden
ahampus@kth.se
[2] Scania, Södertälje, Sweden
mattias.nyberg@scania.com

Abstract. According to the principles of compositional verification, verifying that lower-level components satisfy their specification will ensure that the whole system satisfies its top-level specification. The key step is to ensure that the lower-level specifications constitute a correct decomposition of the top-level specification. In a non-stochastic context, such decomposition can be analyzed using techniques of theorem proving. In industrial applications, especially for safety-critical systems, specifications are often of stochastic nature, for example giving a bound on the probability that system failure will occur before a given time. A decomposition of such a specification requires techniques beyond traditional theorem proving. The first contribution of the paper is a theoretical framework that allows the representation of, and reasoning about, stochastic and timed behavior of systems as well as specifications for such behaviors. The framework is based on traces that describe the continuous-time evolution of a system, and specifications are formulated using timed automata combined with probabilistic acceptance conditions. The second contribution is a novel approach to verifying decomposition of such specifications by reducing the problem to checking emptiness of the solution space for a system of linear inequalities.

Keywords: Specification Theory · Refinement · Contracts

1 Introduction

The principle of *compositional verification* [33] has been proposed as a solution to verify large complex systems built up by smaller components. The key idea is to verify that: (1) each component implements its specification, and (2) the composition of these component specifications refines the top-level system specification. This will then ensure that the whole system implements its top-level specification. The key difficulty is (2), which can also be expressed as to ensure that the component specifications constitute a correct decomposition of the top-level specification.

Supported by Vinnova FFI through the SafeDim project.

Although decomposition of specifications is in general difficult, its importance is stressed by its role in recent industrial standards such as ISO 26262 [20] and ISO 21434 [19]. In these standards, specifications in the form of safety and cyber-security requirements are decomposed into lower-level specifications. The standards also require these decompositions to be correct and complete.

In the present paper, we consider general cyber-physical systems, and have therefore chosen a representation based on continuous time. Based upon logic and various extensions to include time, a number of frameworks are available to express specifications and to verify refinement between specifications, e.g. [10,27,30,35]. A limitation with these frameworks is that they do not consider probabilistic or stochastic behaviors. On the other hand, from an industrial standpoint, the ability to include stochastics is fundamentally important since the exact purpose of many specifications, especially within safety, is to set limits on the probability of undesired events to occur within certain time intervals.

In order to allow the study of stochastic specifications, the present paper proposes, as its first contribution, a novel framework covering: syntax and semantics of stochastic specifications, and composition and refinement of such specifications. To support the industrial applicability of the framework, as the second contribution, the paper proposes also an algorithm for the analysis of whether a composition of stochastic specifications refines another stochastic specification.

The approach taken in the paper is that *behaviors* of components and systems are characterized by traces and probability measures over sets of traces. Rather than being expressed explicitly, behaviors are used as an abstract tool for defining the semantics of *specifications*, as sets of behaviors. The syntax of specifications bears a resemblance to CSL [4,5,17] but views specifications generally as a probabilistic extension to *assume-guarantee contracts* [7,26,37]. In such a specification, denoted $\mathcal{P}_{<p}(\mathcal{A}, \mathcal{G})$, both the assumption $\mathcal{A}$ and the guarantee $\mathcal{G}$ of the contract is represented by a deterministic timed automaton responding to traces. The specification states that, given that the environment satisfies the assumption, the probability that the guarantee is satisfied shall be less than p.

The literature contains some other proposed frameworks for defining stochastic specifications and verifying properties such as refinement, e.g. [8,13,14,16,21,22,24,29,34]. However, in contrast to all of these previous works, the present paper uses continuous time and considers component behaviors purely in terms of traces—no particular modeling formalism for generating the traces is assumed.

The paper is organized as follows. Section 2 uses an example to illustrate the problem and sketch the proposed solution. Section 3 and 4 describe the proposed framework and algorithm. Section 5 applies the framework and the algorithm to an extended version of the example studied in Sect. 2. Finally, Sect. 6 and 7 present related work and conclusions.

2 Problem Illustration

Consider a two-component system consisting of a main and backup power source. The idea is that whenever there is a main power failure, the backup is activated.

The purpose of the backup is to prolong the duration of power output by the system. However, in order for the backup to correctly do this, it needs to first be charged by the main power source for a certain amount of time. Furthermore, even if charged, there is a probability that it will fail prematurely. An example of such a system is depicted in Fig. 1 and 2. In these diagrams, main power failure occurs exponentially with rate $\frac{1}{20}$ (per hour), while the backup component

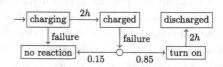

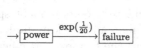

Fig. 1. Possible main power component

Fig. 2. Possible backup component

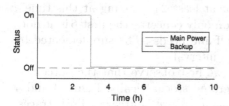

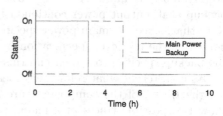

Fig. 3. Failed backup activation

Fig. 4. Successful backup activation

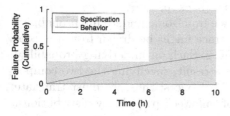

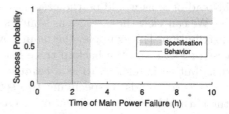

Fig. 5. Main power specification

Fig. 6. Backup specification

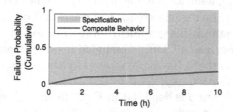

Fig. 7. Top-level specification

responds to this failure probabilistically. More precisely, when main power failure occurs, the backup is activated with 85% probability if it has finished charging and 0% probability otherwise. This fact is represented in Fig. 2 by the edges labeled *failure*. The required charging time for this specific backup is 2 h. Once turned on, the backup will output power also for 2 h, until entering a discharged state.

Assume the top-level specification to be: "the system shall output power continuously during the first 7 h with over 50% probability". Instead of merely verifying that the system composed of the components in Fig. 1 and 2 implements the top-level specification, we want to formulate two component specifications and verify that *any* system composed of a main and backup implementing its component specification is sure to implement the top-level specification. As our attempt for doing so, let the main power source specification be: "main power failure shall occur before 6 h with at most 30% probability". Meanwhile, the backup specification will be an assume-guarantee contract: "assuming main power failure occurs after at least 3 h, then with at least 80% probability, the backup shall output power continuously for at least 2 h starting at this time". Note that, since the main power specification only concerns the first 6 h, it does not refine the top-level specification by itself and needs to be supplemented by the backup specification to extend this time interval.

As a sketch of what refinement means, we first observe that the outcomes, i.e. the *traces*, of the components are generated stochastically. Figure 3 and 4 show two possible traces of a main and backup power source. In both traces, main power failure occurs at exactly 3 h. However, backup power activation fails in Fig. 3 while succeeding in Fig. 4. Once activated, it manages to prolong power output by 2 h, resulting in the system continuously outputting power for 5 h instead of 3, as would be the case without the backup.

We can view these traces as samples drawn from some underlying probability distribution. For example, the main power trace might be drawn from the process of Fig. 1 and the backup trace from Fig. 2. Such an underlying probability distribution is referred to as a *behavior*. As a result, specifying the two components corresponds to specifying two sets of behaviors; thus, we must translate the natural language specifications to sets of "allowed" probability distributions.

Figure 5 depicts the specification for the main power source in terms of the behaviors it contains, represented by the gray region. The convention used here is that a behavior, represented by the cumulative distribution function (CDF) of the time to failure, implements the specification if it lies completely within the gray region. Note that the region extends to positive infinity along the horizontal axis. To better understand this graphical representation of the specification, an example behavior, drawn as a CDF, is included inside the region. Note that this CDF in fact represents the behavior generated by the process of Fig. 1, following the exponential distribution $\exp(\frac{1}{20})$.

The backup specification is depicted in Fig. 6 using a similar approach. However, this region does not represent a set of failure CDFs, but instead a set of success probabilities, given as functions of the time when main power failure occurs. Here, success means that the backup is able to output power for at least 2 h. The example behavior shown within the region corresponds to a backup power source that needs 2 h to charge, and, once charged, has a success rate of 85% regardless of when main power fails. Note that whenever the assumption is unfulfilled, nothing is required of the backup. That is, within the first 3 h, all success rates from 0% to 100% are allowed.

Lastly, the top-level specification is depicted in Fig. 7, showing a region of allowed failure CDFs of total power output, ignoring whether the main or backup is responsible for outputting it. The question now is this: does the composition of the two component specifications refine the top-level specification? The purpose of the rest of the paper is to formalise these notions of *traces*, *behaviors*, and *specifications*, and to provide an algorithm for verifying refinement.

3   A Theory for Specifying Stochastic Behavior

3.1   Traces and Behaviors

A *behavior* is meant to represent the possible executions, or *traces*, of a component, as well as how likely they are. In short, we represent a trace as an assignment of values to variables at each point in time, and a behavior as a distribution over traces. We will also extend behaviors to incorporate input as well as output, calling them input/output behaviors.

We consider a universal set of variables $X = \{x_1, x_2, \ldots, x_n\}, n \geq 1$, each $x_i \in X$ ranging over a non-empty countable set V_{x_i} of values. Given a non-empty set of variables $E \subseteq X$, a *valuation for* E is a function $\nu : E \to \bigcup_{x_i \in X} V_{x_i}$ associating each $x_i \in E$ with a value in its range V_{x_i}. The set of all possible valuations for a non-empty set $E \subseteq X$ is denoted $\mathtt{val}(E)$.

Definition 1 (Trace). *Given a non-empty set of variables $E \subseteq X$, a trace over E is a right-continuous function $\theta : \mathbb{R}_{\geq 0} \to \mathtt{val}(E)$ defined on the timeline.*   □

Let $\mathtt{tr}(E)$ denote the set of all possible traces over E. By convention, let $\mathtt{tr}(\emptyset) = \emptyset$, i.e. the set of all possible traces over the empty set of variables is $\emptyset$.

Definition 2 (Behavior). *Given a non-empty set of variables $E \subseteq X$, a behavior over E is a probability measure defined on a sigma algebra on the set $\mathtt{tr}(E)$.*   □

Let $\mathtt{beh}(E)$ denote the set of all possible behaviors over a non-empty $E \subseteq X$.

We will now extend behaviors into *input-output behaviors*, which intuitively have control over output variables while being dependent on input variables.

Definition 3 (Input/Output Behavior). *Given two disjoint sets of variables $I \subseteq X$ and $O \subseteq X$, where O is non-empty, an input/output behavior from I to O is a function $\beta : \mathtt{tr}(I) \to \mathtt{beh}(O)$ such that for any pair of traces $\theta_1, \theta_2 \in \mathtt{tr}(I)$, the behaviors $\beta(\theta_1)$ and $\beta(\theta_2)$ share the same sigma algebra denoted σ_β.*   □

Given a possibly empty $I \subseteq X$ and a non-empty $O \subseteq X$, let $\mathtt{beh}(I, O)$ denote the set of all possible input/output behaviors from I to O. Furthermore, for an input/output behavior β from I to O, let $\mathtt{in}(\beta)$ and $\mathtt{out}(\beta)$ denote the sets I and O of input and output variables, respectively. From now on, "input/output" will often be abbreviated as I/O.

Example 1. Consider $I = \emptyset$ and $O = \{x\}$. Then an I/O behavior from I to O is a function $\beta : \emptyset \rightarrow \mathtt{beh}(\{x\})$. Thus, the I/O behavior from I to O reduces to a behavior over $\{x\}$, i.e. $\beta \in \mathtt{beh}(\{x\})$.

Composition of Behaviors. When composing two behaviors β_1 and β_2, for the sake of simplicity, we restrict ourselves to the case where β_1 has no input, and its output is exactly the input of β_2, i.e. $\mathtt{in}(\beta_1) = \emptyset$ and $\mathtt{out}(\beta_1) = \mathtt{in}(\beta_2)$. The implication of this is that composing β_1 with β_2 results in yet another behavior without input. The composition of β_1 and β_2, denoted $\beta_1 \| \beta_2$, is the I/O behavior from $\mathtt{in}(\beta_1) = \emptyset$ to $\mathtt{out}(\beta_1) \cup \mathtt{out}(\beta_2)$ formed as follows.

We assume that $\beta_2(\cdot)(\Theta_2)$, for any fixed Θ_2, is a measurable function from the measurable space $(\mathtt{out}(\beta_1), \sigma_{\beta_1})$ to the measurable space $([0, 1], \mathcal{B}([0, 1]))$. Then according to [32] (Thm. 5.8.1 and Thm. 2.4.3), $\beta_1 \| \beta_2(\cdot)$ defined as $\beta_1 \| \beta_2(\Theta_1 \times \Theta_2) = \int_{\Theta_1} \beta_2(\theta_1)(\Theta_2)\beta_1(d\theta_1)$ is a probability of $\Theta_1 \times \Theta_2 \in \sigma_{\beta_1} \times \sigma_{\beta_2}$ and its unique extension a probability measure on the product sigma algebra $\sigma_{\beta_1} \times \sigma_{\beta_2}$. This result is the basis for the following definition.

Definition 4 (Composition of I/O Behaviors). *Let β_1 and β_2 be two I/O behaviors such that $\mathtt{in}(\beta_1) = \emptyset$, $\mathtt{in}(\beta_2) = \mathtt{out}(\beta_1)$, and $\beta_2(\cdot)(\Theta_2)$ is a measurable function from $(\mathtt{out}(\beta_1), \sigma_{\beta_1})$ to $([0, 1], \mathcal{B}([0, 1]))$. The composition of β_1 and β_2, denoted $\beta_1 \| \beta_2$, is an I/O behavior from $\emptyset$ to $\mathtt{out}(\beta_1) \cup \mathtt{out}(\beta_2)$, i.e. a probability measure*

$$\beta_1 \| \beta_2 \in \mathtt{beh}(\mathtt{out}(\beta_1) \cup \mathtt{out}(\beta_2)) ,$$

defined by

$$\beta_1 \| \beta_2(\Theta_1 \times \Theta_2) = \int_{\Theta_1} \beta_2(\theta_1)(\Theta_2)\beta_1(d\theta_1)$$

and its unique extension, and defined on $\sigma_{\beta_1} \times \sigma_{\beta_2}$. $\qquad\square$

Note that according to this definition, we only obtain a measure on the sigma algebra $\sigma_{\beta_1} \times \sigma_{\beta_2}$. As a consequence, we assume that any subset of $\mathtt{tr}(\mathtt{out}(\beta_1)) \times \mathtt{tr}(\mathtt{in}(\beta_2))$ that we want to measure the probability of, and that is not an element of $\sigma_{\beta_1} \times \sigma_{\beta_2}$, can be approximated to arbitrary precision by some element in $\sigma_{\beta_1} \times \sigma_{\beta_2}$. Note further that the output of the composition $\beta_1 \| \beta_2$ simply becomes the union of β_1 and β_2 and it is presumed that $\mathtt{in}(\beta_2) = \mathtt{out}(\beta_1)$ and $\mathtt{in}(\beta_1) = \emptyset$. Clearly, a less restrictive definition can be created, but for the sake of simplicity, these generalizations are left out of scope of the current paper.

3.2 Specifications

In short, we view a specification simply as the set of behaviors that implement it. A specification *refines* another if each behavior implementing it also implements the other. This is captured by the following three definitions.

Definition 5 (Specification). *Given two disjoint sets of variables $I \subseteq X$ and $O \subseteq X$ such that O is non-empty, a* specification Σ *from I to O is a subset of the I/O behaviors* $\mathsf{beh}(I,O)$, *i.e.* $\Sigma \subseteq \mathsf{beh}(I,O)$. $\qquad\square$

Definition 6 (Implements). *An I/O behavior β from I to O* implements *a specification Σ from I to O if $\beta \in \Sigma$.* $\qquad\square$

Definition 7 (Refines). *A specification Σ_1 from I to O* refines *a specification Σ_2 from I to O if $\Sigma_1 \subseteq \Sigma_2$.* $\qquad\square$

Given a possibly empty set $I \subseteq X$ and non-empty set $O \subseteq X$, let $\mathsf{spec}(I,O)$ denote the set of all possible specifications from I to O. Given a specification Σ, $\mathsf{in}(\Sigma)$ and $\mathsf{out}(\Sigma)$ are defined in a similar manner as with I/O behaviors.

Note that, according to Definition 4, $\beta_1 \| \beta_2$ is only defined for cases where $\mathsf{in}(\beta_1) = \emptyset$, $\mathsf{in}(\beta_2) = \mathsf{out}(\beta_1)$, and $\beta_2(\cdot)(\Theta_2)$ is a measurable function from $(\mathsf{out}(\beta_1), \sigma_{\beta_1})$ to $([0,1], \mathcal{B}([0,1]))$. Behaviors fulfilling these conditions will be called *compatible*.

In analogy with the notion of compatible behaviors, we say that two specifications Σ_1 and Σ_2 are *compatible* if each $\beta_1 \in \Sigma_1$ is compatible with each $\beta_2 \in \Sigma_2$. Note that a prerequisite for this is that $\mathsf{in}(\Sigma_1) = \emptyset$ and $\mathsf{in}(\Sigma_2) = \mathsf{out}(\Sigma_1)$.

Definition 8 (Parallel Composition of Specifications). *Given two compatible specifications Σ_1 and Σ_2, the* parallel composition of Σ_1 and Σ_2, *denoted $\Sigma_1 \| \Sigma_2$, is the specification $\Sigma_1 \| \Sigma_2 = \{\beta_1 \| \beta_2 \mid \beta_1 \in \Sigma_1, \beta_2 \in \Sigma_2\}$.* $\qquad\square$

The essence of this definition is that we can take any pair $\beta_1 \in \Sigma_1$ and $\beta_2 \in \Sigma_2$, and be sure that $\beta_1 \| \beta_2 \in \Sigma_1 \| \Sigma_2$.

3.3 Trace Automata

The specification language presented in this paper, as well as its semantics and the verification method, are based on *timed automata*, as introduced by Alur and Dill [2,3]. The following definitions follow closely this literature, except that traces are assumed as input, rather than timed words, to fit the current setting.

Let a *clock* be a variable ranging over the entire timeline $\mathbb{R}_{\geq 0}$. We will often use the notation ν_C for a valuation over clocks, as opposed to ν, which is used for a valuation over variables in X. For $t \in \mathbb{R}_{\geq 0}$, let $\nu_C + t$ denote the clock valuation $\{c \mapsto \nu_C(c) + t \mid c \in C\}$. Given a set $C = \{c_1, \ldots, c_m\}$ of clocks, a *clock constraint δ on C* is defined inductively by the grammar

$$\delta ::= c < k \mid c \geq k \mid \delta \wedge \delta,$$

where c ranges over clocks C and k ranges over constant real numbers $\mathbb{R}$. A clock valuation ν_C for C is said to *satisfy* a clock constraint δ on C if $\delta[c_1 \mapsto \nu_C(c_1), \ldots, c_m \mapsto \nu_C(c_m)]$ evaluates to true. Given a set C of clocks, let $\Delta(C)$ denote the set of all possible clock constraints on C.

Definition 9 (Timed Automaton). *A timed automaton is a tuple* $\mathcal{A} = \langle V, L, l_0, C, \rightarrow, F \rangle$ *where V is a countable alphabet, L is a countable set of locations, $l_0 \in L$ is a start location, C is a countable set of clocks, $\rightarrow \subseteq L \times V \times 2^C \times \Delta(C) \times L$ is a transition relation, and $F \subseteq L$ is a set of accepting locations.* □

For a timed automaton $\mathcal{A} = \langle V, L, l_0, C, \rightarrow, F \rangle$, we denote by $V_{\mathcal{A}}$, $L_{\mathcal{A}}$, $l_{0_{\mathcal{A}}}$, $C_{\mathcal{A}}$, $\rightarrow_{\mathcal{A}}$, and $F_{\mathcal{A}}$ the elements V, L, l_0, C, $\rightarrow$, and F, respectively. A timed automaton is said to be *deterministic* if, for each pair of distinct transitions originating from the same location and sharing the same alphabet symbol, there exists no clock valuation satisfying both clock constraints.

In what follows, only a special class of timed automata, called *trace automata*, will be considered. These are characterized by the fact that their alphabets consist of variable valuations, resulting in the ability to read traces as input. This leads us to use the letter ν to denote an input symbol.

Given a timed automaton $\mathcal{A} = \langle V, L, l_0, C, \rightarrow, F \rangle$, locations $l, l' \in L$, clock valuations ν_C, ν'_C for C, and an alphabet symbol $\nu \in V$, we will denote by $(l, \nu_C) \xrightarrow{\nu}_{\mathcal{A}} (l', \nu'_C)$ the logical statement that $\rightarrow$ contains a transition $\langle l, \nu, r, \delta, l' \rangle$ with $r = \{c_1, \ldots, c_m\}$ such that ν_C satisfies δ and $\nu'_C = \nu_C[c_1 \mapsto 0, \ldots, c_m \mapsto 0]$.

In order to give a concise and well-defined semantics for trace automata, we require that only a finite number of transitions are possible within 0 time. This fact is captured in the following definition.

Definition 10 (Trace Automaton). *Given a non-empty set $E \subseteq X$ of variables, a deterministic timed automaton $\mathcal{A} = \langle V, L, l_0, C, \rightarrow, F \rangle$ is a trace automaton for E if $V = \mathtt{val}(E)$ and, for each $l \in L$ and $\nu_C \in \mathtt{val}(C)$, there exists no infinite sequence* $(l, \nu_C) \xrightarrow{\nu}_{\mathcal{A}} (l_1, \nu_{C_1}) \xrightarrow{\nu}_{\mathcal{A}} (l_2, \nu_{C_2}) \xrightarrow{\nu}_{\mathcal{A}} \ldots$ □

Note from Definition 10 that the condition about infinite transition sequences applies both to loops, including self loops, as well as to infinite location spaces with an infinite number of transitions. For instance, trace automata never allow self loops $\langle l, \nu, r, \delta, l \rangle$ in which the set r of clocks to reset is empty.

The semantics of a trace automaton $\mathcal{A} = \langle V, L, l_0, C, \rightarrow, F \rangle$ for a non-empty E is defined as follows. Consider a trace $\theta \in \mathtt{tr}(E)$ to be given. A configuration is a tuple $\mu_i = (l_i, \nu_{C_i}, t_i) \in L \times \mathtt{val}(C) \times \mathbb{R}_{\geq 0}$, containing a location, clock configuration and time value. Initially, $\mu_0 = (l_0, \bar{0}, 0)$, where $\bar{0}$ denotes the clock valuation $\{c \mapsto 0 \mid c \in C\}$. Inductively, consider a configuration $\mu_i = (l_i, \nu_{C_i}, t_i)$ and the smallest time increment t^+ causing the automaton to transition. That is, $t^+ = \min\{t \in \mathbb{R}_{\geq 0} \mid \exists \langle l_i, \theta(t_i + t), r, \delta, l'_i \rangle \in \rightarrow . \nu_{C_i} + t \text{ satisfies } \delta\}$. The successor of μ_i becomes $\mu_{i+1} = (l_{i+1}, \nu_{C_{i+1}}, t_{i+1})$ such that $t_{i+1} = t_i + t^+$ and there exists a maximal transition sequence $(l_i, \nu_{C_i} + t^+) \xrightarrow{\theta(t_{i+1})} \ldots \xrightarrow{\theta(t_{i+1})} (l_{i+1}, \nu_{C_{i+1}})$.

Note that the sequence $\mu_0, \mu_1, \ldots$ generated in this way is unique since $\mathcal{A}$ is deterministic. Thus, we can define *the execution of $\mathcal{A}$ on θ*, denoted $\mathcal{A}(\theta)$, as this sequence $\mu_0, \mu_1, \ldots$. Let furthermore $\mathcal{A}(\theta)|_L$ denote the sequence $l_0, l_1, \ldots$ of locations visited along the execution.

Definition 11 (Path). *Given a set $E \subseteq X$ of variables, a trace automaton $\mathcal{A} = \langle V, L, l_0, C, \rightarrow, F \rangle$ for E, and a location sequence $\pi \in L^*$, the sequence π is a path of $\mathcal{A}$ if there exists a trace $\theta \in \mathtt{tr}(E)$ such that $\pi = \mathcal{A}(\theta)|_L$.* □

Given a trace automaton $\mathcal{A}$ for E, the set of all possible paths of $\mathcal{A}$ is denoted $\mathtt{paths}(\mathcal{A})$. Furthermore, given an infinite path $l_0, l_1, \ldots$ of $\mathcal{A}$, the limit $\lim_{i \to \infty} l_i$ exists if and only if there exists an index $a \in \mathbb{N}$ such that for each $b \geq a$, $l_b = l_a$. For finite paths $l_0, l_1, \ldots, l_k$, we use the convention that $\lim_{i \to \infty} l_i = l_k$. If for each trace $\theta \in \mathtt{tr}(E)$ the path $\mathcal{A}(\theta)|_L = l_0, l_1, \ldots$ has a limit $\lim_{i \to \infty} l_i$, then $\mathcal{A}$ is said to be *terminating*.

Henceforth, we will only consider terminating trace automata. This is done both for the sake of simplicity and to provide a refinement verification algorithm that is guaranteed to terminate. Note that terminating automata still allow us to express safety properties over infinite traces, such as "the system shall never crash". Furthermore, although some types of liveness properties are not possible to express, such as "at all times, each request shall be followed by an answer", we can still express liveness properties such as "the system eventually finishes", or liveness *within bounded time*, such as "during the system lifetime of 10,000 h, each request shall be followed by an answer". Let $\mathbb{A}_E$ denote the set of all terminating trace automata for any non-empty set of variables $E \subseteq X$, and let $\mathbb{A}_\emptyset = \emptyset$ by convention. For a path $\pi = l_0, l_1, \ldots$ of an automaton $\mathcal{A} \in \mathbb{A}_E$, let $\mathtt{last}(\pi)$ denote the last visited location $\lim_{i \to \infty} l_i$. We also extend $\mathtt{last}(\cdot)$ to executions, so that if ω is an execution, then $\mathtt{last}(\omega) = \mathtt{last}(\omega|_L)$. Furthermore, if π is a path of $\mathcal{A} \in \mathbb{A}_E$, then $\Theta_{\mathcal{A}}(\pi)$ will denote the set of all traces $\theta \in \mathtt{tr}(E)$ corresponding to π, i.e. the set $\{\theta \in \mathtt{tr}(E) \mid \mathcal{A}(\theta)|_L = \pi\}$. As an extension, if Π is a set of paths of $\mathcal{A}$, then $\Theta_{\mathcal{A}}(\Pi) = \{\Theta_{\mathcal{A}}(\pi) \mid \pi \in \Pi\}$. Given trace automata $\mathcal{A}_1 \in \mathbb{A}_{E_1}$ and $\mathcal{A}_2 \in \mathbb{A}_{E_2}$, the *composition of $\mathcal{A}_1$ and $\mathcal{A}_2$*, denoted $\mathcal{A}_1 \| \mathcal{A}_2$, is the trace automaton giving their joint execution. More precisely, $\mathcal{A}_1 \| \mathcal{A}_2 \in \mathbb{A}_{E_1 \cup E_2}$ such that $L_{\mathcal{A}_1 \| \mathcal{A}_2} = L_{\mathcal{A}_1} \times L_{\mathcal{A}_2}$, $l_{0_{\mathcal{A}_1 \| \mathcal{A}_2}} = (l_{0_{\mathcal{A}_1}}, l_{0_{\mathcal{A}_2}})$, and $C_{\mathcal{A}_1 \| \mathcal{A}_2} = C_{\mathcal{A}_1} \cup C_{\mathcal{A}_2}$. The transition relation $\rightarrow_{\mathcal{A}_1 \| \mathcal{A}_2}$ is constructed by determining, for each joint location in $L_{\mathcal{A}_1} \times L_{\mathcal{A}_2}$ and individual transition in $\rightarrow_{\mathcal{A}_1} \cup \rightarrow_{\mathcal{A}_2}$, the joint reaction of both component automata arising from each possible valuation for $E_1 \cup E_2$ and clock valuation for $C_1 \cup C_2$ coherent with the transition. For more details, see [18]. Given a joint location $l = (l_1, l_2) \in L_{\mathcal{A}_1 \| \mathcal{A}_2}$, we denote by $l|_{\mathcal{A}_1}$ and $l|_{\mathcal{A}_2}$ the individual locations l_1 and l_2, respectively.

3.4 Probabilistic Automaton Contracts

For specifying I/O behaviors in practice, we will use a contract-based approach. A contract consists of an *assumption* and a *guarantee* together with a probability bound. Intuitively, an I/O behavior implements a contract if, for each input trace satisfying the assumption, the probability over all output traces satisfying the guarantee respects the probability bound. Both the assumption and guarantee are specified using terminating trace automata. For convenience, we will also allow a special non-assumption $\top$ that carries the meaning of always being satisfied. We use the convention that composing any automaton $\mathcal{A}$ with $\top$ results in $\mathcal{A}$ itself, so that $\mathcal{A} \| \top = \top \| \mathcal{A} = \mathcal{A}$.

The choice of using automata for specifying system properties is motivated by their flexibility—while temporal logics offer their own advantages, it may be difficult, or even impossible, to specify some complex systems using them [9]. In general, it is always possible to construct some automaton corresponding to a given temporal logic formula.

Definition 12 (Accepts). *Given a non-empty set $E \subseteq X$ of variables, an automaton $\mathcal{A} \in \mathbb{A}_E$, and a trace $\theta \in \mathrm{tr}(E)$, $\mathcal{A}$ accepts θ if $\mathrm{last}(\mathcal{A}(\theta)) \in F$.* □

We also extend the notion of acceptance to the non-assumption $\top$, so that $\top$ is considered to accept each possible trace $\theta \in \bigcup_{E \subseteq X} \mathrm{tr}(E)$. For an automaton $\mathcal{A} \in \mathbb{A}_E \cup \{\top\}$, let $\mathrm{acc}(\mathcal{A})$ denote the set of all traces that $\mathcal{A}$ accepts.

Definition 13 (Probabilistic Automaton Contract). *Given a set of variables $I \subseteq X$, a non-empty set of variables $O \subseteq X$ disjoint from I, an assumption $\mathcal{A} \in \mathbb{A}_I \cup \{\top\}$, a guarantee $\mathcal{G} \in \mathbb{A}_{I \cup O}$, a probability value $p \in [0,1]$ and a comparison operator $\bowtie \in \{<, \leq, \geq, >\}$, a formula $\phi = \mathcal{P}_{\bowtie p}(\mathcal{A}, \mathcal{G})$ is a probabilistic automaton contract (PAC) from I to O.* □

Once again, $\mathrm{in}(\phi)$ and $\mathrm{out}(\phi)$ are defined for PACs ϕ in a similar manner as for I/O behaviors and specifications. For a PAC $\phi = \mathcal{P}_{\bowtie p}(\mathcal{A}, \mathcal{G})$, we will denote its assumption $\mathcal{A}$, guarantee $\mathcal{G}$, probability value p and comparison operator $\bowtie$ by $\mathcal{A}_\phi$, $\mathcal{G}_\phi$, p_ϕ, and $\bowtie_\phi$, respectively.

To understand *trace composition* in the following definition of *PAC interpretation*, consider two traces θ_1 and θ_2 over disjoint sets of variables E_1 and E_2, respectively. The *composition of θ_1 and θ_2* is the trace $\theta_1 \| \theta_2 : \mathbb{R}_{\geq 0} \to \mathrm{val}(E_1 \cup E_2)$ such that $(\theta_1 \| \theta_2)(t)(x)$ equals $\theta_1(t)(x)$ if $x \in E_1$ and $\theta_2(t)(x)$ if $x \in E_2$.

In the next definition of *PAC interpretation*, given a set $O \subseteq X$ of variables, we will make use of a particular σ-algebra σ_O that, for each automaton $\mathcal{A} \in \mathbb{A}_O$ and each path $\pi \in \mathrm{paths}(\mathcal{A})$, contains the set $\Theta_{\mathcal{A}}(\pi)$.

Definition 14 (PAC Interpretation). *Given a set of variables $I \subseteq X$, a non-empty set of variables $O \subseteq X$, and a PAC $\phi = \mathcal{P}_{\bowtie p}(\mathcal{A}, \mathcal{G})$ from I to O, the interpretation of ϕ, written $[\![\phi]\!]$, is the specification, i.e. the set of I/O behaviors from I to O, with σ-algebra σ_O such that for each $\beta \in [\![\phi]\!]$, it holds:*

1. *in the case $I = \emptyset$, $\beta()(\mathrm{acc}(\mathcal{G})) \bowtie p$,*
2. *in the case $I \neq \emptyset$, for each trace $\theta_I \in \mathrm{tr}(I)$, if $\theta_I \in \mathrm{acc}(\mathcal{A})$, then $\beta(\theta_I)(\{\theta_O \in \mathrm{tr}(O) \mid \theta_I \| \theta_O \in \mathrm{acc}(\mathcal{G})\}) \bowtie p$.* □

Note that the choice of σ_O guarantees the values $\beta()(\mathtt{acc}(\mathcal{G}))$ and $\beta(\theta_I)(\{\theta_O \in \mathtt{tr}(O) \mid \theta_I \| \theta_O \in \mathtt{acc}(\mathcal{G})\})$ in the above definition to be defined. For a PAC $\phi = \mathcal{P}_{\bowtie p}(\mathcal{A}, \mathcal{G})$, we denote by ϕ^c the PAC $\mathcal{P}_{\bowtie^c p}(\mathcal{A}, \mathcal{G})$ in which the comparison operator has been complemented. For instance, the complement of $<$ is $\geq$. The PAC ϕ^c is called the *complement of* ϕ.

Of course, one could imagine the possibility of creating more complex, even nested, contract-based formulae following a recursively defined grammar. For instance, combining PACs using negation, conjunction and disjunction as well as defining an *until* operator and nesting PACs within PACs. Although this possibility is interesting, it lies outside the scope of the present paper. Instead, as will be introduced in the next definition, we will work with *composite PACs*, which consist of multiple PACs and represent their parallel composition. As with composition of behaviors and specifications, in the next definition, we consider only the case of $\mathtt{in}(\phi_1) = \emptyset$ and $\mathtt{in}(\phi_2) = \mathtt{out}(\phi_1)$.

Definition 15 (Composite Probabilistic Automaton Contract). *Given two PACs ϕ_1 and ϕ_2 with compatible interpretations, the term $\phi_1 \| \phi_2$ is a composite probabilistic automaton contract (cPAC) with interpretation $[\![\phi_1 \| \phi_2]\!] = [\![\phi_1]\!] \| [\![\phi_2]\!]$. Inductively, if ϕ_1 is a PAC or cPAC and ϕ_2 is a PAC or cPAC such that $[\![\phi_1]\!]$ and $[\![\phi_2]\!]$ are compatible, then the term $\phi_1 \| \phi_2$ is a cPAC.* □

The notation $\mathtt{in}(\phi)$ and $\mathtt{out}(\phi)$ is extended also to cPACs ϕ, and the notions of *implement* and *refine* are extended to PACs and cPACs by defining that: β *implements* ϕ if $\beta \in [\![\phi]\!]$, and ϕ_1 *refines* ϕ_2 if $[\![\phi_1]\!] \subseteq [\![\phi_2]\!]$.

4   Verification of Refinement

A common technique for formal verification found throughout literature is to formulate specifications using automata and then solve the language inclusion problem using automata theory [9,23]. This is also the foundation for the method developed in this paper, except here, languages are sets of I/O behaviors instead of strings. The intuition for verifying that a composition $\phi = \phi_1 \| \ldots \| \phi_k$ of component specifications refines a top-level specification $\widehat{\phi}$ is as follows. We want to verify that the set $[\![\phi]\!]$ is a subset of $[\![\widehat{\phi}]\!]$. The strategy is to check emptiness of the specification $[\![\phi]\!] \cap [\![\widehat{\phi}^c]\!]$. To do so, we will compose all automata found in the two specifications and map each joint path to the assumptions and guarantees that it satisfies. From this, a set of linear inequalities can be generated, each representing a conditional probability of a guarantee given an assumption. If this system of inequalities has no solutions, it means that no valid probability measure can possibly exist in $[\![\phi]\!] \cap [\![\widehat{\phi}^c]\!]$, thereby proving emptiness. The last step can be calculated using e.g. the simplex method [11,28].

Although this method is a semi-decision procedure, i.e. is not guaranteed to return `true` if refinement holds and `false` otherwise, it is sound in the sense that refinement does indeed hold whenever the algorithm returns `true`.

To verify refinement, the restrictions imposed on the specifications are as follows. While the component specification ϕ can be either a single PAC or a cPAC consisting of multiple PACs $\phi_1, \ldots, \phi_m$, the top-level specification $\widehat{\phi}$ must be a single PAC. Moreover, we require that $\text{in}(\phi) = \text{in}(\widehat{\phi}) = \emptyset$ and $\text{out}(\phi) = \text{out}(\widehat{\phi}) \neq \emptyset$. Each $\bowtie_{\phi_i}$ must be one of $\leq$ or $\geq$, and $\bowtie_{\widehat{\phi}}$ must be either $<$ or $>$. Lastly, given that ϕ is the PAC or cPAC $\phi = \phi_1 \| \ldots \| \phi_m$ for some $m \geq 1$ and denoting $\mathcal{A} = \mathcal{A}_{\phi_1} \| \mathcal{G}_{\phi_1} \| \ldots \| \mathcal{A}_{\phi_m} \| \mathcal{G}_{\phi_m} \| \mathcal{A}_{\widehat{\phi}} \| \mathcal{G}_{\widehat{\phi}}$, we assume that $\text{paths}(\mathcal{A})$ is finite and can be found in finite time. This should be the case for many industrial applications, for instance when the number of transitions is finite.

The algorithm works as follows. Let $\phi = \phi_1 \| \ldots \| \phi_m$, $m \geq 1$, be a PAC or cPAC and $\widehat{\phi}$ be a PAC. The problem is to decide whether ϕ refines $\widehat{\phi}$. We construct the composition $\mathcal{A} = \mathcal{A}_{\phi_1} \| \mathcal{G}_{\phi_1} \| \ldots \| \mathcal{A}_{\phi_m} \| \mathcal{G}_{\phi_m} \| \mathcal{A}_{\widehat{\phi}} \| \mathcal{G}_{\widehat{\phi}}$ and, from that, a system of linear inequalities as follows. For each $\phi_i \in \{\phi_1, \ldots, \phi_m\}$, let $\{\pi_1, \ldots, \pi_q\}$ be the set of paths of $\mathcal{A}$ accepted by the assumption $\mathcal{A}_{\phi_i}$ and let $\{\pi_{j_1}, \ldots, \pi_{j_s}\} \subseteq \{\pi_1, \ldots, \pi_q\}$ be the set of paths of $\mathcal{A}$ accepted by both the guarantee $\mathcal{G}_{\phi_i}$ and assumption $\mathcal{A}_{\phi_i}$. Then we add an inequality

$$\frac{\pi_{j_1} + \cdots + \pi_{j_s}}{\pi_1 + \cdots + \pi_q} \bowtie_{\phi_i} p_{\phi_i} \, .$$

Do the same for $\widehat{\phi}$ except with $\bowtie_{\widehat{\phi}^c}$ substituted for $\bowtie_{\widehat{\phi}}$. To ensure that the probabilities sum to 1, add the equality $1 = \sum_{\pi \in \text{paths}(\mathcal{A})} \pi$. Lastly, if the solution space for this system of inequalities is empty, we conclude that ϕ refines $\widehat{\phi}$.

Pseudocode for this procedure is presented in Algorithm 1. Here, the variable ineqs stores the set of linear inequalities, which is incrementally updated to contain the inequality generated from each conditional probability.

Algorithm 1. Verify that a PAC or cPAC refines a PAC.

1: **function** REFINES($\phi_1 \| \ldots \| \phi_m, \widehat{\phi}$)
2:    $\mathcal{A} = \mathcal{A}_{\phi_1} \| \mathcal{G}_{\phi_1} \| \ldots \| \mathcal{A}_{\phi_m} \| \mathcal{G}_{\phi_m} \| \mathcal{A}_{\widehat{\phi}} \| \mathcal{G}_{\widehat{\phi}}$
3:    $\text{ineqs} \leftarrow \left\{ 1 = \sum_{\pi \in \text{paths}(\mathcal{A})} \pi \right\}$
4:    **for** $\phi \in \{\phi_1, \ldots, \phi_m, \widehat{\phi}^c\}$ **do**
5:       $\Pi_A \leftarrow \{\pi \in \text{paths}(\mathcal{A}) \mid \text{last}(\pi)|_{\mathcal{A}_\phi} \in F_{\mathcal{A}_\phi}\}$
6:       $\Pi_G \leftarrow \{\pi \in \text{paths}(\mathcal{A}) \mid \text{last}(\pi)|_{\mathcal{G}_\phi} \in F_{\mathcal{G}_\phi}\}$
7:       $\Pi_{G \wedge A} \leftarrow \Pi_G \cap \Pi_A$
8:       $\text{ineqs} \leftarrow \text{ineqs} \cup \left\{ \left(\sum_{\pi \in \Pi_{G \wedge A}} \pi \right) / \left(\sum_{\pi \in \Pi_A} \pi \right) \bowtie_\phi p_\phi \right\}$
9:    **end for**
10:   **return true** if the solution space for ineqs is empty; **unknown** otherwise
11: **end function**

Due to the assumption of finitely many paths, the algorithm will terminate in finite time. However, time complexity depends on operations for enumerating these paths. Therefore, practical implementations call for efficient search algorithms and data structures for this. The following theorem states that Algorithm 1 is sound. The proof is given in the report [18].

Theorem 1. *A PAC or cPAC $\phi_1 \| \ldots \| \phi_m$ refines a PAC $\widehat{\phi}$ if the procedure* `Refines`$(\phi_1 \| \ldots \| \phi_m, \widehat{\phi})$ *given by Algorithm 1 returns* `true`. $\square$

5 Case Study

Recall the two-component system from Sect. 2 consisting of a main and backup power source. The purpose of this section is to solve the refinement verification problem for the specifications presented there, using the algorithm from Sect. 4.

Once again, the natural language top-level specification is: "the system shall output power continuously during the first 7 h with over 50% probability". To represent this specification, we can define the PAC

$$\widehat{\phi} = \mathcal{P}_{>0.5}\left(\top, \quad \rightarrow \boxed{ok} \xrightarrow[c_M < 7]{\{p_M \mapsto 0, p_B \mapsto 0\}} \boxed{pre}\right).$$

Here, the non-assumption is used together with a guarantee automaton over the considered variables p_M and p_B, denoting main power and backup power, respectively. Each variable is boolean, where 1 corresponds to power output and 0 corresponds to no power output. The guarantee accepts all traces for which the location *ok* is never left. Looking at the only outgoing transition, this captures the traces such that there exists no time before 7 h with neither main nor backup power. The probability bound put on the guarantee is > 0.5.

Likewise, the natural language specification for the main power source is stated as: "main power failure shall occur before 6 h with at most 30% probability", and for the backup power source as: "assuming main power failure occurs after at least 3 h, then with at least 80% probability, the backup shall output power continuously for at least 2 h starting at this time". These natural language specifications can be represented by the two PACs

$$\phi_M = \mathcal{P}_{\geq 0.7}\left(\top, \quad \rightarrow \boxed{ok} \xrightarrow[c_M < 6]{\{p_M \mapsto 0\}} \boxed{pre}\right),$$

$$\phi_B = \mathcal{P}_{\geq 0.8}\left(\left(\boxed{U} \xrightarrow[c_M \geq 3]{\{p_M \mapsto 0\}} \boxed{T}\right), \quad \rightarrow \boxed{wait} \xrightarrow[c_B := 0]{\{p_M \mapsto 0, p_B \mapsto 1\}} \boxed{ok}\right),$$

with $\{p_M \mapsto 0\}, c_M < 3$ leading to $\boxed{F}$, and $\{p_M \mapsto 0, p_B \mapsto 0\}$ leading to $\boxed{fail}$ with $\{p_B \mapsto 0\}, c_B < 2$.

respectively. Because an assumption is present in the natural language backup specification, the PAC ϕ_B must include a corresponding assumption automaton. Here, the assumption location U denotes undecided, T denotes true and F denotes false. The assumption automaton accepts traces in which main power failure occurs at some time after 3 h. Meanwhile, the guarantee waits for this occurrence, after which failure to turn on the backup results in entering the *fail* location; otherwise the *ok* location is entered. Now, in order for the guarantee to accept the trace, backup power must be held for at least 2 h. After that, the accepting location *ok* can never be left.

Following Algorithm 1, we first construct the composition $\mathcal{A} = \mathcal{A}_{\widehat{\phi}} \| \mathcal{G}_{\widehat{\phi}} \|$ $\mathcal{A}_{\phi_M} \| \mathcal{G}_{\phi_M} \| \mathcal{A}_{\phi_B} \| \mathcal{G}_{\phi_B}$. The resulting automaton is shown in Fig. 8, where only the reachable part is included. Next to each location, there is a tuple giving the initials of the corresponding component automaton locations, where e.g. (p,p,f,f) refers to locations *pre*, *pre*, *F*, and *fail* of $\mathcal{G}_{\widehat{\phi}}$, $\mathcal{G}_{\phi_M}$, $\mathcal{A}_{\phi_B}$, and $\mathcal{G}_{\phi_B}$, respectively. Dashed arrows denote transitions on the valuation $\{p_M \mapsto 0, p_B \mapsto 1\}$ in which the backup correctly responds to main power failure. Solid lines originating from location a denote transitions on the valuation $\{p_M \mapsto 0, p_B \mapsto 0\}$ in which none of the power sources output power, and solid lines originating from any other location denote transitions on valuations in which the backup does not output power, i.e. both $\{p_M \mapsto 0, p_B \mapsto 0\}$ and $\{p_M \mapsto 1, p_B \mapsto 0\}$. Lastly, note that the clock constraints of transitions sharing the same source location and valuation are disjoint, so that e.g. $c_M < 6$ is shorthand for $c_M < 6 \wedge \neg(c_M < 3)$.

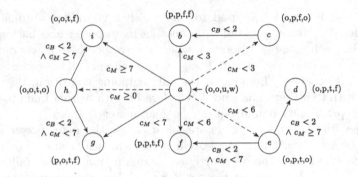

Fig. 8. The composition $\mathcal{A} = \mathcal{A}_{\widehat{\phi}} \| \mathcal{G}_{\widehat{\phi}} \| \mathcal{A}_{\phi_M} \| \mathcal{G}_{\phi_M} \| \mathcal{A}_{\phi_B} \| \mathcal{G}_{\phi_B}$

Identifying the paths ending in accepting locations of each automaton results in the sets $\Pi_{\mathcal{A}_{\widehat{\phi}}} = \Pi_{\mathcal{A}_{\phi_M}} = \text{paths}(\mathcal{A}) = \{a, ab, ac, acb, ae, aed, aef, af, ag, ah,$ $ahg, ahi, ai\}$, $\Pi_{\mathcal{G}_{\widehat{\phi}} \wedge \mathcal{A}_{\widehat{\phi}}} = \{a, ac, ae, aed, ah, ahi\}$, $\Pi_{\mathcal{G}_{\phi_M} \wedge \mathcal{A}_{\phi_M}} = \{a, ag, ah, ahg,$ $ahi, ai\}$, $\Pi_{\mathcal{A}_{\phi_B}} = \{ae, aed, aef, ag, ah, ahg, ahi, ai\}$, and $\Pi_{\mathcal{G}_{\phi_B} \wedge \mathcal{A}_{\phi_B}} = \{ae, ah\}$. This results in the following system of linear inequalities:

$$\begin{cases} a + ag + ah + ahg + ahi + ai \geq 0.7 \\ \dfrac{ae + ah}{ae + aed + aef + ag + ah + ahg + ahi + ai} \geq 0.8 \\ a + ac + ae + aed + ah + ahi \leq 0.5 \\ a + ab + ac + acb + ae + aed + aef + af + ag + ah + ahg + ahi + ai = 1 \,. \end{cases}$$

Running a linear optimization solver, e.g. [1], on this instance shows that the solution space is empty. Thus, we have verified that the composition of ϕ_M and ϕ_B refines $\widehat{\phi}$. Or, in other words, combining any main power source and any backup power source implementing its corresponding specification will surely implement the top-level specification.

6   Related Work

A related field is the area of model checking. In contrast to the present paper, which treats refinement of specifications, the goal of model checking is to verify that a given model implements a given specification, see e.g. [25,31].

The literature contains various proposed specification theories for stochastic systems, supporting for instance constraint Markov chains [8], abstract probabilistic automata [14], interactive Markov chains [16], and a variety of probabilistic transition systems [21,22,24,34]. In the contract context, Nuzzo et al. [29] present a specification theory for probabilistic assume-guarantee contracts. While these previous theories are based on discrete time, the present paper gives explicit support for continuous time. Also in the continuous setting, simulation and bisimulation have been studied for continuous-time Markov chains (CTMCs) [6]. However, this theory assumes that systems follow a particular stochastic process. Similarly, the rest of the papers above assume a particular formalism or system structure, in contrast to the purely trace-based approach of the present paper. The contract theory of [13] is also trace-based, but in discrete time.

Both automata and temporal logics can be used for specifying properties of systems. For specifying stochastic systems in continuous time, Continuous Stochastic Logic (CSL) is commonly used [17]. The extension CSL^{TA} allows specifying properties through single-clock automata and has been used for model checking CTMCs [15]. A specification theory allowing compositional reasoning has been developed for timed I/O automata [12]; however, this framework gives no explicit support for probabilities. In a discrete-time setting, temporal operators defined by finite automata are included in a temporal logic presented by [36], and in an extension to computation tree logic, called ECTL [9].

7   Conclusions

In industrial applications, especially for safety-critical systems, specifications are often of stochastic nature, for example giving a bound on the probability that system failure will occur before a given time. A decomposition of such a specification requires techniques beyond traditional theorem proving.

As presented in Sect. 3, the first contribution of the paper is a theoretical framework that allows the representation of, and reasoning about, stochastic and continuous-time behaviors of systems as well as specifications for such behaviors. The main goal has been to provide a framework that can handle reasoning of *refinement* between specifications in the form of assume-guarantee contracts. This is needed to support compositional verification, which in turn is a key solution to specify and verify large-scale complex systems. A main goal has also been to approach the problem from a general perspective, leading to our choice of representing behaviors of components as probability measures on sets of traces. The second contribution, presented in Sect. 4, is an algorithm for the verification of stochastic specification refinement by reducing the problem to checking emptiness of the solution space for a system of linear inequalities. Future work includes investigating more efficient implementations of the algorithm, e.g. by replacing explicit path enumeration, and experimental evaluation using larger and more realistic case studies motivated by industry.

References

1. Linear optimization. https://online-optimizer.appspot.com. Accessed 27 May 2022
2. Alur, R., Dill, D.: Automata for modeling real-time systems. In: Paterson, M.S. (ed.) ICALP 1990. LNCS, vol. 443, pp. 322–335. Springer, Heidelberg (1990). https://doi.org/10.1007/BFb0032042
3. Alur, R., Dill, D.L.: A theory of timed automata. Theoret. Comput. Sci. **126**(2), 183–235 (1994)
4. Aziz, A., Sanwal, K., Singhal, V., Brayton, R.: Verifying continuous time Markov chains. In: Alur, R., Henzinger, T.A. (eds.) CAV 1996. LNCS, vol. 1102, pp. 269–276. Springer, Heidelberg (1996). https://doi.org/10.1007/3-540-61474-5_75
5. Aziz, A., Sanwal, K., Singhal, V., Brayton, R.: Model-checking continuous-time Markov chains. ACM Trans. Comput. Logic (TOCL) **1**(1), 162–170 (2000)
6. Baier, C., Katoen, J.P., Hermanns, H., Wolf, V.: Comparative branching-time semantics for Markov chains. Inf. Comput. **200**(2), 149–214 (2005)
7. Benveniste, A., Caillaud, B., Ferrari, A., Mangeruca, L., Passerone, R., Sofronis, C.: Multiple viewpoint contract-based specification and design. In: de Boer, F.S., Bonsangue, M.M., Graf, S., de Roever, W.-P. (eds.) FMCO 2007. LNCS, vol. 5382, pp. 200–225. Springer, Heidelberg (2008). https://doi.org/10.1007/978-3-540-92188-2_9
8. Caillaud, B., Delahaye, B., Larsen, K.G., Legay, A., Pedersen, M.L., Wasowski, A.: Compositional design methodology with constraint Markov chains. In: 2010 Seventh International Conference on the Quantitative Evaluation of Systems, pp. 123–132. IEEE (2010)
9. Clarke, E.M., Grumberg, O., Kurshan, R.P.: A synthesis of two approaches for verifying finite state concurrent systems. In: Meyer, A.R., Taitslin, M.A. (eds.) Logic at Botik 1989. LNCS, vol. 363, pp. 81–90. Springer, Heidelberg (1989). https://doi.org/10.1007/3-540-51237-3_7
10. Cuoq, P., Kirchner, F., Kosmatov, N., Prevosto, V., Signoles, J., Yakobowski, B.: Frama-C. In: Eleftherakis, G., Hinchey, M., Holcombe, M. (eds.) SEFM 2012. LNCS, vol. 7504, pp. 233–247. Springer, Heidelberg (2012). https://doi.org/10.1007/978-3-642-33826-7_16
11. Dantzig, G.B.: Origins of the simplex method. In: A History of Scientific Computing, pp. 141–151 (1990)
12. David, A., Larsen, K.G., Legay, A., Nyman, U., Wasowski, A.: Timed I/O automata: a complete specification theory for real-time systems. In: Proceedings of the 13th ACM International Conference on Hybrid Systems: Computation and Control, pp. 91–100 (2010)
13. Delahaye, B., Caillaud, B., Legay, A.: Probabilistic contracts: a compositional reasoning methodology for the design of systems with stochastic and/or nondeterministic aspects. Form. Methods Syst. Des. **38**(1), 1–32 (2011)
14. Delahaye, B., et al.: Abstract probabilistic automata. In: Jhala, R., Schmidt, D. (eds.) VMCAI 2011. LNCS, vol. 6538, pp. 324–339. Springer, Heidelberg (2011). https://doi.org/10.1007/978-3-642-18275-4_23

15. Donatelli, S., Haddad, S., Sproston, J.: Model checking timed and stochastic properties with CSL^{TA}. IEEE Trans. Softw. Eng. **35**(2), 224–240 (2008)
16. Gössler, G., Xu, D.N., Girault, A.: Probabilistic contracts for component-based design. Form. Methods Syst. Des. **41**(2), 211–231 (2012)
17. Grunske, L.: Specification patterns for probabilistic quality properties. In: 2008 ACM/IEEE 30th International Conference on Software Engineering, pp. 31–40. IEEE (2008)
18. Hampus, A., Nyberg, M.: Formally verifying decompositions of stochastic specifications (with proofs). Technical report (2022). http://urn.kb.se/resolve?urn=urn:nbn:se:kth:diva-315290. oai:DiVA.org:kth-315290
19. ISO 21434: Road vehicles - Cybersecurity engineering (2021)
20. ISO 26262: Road vehicles - Functional safety (2018)
21. Jonsson, B., Larsen, K.G.: Specification and refinement of probabilistic processes. In: Proceedings 1991 Sixth Annual IEEE Symposium on Logic in Computer Science, pp. 266–267. IEEE Computer Society (1991)
22. Jonsson, B., Yi, W.: Testing preorders for probabilistic processes can be characterized by simulations. Theoret. Comput. Sci. **282**(1), 33–51 (2002)
23. Kern, C., Greenstreet, M.R.: Formal verification in hardware design: a survey. ACM Trans. Des. Autom. Electron. Syst. (TODAES) **4**(2), 123–193 (1999)
24. Lanotte, R., Maggiolo-Schettini, A., Troina, A.: Parametric probabilistic transition systems for system design and analysis. Formal Aspects Comput. **19**(1), 93–109 (2007)
25. Mereacre, A., Katoen, J.P., Han, T., Chen, T.: Model checking of continuous-time Markov chains against timed automata specifications. Log. Methods Comput. Sci. **7** (2011)
26. Meyer, B.: Applying 'design by contract'. Computer **25**(10), 40–51 (1992)
27. de Moura, L., Bjørner, N.: Z3: an efficient SMT solver. In: Ramakrishnan, C.R., Rehof, J. (eds.) TACAS 2008. LNCS, vol. 4963, pp. 337–340. Springer, Heidelberg (2008). https://doi.org/10.1007/978-3-540-78800-3_24
28. Nash, J.C.: The (Dantzig) simplex method for linear programming. Comput. Sci. Eng. **2**(1), 29–31 (2000)
29. Nuzzo, P., Li, J., Sangiovanni-Vincentelli, A.L., Xi, Y., Li, D.: Stochastic assume-guarantee contracts for cyber-physical system design. ACM Trans. Embed. Comput. Syst. (TECS) **18**(1), 1–26 (2019)
30. Nyberg, M., Westman, J., Gurov, D.: Formally proving compositionality in industrial systems with informal specifications. In: Margaria, T., Steffen, B. (eds.) ISoLA 2020. LNCS, vol. 12478, pp. 348–365. Springer, Cham (2020). https://doi.org/10.1007/978-3-030-61467-6_22
31. Paolieri, M., Horváth, A., Vicario, E.: Probabilistic model checking of regenerative concurrent systems. IEEE Trans. Software Eng. **42**(2), 153–169 (2015)
32. Resnick, S.: A Probability Path. Birkhäuser Boston (2019)
33. Roever, W.-P.: The need for compositional proof systems: a survey. In: de Roever, W.-P., Langmaack, H., Pnueli, A. (eds.) COMPOS 1997. LNCS, vol. 1536, pp. 1–22. Springer, Heidelberg (1998). https://doi.org/10.1007/3-540-49213-5_1
34. Segala, R., Lynch, N.: Probabilistic simulations for probabilistic processes. In: Jonsson, B., Parrow, J. (eds.) CONCUR 1994. LNCS, vol. 836, pp. 481–496. Springer, Heidelberg (1994). https://doi.org/10.1007/978-3-540-48654-1_35
35. Slind, K., Norrish, M.: A brief overview of HOL4. In: Mohamed, O.A., Muñoz, C., Tahar, S. (eds.) TPHOLs 2008. LNCS, vol. 5170, pp. 28–32. Springer, Heidelberg (2008). https://doi.org/10.1007/978-3-540-71067-7_6

36. Vardi, M.Y., Wolper, P.: Reasoning about infinite computations. Inf. Comput. **115**(1), 1–37 (1994)
37. Westman, J., Nyberg, M.: Conditions of contracts for separating responsibilities in heterogeneous systems. Form. Methods Syst. Des. **52**(2), 147–192 (2017). https://doi.org/10.1007/s10703-017-0294-7

Verification of Behavior Trees using Linear Constrained Horn Clauses

Thomas Henn[1]($\boxtimes$)(iD), Marcus Völker[1](iD), Stefan Kowalewski[1](iD), Minh Trinh[2](iD), Oliver Petrovic[2](iD), and Christian Brecher[2](iD)

[1] Informatik 11 - Embedded Software, RWTH Aachen University, Aachen, Germany
{henn,voelker,kowalewski}@embedded.rwth-aachen.de
[2] Laboratory for Machine Tools and Production Engineering, RWTH Aachen University, Aachen, Germany
{m.trinh,o.petrovic,c.brecher}@wzl.rwth-aachen.de

Abstract. In the field of industrial production the usage of Behavior Trees sparks interest due to their modularity and flexibility. Considering Behavior Trees are used in a safety-critical domain, there is increased interest for methods to verify a Behavior Tree's safety. Current approaches for Behavior Trees are only semi-automatic since they require manually added low-level details about the action's behavior.

In this paper, we describe an automatic verification method for safety properties on Behavior Trees using Linear Constrained Horn Clauses (LCHCs). Our approach encodes all components of the verification task as CHCs, that is, the structure and semantics of the Behavior Tree, the implemented actions in the leaf nodes and the safety property itself. These clauses are then solved by a state-of-the-art SMT solver, leading to an efficient algorithm for Behavior Tree verification, which we evaluate by comparing our method against a general purpose verification framework.

Keywords: behavior tree · formal verification · constrained horn clauses · software safety

1 Introduction

Behavior Trees describe the executions of agents and systems. One of the major advantages is their modularity [10]. Complex tasks are composed of simpler tasks, without further knowledge about the implementation of the simple tasks, since all nodes share a common interface. This advantage and the visualization of Behavior Trees (e.g., see Fig. 1) contribute to their popularity and helps to design, develop, and test Behavior Trees. At first, Behavior Trees were used to characterize the behavior of non-player characters (NPCs) in video games

J. F. Groote and M. Huisman (Eds.): FMICS 2022, LNCS 13487, pp. 211–225, 2022.
https://doi.org/10.1007/978-3-031-15008-1_14

[14]. Since then, other communities, like the robotics [5,6,12,13] and artificial intelligence communities [9,11], have used Behavior Trees to model their agents.

This usage of Behavior Trees in safety-critical environments leads to an increasing interest in the application of formal methods on Behavior Trees. However, the clear and intuitive graphical representation of Behavior Trees is achieved by defining the control flow implicitly. Therefore, execution paths can easily be overlooked.

Previous work focuses mostly on defining a clear syntax and semantics, since no common standard, for representing Behavior Trees, exists [2–4]. A first approach to verify Behavior Trees looks promising, but still needs additional input in form of logical formulas from the user about the low-level behavior [1].

In this paper, our contribution is the demonstration of a viable approach for an automatic (i.e., no further input about the Behavior Tree is required) verification of Behavior Trees. Our approach is based on a logical encoding of the Behavior Tree's semantics. We utilize Linear Constrained Horn Clauses (LCHCs), because solving LCHCs has been proven to be efficient [7] and their successful usage in software verification has been presented in [8,9].

The paper is structured as follows: Sect. 2 shows the current state-of-the-art concerning the verification and analysis of Behavior Trees. In Sect. 3, we introduce the notion of a Behavior Tree and Constrained Horn Clauses. In Sect. 4, we present the encoding of Behavior Trees using CHCs. The presented approach is then evaluated on several verification tasks and compared to a general purpose verification framework in Sect. 5. We finish with a summary and outlook in Sect. 6.

2   Related Works

In several other works, alternative encodings of Behavior Trees which could be used for verification purposes, are presented. In [2], the authors show how Behavior Trees can be encoded as Communicating Sequential Processes (CSP). The motivation behind this work is to provide a more precise formalization for Behavior Trees since there is no standardized formalism or rigorous semantics for Behavior Trees. CSPs are no intended to be used as a control architecture but is suited for verifying and specifying concurrent systems. To use the CSP formalism for verification purposes was left for future work.

Another approach which encodes Behavior Trees in a description logic is presented in [3]. The shown encoding in description logic could be utilized for a runtime verification that checks whether a proper action is executed. The extension of the approach was left for future work as well as the verification whether a given Behavior Tree is guaranteed to execute successfully.

In [21] another approach for runtime monitoring is presented. Behavior Trees are translated into a communication channel system. The, in the paper, introduced Behavior Trees only model a subset of the "classical" Behavior Trees since parallel nodes are omitted. Also the environment is not part of the formal model and therefore the properties can only be analyzed in a simulation or in a real world scenario.

The authors of [4] present an correct-by-construction approach. Linear Temporal Logic (LTL) formulas are used to define the correct behavior which the synthesized Behavior Tree has to exhibit. The approach does not allow the verification of already existing Behavior Trees.

In [1] a verification approach is presented which is based on the transformation of (sub-)trees to a collection of LTL formulas. These constructed LTL formulas, representing the semantics of the Behavior Tree, are then checked against properties encoded as other LTL formulas. The need of LTL formulas, given by the user, which describe the semantics of the action and condition nodes, prevent an automatic usage of the verification algorithm. The necessary level of detail differs from property to property and should be adapted for every verification run.

3   Preliminaries

In Sect. 3.1, we introduce the structure as well as the semantics of behaviour trees. Afterwards, we give a short introduction to Constrained Horn Clauses in Sect. 3.2.

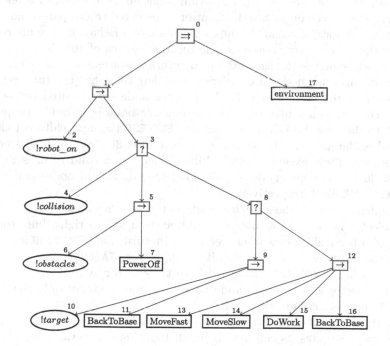

Fig. 1. Example behavior tree with collision and obstacle detection.

3.1 Behavior Trees

A Behavior Tree, as depicted in Fig. 1, is a directed acyclic graph with a distinguished root node [10]. It describes the control flow between the possible actions. All nodes in a Behavior Tree have the same interface when it comes to the execution. A node starts its execution when it receives a *tick*. Each node returns one of the following three statuses: SUCCESS, FAILURE and RUNNING. The status indicates that the subtree performed its task successfully, unsuccessfully or that the task is still in execution, respectively. The possibility, to return RUNNING, shows that Behavior Trees are not an extension of (hierarchical) finite state machines since a Behavior Tree does not stay in a node until the execution is complete. The whole tree is executed by ticking the root node. Usually, this is done in an infinite cycle, i.e. the root node is ticked again as soon as it returns SUCCESS, RUNNING or FAILURE.

The leaves encode *actions* (drawn as a box) and *conditions* (drawn as a ellipse). Condition nodes only return SUCCESS or FAILURE and check the condition of the system, described by the Behavior Tree, or the environment. They also have no side effects (i.e. do not alter variables or the state of the system). Ticking an action node corresponds to a function call which triggers the action to be performed. If the execution of the action is not finished, RUNNING is returned. Otherwise the successful or failed execution is reported to the parent node.

The inner nodes, also called composite nodes, of a Behavior Tree are responsible for the control flow. Based on the returned status of their subtrees, they decide which subtrees to tick next or to return a status to their parent. The children of an inner nodes are ordered from left to right (i.e. the first child is depicted as the leftmost child). A *sequence* node (represented by →) executes is children consecutively. When a sequence node is ticked it propagates the tick to the first child. If a child returns SUCCESS the next child is ticked. If the child is the last one the sequence node returns SUCCESS instead since the whole sequence was executed successfully. Whenever a child returns FAILURE or RUNNING the sequence node stops ticking the other child nodes and returns FAILURE or RUNNING, respectively.

Complementary to the sequence node is the *selector* node (represented by ?). A selector node also executes its children from left to right, but stops the ticking of other child nodes whenever a child returns SUCCESS or RUNNING and returns the same value to its parent. If a child returns FAILURE the next child in order is ticked or FAILURE is returned from the selector node if the child is the last one. Selector and sequence node have the same behavior; only the roles of SUCCESS and FAILURE are switched.

The third type of composite node is the *parallel* node (represented by ⇉). A parallel node executes its children in parallel and returns a value based on the accumulated return values of its children. Parallel nodes are parametrized with a variable $m \in \mathbb{N}$ which is less than or equal to the number of children. SUCCESS is returned when at least m children finished their execution with SUCCESS. If $n - m + 1$ children returned FAILURE the parallel node returns FAILURE. In all other cases RUNNING is returned.

Behavior Trees composed of these node types are sometimes called *classic* Behavior Trees. In practice there are custom nodes and extensions since no standard exists. The idea, that sequences do not necessarily start from the beginning, but from a child which returned RUNNING, is incorporated in *sequence with memory* nodes (represented by $\rightarrow_m$). These nodes behaves similar to the regular sequence nodes except that if the last value returned was RUNNING, the corresponding child is ticked instead of the first child when the sequence with memory node is ticked again. The same extension exists for selector nodes which are called *selector with memory* (represented by $?_m$).

The BT in Fig. 1 corresponds to assembly robot which performs at task (DoWork) if no collisions & obstacles are detected and a target is selected.

3.2 Constrained Horn Clauses

Constrained Horn Clauses (CHCs) are a structure for clauses from a first-order logic [8]. Given sets of predicates $\mathcal{P}$, functions $\mathcal{F}$, and variables $\mathcal{V}$ a Constrained Horn Clause is defined as formula of the following structure:

$$\forall \mathcal{V}.\mathbf{p_1}(\overrightarrow{X_1}) \wedge \cdots \wedge \mathbf{p_k}(\overrightarrow{X_k}) \wedge \varphi \rightarrow \mathbf{h}(\overrightarrow{X}), \quad k \geq 0 \tag{1}$$

where $\mathbf{p}$ are predicates, $\overrightarrow{X_i} \subseteq \mathcal{V}$ are subsets of variables, φ is a quantifier-free formula over $\mathcal{X}$ and $\mathcal{F}$, and $\mathbf{h}$ can be either a predicate or a quantifier-free formula. A Constrained Horn Clause is called linear if $k \leq 1$.

A set of CHCs is satisfiable when there exist an interpretation of all predicates such that all implications hold. Since all variables are universal quantified, we omit the quantifier and in the style of logic programming languages we replace $\wedge$ by comma and reverse the implication:

$$\mathbf{h}(\overrightarrow{X}) \leftarrow \mathbf{p_1}(\overrightarrow{X_1}), \cdots, \mathbf{p_k}(\overrightarrow{X_k}), \varphi \tag{2}$$

4 Encoding of Behavior Trees

In this section, we present our approach how the Behavior Trees semantics can be encoded in linear Constrained Horn Clauses. Section 4.1 explains the general idea and introduces a common interface and some auxiliary definitions to simplify further explanations. The following sections propose how every node type can be encoded using only the knowledge of their direct children which creates a logical representation of the Behavior Tree which is as modular and flexible as the Behavior Tree itself. After we presented the encoding of the Behavior Tree, we show how safety properties and the environment is transformed in linear Horn Clauses in Sect. 4.9 and 4.10 respectively.

4.1 Idea

The approach of encoding procedures with Constrained Horn Clauses, presented in [8,9], is based on creating uninterpreted predicates which corresponds to program locations. The SMT solver finds an over-approximation of variable valuations which are valid at these specific program locations. E.g., the interpretation of a predicate loc_1 with $x > 0$ characterizes all states at location loc_1 where x is positive.

To identify the different nodes, which could have the same type, we assign an index $i \in \mathbb{N}$ to each node where the root node always has the index 0. The number of children of node i is denoted with n_i and the index of the j-th child of node i is the result of the auxiliary function $child(i, j)$. The parameterized threshold for parallel node i is given as m_i.

We also introduce two vectors of variables X and X' where X is a vector containing all program variables as well as all variables introduced by our encoding. X' is a primed copy of the vector X which is used to distinguish variables before and after some changes. E.g., the formula $y' = y + 1$ encodes the increment of the variable y by 1.

For every node i, we add the following predicates: $tick_i(X)$, $success_i(X)$, $failure_i(X)$ and $running_i(X)$. These predicates represent the states when a node is ticked and when the node returns SUCCESS, FAILURE or RUNNING.

Since these four predicates exist for all nodes and the behavior of the composite nodes only depends on the return value of their children, we can use these predicates as a means to encode the semantics with CHCs.

4.2   Action Node

As mentioned before, an action node corresponds to a function a program. These functions are represented as Control Flow Automata (CFA) which are directed graphs. The nodes (in the CFA) are called locations and the edges correspond to the instructions which are performed in order to move from one location to the next location. We omit a detailed definition of CFAs since more information can be found in the literature [20]. These CFA have four designated locations for the entry and exit. One entry location l_0 and one for each return value and exit location named $l_{success}, l_{running}, l_{failure}$.

In [20] is shown how CFAs can be encoded using Constrained Horn Clauses. We use presented approach for the encoding of CFAs: e.g., the clause $l_i(X') \leftarrow x' = x + 1, l_j(X)$ encodes the transition from location j to location i which is the labeled with x = x + 1.

The predicates used for the location representation need to be connected with the predicates for the action node. The semantics of an action node i are encoded by the following clauses:

$$l_0(X) \leftarrow tick_i(X)$$
$$success_i(X') \leftarrow l_{success}(X)$$
$$running_i(X') \leftarrow l_{running}(X)$$
$$failure_i(X') \leftarrow l_{failure}(X)$$

Intuitively, the first clause states that if the action node i is ticked with the variables X the execution continues at the initial location of the corresponding

CFA. The remaining clauses propagate the state reaching one of the exit location of the CFA to the predicates of the BT.

In order to model asynchronous function calls to external libraries, we allow the use of nondeterministic values. This method is also used for modeling the environment which is explained in Sect. 4.10.

4.3   Condition Node

Condition nodes are represented by functions in the same way as action nodes. Therefore, they can be encoded in the same way as in Sect. 4.2 and we can construct predicates and clauses for the CFA of condition node i. Note, that we only have two exit locations for condition nodes, since condition nodes never return RUNNING.

The clauses for encoding a condition node i are the following:

$$l_0(X) \leftarrow tick_i(X)$$
$$success_i(X') \leftarrow l_{success}(X)$$
$$running_i(X') \leftarrow l_{running}(X), false$$
$$failure_i(X') \leftarrow l_{failure}(X)$$

The boolean condition $false$ encodes that $l_r(X)$ is not reachable.

4.4   Sequence Node

Clause 3 encodes the propagation of a tick from a sequence node i to its first child.

$$tick_{child(i,1)}(X) \leftarrow tick_i(X) \tag{3}$$

When a child returns FAILURE or RUNNING the value is propagated to the parent of the sequence node. Since the sequence stops its execution independent from the child node which returns FAILURE or RUNNING, we use a clause for each child to propagate the return value, as shown in clauses 4 and 5.

$$failure_i(X) \leftarrow failure_{child(i,j)}(X) \quad \forall 1 \leq j \leq n_i \tag{4}$$
$$running_i(X) \leftarrow running_{child(i,j)}(X) \quad \forall 1 \leq j \leq n_i \tag{5}$$

The successful execution of a child triggers the tick of the next child in the sequence which is encoded in the set of clauses 6. Only if the last child returns SUCCESS the value is propagated to the parent of the sequence node (see clause 7).

$$tick_{child(i,j+1)}(X) \leftarrow success_{child(i,j)}(X) \quad \forall 1 \leq j < n_i \tag{6}$$
$$success_i(X) \leftarrow success_{child(i,n_i)}(X) \tag{7}$$

The clauses generated for node 1 from Fig. 1 are shown in the following enumeration. Since the control flow is determined directly by the return values, there is no modification of variables.

$$tick_2(X) \leftarrow tick_1(X)$$
$$tick_3(X) \leftarrow success_2(X)$$
$$running_1(X) \leftarrow running_2(X)$$
$$failure_1(X) \leftarrow failure_2(X)$$
$$success_1(X) \leftarrow success_3(X)$$
$$running_3(X) \leftarrow running_3(X)$$
$$failure_3(X) \leftarrow failure_3(X)$$

4.5 Sequence Node with Memory

A sequence node with memory needs to keep track which of its children needs to be ticked when the sequence node itself is ticked next time. We introduce a fresh variable $next_i$ for every sequence node i with memory to store the information. The variable is initialized with the index of the first child to ensure that the first time the sequence node with memory is ticked, it starts from the beginning.

Since every child can return RUNNING, we encode the propagation of the tick with clauses 8. In contrast to clause 3, the propagation of the tick is no longer unconditional, but we enforce that the value of the variable $next_i$ is the same as the index of the child being ticked.

$$tick_{child(i,j)}(X) \leftarrow tick_i(X), next_i = j \quad \forall 1 \leq j \leq n_i \qquad (8)$$

The value of $next_i$ must be set whenever a child returns RUNNING. In clauses 9 the value is changed. To prevent that other variables change their values, we use another auxiliary function id which ensures that variables keep their value if they are elements of the passed set.

$$running_i(X') \leftarrow running_{child(i,j)}(X), next'_i = j,$$
$$id(X \setminus \{next_i\}) \quad \forall 1 \leq j \leq n_i \qquad (9)$$

The clauses for FAILURE and SUCCESS must be adapted as well. The clauses 10 for the FAILURE cases are similar to the clauses 9 for RUNNING. They differ in the index which is assigned to $next_i$. For the clauses concerning the SUCCESS case, only the last one, clause 12, must be adapted in order to reset the variable $next_i$. The clauses 11 are identical to the ones for sequence nodes without memory, since they trigger the tick of the next child.

$$failure_i(X') \leftarrow failure_{child(i,j)}(X),$$
$$next_i = child(i,1),$$
$$id(X \backslash \{next_i\}) \quad \forall 1 \le j \le n_i \tag{10}$$
$$tick_{child(i,j+1)}(X) \leftarrow success_{child(i,j)}(X) \quad \forall 1 \le j < n_i \tag{11}$$
$$success_i(X') \leftarrow success_{child(i,n_i)}(X),$$
$$next_i = child(i,1), id(X \backslash \{next_i\}) \tag{12}$$

4.6   Selector Node

The selector node is complementary to the sequence node, as explained in Sect. 3.1. The Constrained Horn Clauses needed to encode the semantics for a selector node, with or without memory, are similar to the clauses for sequence nodes. We use the same clauses but switch the occurrences of SUCCESS and FAILURE in the Constrained Horn Clauses. The exact formalization is trivial and omitted in this paper.

4.7   Parallel Node

Verifying programs with concurrency and modelling interleaving semantics is challenging when using linear Constrained Horn Clauses. It also creates more complex and larger models which in turn impacts the time needed for verification. Often the precise modeling of concurrency is not necessary, depending on the properties which are to be verified. Therefore, we assume that it is sufficient to model the execution of a parallel node's children as atomic.

Similar to the encoding of sequence nodes with memory, we introduce new fresh variables to keep track of the execution status of the parallel node i. $cnt\_success_i$, $cnt\_running_i$ and $cnt\_failure_i$ are new integer variables which are used to store the amount of returned SUCCESS, RUNNING and FAILURE values. Also for every child j, we add a boolean variable $executed_j$ to memorize whether a child has been executed and in order to prevent that a child is ticked more than once.

For every parallel node i, we introduce a new predicate $intermediate_i(X)$ which represents all states before and after children of the parallel node are executed. The following formulas representing the different conditions when the parallel node stops executing and return either SUCCESS, FAILURE or RUNNING. The formula $continue_i$ evaluates to true when none of the the conditions are fulfilled.

$$cond\_success_i := cnt\_success_i \geq m_i$$
$$cond\_failure_i := cnt\_failure_i \geq n_i - m_i + 1$$
$$cond\_running_i := (cnt\_failure_i +$$
$$cnt\_running_i \geq n_i - m_i + 1)$$
$$\land (cnt\_success_i + cnt\_running_i \geq m_i)$$
$$continue_i := \neg(cond\_success_i \land cond\_failure_i$$
$$\land cond\_running_i)$$

While propagating the tick to the predicate $intermediate_i(X)$, the newly introduced variables are initialized. The counter variables are set to 0 while the *executed* flag for the children is set to `false`. The other variables keep their values and for the sake of readability we omitted the argument for the *id* function.

$$intermediate_i(X') \leftarrow tick_i(X), cnt\_success'_i = 0,$$
$$cnt\_running'_i = 0, cnt\_failure'_i = 0,$$
$$\bigwedge_{j=1}^{n_i} executed'_{child(i,j)} = \texttt{false}, id(\dots)$$

From the *intermediate* predicate the tick is propagated to the children, when the *executed* flag is still `false` and none of the return conditions for the parallel node holds.

$$tick_{child(i,j)}(X) \leftarrow intermediate_i(X), executed_i = \texttt{false},$$
$$continue_i \quad \forall 1 \leq j \leq n_i$$

In the following, we only present clauses when a child returns SUCCESS, clause 13, and when the parallel node returns SUCCESS, clause 14. The clauses for RUNNING and FAILURE are analogous. In case the child execution ends successfully, the counter $cnt\_success$ is incremented by one and the *executed* flag is set to `true` in order to prevent that from the *intermediate* predicate the *tick* of the child is again reachable.

$$intermediate(X')_i \leftarrow success_{child(i,j)}(X),$$
$$executed'_{child(i,h)} = \texttt{true},$$
$$cnt\_success'_i = cnt\_success_i + 1,$$
$$id(\dots) \quad \forall 1 \leq j \leq n_i \qquad (13)$$

Clause 14 encodes that once the success condition is fulfilled, the result is propagated to the parent.

$$success_i(X) \leftarrow intermediate_i(X), cond\_success \qquad (14)$$

4.8   Root Node

The root node with index 0 can be any arbitrary node type, but there are some additional clauses which model the initialization, clause 15, and the repeatedly ticking, clauses 16.

The variables used in the action nodes as well as the variables we introduced for the encoding must be initialized. The initialization can be interpreted as a sequence of assignment to variables. These assignments can be encoded in a formula *init*.

$$tick_0(X) \leftarrow init \tag{15}$$

The complete Behavior Tree is usually ticked repeatedly. A Behavior Tree is only ticked again, when it is not currently executing. Therefore, clauses 16 encode a tick, after the root node finished its execution

$$tick_0(X) \leftarrow success_0(X)$$
$$tick_0(X) \leftarrow running_0(X)$$
$$tick_0(X) \leftarrow failure_0(X) \tag{16}$$

4.9   Safety Property

In the previous sections, we presented how behaviour trees can be encoded using linear Constrained Horn Clauses. In this section, we present how to encode the safety properties of interest. Safety properties are equivalent to the reachability problem. Here, we show how additional clauses can be used to assert a condition over the Behavior Trees' variables. Given the safety condition $safe(X)$, clause 17 encodes whether the safety property holds at every tick of the root node. This encoding of invariants is not limited to the root node's *tick* predicate. Any introduced predicate can be used, depending on where in the Behavior Tree the property should hold.

$$\textbf{true} \leftarrow tick_0(X), \neg safe(X) \tag{17}$$

A possible safety property for the example behavior tree in Fig. 1 is that the robot is executing the action node *DoWork* if no collision or obstacle is detected.

If adding clause 17 leads to the SMT solver not finding a satisfying interpretation, the Behavior Tree fulfills the safety property since there exists no variable valuation which holds at the tick of the root node and is unsafe.

4.10   Environment

In many use cases, the system described by the Behavior Tree interacts with its environment. As in Fig. 1 the environment can be modeled as an subtree and is connected via a parallel node with the Behavior Tree of the system. To model the environment adequately, it is necessary to allow nondeterminism

since some events only occur randomly or do not follow specific steps. In order
to accommodate this, we added the possibility of assigning a random value to a
variable.

$$p_2(X') \leftarrow id(X \backslash \{y\}), p_1(X) \tag{18}$$

Clause 18 illustrates the idea of modeling nondeterminism. Predicate p_2 is reachable from predicate p_1 where all variables except variable y retain their value. In
the Horn Clause, y' is unconstrained and therefore can take any nondeterministic
value.

5   Experiments

We implemented the linear encoding in our verification tool ARCADEBT which
is a spin-off from ARCADEPLC [19], a verification tool for Programmable Logic
Controller programs. ARCADEBT is written in C++ and uses the open source
SMT solver Z3 [16] in version 4.8.15. In this version Z3 uses the SPACER algorithm [17] to solve Constrained Horn Clauses.

Since, to the best of our knowledge, no publicly available verification tool,
which targets safety properties of Behavior Trees, exists, we compare our implementation against the general purpose verification framework SEAHORN [15]. It
analyzes C programs by encoding the semantics in Constrained Horn Clauses
which are then solved using Z3. In this section, we show the performance
improvements, gained by exploiting the structure of Behavior Trees and the
direct encoding of the semantics in Constrained Horn Clauses in contrast to
transforming the Behavior Tree to a C program which is then analyzed by a general purpose verification framework which uses a similar encoding in Constrained
Horn Clauses, and the same SMT solver Z3.

Our implementation currently does not contain a counterexample generator, as Z3 does not store the necessary information during the execution to
reconstruct a counterexample. In the future, it should be possible to extract a
counterexample from the derivation tree [18].

5.1   Benchmark

We used 39, from us created, different Behavior Trees for our benchmark. Each
verification tasks consists of one or more safety properties. In these 39 tasks, there
are 26 satisfiable tasks and 13 unsatisfiable tasks. The size of the verification
tasks ranges from small (less than 5 nodes) to medium size Behavior Trees with
18 nodes.

Although our experiments with Behavior Trees containing parallel nodes
show similar performance, we excluded them for reasons of fairness, since the
simplified semantic could not be easily represented in C code which is the input
for the SEAHORN framework. The generated C code does not use arrays, external header files, pointer arithmetic or dynamic memory allocation which would
create are more challenging verification task.

All benchmarks were executed on a Linux 5.10 computer with 2 GHz, 16 GB memory and a timeout of 10 s. The implementation and the tasks can be found on GitHub[1].

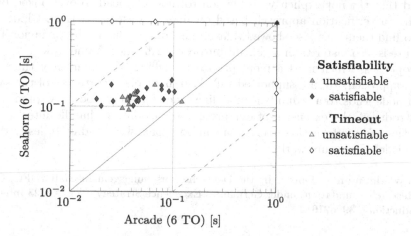

Fig. 2. Time spent by Arcade and Seahorn on verification of each task.

5.2   Discussion

Figure 2 illustrates the time needed for ARCADEBT and SEAHORN to solve the 39 tasks. Each data point represents one of the verification tasks. The solid diagonal line splits the coordinate system into an area where ARCADEBT performs better (above the line) and where SEAHORN performs better (below the line). Since both projects only share the SMT solver Z3 as a shared component, the time is measured for the complete execution of the respective verification tool.

In most cases ARCADEBT is 2 to 3 times faster than SEAHORN and it does not matter whether the safety property is satisfiable or unsatisfiable. Both tools have 6 tasks where the time limit is reached and they do not return an answer. In four cases both tools cannot find an answer. The reason is likely a shortcoming in Z3 which in some cases has difficulties finding linear invariants for the predicates. The other two cases in which SEAHORN needs more than 10 s, are the only tasks which contains the modulo operator in at least one arithmetic expression. Since ARCADEBT can solve both tasks in reasonable time, it is very likely that this is due to a minor bug in SEAHORN. On the other hand, the two tasks where ARCADEBT needs more than 10 s, are not very different from other tasks which can be solved. A possible explanation is that these are also cases where Z3 has difficulties in finding linear invariants. SEAHORN may be able to find the solution since it does not only use SMT solving, but also code optimization techniques and static analysis (e.g., value set analysis) which might simplify the Constrained Horn Clauses given to the SMT solver.

---

[1] https://github.com/embedded-software-laboratory/ArcadeBT.

6   Conclusion and Outlook

Behavior Trees are models which can visualize complex systems clearly. We showed that the not explicitly visible control flow can lead to overlooked bugs and that a verification approach based on linear Constrained Horn Clauses is able to find them. We also showed that an encoding utilizing the Behavior Tree structure is also faster than a general purpose verification framework.

Properties, which need a more precise modelling of concurrency than our atomic approach, are not supported yet. Also, multiple occurrences of the same action node leads to a redundant modeling since for every node new predicates are introduced. An extension of our presented encoding to handle interleaving semantics and model action nodes in a compositional way, leading to less redundancy, is left for future work.

Acknowledgements. Funded by the Deutsche Forschungsgemeinschaft (DFG, German Research Foundation) under Germany's Excellence Strategy – EXC-2023 Internet of Production – 390621612.

References

1. Biggar, O., Zamani, M.: A framework for formal verification of behavior trees with linear temporal logic. IEEE Robot. Autom. Lett. **5**(2), 2341–2348 (2020). https://doi.org/10.1109/LRA.2020.2970634
2. Colvin, R., Hayes, I.: A semantics for behavior trees using CSP with specification commands. Sci. Comput. Program. **76**, 891–914 (2011). https://doi.org/10.1016/j.scico.2010.11.007
3. Klöckner, A.: Interfacing behavior trees with the world using description logic. In: AIAA Guidance, Navigation, and Control Conference (2013). https://doi.org/10.2514/6.2013-4636
4. Colledanchise, M., Murray, R.M., Ögren, P.: Synthesis of correct-by-construction behavior trees. In: 2017 IEEE/RSJ International Conference on Intelligent Robots and Systems (IROS), pp. 6039–6046 (2017). https://doi.org/10.1109/IROS.2017.8206502
5. Klöckner, A.: Behavior Trees for UAV Mission Management (2013)
6. Ogren, P.: Increasing Modularity of UAV Control Systems using Computer Game Behavior Trees (2012). https://doi.org/10.2514/6.2012-4458
7. Beyer, D.: Software verification and verifiable witnesses. In: Baier, C., Tinelli, C. (eds.) TACAS 2015. LNCS, vol. 9035, pp. 401–416. Springer, Heidelberg (2015). https://doi.org/10.1007/978-3-662-46681-0_31
8. Bjørner, N., Gurfinkel, A., McMillan, K., Rybalchenko, A.: Horn clause solvers for program verification. In: Beklemishev, L.D., Blass, A., Dershowitz, N., Finkbeiner, B., Schulte, W. (eds.) Fields of Logic and Computation II. LNCS, vol. 9300, pp. 24–51. Springer, Cham (2015). https://doi.org/10.1007/978-3-319-23534-9_2
9. Komuravelli, A., Bjorner, N., Gurfinkel, A., Mcmillan, K.: Compositional verification of procedural programs using horn clauses over integers and arrays, pp. 89–96 (2015). https://doi.org/10.1109/FMCAD.2015.7542257
10. Colledanchise, M., Ögren, P.: Behavior Trees in Robotics and AI: An Introduction. arXiv abs/1709.00084 (2017)

11. Colledanchise, M., Parasuraman, R., Ogren, P.: Learning of behavior trees for autonomous agents. IEEE Trans. Comput. Intell. AI Games **11**, 183–189 (2018). https://doi.org/10.1109/TG.2018.2816806
12. Coronado, E., Mastrogiovanni, F., Venture, G.: Development of Intelligent Behaviors for Social Robots via User-Friendly and Modular Programming Tools, pp. 62–68 (2018). https://doi.org/10.1109/ARSO.2018.8625839
13. Colledanchise, M., Natale, L.: Improving the Parallel Execution of Behavior Trees, pp. 7103–7110 (2018). https://doi.org/10.1109/IROS.2018.8593504
14. Isla, D.: Handling complexity in the halo 2 AI. In: Game Developers Conference (2005)
15. Gurfinkel, A., Kahsai, T., Komuravelli, A., Navas, J.A.: The SeaHorn verification framework. In: Kroening, D., Păsăreanu, C.S. (eds.) CAV 2015. LNCS, vol. 9206, pp. 343–361. Springer, Cham (2015). https://doi.org/10.1007/978-3-319-21690-4_20
16. de Moura, L., Bjørner, N.: Z3: an efficient SMT solver. In: Ramakrishnan, C.R., Rehof, J. (eds.) TACAS 2008. LNCS, vol. 4963, pp. 337–340. Springer, Heidelberg (2008). https://doi.org/10.1007/978-3-540-78800-3_24
17. Komuravelli, A., Gurfinkel, A., Chaki, S.: SMT-based model checking for recursive programs. In: CAV (2014)
18. Paulson, L.C.: The foundation of a generic theorem prover. J. Autom. Reason. **5**, 363–397 (1989)
19. Biallas, S., Frey, G., Kowalewski, S., Schlich, B., Soliman, D.: Formale Verifikation von Sicherheits-Funktionsbausteinen der PLCopen auf Modell- und Code-Ebene. Tagungsband Entwicklung und Betrieb komplexer Automatisierungssysteme. EKA (2010)
20. Bohlender, D., Kowalewski, S.: Compositional verification of PLC software using horn clauses and mode abstraction. IFAC-PapersOnLine **51**, 428–433 (2018)
21. Colledanchise, M., Cicala, G., Domenichelli, D.E., Natale, L., Tacchella, A.: Formalizing the execution context of behavior trees for runtime verification of deliberative policies. In: IROS (2021)

A Multi-level Methodology for Behavioral Comparison of Software-Intensive Systems

Dennis Hendriks[1,2(✉)], Arjan van der Meer[1,3], and Wytse Oortwijn[1]

[1] ESI (TNO), Eindhoven, The Netherlands
dennis.hendriks@tno.nl
[2] Radboud University, Nijmegen, The Netherlands
dennis.hendriks@ru.nl
[3] Capgemini Engineering, Eindhoven, The Netherlands

Abstract. Software-intensive systems constantly evolve. To prevent software changes from unintentionally introducing costly system defects, it is important to understand their impact to reduce risk. However, it is in practice nearly impossible to foresee the full impact of software changes when dealing with huge industrial systems with many configurations and usage scenarios. To assist developers with change impact analysis we introduce a novel multi-level methodology for behavioral comparison of software-intensive systems. Our fully automated methodology is based on comparing state machine models of software behavior. We combine existing complementary comparison methods into a novel approach, guiding users step by step through relevant differences by gradually zooming in on more and more details. We empirically evaluate our work through a qualitative exploratory field study, showing its practical value using multiple case studies at ASML, a leading company in developing lithography systems. Our method shows great potential for preventing regressions in system behavior for software changes.

Keywords: Cyber-Physical Systems · Software Behavior · State Machines · Behavioral Comparison · Change Impact Analysis

1 Introduction

Software-intensive systems, e.g., cyber-physical systems, become more and more complex. They often employ a component-based software architecture to manage their complexity. Over the years such systems continuously evolve by adding new features and addressing defects, more and more layers are built on top of each other [11], and components that are not well-maintained become legacy [13,19].

Changing the software is often considered risky as any change can potentially break a system. If a software change leads to a system defect, then the impact

This research is carried out as part of the Transposition project under the responsibility of ESI (TNO) in co-operation with ASML. The research activities are supported by the Netherlands Ministry of Economic Affairs and TKI-HTSM.

J. F. Groote and M. Huisman (Eds.): FMICS 2022, LNCS 13487, pp. 226–243, 2022.
https://doi.org/10.1007/978-3-031-15008-1_15

can be tremendous due to system downtime and productivity loss [19]. This may even lead to software engineers becoming afraid to make changes for which they cannot properly foresee the impact on (other parts of) the system.

To reduce the risks, it is essential to understand the impact of software changes. However, for large complex industrial code bases consisting of tens of millions of lines of code, no single person has the complete overview. This makes it difficult to understand the impact of software changes on the overall system functionality [4]. This is especially true when the system can behave differently for different configurations and usage scenarios [29].

It is thus important that: 1) software developers understand how the system currently behaves for different configurations and usage scenarios, and 2) they understand how software changes impact that system behavior.

To address these needs, in this paper we introduce a novel multi-level methodology for behavioral comparison of (large) software-intensive systems. The power of our methodology is that it quickly guides users to relevant differences. This avoids the laborious and error-prone practice of looking into many thousands of lines of code, or plough through gigabytes of execution logs. Our method is fully automated, making it possible to consider huge (sub-)systems, for which due to their sheer size it is practically impossible to compare their behavior manually.

Our methodology is based on comparing state machine models rather than source code or execution logs, which makes it generally applicable. State machines can compactly and intuitively represent system behavior as a collection of software function calls and the order in which they are called. Such models are general and can be obtained by any means of model learning or construction.

Methods to compare state machines can be divided into two classes that complement each other [28]. Language-based methods compare state machines in terms of their allowed sequences of function calls, while structure-based methods compare them in terms of their states and transitions.

However, two important things are missing in the literature: 1) a single automated method integrating these individual methods to allow large-scale industrial application, and 2) an approach to inspect the resulting differences at various levels of detail, and step by step zoom in on relevant differences, to manage the complexity of huge systems. Our methodology tackles both these challenges.

Our methodology takes any number of sets of state machines representing software behavior of, e.g., different software versions, different configurations or different usage scenarios. We automatically compare the provided sets by comparing the languages and structures of their state-machine models. The comparison results can be inspected at six levels of abstraction, ranging from very high-level differences to very detailed ones. Users are guided through the differences in a step by step fashion tailored to allow them to zoom in on relevant behavioral differences, wasting no time on irrelevant ones.

We empirically evaluate the practical potential of our methodology through a qualitative exploratory field study [18,23]. Using multiple case studies at ASML, a leading company in developing lithography systems, we demonstrate that our approach can be applied to large industrial (sub-)systems, provides developers and architects insight into their behavioral differences, and allows them to find unintended regressions. The company wants to broadly adopt our work.

The remainder of this paper is organized as follows. In Sect. 2 we introduce the concepts, definitions and methods on which we build our methodology. Section 3 introduces our methodology, both conceptually and formally. We evaluate our methodology in Sect. 4, before concluding in Sect. 5.

2   Background

2.1   Software Behavior

Programming languages typically have a notion of *function, procedure* or *method.* The behavior of software implemented in such languages can then be seen as all the *calls* to or *invocations* of these functions, and the constraints on the order in which they may be called.

Large systems often employ a component-based software architecture to manage their complexity. The many components are independent units of development and deployment, encapsulate functionality and allow for re-use [14,24,27]. Functions may then be called internally within a component and to communicate between components connected via interfaces, e.g., remote procedure calls.

2.2   State Machines

We consider software behavior in terms of sequences of discrete *events*, e.g., the start and end of function calls. We define an *alphabet* Σ to be a finite set of events of interest. A *trace* $t \in \Sigma^*$ represents a single finite execution, with $*$ the Kleene star. The length of t is denoted by $|t|$ and its i-th event by t_i for $1 \leq i \leq |t|$. An execution *log* is a set of observed traces, and can for instance be obtained by explicit logging or through sniffing tools.

A *state machine* or *automaton* compactly and intuitively represents multiple executions. We define a *Non-deterministic Finite Automaton* (NFA) $A = (S, \Sigma, \Delta, I, F)$ as a 5-tuple, with S a finite set of states, Σ a finite set of events (the alphabet), $\Delta \subseteq S \times \Sigma \times S$ a set of transitions, $I \subseteq S$ a set of *initial states*, and $F \subseteq S$ a set of *accepting states*. *Deterministic Finite Automata* (DFAs) are a sub-class of NFAs allowing for each source state and event only a single target state. An NFA can be determinized to a DFA [25].

A trace $t \in \Sigma^*$ is *accepted* by an NFA $A = (S, \Sigma, \Delta, I, F)$ iff there exists a sequence $(s_0, t_1, s_1), (s_1, t_2, s_2), \dots, (s_{|t|-1}, t_{|t|}, s_{|t|}) \in \Delta^*$ with $s_0 \in I$ and $s_{|t|} \in F$. Traces that are not accepted are *rejected*. The *language* $\mathcal{L}(A)$ of an NFA A is the set of all its accepted traces, i.e., $\mathcal{L}(A) = \{t \in \Sigma^* \mid A \text{ accepts } t\}$. The behavior presence predicate $B(A)$ indicates whether A has any behavior, i.e., $B(A) = (\mathcal{L}(A) \neq \emptyset)$. State machines can be *minimized* to a representation with the least number of states possible, while still accepting the same language [8,16]. Given two NFAs A_1 and A_2, union and intersection are defined as operations that reflect the effect on their resulting languages, i.e., $\mathcal{L}(A_1 \cup A_2) = \mathcal{L}(A_1) \cup \mathcal{L}(A_2)$ and $\mathcal{L}(A_1 \cap A_2) = \mathcal{L}(A_1) \cap \mathcal{L}(A_2)$, respectively [20].

A (minimal) state machine can be obtained from an execution log through model learning, e.g., using state machine learning algorithms [3,6,7,12] or through active automata learning [6,9]. Their details are beyond the scope of this paper.

2.3 State Machine Comparison

State machines can be compared in various ways. Walkinshaw and Bogdanov [28] differentiate two perspectives: language-based and structure-based comparisons.

The language perspective considers to which extend the languages of state machines overlap. Two state machines A_1, A_2 are *language equivalent* ($=_L$) iff they accept exactly the same language, i.e., $A_1 =_L A_2 \Leftrightarrow \mathcal{L}(A_1) = \mathcal{L}(A_2)$. A state machine A_1 is related by *language inclusion* ($\leq_L$) to state machine A_2 iff the language of A_1 is included in that of A_2, i.e., $A_1 \leq_L A_2 \Leftrightarrow \mathcal{L}(A_1) \subseteq \mathcal{L}(A_2)$. Various other types of well-known binary equivalence and inclusion relations exist [26], as well as non-binary ones such as precision and recall [21,28]. We use language equivalence and inclusion as these are commonly used in automata theory, are sufficient to capture the order of function calls, and can be easily explained even to engineers without a formal background. For finite state machines these relations can be computed on their finite structures [2].

Language-based comparison considers the externally observable behavior of state machines. Complementary to it, structure-based comparison considers the overlap of their internal representations in terms of states and transitions.

Walkinshaw and Bogdanov define the *LTSDiff* algorithm [28] that takes two state machines and computes a *diff* state machine: a compact representation of their differences. Figure 1 shows an example. A diff state machine is a regular state machine with its states and transitions annotated to represent difference information, i.e., 'unchanged' (black), 'added' (green) and 'removed' (red).

The algorithm has three steps: 1) Compute similarity scores for all possible pair-wise combinations of states from the two NFAs being compared. A local score considers only the overlap in directly connected incoming and outgoing transitions of the states. It is extended to a global score by recursively considering all context, using an attenuation factor to ensure closer-by context counts more towards the score than further away context. 2) Use the scores to heuristically compute a matching between states of the two NFAs based on landmarks, a percentage of the highest scoring pairs that score at least some factor better than any other pairs, with a fallback to the initial states. The most obviously equivalent state pairs are matched first and these are then used to match the surrounding areas, rejecting any remaining conflicting state pairs. The next-best

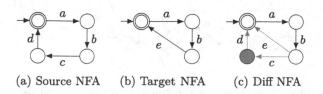

(a) Source NFA   (b) Target NFA   (c) Diff NFA

Fig. 1. Source and target NFAs and their structural differences as a diff NFA.

remaining state pair is then selected and matched, etc., until no state pairs are left to consider. 3) Use the matching to compute the diff state machine.

The LTSDiff algorithm has the advantage that it does not require states to be reachable from initial states, does not require state machines to be deterministic or minimal, does not rely on state labels, and that it produces relatively small diffs in practice, unlike some other approaches [10,15,17,22].

For a more extensive overview of alternative approaches to compare state machine languages and structures, see the work of Walkinshaw and Bogdanov [28].

3   Behavioral Comparison Methodology

The language and structure-based state machine comparison approaches are complementary. However, to the best of our knowledge there is no work that fully exploits the complementary nature of these approaches, to provide intuitive insights into the behavioral impact of changes for industrial-scale software-intensive systems. Our methodology takes advantage of their complementary nature in a novel way, to allow handling the complexity of such scale.

As input our methodology takes any number of *model sets* representing, e.g., different software versions, configurations or usage scenarios. They contain state machines that represent behaviors of a number of *entities* representing, e.g., software functions or components. Formally, let E be a finite set of (behavioral) entities and $\mathcal{N}$ the set of all NFAs. A model set $S \in E \to \mathcal{N}$ is a complete mapping of entities to models (NFAs). An incomplete mapping can be made complete using $(\emptyset, \emptyset, \emptyset, \emptyset, \emptyset)$ as NFA for unmapped entities. As input our methodology takes a finite entities set E and a finite set of model sets $\mathbb{S} = \{S_1, ..., S_n\} \subseteq E \to \mathcal{N}$.

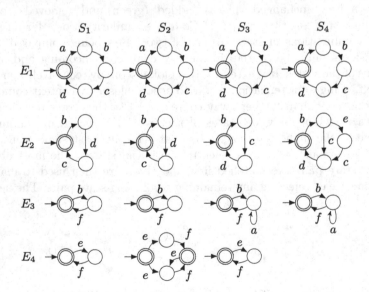

Fig. 2. The input state machines for the running example, for entities E_1 through E_4 (rows) and model sets S_1 through S_4 (columns). $S_4(E_4) = (\emptyset, \emptyset, \emptyset, \emptyset, \emptyset)$.

Model sets			Models		
Level 1	Level 2	Level 3	Level 4	Level 5	Level 6
Variants	Variant relations	Variant differences	Variants	Variant relations	Variant differences
L	L	L	L	L / S	S

Fig. 3. Methodology overview: six levels of detail to inspect comparison results.

Figure 2 shows the model sets that we use as a running example. For model set S_4 (e.g., configuration 4) there is no model for entity E_4 (e.g., function 4). If these models were obtained through model learning on execution logs, no behavior was observed for function 4 using configuration 4.

Our methodology compares the state machines of all input model sets. The results are represented at six levels of abstraction (Fig. 3). The first three levels focus on model sets and the last three on individual (models of) entities within them. For both model sets and models, the first level considers different behavioral variants, the second level relates the variants, and the third level elaborates on variant differences. Users are guided step by step through the levels, by gradually zooming in on more details, letting them focus on relevant differences. Levels 1–5 contain information from the language perspective (L), while levels 5 and 6 contain information from the structural perspective (S). Next, we further elaborate on each of the six levels.

3.1   Level 1: Model Set Variants

Level 1 provides the highest level overview. It shows whether model sets have the same behavior, i.e., their entity models are language equivalent. Two model sets $S_i, S_j \in \mathbb{S}$ have the same behavior, denoted $S_i =_L S_j$, iff $\forall_{e \in E} S_i(e) =_L S_j(e)$.

We compare model sets against each other and determine unique model set behavior variants. Variants are formally defined to be equivalence classes of $\mathbb{S}$ under $=_L$, so that $\mathbb{S}/=_L$ is the set of all variants. For presentational clarity we enumerate and refer to different variants of $\mathbb{S}$ in alphabetical order: A, B, etc. We choose a structural representative for each behavioral equivalence class.

Figure 4a shows the level 1 result for our running example. Model sets S_1 and S_2 have the same behavior for all four functions and thus get variant A, even though their models for E_4 are structurally different. Model sets S_3 and S_4 get variants B and C as they differ from the other model sets (and each other).

Level 1 thus provides a very high level overview of which model sets have the same or different behavior, and how few or many variants there are. We can see whether this matches our expectations. Depending on the use case, we may be satisfied already after looking at these results. For instance, if we want to know whether different configurations have the same behavior, and if they all have the same variant, we can already conclude that there are no differences in their behavior. If we do go to the other levels, we can ignore model set S_2 as it has the same behavior as S_1. In fact, from the language perspective we can focus on (representatives of) model set variants, each representing one or more models with the same behavior, rather than on individual model sets. Finally, in Fig. 4a variants are colored using shades of blue like a heat map. In case of many model sets this may reveal patterns, as we will see in Sect. 4.

3.2 Level 2: Model Set Variant Relations

Level 1 provides us with model set variants that each have different behavior. Level 2 provides more details. It considers whether the behavior of one model set variant is completely included in the behavior of another variant, i.e., it has less behavior. Formally, for two model sets $S_i, S_j \in \mathbb{S}$, S_i is related to S_j by language inclusion, denoted $S_i \leq_L S_j$, iff $\forall_{e \in E} S_i(e) \leq_L S_j(e)$. Given that all model set variants have different behavior, S_i thus has less behavior for at least one entity. Partially ordered set $(\mathbb{S}/\!\!=_L, \leq_L)$ can be extended into a finite lattice by computing unions (as supremum) and intersections (as infimum) of representatives of model set variants until a fixed point is reached. The union or intersection of two model sets constitutes the per-entity pairwise combination of their entity models, using state machine union or intersection, respectively.

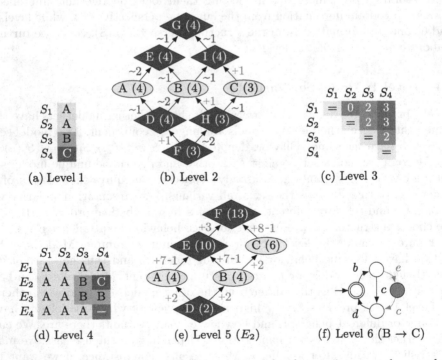

Fig. 4. Behavioral comparison methodology output for the running example: complete levels 1–4, level 5 for E_2, and level 6 for E_2 variants B $\rightarrow$ C.

Figure 4b shows the level 2 lattice for our running example. The variants from level 1 are indicated by ellipses containing the variant and number of entity models that have behavior. The extra variants computed to complete the lattice are indicated by diamonds. Arrows indicate inclusion relations, e.g., the behavior of variant D is included in that of variants A and B (and E, I and G, by transitivity). The arrows are labeled with the number of entities with different present behavior (e.g., ~1) and the number of entities with newly present behavior (e.g., +1). Formally, for model set variants S_i, S_j and $S_i \leq_L S_j$, these are computed by $|\{e \in E \mid B(S_i(e)) \wedge B(S_j(e)) \wedge S_i(e) \neq_L S_j(e)\}|$ and $|\{e \in E \mid \neg B(S_i(e)) \wedge B(S_j(e))\}|$, respectively.

Level 2 provides information on which variants have more or less behavior than other variants, whether variants are closely related (direct arrow) or less closely related (via several arrows), and it has quantitative information on the models within the model sets by means of the labels on the arrows. As for level 1, we can check whether this conforms to our expectations, or not. For instance, if we compare two software versions and we only added new functionality (e.g., new entities), we would reasonably expect the behavior of the old software version to be included in that of the new software version, and we can check whether that is indeed the case. If this is all that we want to know, we can stop here and we do not need to proceed to level 3.

3.3   Level 3: Model Set Variant Differences

Level 2 shows us the quantitative differences between model sets via the arrow labels. However, some model set variants are not directly related by an inclusion arrow (e.g., variants A and B). The number of entities with different behavior between them cannot be determined from the lattice, as simply summing labels (e.g., ~1, +1) could count the same entity multiple times. Level 3 provides more details, showing the number of entities with different behavior between all input model sets. That is, for model sets $S_i, S_j \in \mathbb{S}$ it shows $|\{e \in E \mid S_i(e) \neq_L S_j(e)\}|$.

Figure 4c shows the level 3 matrix for our running example. Rows and columns are labeled with the input model sets. Cells indicate the number of entities with different behavior. As language (in)equality is a symmetric and reflexive relation, only the upper-right part of the matrix is filled, and the diagonal is labeled with '=' symbols. As expected, model sets S_1 and S_2 have zero entities with different behavior, as they have the same model set variant. Model sets S_1 (variant A) and S_4 (variant C) have three entities with different behavior.

Level 3 provides more detailed quantitative information. It shows not just whether model sets are different, and how many model sets have differences, but also how different they are. The diagonal is colored gray as it is not relevant. Numbered cells are colored like a heat map based on a gradient from green (no entities with differences) via yellow and orange to red (most entities with differences). In case of many model sets this may again reveal patterns. Similarly to the previous levels, we can check whether all information matches our expectations, and whether we want to proceed to level 4, or not.

3.4   Level 4: Model Variants

Levels 1–3 focus on model sets. Level 4 zooms in even further and considers the (entity) models within the model sets. Similar to how level 1 identifies model set variants, level 4 identifies model variants for each entity. Formally, for an entity $e \in E$, let $\mathbb{S}_e = \{S(e) \mid S \in \mathbb{S}\}$. We consider equivalence classes $\mathbb{S}_e/{=}_L$ for each $e \in E$ and enumerate and represent them in alphabetical order: A, B, etc. Note that variants are determined per entity and thus variant A of one entity does not necessarily have the same behavior as variant A of another entity.

Figure 4d shows the level 4 matrix for our running example. The cells indicate the behavior variant of the model for the corresponding entity (row) in the corresponding model set (column).

Level 4 is the first level to provide details on which entities differ between model sets. This provides a high level overview of the behavior variants for entity models, similar to how level 1 provides it for model sets. We can see the variants, how many there are, for which models sets, and whether this is expected or not. Depending on the use case, we may again stop at this level if it answers our questions, e.g., in case of checking for regressions if each entity has only a single behavior variant. Otherwise, we can reduce the number of entities to consider for subsequent levels, e.g., skip the ones without regressions (only a single variant, no differences). Furthermore, we may then focus only on unique entity model variants instead of all individual entity models. Finally, the matrix cells are again colored using shades of blue like a heat map. Models without behavior are indicated as a red cell labeled '−' to make them stand out. Here too, in case of many model sets this may reveal patterns.

3.5   Level 5: Model Variant Relations

Level 5 shows relations between entity model variants of level 4, similar to how level 2 shows relations between model set variants of level 1. Formally, for an entity $e \in E$ we have a partially ordered set $(\mathbb{S}_e/{=}_L, \leq_L)$, which we extend to a finite lattice using unions and intersections, similar to level 2.

Figure 4e shows the level 5 lattice for our running example, for entity E_2. We use a representative model for each entity model variant (set of equivalent models). The node shapes and arrows are as in level 2. The node labels now indicate the number of transitions of the model, and the arrow labels indicate the number of added (e.g., +7) and removed transitions (e.g., -1). These are based on the structural comparison that we use and will explain further for level 6. In our example, the behavior of variant B is included in the behavior of variant C.

Level 5 provides information on which entity model variants have more or less behavior, how closely they are related, and the amount of changes between them. As for previous levels, we can check whether this conforms to our expectations, or not. We can also use it to decide what to inspect in more detail in level 6.

3.6   Level 6: Model Variant Differences

Level 6 is the last level. It shows all structural differences between two entity model variants of level 5 as a diff NFA, computed with the LTSDiff algorithm.

Figure 4f shows the level 6 diff NFA for our running example, for variants B and C of entity E_2. Variant C (from model set S_4) has two extra transitions in its state machine, and this is clearly visible as two green arrows in this figure.

Level 6 provides the most detailed behavioral differences. Diff NFAs show differences in terms of states and transitions within models. As with the other levels, we can check whether this matches our expectations, or not.

4   Evaluation

We perform an empirical evaluation of our methodology through an exploratory field study [18,23]. To gain some first evidence of both its practical potential and its ability to handle large systems, we perform two case studies at ASML. The first case study provides some preliminary evidence of our methodology's practical value by finding a regression. The second case study shows that our methodology can be applied to a large industrial system, providing insights into its behavior. We have completely automated our approach, in a (for now) company-internal prototype tool.

ASML develops photolithography systems for the semiconductor industry. These systems process *wafers* (thin circular slices of silicon) in batches (*lots*). Multiple circuits (*dies*) are produced on a single wafer. After the wafer's height profile is *measured*, a light source *exposes* the chip pattern onto a wafer through a projection mask (a *reticle*). A reticle may contain a full-sized pattern (*full field*) or a smaller one (*narrow field*). Computational lithography software uses the *measurements* to compensate for nano-scale imperfections during *exposure*.

In this section the start of function call f is denoted as $f^\uparrow$ and its end as $f^\downarrow$.

4.1   Case Study 1: Legacy Component Technology Migration

For the first case study, we look at a relatively small computational lithography component, developed and maintained by two engineers. It is internally implemented using legacy end-of-life technology and is migrated to new technology, without changes to its external interface. The engineers thus expect to see the same external behavior in communications with the other components, and we apply our approach to see whether this is indeed the case.

We observe six executions, using three different test sets for both the legacy and new implementations. The *integration* test set contains integration tests. The *overruling* and *verification* test sets both test different configuration options and functionality of the component. Each test set contains multiple tests. For reasons of confidentiality we do not explain them in more detail. For each observed execution, we obtain an execution log capturing the component's runtime communications with other components. The log for each execution is split into separate logs for each of the functions in the component's external interface. Using model learning [7], we obtain six model sets (one for each execution), with 11 interface functions of the component as entities. The model sets together contain 46 models with behavior, with 2 to 578 states per model, and a sum total of 1,330 states. We run our tool, which takes about 3.38 hours on a standard laptop, mostly spent on executing LTSDiff, and discuss the results per level.

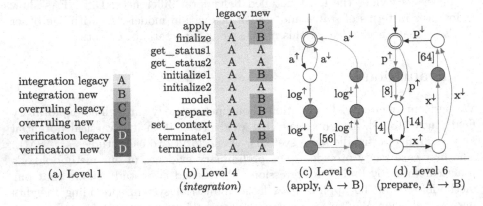

			legacy	new
		apply	A	B
		finalize	A	B
		get_status1	A	A
		get_status2	A	A
integration legacy	A	initialize1	A	B
integration new	B	initialize2	A	A
overruling legacy	C	model	A	B
overruling new	C	prepare	A	B
verification legacy	D	set_context	A	A
verification new	D	terminate1	A	B
		terminate2	A	A

(a) Level 1   (b) Level 4   (c) Level 6   (d) Level 6
(*integration*)   (apply, A → B)   (prepare, A → B)

Fig. 5. First results for case study 1: complete level 1, level 4 for the *integration* test set, and level 6 with variants A vs B for functions 'apply' and 'prepare'.

Level 1 (Fig. 5a): Only for *integration* there are differences in behavior between the legacy and new implementations. As the other two test sets show no differences, they do not need further inspection. Given that we then have only two model sets left, we skip levels 2 and 3, and proceed directly to level 4.

Level 4 (Fig. 5b): We see the 11 functions, anonymized for confidentiality reasons, and their behavioral variants. Only 6 out of 11 entities show differences in behavior, to be inspected in more detail. Given that they all have only two variants per entity, we skip level 5 and proceed directly to level 6.

Level 6 (Figs. 5c and 5d): Figure 5c shows the diff NFA for function 'apply' (abbreviated to 'a'), for variant A to variant B. The figure shows that the new implementation involves only the start and end of this function. The legacy implementation has more behavior, as within the 'apply' function it has 30 calls (with returns) to a 'log' function. In the figure, only the first and last of these calls (with their returns) are shown, and the remaining sequence of 56 transitions, representing 28 calls and their returns, is abbreviated to '[56]'. Figure 5d shows the diff NFA for function 'prepare' (abbreviated to 'p'), for variant A to variant B. For reasons of confidentiality and presentational clarity again several sequences of transitions are abbreviated. Here, the figure shows that the legacy implementation invokes the 'log' function 4 and 32 times, indicated as '[8]' and '[64]', respectively, while the new implementation does not.

Having inspected the differences for only two entities, it appears that all 'log' function calls are missing in the new implementation. The component engineers confirmed that indeed for the new implementation the component was not yet hooked up to the logging framework. Our approach clearly shows this regression.

To look for other differences in behavior, we remove all 'log' function calls and returns from the models of the legacy implementation. To do so, we rename all 'log' function call and return events to ε and apply weak-language normalization [20]. We run our tool again, which now only takes a mere 19 seconds.

Level 1 (Fig. 6): Looking at the new results for level 1, we immediately see that there are no more observed differences in behavior for the legacy and new implementations, for all three test sets. We do not see any further regressions in behavior, and we thus do not have to go to further levels.

Given that the engineers consider this component to have quite a good test set with adequate coverage, our approach is applied as an extra safety net that complements traditional testing, akin to differential testing [4]. As any change in the (order of) communications with other components will show up in our models and comparisons, it is like having assertions for all external communications. Both engineers find this valuable. They would like to apply our methodology also for larger and more complex technology migrations, where they foresee even more value.

integration legacy	A
integration new	A
overruling legacy	B
overruling new	B
verification legacy	C
verification new	C

Fig. 6. New results for case study 1: level 1.

The full version [5] of this paper includes a comparison and analysis of the behaviors of the different test sets, highlighting the value of levels 2 and 5.

4.2 Case Study 2: System Behavior Matching Recipe

For the second case study, we investigate how *recipes* containing information on the number of wafers and used reticles relate to the system behavior. ASML's customers can specify their own recipes to configure their lithography systems for their purposes, e.g., to create CPU or memory chips. The software running on the systems will exhibit different behavior for different recipes, and thus software behavior offers a lens to look at system behavior.

Figure 7 shows the recipes that we consider for this case study. For reasons of confidentiality, we do not explain the origin of these recipes and we consider only the details relevant for this case study. There are six lots, each with their own recipe. Lots 1 and 2 have five wafers each and the other lots have 15 wafers each. There are two reticles, X and Y. For lot 1, reticle X is used 96 times, one for each die. Lot 5 uses both reticles. Exposure can be done using full field or narrow field, where narrow field leads to more exposures (125 rather than 96).

	Lot 1	Lot 2	Lot 3	Lot 4	Lot 5	Lot 6
Wafers	5	5	15	15	15	15
Reticle	96*X	96*Y	96*X	96*Y	124*X, 1*Y	125*X
Field	Full	Full	Full	Full	Narrow	Narrow

Fig. 7. Case study 2: recipes for the different lots.

We consider the behavior of the exposure sub-system, i.e., 32 software components involved in the high-level exposure control. Observing the system execution for about an hour as it initializes and processes lots, we obtain a single execution log capturing all observed inter-component communications. This log is split into multiple logs, one for each of the 85 exposures (one per wafer and for lot 5 twice per wafer as it uses two reticles). The exposure logs are further split into separate logs for each of the components, containing only their interactions with the other components. Using model learning [7], we obtain 85 model sets (one per exposure), containing models of the 32 components (entities). Model sets may lack a certain component model if that component did not interact with other components during the corresponding exposure. Figure 8 shows the sizes of the input models in number of states. The 85 model sets together contain 2,386 models with behavior, with 2 to 7,070 states per model, and a sum total of 495,505 states, making this a large case study.

We run our tool, skipping levels 2 and 5 as they are less relevant for this case study. For LTSDiff, local instead of global scoring is used when state machines with more than 100 states are involved, sacrificing accuracy for performance. Running the tool takes about 1.23 hours. We discuss the results per level.

Level 1 (Fig. 9): We discuss multiple observations based on patterns that are visible in level 1. Different gradient colors are used for presentational clarity.

a) *First exposure of a lot*: For lots 1 – 4, the main behavior variant is variant B. The first exposures of these lots however all have different behavior (A, D).
b) *Changes during a lot*: For lots 2 – 4 we also see different behavior for some exposures later during the lot (C, E).

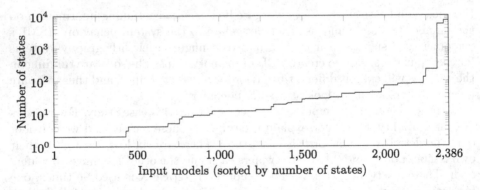

Fig. 8. Case study 2: sizes of the input models with behavior.

1-1 A	3-1 A	4-1 D	5-1A F		6-1 M
1-2 B	3-2 B	4-2 B	5-1B G	5-9A K	6-2 N
1-3 B	3-3 B	4-3 B	5-2B H	5-9B G	6-3 N
1-4 B	3-4 B	4-4 B	5-2A I	5-10B H	6-4 N
1-5 B	3-5 B	4-5 B	5-3A J	5-10A I	6-5 N
	3-6 B	4-6 B	5-3B G	5-11A K	6-6 N
	3-7 B	4-7 B	5-4B H	5-11B G	6-7 N
	3-8 B	4-8 B	5-4A I	5-12B H	6-8 N
2-1 A	3-9 B	4-9 B	5-5A J	5-12A I	6-9 O
2-2 B	3-10 B	4-10 B	5-5B G	5-13A K	6-10 N
2-3 B	3-11 C	4-11 B	5-6B H	5-13B L	6-11 N
2-4 C	3-12 B	4-12 B	5-6A I	5-14B H	6-12 N
2-5 B	3-13 B	4-13 E	5-7A K	5-14A I	6-13 N
	3-14 B	4-14 B	5-7B G	5-15A K	6-14 N
	3-15 B	4-15 B	5-8B H	5-15B L	6-15 O
			5-8A I		

Fig. 9. Results for case study 2: level 1.

c) *Reticle swaps*: All exposures of lots 5 (F–L) have behavior different than the other lots (A–E, M–O). Lot 5 is the only lot where two reticles are used per wafer, and thus reticles must be swapped regularly. To minimize the number of swaps, the system uses an 'XYYX' pattern for every two wafers (first wafer reticle 'X', first wafer reticle 'Y', second wafer reticle 'Y', second wafer reticle 'X'). These patterns of four exposures are clearly visible in the model set variants (J–G–H–I, K–G–H–I).

d) *Full field vs narrow field*: The difference between lots 1 and 3 compared to lot 6 is the use of full vs narrow field. The behavior for lots 1 and 3 (A–C) and lot 6 (M–O) differ, but they have similar structure (mostly the same variant, first exposure and some exposures during the lot are different).

For brevity, we only zoom in on the *first exposure of a lot* differences in further levels, and therefore only consider parts of the views for those levels. For a discussion of the other differences, see the full version [5] of this paper.

Level 3 (Fig. 10a): For lots 1–3, we mainly see regular behavior (dark green, 0 components with different behavior). For the first exposures of these lots we do see differences (yellow lines, 2 components with different behavior).

Level 4 (Fig. 10b): The two components with differences for the first exposures of lots 1–3 are components C1 and C21.

Level 6 (Fig. 10c): We inspect level 6 for variants A and B of component C21. Figure 10c shows a part of the diff state machine, with 'l' a logging function, 'i' a function to get some information, and 'q' a query function. For confidentiality reasons we do not explain the functions in more detail. The upper and lower paths indicate that both versions can skip the calls to 'q'. The only difference is that variant A (first wafer, in red) calls 'i' before calling 'q', while variant B (other wafers, in green) does not. The company's domain experts are well aware of such 'first wafer effects'.

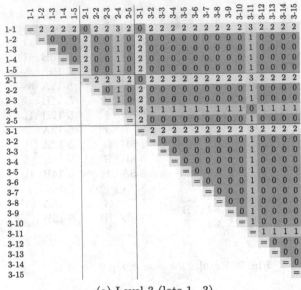

(a) Level 3 (lots 1−3)

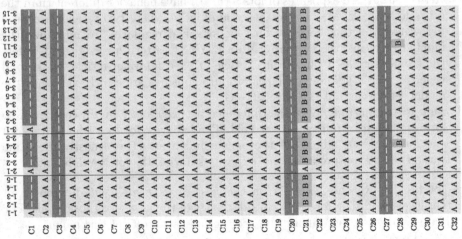

(b) Level 4 (lots 1−3), rotated 90 degrees counterclockwise

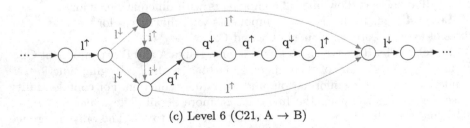

(c) Level 6 (C21, A → B)

Fig. 10. Results for case study 2: partial results for levels 3, 4 and 6. The component names have been anonymized for confidentiality reasons.

The system behavior differs between wafers, and by going through the levels of our methodology we obtain progressive insights into these behavioral differences. While the input contains a large number of state machines, with an even larger number of states, our methodology allows engineers to step by step zoom in on parts of this behavior, thus making it suitable to analyze this large system.

5   Conclusions and Future Work

We contribute a novel multi-level methodology for behavioral comparison of software-intensive systems. It integrates multiple existing complementary methods to automatically compare the behavior of state machines. Our methodology takes advantage of their complementary nature in a novel way, using six levels with progressive detail to handle the complexity of large industrial systems.

Our qualitative exploratory field study suggests that our approach allows one to inspect the behavioral differences of large systems, and that it has practical value for getting insight into system behavior for various configurations and scenarios, and preventing regressions. However, a more rigorous and quantitative evaluation of our methodology is still needed.

Our work is generically applicable as it works on state machines, which are widely used and understood in both computer science and industry. We plan to research the generality of our approach by also applying it at other companies with software-intensive systems that have suitable state machine models [1], and make the company-internal prototype tool publicly available.

Other future work includes extensions beyond comparing NFAs to consider also Extended Finite Automata and Timed Automata as input to our approach, and adding actionable insights beyond merely behavioral differences to further support change impact analysis. Our methodology could also be applied to different use cases such as diagnosis of unstable tests and field issues.

Acknowledgments. The authors would like to thank ASML for making this work possible and for supporting it.

References

1. Bera, D., Schuts, M., Hooman, J., Kurtev, I.: Reverse engineering models of software interfaces. Comput. Sci. Inf. Syst. **18**(3), 657–686 (2021). https://doi.org/10.2298/CSIS200131013B
2. Cleaveland, R., Sokolsky, O.: Equivalence and Preorder checking for finite-state systems. In: Handbook of Process Algebra, pp. 391–424 (2001). https://doi.org/10.1016/B978-044482830-9/50024-2
3. Gold, E.M.: Language identification in the limit. Inf. Control **10**(5), 447–474 (1967). https://doi.org/10.1016/S0019-9958(67)91165-5
4. Gulzar, M.A., Zhu, Y., Han, X.: Perception and practices of differential testing. In: 2019 IEEE/ACM 41st International Conference on Software Engineering: Software Engineering in Practice (ICSE-SEIP), pp. 71–80. IEEE (2019). https://doi.org/10.1109/ICSE-SEIP.2019.00016

5. Hendriks, D., van der Meer, A., Oortwijn, W.: A multi-level methodology for behavioral comparison of software-intensive systems. arxiv (2022). https://doi.org/10.48550/arxiv.2205.08201
6. De la Higuera, C.: Grammatical Inference: Learning Automata and Grammars. Cambridge University Press, New York (2010). https://doi.org/10.1017/CBO9781139194655
7. Hooimeijer, B., Geilen, M., Groote, J.F., Hendriks, D., Schiffelers, R.: Constructive Model Inference: model learning for component-based software architectures. In: Proceedings of the 17th International Conference on Software Technologies - ICSOFT, pp. 146–158 (2022). https://doi.org/10.5220/0011145700003266
8. Hopcroft, J.: An n log n algorithm for minimizing states in a finite automaton. In: Theory of Machines and Computations, pp. 189–196. Elsevier (1971). https://doi.org/10.1016/B978-0-12-417750-5.50022-1
9. Howar, F., Steffen, B.: Active automata learning in practice. In: Bennaceur, A., Hähnle, R., Meinke, K. (eds.) Machine Learning for Dynamic Software Analysis: Potentials and Limits. LNCS, vol. 11026, pp. 123–148. Springer, Cham (2018). https://doi.org/10.1007/978-3-319-96562-8_5
10. Kelter, U., Schmidt, M.: Comparing state machines. In: Proceedings of the 2008 International Workshop on Comparison and Versioning of Software Models, pp. 1–6 (2008). https://doi.org/10.1145/1370152.1370154
11. Klusener, S., Mooij, A., Ketema, J., Van Wezep, H.: Reducing code duplication by identifying fresh domain abstractions. In: 2018 IEEE International Conference on Software Maintenance and Evolution (ICSME), pp. 569–578. IEEE (2018). https://doi.org/10.1109/ICSME.2018.00020
12. Lang, K.J., Pearlmutter, B.A., Price, R.A.: Results of the Abbadingo one DFA learning competition and a new evidence-driven state merging algorithm. In: Honavar, V., Slutzki, G. (eds.) ICGI 1998. LNCS, vol. 1433, pp. 1–12. Springer, Heidelberg (1998). https://doi.org/10.1007/BFb0054059
13. Lehman, M.M.: Programs, life cycles, and laws of software evolution. Proc. IEEE 68(9), 1060–1076 (1980). https://doi.org/10.1109/PROC.1980.11805
14. McIlroy, M.D., Buxton, J., Naur, P., Randell, B.: Mass produced software components. In: Proceedings of the 1st International Conference on Software Engineering, Garmisch Partenkirchen, Germany, pp. 88–98 (1968)
15. Nejati, S., Sabetzadeh, M., Chechik, M., Easterbrook, S., Zave, P.: Matching and merging of Statecharts specifications. In: 29th International Conference on Software Engineering (ICSE 2007), pp. 54–64. IEEE (2007). https://doi.org/10.1109/ICSE.2007.50
16. Paige, R., Tarjan, R.E.: Three partition refinement algorithms. SIAM J. Comput. 16(6), 973–989 (1987). https://doi.org/10.1137/0216062
17. Quante, J., Koschke, R.: Dynamic protocol recovery. In: 14th Working Conference on Reverse Engineering (WCRE 2007), pp. 219–228. IEEE (2007). https://doi.org/10.1109/WCRE.2007.24
18. Runeson, P., Höst, M.: Guidelines for conducting and reporting case study research in software engineering. Emp. Softw. Eng. 14(2), 131–164 (2009). https://doi.org/10.1007/s10664-008-9102-8
19. Schuts, M., Hooman, J., Vaandrager, F.: Refactoring of legacy software using model learning and equivalence checking: an industrial experience report. In: Ábrahám, E., Huisman, M. (eds.) IFM 2016. LNCS, vol. 9681, pp. 311–325. Springer, Cham (2016). https://doi.org/10.1007/978-3-319-33693-0_20
20. Sipser, M.: Introduction to the Theory of Computation. Cengage Learning, 3rd edn. Cengage, Boston (2013)

21. Sokolova, M., Lapalme, G.: A systematic analysis of performance measures for classification tasks. Inf. Process. Manag. **45**(4), 427–437 (2009). https://doi.org/10.1016/j.ipm.2009.03.002
22. Sokolsky, O., Kannan, S., Lee, I.: Simulation-based graph similarity. In: Hermanns, H., Palsberg, J. (eds.) TACAS 2006. LNCS, vol. 3920, pp. 426–440. Springer, Heidelberg (2006). https://doi.org/10.1007/11691372_28
23. Storey, M.-A., Ernst, N.A., Williams, C., Kalliamvakou, E.: The who, what, how of software engineering research: a socio-technical framework. Emp. Softw. Eng. **25**(5), 4097–4129 (2020). https://doi.org/10.1007/s10664-020-09858-z
24. Szyperski, C., Gruntz, D., Murer, S.: Component Software: Beyond Object-Oriented Programming. 2nd edn. Pearson Education, Upper Saddle River (2002)
25. Van Glabbeek, R., Ploeger, B.: Five Determinisation Algorithms. In: Ibarra, O.H., Ravikumar, B. (eds.) CIAA 2008. LNCS, vol. 5148, pp. 161–170. Springer, Heidelberg (2008). https://doi.org/10.1007/978-3-540-70844-5_17
26. Van Glabbeek, R.J.: The linear time — branching time spectrum II. In: Best, E. (ed.) CONCUR 1993. LNCS, vol. 715, pp. 66–81. Springer, Heidelberg (1993). https://doi.org/10.1007/3-540-57208-2_6
27. Vitharana, P.: Risks and challenges of component-based software developmen. Commun. ACM **46**(8), 67–72 (2003). https://doi.org/10.1145/859670.859671
28. Walkinshaw, N., Bogdanov, K.: Automated comparison of state-based software models in terms of their language and structure. ACM Trans. Softw. Eng. Methodol. **22**(2), 1–37 (2013). https://doi.org/10.1145/2430545.2430549
29. Yang, N., Cuijper, P., Schiffelers, R., Lukkien, J., Serebrenik, A.: An interview study of how developers use execution logs in embedded software engineering. In: 2021 IEEE/ACM 43rd International Conference on Software Engineering: Software Engineering in Practice (ICSE-SEIP), pp. 61–70. IEEE (2021). https://doi.org/10.1109/ICSE-SEIP52600.2021.00015

Author Index

Printed in the United States
by Baker & Taylor Publisher Services